BIRD

BIRD

EXPLORING
THE WINGED
WORLD

Phaidon Press Limited
2 Cooperage Yard
London E15 2QR

Phaidon Press Inc.
65 Bleecker Street
New York, NY 10012

phaidon.com

First published 2021
© 2021 Phaidon Press Limited

ISBN 978 1 83866 140 3

A CIP catalogue record for this book is available from
the British Library and the Library of Congress.

Commissioning Editor: Victoria Clarke
Project Editor: Tom Furness
Production Controller: Adela Cory
Design: Hans Stofregen
Layout: Ana Teodoro

Printed in China

Arrangement
The illustrations in this book have been
arranged in pairs to highlight interesting
comparisons and contrasts based loosely on
their subject, age, purpose, origin or appearance.
This organizational system is not definitive and
many other arrangements would have been
possible. A chronological survey of ornithology
can be found in the timeline at the back.

Dimensions
The dimensions of works are listed by height
then width. Digital images have variable
dimensions. Where differences in dimensions
exist between sources, measurements listed
refer to the illustrated version.

You only have to look up to see a bird. In town or country, birds are there, advertising their presence with their songs, visiting garden feeders, making use of artificial nest sites and staking their claim to every pond, lake or waterway. High-speed screaming parties of swifts race through the narrow streets of ancient towns on summer evenings (p.45, p.262), while sparrows hop around café tables searching for crumbs. In the heart of our cities, peregrine falcons have made their home on the ledges of buildings, feeding on pigeons, just as they have for millennia on the natural ledges of sea cliffs. Even in the dead of night, an acute observer with a good ear might hear the subtle calls of small birds as they pass overhead on their autumn migrations. The ubiquity of birds means that they can be enjoyed equally by everyone, whether travelling the four corners of the world in search of 'lifers' (a birder's first sighting of a bird to tick off a life list), or from an armchair by a window. Birds belong to us all.

Bird imagery surrounds us too. All civilizations, even in the farthest outposts of humanity, at virtually every period in recorded history, have incorporated images of birds into the very fabric of daily life. Wood, textile, clay, metal, paper, stone and innumerable other materials have all been shaped into bird form or had bird images drawn onto, carved or woven into, or printed from, their surfaces. Universal, transcendental and tenacious; there is no niche in human culture or imagination that isn't inhabited by birds.

Just how birds have ingrained themselves in our collective psyche can be explored by taking a closer look at exactly what they are and how they live their lives. Birds are bipedal, walking on two legs, like us. They have a beak, and two wings formed for flight. Many other animals possess some of these features, although none except birds possesses them all. But birds have one characteristic unique to them alone: feathers. Any milliner, fly fisher, bedding manufacturer or cabaret dancer will attest to the unique qualities of feathers. Feathers have allowed arrows to fly, and poetry to be scribed. Only birds have feathers and birds have only feathers. Bristles, quills, down, even their eyelashes; all are modified feathers.

There are around 10,000 species of bird recognized in ornithology (the study of birds), compared with only 5,800 species of mammals. Birds are classified according to their supposed evolutionary relationships, with species grouped into genera, families and orders - often represented as an avian phylogenetic tree - from the Struthioniformes containing just two species of ostrich, to the Passeriformes or songbirds, which contains over 60 per cent of all avian species (pp.336–7). Mammals are, admittedly, more structurally diverse, having, for example, re-invented their quadrupedal body-plan as wings, fins, flippers, hooves and gripping hands, but birds make up for this in the dazzling diversity of their plumage. While this natural display has provided rich and vibrant inspiration for the palettes of artists, birds in fact see the world, and each other, in colours we can only imagine: a whole spectrum of ultraviolet invisible to the human eye (p.218–9).

Some pigments, like melanins, occur throughout the animal kingdom, and produce every shade of black, brown and grey, such as the subtly camouflaged coloration of owls and nightjars. The splendid scarlet of Mark Catesby's ibis, the pink of flamingos, or the red face and golden wing of Fabritius's iconic goldfinch (p.209, p.240, p.250) are caused by carotenoids: pigments synthesized from the diet. However, the metallic iridescence of peacocks, starlings and hummingbirds (p.148) is due not to pigments, but to the optical effects in the feathers' microstructure, meaning that beauty really is in the eye of the beholder. Bird species can even be identified by the microstructure of their feathers, a technique used, among others, in cutting-edge forensic research to investigate bird-aircraft strike hazards.

The wings of birds are formed from an independent aerofoil of stiff flight feathers protruding from the forelimb, leaving the legs free to adapt to other purposes: grasping tree trunks or prey, scratching, wading, fighting, underwater swimming or even showing off their colour to prospective partners (p.312, p.279). Bat wings, in contrast, are formed from a membrane of skin stretched between elongated fingers and their hind limbs, as were those of the extinct flying reptiles, the pterosaurs.

The Allegorical Bird

Flight - the concept of ascension to the heavens and unbounded freedom - is probably the single quality that connects birds most closely with the human spirit and has been most envied and emulated. From the fabled Icarus who flew too close to the sun on wings of feathers and wax, to the Renaissance 'flying machines' of Leonardo da Vinci, an enthusiastic observer of birds, and the nineteenth-century German aeronautical pioneer Otto Lilienthal, the first successful glider pilot, birds have inspired countless pioneers, inventors and aeronauts in their attempts at human flight, as well as many untimely deaths.

Existing in both the realms of earth and sky, birds inhabit the shaman spirit world, seemingly crossing the boundaries at the very transition between life and death, personified by the Thunderbird in Native American mythology or the white dove of the Christian Eucharist (p.187). Ornithomancy - reading omens from the actions of birds - was practised by many ancient cultures in the Mediterranean: the sight of a soaring eagle could predict the outcome of war or the birth of a son. An allegorical take on the transcendental symbolism of birds can be found in the English writer Barry Hines' tragic 1968 story *A Kestrel for a Knave* (later filmed by Ken Loach under the title *Kes*), in which a working-class boy in a coalmining community experiences a few short months of joy with a revered creature of the air, until its cruel loss consigns him to a bleak future underground (p.84). Bats, by comparison, have never had associations with the heavens. Quite the opposite, in fact. Denizens of caves and dark places, they are more demon than angel, though in medieval bestiaries bats were considered honorary birds by virtue of their ability to fly.

Birds are the messengers, the sidekicks and sometimes the very personification of the gods themselves. The Egyptian god Horus was depicted as a falcon (p.85), befitting a deity of the sky. Zeus, the ruler of the ancient Greek gods on Mount Olympus, regularly transformed into an eagle, but for the seduction of Leda – a union which would produce the beautiful Helen and eventually bring about the Trojan War – only the form of a swan would do. A peacock symbolizes the proud, regal (and long-suffering) wife of Zeus, Hera, while owls are sacred to the wise Athene, and one genus bears her name. Even today we talk about wise owls, proud peacocks and mighty eagles, and the personification of birds in proverb and folklore has been used for amusement and moral instruction from Aesop to the present day (p.98, p.227).

The eagle of Zeus was likewise the bird of his Roman equivalent, Jupiter, and hence the choice of emblem of the Roman Empire – an association that would spread through heraldry and nationalism from powerhouse to powerhouse across centuries of European political upheaval. Still the favourite bird of leaders and statesmen, an eagle, with one head or two, is the national symbol of at least fourteen countries across the world.

The bald eagle is the symbol of the United States, and most depictions of them are weighted with metaphors of national identity (p.119). There's even a US museum, the National Eagle Center in Minnesota, with a gallery dedicated to bald-eagle imagery. This species hasn't always been a popular choice, however. In the eighteenth century the Founding Father Benjamin Franklin criticized the eagle as a rank coward and bird of bad moral character. He thought the turkey, now the symbol of American Thanksgiving (p.304), a much more respectable bird. The American bird artist John James Audubon shared this opinion and chose a wild turkey as the iconic first plate in his magnificent 'double elephant folio edition' of *The Birds of America* (1827–38).

Birds are regular embodiments of allegorical meaning in visual art. The seaside gull or town pigeon (p.229, p.123), for example, can be less bird portraits than symbols of the commonplace. Half-hidden allusions to the political and religious turmoil of past centuries, like *The Threatened Swan* by Dutch Golden Age painter Jan Asselijn (p.97) and *The Wounded Eagle* by the nineteenth-century French animal painter Rosa Bonheur (p.118), are aesthetically triumphant as bird images in their own right.

The ownership of rare and valuable birds is in itself a symbol of status and wealth – though it is prudent also to commission a portrait that will still exist after the bird has died. Beautiful paintings are often all that are left to honour the prized falcons and exotic treasures of long-forgotten patrons (p.57, p.74). Many birds and bird-like creatures in mythology bear no resemblance to real species. The Stymphalian birds slain by Heracles for his sixth labour were man-eating creatures with metallic feathers and beaks of bronze (p.78). Likewise, the sirens that lured sailors to their doom in the *Odyssey* and the terrorizing harpies of Greek and Muslim mythology have attributes relating more to women than to birds. The phoenix (pp.52–3, pp.86–7, p.235) however, has one foot – a webbed, pink foot – in the real world. Flamingos, inhabiting caustic and deadly soda lakes seemingly to be reborn from the steaming, noxious surface, have been granted some of the attributes of the mythical bird (p.264) and 'phoenix' is preserved in their scientific name, Phoenicopteridae.

Feathered Bounty

Deserving of even greater reverence than the spirituality of flight is the role of birds as earthly providers. With few exceptions, all major bird groups are, or have been at some time in their history, taken as food by humans, or have been used to obtain food. Their flesh and eggs sustain us, and their feathers can be repurposed for clothing and adornment. From this basic bodily need, a complex and intricate relationship has evolved between birds and people, intertwining human cultures with birds in a myriad of ever-evolving ways.

Our wealth of exhibition varieties and rare breeds, birds kept for their usefulness as guards, their homing ability and their attractiveness or curiosity, all largely owe their existence to livestock initially bred for consumption. These same varieties, like the fancy pigeons studied by English naturalist Charles Darwin during his investigation into inheritance and evolution, continue to contribute to our understanding of the origins of life on Earth.

It is no coincidence that some of the most beautifully observed depictions of birds are those representing them as food sources. Our ancestors pondered the mysteries of migration while exploiting the sudden landfalls of fresh meat, like the Biblical arrival of quails (the only migratory gamebird) feeding the Children of Israel on their passage from Egypt. The sudden arrival of migrating birds feeding in the fertile marshlands and meadows of the Nile delta must have provided rich pickings for ancient Egyptians and were rendered with the intimacy that comes surely from a direct culinary connection (p.104, p.277). The pigeons shown drinking at a fountain, perfectly and accurately recorded in mosaic at Pompeii (p.170), are domesticated birds that would have provided a regular supply of meat throughout the year. Little wonder they're depicted so lovingly.

Much of the accurate observation of wild and domesticated birds in art history can be attributed to the hunting tradition.

The bird tables of today are the baited traps of the past, and much of our field-craft and knowledge of birds has its roots in practices initially adopted for trapping and killing. Likewise, our close knowledge of bird form and anatomy began with the butchering and preparation of carcasses for the table. This also provided unparalleled opportunities for the close inspection and appreciation of the subtleties and beauty of bird plumage recorded in the highly realistic still-life paintings from seventeenth-century northern Europe (p.102). Too exquisite to waste, the freshly dead birds – even those not destined for the table – recorded in studies such as those of British twentieth-century artist Charles Tunnicliffe's 'measured drawings' (p.210) and German Renaissance master Albrecht Dürer's wing of a roller (p.166), have a lasting and undeniable beauty.

The intimacy between human and bird, not just between predator and prey, but between two predators working together, reaches its height in the art of falconry. From tiny falcons used to hunt songbirds in Europe, to the pursuit of wolves with large eagles in Mongolia: with a rich historical and cultural legacy and a language and folklore all its own, it is not surprising that this sport has endured through so many centuries (p.190).

The intimate knowledge required by the human predator of avian prey can be adapted to less bloodthirsty pursuits and serve the needs of the modern eco-tourist. A visitor to New Guinea will need the services of a local guide if they want to photograph displaying birds of paradise (p.141), and doubtless the guide will have learned his field-craft as a plume hunter, employing the same skills and local knowledge as his forebears have for generations. The skills of luring and trapping birds, including the use of duck decoys (pp.192–3), are likewise now additionally repurposed to capture birds for scientific study and release.

While watching birds may have replaced hunting them in many parts of the world, the rule of thumb remains the same: the greater the knowledge of bird behaviour, the greater the prize. Perhaps the principal source of reverence of hunters for their sport is not the quarry itself, but the very communion with nature and wild places. This may explain why former hunters often become the most ardent conservationists; the British ornithologist and painter Sir Peter Scott, for example, founder of the UK conservation charity the Wildfowl and Wetlands Trust was, in his youth, an ardent wildfowler. His paintings show a deep love not just for wildfowl but for wetland habitats worldwide (p.316). It might be hard for us, as bird lovers, to imagine that modern-day hunters in Mediterranean countries like Malta, Egypt and Lebanon, slaughtering migrating birds wholesale with automatic weapons, share a deep affinity with them, as did the ancient Egyptians. Perhaps in time they too will eventually choose to put down their weapons and turn from carnage to conservation.

Preservation and Integrity

From the earliest days of the Age of Exploration, from the 1400s onwards, dried and salted skins of exotic birds reached Europe by the shipload. There they were reassembled by taxidermists, and eventually found homes in the private museums – the 'cabinets of curiosity' – of wealthy collectors, such as Sir Ashton Lever's famed museum of zoological and ethnographic specimens in central London (p.232). These collections, often just amalgamations of the colourful, interesting or exotic, were the principal source of raw materials for the scientific study of birds.

Information about a specimen, even as basic as a country of origin, if any had been recorded, was often lost or muddled. It wasn't unusual for missing parts of specimens to be patched up with others of entirely different species, though whether these were innocent mistakes or deliberate attempts at falsification is a secret lost to time. Many a 'species', never seen before or since, and even declared officially extinct, has been revealed as one of these taxidermy chimeras (p.19).

After the death of a bird, the colours of the skin, legs and bill (known as the 'soft parts') rapidly change. The eyes are removed when the bird is skinned, and sometimes even the colours of the feathers fade. So the mounted specimen, with soft-part colours and glass eyes of the taxidermist's own choosing, could look entirely unlike the species in life. The posture, too, would be open to interpretation. There's little in the skin of petrels and shearwaters (tube-nosed seabirds that nest in burrows on isolated sea cliffs), for example, to suggest that these birds shuffle along on their belly on land, so they were mounted standing misleadingly tall with their legs straight beneath them. Similarly, it could easily be assumed that grebes and divers (or loons) sit bolt upright on land, instead of virtually never even leaving the water.

Bird of paradise plumes reaching Europe from the Dutch colonies in New Guinea were a valuable trading commodity for centuries; roughly skinned and with the legs removed, they were intended simply to preserve the lavish feathers of the flanks, head and tail. However, when Europeans saw these 'trade skins' for the first time, they marvelled not just at the plumage, but at the lack of legs, assuming these birds to remain airborne in perpetuity, feeding from the dews of Heaven. This is the reason for their name 'birds of paradise' and for the scientific name of the greater bird of paradise, *Paradisaea apoda*, meaning 'without feet' (p.140).

Bit by bit, the inaccuracies resulting from the lack of opportunity for direct observation accumulated and were passed on like a game of Chinese whispers. The errors of taxidermists were innocently copied by artists of the day, and their work was copied by others to create a perpetual chain of ornithological inaccuracy throughout the historical literature. This is why scientific research collections from the nineteenth century onwards use skins of birds with no attempt to recreate an artificially lifelike appearance (p.33). As a tool for recording bird sightings, the camera has now largely replaced the shotgun, and with it the old adage 'what's hit is history; what's missed is mystery'.

Artists working in two dimensions from taxidermy specimens have the choice of using the specimen as reference only, or representing it as it is, with all its faults. While many do this in ignorance, for others it's a deliberate comment on the history of ornithology and the rich historical legacy of museum collections. The remarkable *trompe l'oeil* paintings of the French painter Leroy de Barde around 1800 faithfully re-created not just the specimens, but eerily lifelike copies of the exact same cabinets in Lever's collection (p.178).

Taxidermy is a fine-art sculpture and installation medium in its own right, allowing pertinent observations about our attitudes to animals, and playing on the fashions of bygone eras. Often the aim is to produce taxidermy that's deliberately poor in quality or taste. Or, in contrast, like the contemporary British artist Polly Morgan, making poignant use of taxidermy to portray an animal not animated, but inanimate, like the sad little blue tit lying dead in its glass dome (p.40).

Taxidermy itself has a rich cultural history, with changing styles and trends reflecting our attitudes to animals and the particular aesthetic leanings of individual craftsmen. Nowhere is it used to better naturalistic and educational effect than in the spectacular dioramas at the American Museum of Natural History in New York City, re-creating scenes from nature with the use of a cleverly painted curved background that gives the illusion of infinity. The creation of the Florida Everglades diorama (pp.136–7) played an important role in highlighting the devastating effects of the trade in exotic plumes for hats, clothing and jewellery, which decimated bird populations throughout the nineteenth and early twentieth centuries. The sheer scale of slaughter is barely conceivable. It is difficult today to comprehend that items like birds'-head earrings could ever have been considered good taste (p.300). Women's fashions drove the carnage and, on both sides of the Atlantic, women's passion ended it. The bravery and tenacity of a handful of women resulted in the establishment of the major organizations still working for bird conservation today: the Royal Society for the Protection of Birds in the UK, and the National Audubon Society in the US.

Icons and Origins

The word 'bird' yields a myriad of meaning. For some it evokes the sublime; for others, the ridiculous. In 'bird' there is 'food', and there is 'freedom'. There is 'pet', and also 'pest'. 'Bird' is the wilderness, and 'bird' is our feathered friend. With enough synonyms for 'bird' to fill a pocket thesaurus, it's not surprising that bird imagery, too, is inconceivably rich and varied. This book represents the tiniest fraction of that imagery. Much of it is art, but this is more than a book about bird art and its history; it's about culture in a far wider sense. The images contained in these pages are united only by a single theme – 'bird'. Like every good seating plan at a banquet, the traditional cliques have been broken up and rearranged to work together in unexpected ways, juxtaposed in pairs to be sometimes startling, usually thought-provoking, occasionally amusing and always more than the sum of the parts. There is more than enough iconic content to give the reassurance of being among friends, and enough surprises to provide the excitement of making new ones.

One of the messages of this book is that iconic imagery is often incidental – a byproduct of another process, recording a pivotal moment in history or science. An informal portrait may capture an isolated event in the career of an artist or researcher (p.13, p.153). A pioneering experimental attempt to understand locomotion through time-lapse photography or the use of photographs taken under ultra-violet light in ongoing research in avian biology may be striking images in their own right (p.263, pp.218–9). Likewise, that imagery might be a preliminary sketch or study for a 'finished' studio painting, never intended for wider circulation, or a drawing made as a scientific record by an expedition artist (p.126).

Technical advances in optical aids have made it possible to observe, film and photograph living, wild birds engaged in natural behaviour even at considerable distances, making one wonder how we ever managed to produce closely observed studies of birds before. But as these images show, the quality of art and observation has remained steadfastly excellent throughout; every human age has included individuals who recorded birds with equal acuity and sensitivity.

Whether birds are portrayed as art or for science – whether stylized, exaggerated, simplified or abstracted – observation is everything. You only have to look at the hummingbird gouged into the soil of the Nazca Desert in Peru (pp.108–9) to see that good observation doesn't necessarily mean detail or even realism. Observation of living birds allows artists to capture what birders call the 'jizz' – that certain, indefinable something which gives each species its particular character. Today the immediacy and expression of 'unfinished' field sketches, celebrating the very transitory nature of birds, have gained appreciation for the masterpieces they really are.

It is easy to forget the influence of technology on the images we see, and particularly on published images. All reproduction involves some degree of translation imposed by the medium, though nowadays high-quality digital scanning and printing mean that the changes are minimal. Crude printed illustrations from the sixteenth century, such as those in *Historia Animalium* (p.302) by the Swiss Renaissance polymath Conrad Gessner, reflect not the artistry of the period, but the limited capacity of woodcut prints to show detail. Moving on through history, very few artists had the skills in copperplate 'intaglio' techniques to reproduce their own work, so the published bird books of much of the eighteenth and early nineteenth centuries are as much attributable to the engravers as they are to the artists. Audubon's celebrated life-sized American birds, for example, owe much of their profound beauty to the skills of the engraver Robert Havell (p.177). The intricate wood engraving technique of the English naturalist Thomas Bewick (p.16) and others was only possible because of the earlier invention of tools employed for the process of metal engraving, themselves developed for engraving on weaponry. Likewise, the subtle technology of lithography – literally, 'drawing on stone' – was initially developed as a means of reproducing sheet music, and only afterwards adopted by artists including William Swainson, Edward Lear and John Gould for illustrating bird books (p.43, p.106). Lithography has a softness and delicacy that all earlier print processes lacked, and unlike previous copperplate print processes, the image could be drawn directly onto the stone by the artists themselves, so the lines were their lines and not transcribed by a third party.

Invented for music and perfected for birds, there's a final ornithological twist to the tale of lithography. The fine-grained sediment laid down 150 million years ago in the Late Jurassic period, in what would become the Solnhofen region of Bavaria, did not only yield superlative printing slabs. When the rock strata were split, quarry workers found fossils – fish, dragonflies, crustaceans, a complete feather and, around 1875, a bird attributed to the same species – perfectly preserved in exquisite detail. With characteristics of both living birds and reptiles, it was considered a 'missing link', supporting Charles Darwin's recently published theory of evolution by natural selection. It was named, most appropriately, *Archaeopteryx lithographica* (p.26).

I'll leave you here, with *Archaeopteryx*, at the very foot of the avian tree. The winged world and our relationship with it have the power to lead in marvellous and unexpected directions, to inspire and enthral. I hope you'll enjoy exploring its branches.

Katrina van Grouw
Ornithologist, author, illustrator and artist
Author of *The Unfeathered Bird* and *Unnatural Selection*

Jakob Bogdány

Still Life with Fruit, Parrots and a Cockatoo, c.1700
Oil on canvas, 81 × 116 cm / 32 × 45⅝ in
Private collection

A collection of tropical birds pose above a stone plinth laden with ripe fruits, and peer at the viewer with sharply focused, bright beady eyes. To the right of the picture, on a broken column, is a scarlet macaw (*Ara macao*), while at the centre a yellow-crested cockatoo (*Cacatua sulphurea*) greedily draws a plum up to its beak and another parrot, possibly based on a sun parakeet (*Aratinga solstitialis*), swoops in to take its pick of the cornucopia. The Hungarian-born artist Jakob Bogdány (1658-1724), a renowned painter

of birds, characteristically depicts them with their heads in profile, carefully arranged in dioramas. The composition's somewhat stiff - almost stuffed - impression belies the studies from nature Bogdány made in King William III's aviary at Hampton Court, a wonderful resource for an artist. Bogdány moved to the Netherlands as a young man and initially specialized in still lifes before settling in England after the Glorious Revolution of 1688 and shifting his focus to large compositions with living birds,

occasionally in combination with other animals. Such works were highly popular, and Bogdány became a successful supplier to the English aristocracy, as well as working for Queen Mary and later for Queen Anne, thus gaining access to the renowned royal collection of exotic birds from all over the world. This painting may have served as an attractive decoration of an aristocratic salon, probably as an overdoor, where guests conversed about these curious, enchanting and quirky creatures.

Frans Lanting

Macaws over river, Peru, 1992
Photograph, dimensions variable

Taken in Amazonia, this remarkable image captures the vivid colours of three macaw species: the blue-and-yellow macaw (*Ara ararauna*), with entirely blue back and upper tail; the scarlet macaw (*A. macao*), with large yellow patches on the wings and minimal striping of the face; and the red-and-green macaw (*A. chloropterus*), which has less yellow on the upperwing and more facial striping. The three species are widespread in the Amazonian forests of Brazil and neighbouring countries, where they primarily eat fruits and nuts. This diet

is low on minerals and some of the most famous macaw images are of birds gathered at salt licks to supplement these essential nutrients. Altogether there are around seventeen macaw species still extant, all dwelling in the American tropics and all colourful. The red coloration in macaws and other parrots is produced in a unique way by pigments called psittacofulvins, which are different from carotenoids, the pigments responsible for reds, oranges and yellows in the feathers of most other birds. Meanwhile, the

blue of parrots, like that of some other birds, is mainly due to tiny structures in the feathers that absorb and cancel out some light wavelengths while reflecting others, including blue. Renowned Dutch wildlife photographer Frans Lanting (born 1951) has travelled the world on assignment for *National Geographic* and other prestigious publications.

Frida Kahlo

Me and My Parrot, 1941
Oil on canvas, 82 × 62.8 cm / 32¼ × 24¾ in
Private collection

In one of fifty-five self-portraits she painted with various animals and birds, the Mexican artist Frida Kahlo (1907–54) depicts four colourful parrots – lilac-crowned amazon (*Amazona autumnalis*) and yellow-headed amazon (*A. oratrix*) – with textural feathers perching on her shoulders and sitting in her lap. Kahlo had a great love of animals and lived with many pets, including hairless dogs, monkeys and a deer, as well as birds, in her home Casa Azul (Blue House) in Coyoacán, Mexico City. Parrots are birds of around 400 species, which inhabit tropical and subtropical regions. The order Psittaciformes can be subdivided into three families, the Psittacidae (perhaps the most typically recognizable parrot), the Cacatuidae (cockatoos) and the Strigopidae (New Zealand parrots) – with the greatest diversity occurring in South America. The birds are known for their intelligence, and many can imitate human speech. Like all birds, they produce sounds by expelling air across the syrinx – an organ at the mouth of the trachea – changing its shape to produce different sounds. Some grey parrots can associate words with their meanings, as well as forming simple sentences. Kahlo, who suffered from polio at the age of six and at eighteen was involved in a bus crash that left her with spinal and pelvic damage, started painting while she was convalescing, representing herself with the aid of a mirror above her bed. Having married and divorced the artist Diego Rivera, she painted this portrait just after the couple remarried.

Oskar Heinroth

Magdalena Heinroth with Three Hand-Raised Jackdaws, 1919
Photograph
Staatsbibliothek zu Berlin

A young woman regards three Eurasian jackdaws (*Corvus monedula*) perched on her arms. Her tired-looking face is a contrast to their curiosity and expectation, but the bond between them is clear – and no wonder, for the woman, German ornithologist Magdalena Heinroth (1883–1932), had hand-reared the jackdaws in her Berlin apartment, together with her husband Oskar (1871–1945), feeding them until they could feed themselves. For thirty years, the Heinroths ran a household that remains difficult even to imagine

today, sharing their home over twenty-eight years with around a thousand birds (from 286 species), which they raised, observed, documented and photographed together around the clock: this might explain the worn expression on Magdalena's face. The two were passionate ornithologists, Magdalena as a trained taxidermist and Oskar as a doctor and zoologist. Their pioneering work on the birds in their home laid the foundations for modern behavioural research in birds. The resulting four-volume work

Die Vögel Mitteleuropas ('Birds of Middle Europe'), published between 1924 and 1933, contains 4,040 photos. It has a chapter dedicated to each of the Heinroths' 286 bird species, giving specific information based on the couple's direct observations on their rearing, communication, nutrition and courtship behaviour. Throughout the work, the authors' love for and amazement at their avian subjects is clearly evident, making their magnum opus unique among natural research surveys, in addition to its huge scientific value.

Charles and Ray Eames

*Eames House Bird, c.*1910
Carved wood and steel wire, H. *c.*27.5 cm / 10¾ in
Eames Foundation, Pacific Palisades, California

Cherished by its owners Charles and Ray Eames, this small wooden black bird stood in the industrial designers' living room for more than fifty years. With its elegant curves, discreet steel legs and beady eye, the painted bird is one of the couple's most famous pieces. But though it was used in many of their furniture photo-shoots, and even appeared nestled amid a cluster of wire-frame chairs on a 1952 cover of *Architectural Review*, the bird is not an original Eames design. It was purportedly acquired on a visit to the Appalachian Mountains. Husband-and-wife team Charles (1907-78) and Ray (1912-88) were keen travellers and often returned from their trips laden with ornaments and American folk art to decorate their Modernist home, The Eames House, in Pacific Palisades, Los Angeles. However, the bird's form is remarkably similar to the popular decoys and wildfowl sculptures produced by wood carvers Charles Perdew (1874-1963) and his wife Edna (1882-1974) for local hunters in Illinois. Whatever its true origin, the bird's craftsmanship and simple design appealed greatly to Charles and Ray Eames, echoing in its simplicity the innovative plywood furniture that they designed. Today, official reproductions of the Eames House Bird are produced by Swiss furniture company Vitra. While some question whether the Eames name should be attached to it at all, this Mid-Century design icon would probably be languishing in obscurity without the keen eyes of this visionary couple.

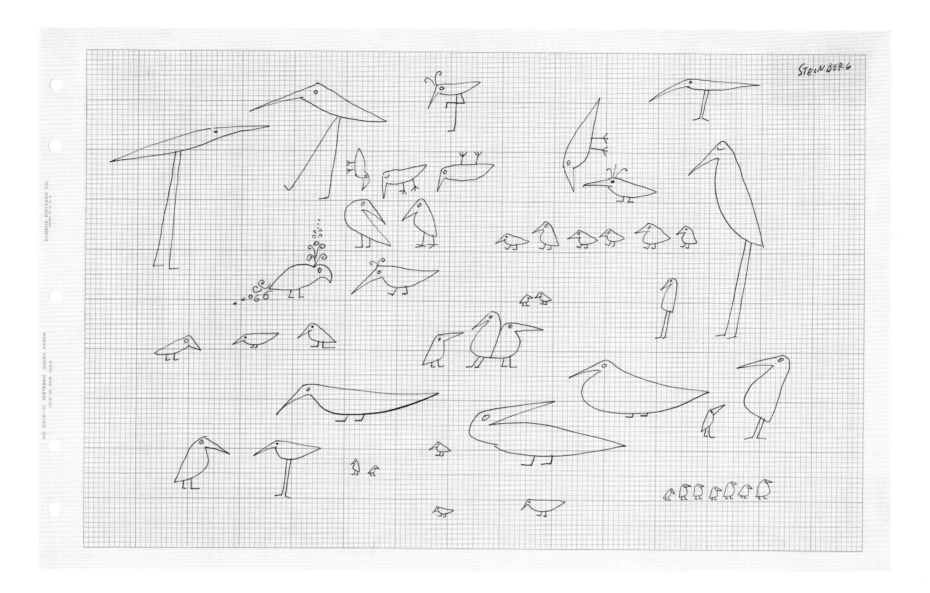

Saul Steinberg

Birds, 1945-54
Pen and black ink on ivory-wove graph paper, 27.8 × 41.9 cm / 11 × 16½ in
Art Institute of Chicago, Illinois

A playful avian flock parades about a page of graph paper. Their procession is directionless, as they move along rigid lines yet adhere to no order, giving each other meaningful glances as they interact. The shapes are simple caricatures, yet we can venture a guess as to which species may have inspired this lively grouping: perhaps the waddling dance of the American woodcock (*Scolopax minor*) or the stately stature of a stork. It is up to the viewer to decide, for the appeal of the American artist Saul Steinberg

(1914-99) lies in his absurdist sense of humour rather than literal description. Steinberg, born in Romania, spent his youth in Bucharest during a time when Western styles were converging with traditional Ottoman influence. The vibrant city with its many cultures would shape his prolific career. Following a move to Milan to study architecture, Steinberg was detained as anti-Semitic nationalism heightened in Italy. Upon his release in 1941, Steinberg fled for the United States via the Dominican Republic,

where he was when his drawings were first published by *The New Yorker*, thus beginning a relationship spanning six decades that included his famous map, *View of the World from 9th Avenue*. His uniquely witty style and the charm of his drawings earned him acclaim across multiple disciplines. In addition to magazine publications, Steinberg's paintings, textiles, collages and murals are exhibited in galleries and museums internationally.

Thomas Bewick

The Magpie, from *A History of British Birds, Vol. 1 Land Birds*, 1797
Wood engraving

In an age of lavish, coloured ornithological monographs for a privileged and specialized market, Thomas Bewick's exquisite illustrated books, cheap to produce and confined to minuscule dimensions, brought nature to new audiences. His first book, the two-volume *A History of British Birds*, included familiar birds like this Eurasian magpie (*Pica pica*) as well as less familiar rarities; it became one of the best-loved books of the age, encouraging people of every social class to take an interest in the birdlife around them. Magpies are members of the crow family (Corvidae), highly intelligent and opportunistic birds with glossy blue-black and white plumage. The son of a tenant farmer, Bewick (*c.*1753–1828) had no academic training. His education came from the countryside itself and contact with fellow craftsmen. A metal engraver by trade, Bewick discovered that the tools (called burins) used in his daily work were equally suitable for making precise wood engravings in the hard end-grain of slow-growing box wood. Bewick's name is synonymous with wood engraving – not to be confused with wood*cut*, which was the first and comparatively crude print medium. Unlike his contemporaries, whose original drawings were prepared for printing by other artisans, Bewick was, first and foremost, a printmaker. He engraved and printed his own blocks, a process requiring considerable skill. Bewick's illustrations, monochrome and seldom exceeding 10 cm (4 in) across, have touched the hearts of millions and continue to inspire new generations of naturalists.

Edward Bawden

The Peacock and the Magpie, from *Aesop's Fables*, 1970
Colour printed linocut, 40.5 × 56 cm / 16 × 22 in
Fry Art Gallery, Saffron Walden

Simple, understated and elegant, this narrative linocut by British artist Edward Bawden (1903–89), one of a series of illustrations from *Aesop's Fables*, is a masterpiece of modern graphic art. The peacock, basking in his own splendour, is about to be elected king of the birds by an admiring throng when a magpie intervenes, cunningly raising questions about the peacock's usefulness in deterring predators, and showing the birds that there are other qualities more desirable in a leader than physical beauty. The peacock gained a reputation for useless vanity, while the magpie became esteemed for his cleverness. Linocuts belong to the group of processes called relief prints, in which ink is transferred onto paper from a raised, flat surface. Despite its apparent simplicity, the creation of coloured relief prints like this one involves some complex techniques – for example, applying ink only to selected areas, overlaying inks of varying opacity to produce additional colours, or using multiple printing blocks to produce a single image. Traditional print forms were initially developed purely as a means of repro-

duction, the aim being to create quickly as close a likeness as possible of a pre-existing work. Freed from commercial constraints and working experimentally, graphic artists taking the time to print by hand were able to explore what these techniques could offer as expressive media in their own right. While we use the term 'printing' for commercial reproduction, the creation of these 'original prints' is known as 'printmaking'.

Joseph Chaumet

Hummingbird aigrette transformable into a brooch, *c.*1880
Gold, silver, diamonds and rubies, H. 10 cm / 4 in
Collections Chaumet, Paris

Two, long tail 'feathers' ending in large, racket-shaped spatules indicate that this aigrette - a piece of jewellery worn attached to a hat or other piece of headwear - was most likely modelled on a male marvellous spatuletail (*Loddigesia mirabilis*), a Peruvian hummingbird that performs a courtship display for females by holding its extended feathers outwards while hovering. Crafted by the French jeweller Joseph Chaumet (1852–1928) early in the Belle Époque of the late nineteenth century, the bird is resplendent with precious stones, while still reflecting the animal's true form. The 'plumage' created by a tight pavé setting of rubies and diamonds mirrors the refracting feathers hummingbirds use to attract mates. Chaumet's hummingbird is a dynamic object: as an aigrette, the feathers would tremble and shake, caught by the wind while perched atop a fabulously rich Parisian headdress. It could also be transformed from an aigrette into a brooch by removing the additional feathers. The maison, now known as Chaumet, which originated in 1780, had been producing luxury, high-end jewellery for over a century when Chaumet married the owner's daughter and gave it his name. The maison has continued to be inspired by the natural world. By building birds out of diamonds - quite aside from creating a poetic language of aesthetic symbols - Chaumet brings together two sides of natural history, albeit in singularly inaccessible structures: the active, vivacity of life and the motionless, enduring chemical lattices of geology.

Le Nébuleux, étalant ses parures. Pl. 16.

Jacques Barraband

Le Nébuleux, étalant ses parures, from *Histoire Naturelle des Oiseaux de Paradis et des Rolliers: suivie de celle des toucans et des barbus* by François Levaillant, 1806
Etching, printed in colour à la poupée, 51 × 33 cm / 20⅛ × 13 in

Among the most exquisite of all ornithological illustrations were those produced by the French artist Jacques Barraband (c.1767–1890) for the published works of naturalist François Levaillant (1753–1824). Working closely with the finest engravers and printers of his day, Barraband developed a distinctive style for reproducing his illustrations. Instead of printing in black then painting the prints with watercolour, they used a technique called *à la poupée* ('with the dolly') in which coloured inks are applied directly to the copper printing plate with a 'dolly' of twisted rag before printing. He produced his drawings directly from specimens described by Levaillant, many of which are now at the Netherlands National Museum of Natural History in Leiden, including this unique 'cloudy bird of paradise'. Barraband himself was confused by it – and with good reason. The specimen has been carefully studied by modern ornithologists and revealed to be a chimera of parts put together from other birds. The wirelike feathers and white plumes are from the twelve-wired bird of paradise (*Seleucidis melanoleucus*) though in nature these plumes are a deep yellow (they fade soon after death) and are not positioned on the back. The wings are from a woodpecker, and the upper mandible of the bill is in fact an inverted lower mandible of another species completely. Although Levaillant's many errors have undermined his reputation as a scientist, this does not diminish appreciation of Barraband's beautiful and accurately observed illustrations.

Allen & Ginter

Birds of the Tropics, 1889
Chromolithograph, 7.3 × 8.3 cm / 2⅞ × 3¼ in
Metropolitan Museum of Art, New York

This colourful selection of twelve cigarette cards celebrating birds of the tropics - part of a set of fifty - begins with the Alexandrine parakeet (*Psittacula eupatria*, top left), ends with the scarlet macaw (*Ara macao*, bottom right) and includes such exotic species as the black swan (*Cygnus atratus*, bottom left), the fire-tailed sunbird (*Aethopyga ignicauda*, top, second right) and the golden pheasant (*Chrysolophus pictus*, bottom, second left). The cards were created in 1889 by the Richmond, Virginia, tobacco company Allen

& Ginter and proved so popular that the company produced two versions. A set of smaller cards included only the original portraits of each bird, while this larger set reused those portraits - the darker panels - and added some paler, atmospheric background. Certain of the portraits and poses can be traced to their artistic inspirations, such as the macaw by Edward Lear (see p.43) or the resplendent quetzal (*Pharomachrus mocinno*) from John Gould's (see p.106) *A Monograph of the Trogonidae* (1838). Birds were a

popular subject that also featured in three more sets of cards: *Birds of America*, *Game Birds* and *Song Birds of the World*. Allen & Ginter were the first company to produce trading cards with their cigarettes - in part the card reinforced the flimsy paper packaging - but the practice later became widespread. Allen & Ginter's own card sets ranged from world sovereigns and naval flags to actresses and Native American chiefs, but the most popular by far were the baseball cards they first produced in 1887.

Thomas Poulsom

Nina the Northern Lapwing, 2013
Lego bricks, H. *c*.14.4 cm
Private collection

A handful of Lego bricks has been snapped together to form the recognizable likeness of a northern lapwing (*Vanellus vanellus*). Lapwings are wading birds common to much of Europe whose name is thought to derive from the 'lapping' sound of their wings in flight. Balanced on lurid pink legs, this work by British garden designer and artist Thomas Poulsom – one of tens of similar works featured in his book *Birds from Bricks* (2016) – may echo taxidermy of the nineteenth century in its impressive ability to represent a living creature,

irrespective of its immobility. And yet, in stark contrast to those who conjured life from dead specimens, no natural material has been used in this recreation of a living organism: the ABS plastic is non-biodegradable and difficult to recycle. In that way, Lego bricks could be seen as an ironic medium with which to introduce the subjects of ornithology and biodiversity to toy-lovers. Indeed, images of Poulsom's work shared online have been so popular that Lego have turned a number of his designs into official sets, packaged and distributed by

the company, while his larger scale models have been acquired by the United Kingdom's Wildfowl and Wetlands Trust to decorate the paths through some of their conservation wetlands. Seen on these trails, Poulsom's works are doubly arresting thanks to the juxtaposition of their crisp, cellular makeup with the semi-wild environments, and seem to ask their viewers just how far animals' forms can be reduced and simplified and yet remain identifiable.

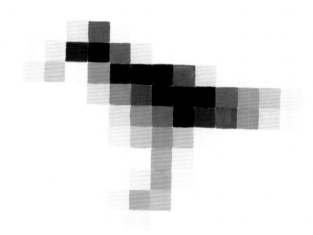

Marcus Coates

Common Sandpiper, 2019
Gouache on watercolour paper, 48 × 65.5 cm / 18⅞ × 25¾ in
Private collection

A simple collection of coloured squares sit adjacent to each other – black, grey and brown – starkly placed against a featureless background, but the viewer is left with no doubt that the life-sized image is that of a bird, standing erect, facing to the left. *Common Sandpiper* appears as part of a collection British artist and ornithologist Marcus Coates (born 1968) painted of animals with the word 'common' as part of their non-scientific name, a series intended to question the value attached to common species. Indeed, the work's title leads us to assume that the assorted pixels are representative of the common sandpiper (*Actitis hypoleucos*), a medium-sized migratory wading bird widespread throughout most of Eurasia at various times of the year – but we must take the artist's word for it. The details of the animal's body, required by naturalists to make species identifications, are all hidden: the crescent of white feathers framing the front of the closed wing, the tip of dark on the end of the bill, the bar of dark feathers transecting the pale eye ring, have all been subsumed into blocks of uninformative colour. As well as asking us to look again at more common UK species, Coates' reduction of the bird to fifty coloured squares resembles a heavily magnified section of a digital photograph, or an enormously compressed JPEG or TIFF, highlighting the largely digital nature of our interactions with wildlife in the twenty-first century.

Shen Quan

Flowers and Birds, 1750
Hanging scroll, ink and colour on silk, 116.4 × 50 cm / 45¾ × 19¾ in
Metropolitan Museum of Art, New York

This bird-and-flower painting, signed 'Spring 1750, Chaohengzai, Shen Quan', draws on one of the three main traditions in Chinese painting, alongside landscapes and figure painting. The accompanying calligraphy was considered a vital part of the painting. The artist Shen (c.1682–1762), who was already well-known in China, spent two years in Nagasaki from 1731 – during Japan's Edo period, it was the only Japanese city open to foreigners – teaching local painters his meticulously realistic, three-dimensional style of painting, and founding what would become the Nagasaki school. Nagasaki was a centre for the transmission of Chinese culture within Japan, and the Chinese there also acted as conduits for the diffusion of Western science and art. It has been suggested that the Nagasaki school style may have been inspired by the naturalistic illustrations in eighteenth-century Chinese and Western treatises on botany, zoology and mineralogy. Shen's realistic treatment of the birds in his painting would have been subordinate to his ideas about their essence, however, reflecting the emotions and personality of the artist – particularly literati scholar-painters, who were intent on capturing not only the outward appearance of their subjects but also their internal spirit. Shen based the birds on the red-billed blue magpie (*Urocissa erythroryncha*), with its extraordinarily long tail, but he has taken liberties in the details of plumage, with the result that the birds are effectively creatures of his imagination.

Ito Jakuchu

Golden Pheasants in Snow, from *Colorful Realm of Living Beings*, c.1761-65
Hanging scroll, ink and colour on silk, 142.1 × 79.5 cm / 56 × 31⅜ in
Museum of Imperial Collections, Tokyo

In addition to the careful observation and technical skill that helped make him a popular artist of the Edo period in Japan, Ito Jakuchu (1716-1800) heightened the level of realism in his depiction of golden pheasants (*Chrysolophus pictus*) by applying powdered white paint to create a subtle three-dimensional effect and a powdery texture for the snow. Birds were among Jakuchu's most frequent subjects, and he captures the distinctive golden cape, bright red body and long mottled tail of the male golden pheasant, which is native to the mountains of Western China. Next to the male is a female with typically more muted colours. These birds, which only fly in short bursts and prefer to walk along the ground, are sometimes known to stay near human residences in winter to find food more easily. This work is one of a set of thirty paintings of birds, animals and flowers that are considered Jakuchu's masterpiece: *Colourful Realm of Living Beings* (Doshoku sai-e), which was painted between 1757 and 1766 and gifted to the Shokoku-ji, a Buddhist temple in Kyoto, as a personal expression of the artist's Buddhist devotion. The son of a grocer, Jakuchu was considered one of the eccentrics of the period and experimented with a variety of distinctive painting and printing styles that resulted in dramatically colourful and dynamic compositions that are highly decorative and patterned, as can be seen here.

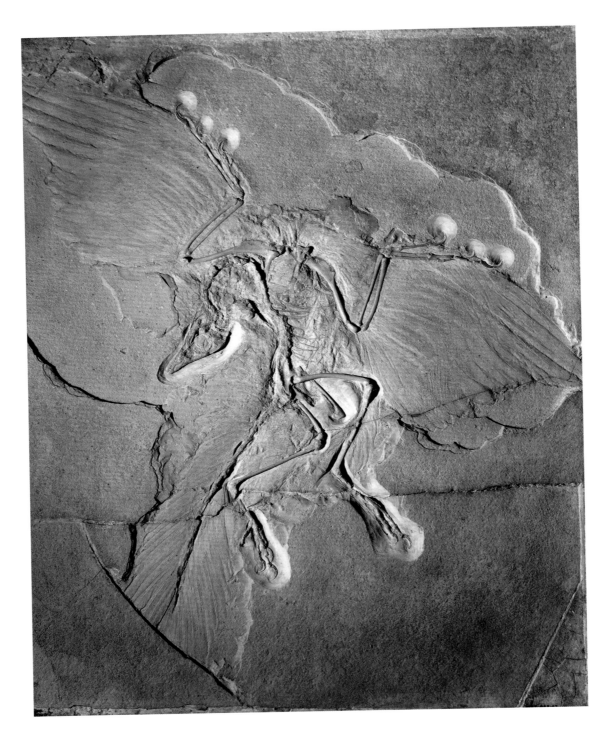

Unknown

Archaeopteryx siemensii, *c*.150 million years ago
Solnhofen limestone, 46 × 38 cm / 18 × 15 in
Museum für Naturkunde, Berlin

Characterized by what palaeontologists call a 'death pose', the head and neck of this *Archaeopteryx* ('ancient wing') are arched back from the stiffening of the muscles and tendons of the neck after death. The fossil shows features of both reptiles (teeth, a bony tail and claws on its wings) and later birds (asymmetrical flight feathers, a wishbone and possibly a partially reversed first toe), and may thus represent a transitional stage between the two. Roughly the size of a raven, the creature did not possess the keeled sternum that anchors the flight muscles of modern birds, though a cartilaginous sternum may have enabled a modified flight stroke. If it did fly, it was probably in short bursts, followed by a glide. It had three claws on each wing, and the lack of a fully reversed toe may indicate it could not grasp a perch and may have lived mostly on the ground (though many modern birds without a grasping hallux still perch in trees). The first *Archaeopteryx* skeleton was identified in 1861, near Langenaltheim, Germany. The discovery coincided with the publication of Darwin's *On the Origin of Species*, and the specimen, which was sold to the Natural History Museum in London, seemed serendiptiously to confirm Darwin's theory. The Berlin Specimen illustrated here, is the most complete skeleton discovered to date, and the first with an intact head; it was found in 1874 or 1875 near Eichstatt, Germany. Since its initial discovery, *Archaeopteryx* has become central to an understanding of evolution.

differing from the Progne purpurea of both Americas, only in being rather duller coloured, smaller, and slenderer, is considered by Mr. Gould as specifically distinct. Fifthly, there are three species of mocking-thrush—a form highly characteristic of America. The remaining land-birds form a most singular group of finches, related to each other in the structure of their beaks, short tails, form of body, and plumage: there are thirteen species, which Mr. Gould has divided into four sub-groups. All these species are peculiar to this archipelago; and so is the whole group, with the exception of one species of the sub-group Cactornis, lately brought from Bow island, in the Low Archipelago. Of Cactornis, the two species may be often seen climbing about the flowers of the great cactus-trees; but all the other species of this group of finches, mingled together in flocks, feed on the dry and sterile ground of the lower districts. The males of all, or certainly of the greater number, are jet black; and the females (with perhaps one or two exceptions) are brown. The most curious fact is the perfect gradation in the size of the beaks in the different species of Geospiza, from one as

1. Geospiza magnirostris.
2. Geospiza fortis.
3. Geospiza parvula.
4. Certhidea olivaºea.

large as that of a hawfinch to that of a chaffinch, and (if Mr. Gould is right in including his sub-group, Certhidea, in the main

Unknown

Four species of Galápagos finch, from *Journal of Researches into the Geology and Natural History of the Various Countries Visited by H.M.S.* Beagle, *1832–6* by Charles Darwin, 1845
Etching, 17.3 × 11.3 cm / 6¾ × 4½ in
Natural History Museum, London

On his voyage around the world on HMS *Beagle* from 1831 to 1836, the young British naturalist Charles Darwin spent only five weeks in the Galápagos Islands. Nonetheless the finches of the Galápagos shown here – now known as Darwin's finches – have become inextricably linked with Darwin's insight that natural selection was the mechanism behind evolution. At the time he collected finches on the various islands, however, Darwin did not even appreciate that they were related, an understandable error given the birds' variety of bill shapes, from massive (Fig. 1; *Geospiza magnirostris*) to fine and warbler-like (Fig. 4; *Certhidea olivacea*). It was only when the finches were examined by the ornithologist John Gould (see p.106) in 1837 that he – and Darwin – appreciated that they were related species whose bills had adapted to their specialized diets, from insects or pollen to seeds and nuts. In the second edition of *Voyage of the Beagle* in 1845, Darwin wrote, 'Seeing this gradation and diversity of structure in one small group of birds, ... one might really fancy that from an original paucity of birds in this archipelago, one species had been taken and modified for different ends.' Darwin's fancy has been vindicated by modern DNA analysis. From a single ancestral species, Darwin's finches – in fact, they are members of the tanager family – have diverged into fourteen species (arguably one or two more) plus a further species on Cocos Island some 750 km (466 miles) north west of the Galápagos.

Ulisse Aldrovandi

Golden eagles, from *Ornithologiae, hoc est, De avibus historiae libri XII*, 1599
Printed book, 35 × 21 cm / 13¾ × 8¼ in
Library of Congress, Washington, DC

These two drawings of golden eagles (*Aquila chrysaetos*) appear in a book that described species of birds with varying degrees of information on their ecology, distribution and cultural significance, many accompanied by coloured illustrations. The author was one of the first natural historians in Europe, the Italian Ulisse Aldrovandi (1522–1605), who became the first known professor of natural sciences at the University of Bologna in 1561. One of his greatest works is this thirteen-volume illustrated series on natural history – including dragons – of which he dedicated three volumes to birds: *Ornithologiae, hoc est, De avibus historiae* ('Ornithology, that is, the history of birds'), published in 1599. The golden eagle was probably much more common in Aldrovandi's time than it is now, when only about 9,000–12,000 pairs remain in Europe. In Italy, they are found in the Alps and Apennines, where they feed on mammals and other birds, such as grouse and partridge. They are revered by humans across their range, including the indigenous cultures of North America, and are the national animal of five countries (Albania, Germany, Austria, Mexico and Kazakhstan). In the Roman military, each legion caried an aquila, or eagle standard modelled after the golden eagle (see p.266). Aldrovandi's four-and-a-half-page description of the bird is short compared with those of other species, perhaps because it was so well known.

Johann Jakob Walther

*Sparrowhawk and Eagle Owl, c.*1639
Watercolour and gouache on paper
Musées de la Ville de Strasbourg

One of a set of twenty watercolours by the German ornithologist and artist Johann Walther (1650-1717) held in the collections of Strasbourg museums, this fine painting depicts a male Eurasian sparrowhawk (*Accipiter nisus*) and a Eurasian eagle owl (*Bubo bubo*). The birds are not shown to scale; male sparrowhawks are tiny and would be dwarfed by the massive owl, the largest owl species in western Europe. The names at the top of the painting are in Latin; the word *muscetus* might be familiar to some as 'musket', the falconers'

term for a male sparrowhawk. In most birds of prey, the female is considerably larger than the male, which accounts for this distinction in names. Despite their predatory habits, hawks and owls are not closely related. Neither do they hunt the same prey. The short rounded wings and long tail of sparrowhawks enable them to pursue birds in flight with remarkable agility even through thick foliage, and their long legs afford them extra reach to pluck birds from the air. Owls, by contrast, are mammal specialists, swooping on

stationary prey hiding among leaves at ground level. In case their prey bites back, they have a protective layer of feathering covering each of their toes. Little is known of Johann Walther, other than that he and his son produced illustrations for fisherman and hunter Leonard Baldner of his quarry along the Rhine.

GOLDFINCH AND CANARY MULE.

DARK MEALY.   CINNAMON

DARK JONQUE

W. A. Blakston, W. Swaysland and August F. Wiener

Goldfinch and Canary Mule, from *The illustrated Book of Canaries and Cage-Birds, British and Foreign, c.1878*
Chromolithograph
Harvard University, Cambridge, Massachusetts

Songbirds have been kept in cages to delight their owners with colourful plumage and melodious song since at least Roman times. For about 400 years, a particular branch of the pastime has involved cross-breeding different species to generate an ever-greater range of plumages. Finch species have been at the forefront of this cross-breeding enterprise, with finch × finch crosses known as hybrids and finch × canary crosses known as mules which, like their equine counterparts, are likely to be infertile. Among the easiest to breed are goldfinch mules, the result of interbreeding a goldfinch (*Carduelis carduelis*) and a canary. All such mules have the red face mask of their goldfinch parent, but the body plumage varies according the gender of the species used. Illustrated here are three plumage shades: dark mealy, dark jonque and cinnamon. Exhibitors at competitive cagebird shows may place their birds in separate categories reserved for different shades. There are categories reserved for, for example, greenfinch (*Chloris chloris*) and bullfinch (*Pyrrhula pyrrhula*) mules. While this book from 1878 focuses on canaries, it also includes information about other cagebirds such as parrots and starlings, and it offers detailed practical advice, for example explaining the intimate process of safely washing one's canary. The book is now a collector's item, a quality first edition commanding a price in excess of £1,300.

Blaise Bontems

Octagonal bird cage with three singing birds, *c.*1870
Gilt-brass, porcelain, 48.5 × 26 cm × 26 cm / 19 × 10¼ × 10¼ in
Private collection

The bars of this octagonal brass cage are unnecessary. The three songbirds swivel their heads, flap their tails and move their beaks as they chirp – yet they will never escape. They are metal shells covered with feathers and driven by a clockwork mechanism in the base, with its inset plaques of Sèvres porcelain depicting pairs of lovers. French watchmaker Blaise Bontems (1814–93) began creating his singing automata in the mid-1800s, when he stumbled upon the idea after being asked as an apprentice in the Vosges to repair a snuffbox with a mechanical bird. Bontems studied the songs of the common nightingale (*Luscinia megarhynchos*) before modifying the gears of the snuffbox to produce a song that sounded real. As demand for Bontems' birds grew, he opened his own workshop in 1849. His novelties were immensely popular. Some 90 per cent of Bontems' output was sold abroad; at the Great Exhibition in London in 1851 his automata were described as 'toys for adults rather than children'. At a time when cagebirds were valued for their song, an artificial bird that looked and sounded natural – on a flower or a branch, or in a cage – was a status symbol. In an arrangement like this, the birds could be set to sing continuously or intermittently. Bontems retired in 1881, and was replaced by his son, Charles, under whom the company continued to thrive, employing more than twenty workers to produce about 400 pieces a year.

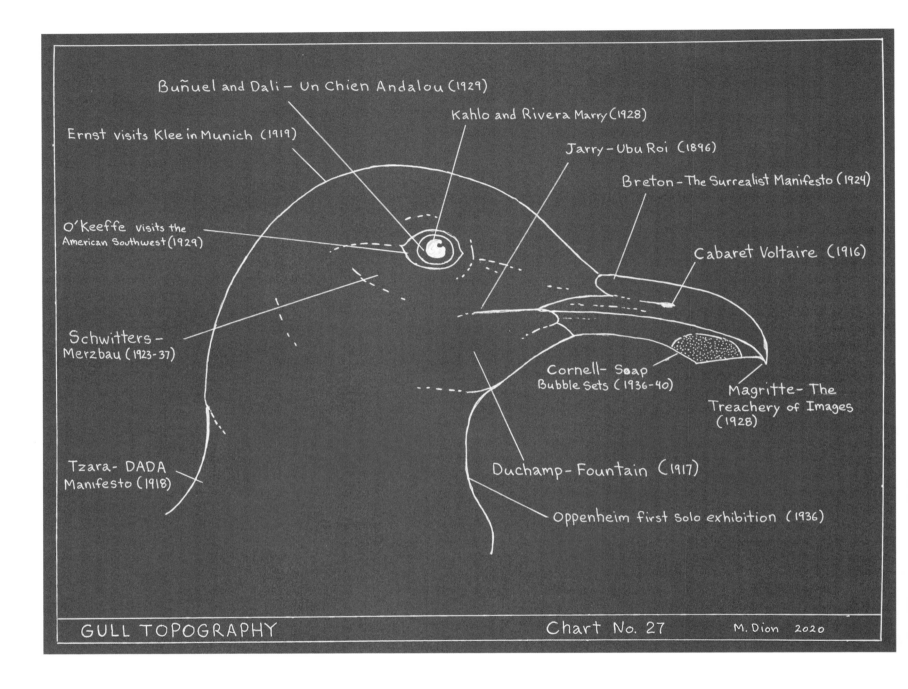

Buñuel and Dali — Un Chien Andalou (1929)

Kahlo and Rivera Marry (1928)

Ernst visits Klee in Munich (1919)

Jarry — Ubu Roi (1896)

Breton — The Surrealist Manifesto (1924)

O'Keeffe visits the American Southwest (1929)

Cabaret Voltaire (1916)

Schwitters — Merzbau (1923-37)

Cornell — Soap Bubble Sets (1936-40)

Magritte — The Treachery of Images (1928)

Tzara — DADA Manifesto (1918)

Duchamp — Fountain (1917)

Oppenheim first solo exhibition (1936)

GULL TOPOGRAPHY   Chart No. 27   M. Dion 2020

Mark Dion

Gull Topography Chart No. 27, 2020
Coloured pencil on paper, 38 × 50.5 cm / 15 × 19⅞ in

As even a novice birdwatcher will know, when opening a new field guide the reader is often confronted with a series of scientific drawings indicating various feather types and body parts of birds, referred to as 'topography' – the arrangement of parts or features on the outside surface of an organism. In books, these illustrations highlight features that will come up in the nuanced identifications in the pages that follow. A notoriously challenging group to identify, gulls (Laridae) present an often-bewildering array of subtle field marks and barely perceptible colour differences. American artist Mark Dion (born 1961) takes this structure and transposes it with late nineteenth and early twentieth-century artistic landmarks in the same way as a field-guide illustrator would point out the features differentiating two similar species. The landmarks are largely drawn from Surrealism or Dadaism, avant-garde artistic styles of the time, with the dates when they occurred. Ranging from the first performance of Alfred Jarry's play *Ubu Roi* in 1896 to Joseph Cornell's (see p.273) Soap Bubble Sets of the 1940s, they cover the fifty years of the rise – and possibly the fall – of modern Surrealism. By super-imposing these on the head and neck of a gull (modelled after a herring gull, *Larus argentatus*), Dion contributes his own Surrealism to the topic.

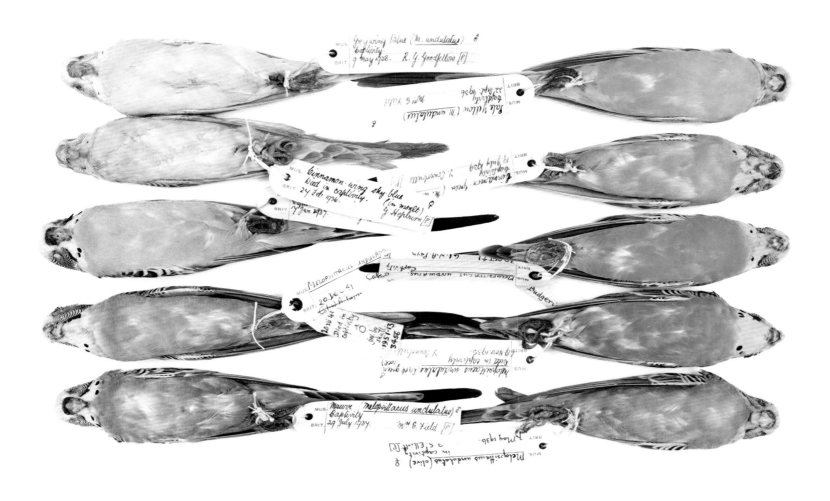

Harry Taylor for the Natural History Museum

Budgerigar specimens illustrating colour variations, 2014
Photograph, dimensions variable
Natural History Museum, London

Wild budgerigars (*Melopsittacus undulatus*) are green. This is because they produce yellow psittacofulvin pigment, and also 'blue' melanin pigment. The rule of blue and yellow making green applies equally to colours in animals as it does to overlying washes in a watercolour painting. Very occasionally a naturally occurring mutation removes one or other of the pigments to produce a yellow or a blue budgie. It's equally likely to occur in wild or captive populations. However, it was only when these diminutive

Australian parakeets were first introduced to Europe as pets in the mid-nineteenth century that breeders began to deliberately propagate these spontaneous colour variants, interbreeding birds to remove all colour or, when combined with additional traits, broadening the spectrum still further. Mutations can substitute one colour for another, for example, or dilute a colour to a paler version. And finally, the feathers' structure also influences the colours we perceive. The 'blue' melanin is actually grey-black,

and only appears blue because of the peculiar formation of the feather barbs. Yet another mutation increases this optical illusion and with two paired together the effect is doubled. Skilled breeders are artists in their own right, and the seemingly endless colour range of budgies represents a veritable masterpiece of selective breeding. This photo was taken to illustrate an article on colour varieties for a breeders' journal, and later featured in the Wellcome Collection's exhibition, *Making Nature* (2016-17).

Lorna Simpson

Unanswerable (The Bird, detail*)*, 2018
Found photographs and collage on paper, 40 framed collages, installation dimensions variable
Private collection

The collages of US artist Lorna Simpson (born 1960) are an extension of the appropriationist gauntlet that informed her practice from the very beginning of her career. Having found a large collection of back issues of *Ebony* and *Jet* magazines from the 1950s to 1970s in her grandmother's house – a common presence in many African-American households – Simpson started combining editorial and fashion images, sometimes with her own drawings, thus referencing both the mechanical aspect of pop art and the manual labour of the artist. A particularly successful episode in this exploration was Simpson's 2018 exhibition *Unanswerable* at the Hauser & Wirth gallery in London, where the personal and collective significance of her source material was emphasized in the series of forty collages that titled the show and provided a snapshot of the past while addressing the present. The female protagonists in each composition are juxtaposed with architectural features, natural elements or animals, like this elegantly feathered bird stretching its wings in an apparently institutional context; the austerity of the moment, reinforced by the black and white tone, doesn't seem to affect the smiling woman, who emerges as the true winner in this fragmented context. Conjectures about the relationship of the bird and the woman are inviting but, as Simpson noted when she chose the title for this body of work, 'There is no answer, not because it's "unanswerable" but because the nature of the question makes it unable to be answered.'

Alfred Hitchcock

Still from *The Birds*, 1963
Film, dimensions variable
Alfred J. Hitchcock Productions / Universal Pictures

Blonde socialite Melanie Daniels, played by Tippi Hedren, and her children flee as threatening black shapes loom over them in this still from the 1963 masterpiece, *The Birds*, by British director Alfred Hitchcock (1899-1980), considered one of the most unsettling horror movies ever made. In the film, birds begin to attack people and their aggressive behaviour escalates, leading the main characters to flee their homes to seek refuge in nearby San Francisco. As they flee, the car radio reports new bird attacks on nearby communities and hints that the military may intervene. The narrative ends unresolved, suggesting that life might not return to normality any time soon. As absurd as the film's plot might at first seem, a flock of birds' coordinated attack is not such a remote possibility. Gulls, crows, starlings and geese and many other birds have been known to strike if humans inadvertently venture too close to thier nests. However, more than referencing real events, Hitchcock's bird revolt has been understood to symbolize the fear-mongering and nervousness of the Cold War period, when terror raining down from the sky was a constant threat in the American popular consciousness. To other viewers, the film represents a more literal form of animal retaliation: payback time for humans who have decimated bird colonies and destroyed nesting environments. Hitchcock spent more than $200,000 building mechanical birds for the film, but most were unconvincing in appearance - leaving him no choice but to use live birds instead.

Kerry James Marshall

Black and Part Black Birds in America (Grackle, Cardinal & Rose-breasted Grosbeak), 2020
Acrylic on PVC panel, 90 × 80 cm / 35½ × 31½ in
Private collection

A grackle (*Quiscalus* sp.), a northern cardinal (*Cardinalis cardinalis*) and a rose-breasted grosbeak (*Pheucticus ludovicianus*) fly around a white bird house in an oil painting by the contemporary US artist Kerry James Marshall (born 1955), whose bright, cheerful colours jar with the questions it provokes about race and identity. Behind the apparently innocuous representation lies Marshall's analysis of the One-Drop rule, a controversial racial classification formula established in the United States in the 1800s, where people with even a single drop of African blood were deemed as black, whether or not their heritage showed in their physical appearance. Marshall applies the absurdity of such a system to the world of birds, where some species are clearly 'black' but where the One-Drop rule would also define as black far brighter species, such as cardinals. An added poignancy may come from an allusion to John James Audubon (see p.177), the artist who created the renowned ornithological masterpiece, *The Birds of America* (1838). A French immigrant from Haiti, Audubon is thought by some historians to have been the mixed-race offspring of a colonial plantation owner and one of his slaves, although his family chose not to disclose his origins when they sent him to the United States in 1803 to escape conscription in the Napoleonic Wars. First publicly exhibited in spring 2020, Marshall's painting articulates the complexity of the racial debate during a particularly tense time in America.

William Holman Hunt

The Festival of St Swithin (The Dovecote), 1865–66
Oil on canvas, 73 × 91 cm / 28¾ × 35⅞ in
Ashmolean Museum of Art and Archaeology, Oxford

This moody and atmospheric painting of a dovecote by William Holman Hunt (1827–1910) is one of the most detailed works ever made by the artist, a founder of the Pre-Raphaelite Brotherhood. Hunt's meticulous style was strongly inspired by early Renaissance painting and the daguerreotype, the early photographic medium that mesmerized Victorian Britain. Impressed on metal plates, daguerreotypes had a highly reflective surface that recorded minute detail, something the Pre-Raphaelites greatly admired. Hunt's desire to reproduce the utmost realism was such that, instead of composing the scene by borrowing from other artists' paintings or natural history illustrations, as was common at the time, he bought some pigeons and a dovecote to copy them accurately from life. The oldest dovecotes, or columbaria, have been found in Egypt and Iran, where the birds' eggs were an important food and their dung was used as fertilizer. In medieval Europe, the dovecote became an aristocratic status symbol. Like the other members of the Pre-Raphaelite Brotherhood, Hunt was highly religious, which might explain his choice of subject, since doves are traditionally symbols of the Holy Spirit. The title of the painting also refers to St Swithin's Day, or 15 July. According to folklore, the weather on that day determines that of the rest of summer. If it rains on St Swithin's Day, it will rain for forty days, but if it is fair, forty days of fair weather will follow.

Wat baet keers off bril, als den WL niet sien en wil.

Cornelis Bloemaert II, after Hendrik Bloemaert

Owl with Glasses and Books, c.1625
Engraving, 22.2 × 18.1 cm / 8¾ × 7⅛ in
Rijksmuseum, Amsterdam

The owl as a symbol of wisdom – this common association is taken for granted today, but was a different story in the seventeenth century. In this copper engraving by the Dutch painter and engraver Cornelis Bloemaert II (1603-92), an alternative interpretation of the owl as champion of wilful ignorance comes to the fore: 'What use are candles or glasses if you don't want to see?' asks the inscription. This copper engraving of a delicately depicted barn owl (*Tyto alba*) offers a kind of social satire and caution against reprehensible characteristics. The owl is crouching on a book in which a scrap of paper reads: 'T`is omt profyt' ('It happens out of greed for profit'), and trying its best to ignore the Ten Commandments open next to it, of which two can be read: 'You shall not kill; You shall not steal.' The mortal sins of greed and sloth, it suggests, can lead to heinous crimes of robbery and even murder. The motif of the bespectacled owl, heedless of its surroundings, can also be found as a picture-within-a-picture in several other works of art, where its almost surreptitious appearance refers to the folly of the foreground action – often groups of drunken revellers and even in quieter genre representations of agricultural life. In reality, the most intelligent birds are thought to be those in the corvid family, including ravens and crows, magpies and jays, that, unlike very solitary owls, are highly social.

John Tenniel

Alice and the Dodo, from *Alice's Adventures in Wonderland* by Lewis Carroll, 1890
Chromolithograph, 17.7 × 12.7 cm / 7 × 5 in
Private collection

'Everybody has won, and all must have prizes!' It is a commendable attitude, although, of course, someone had to provide the prizes. In Lewis Carroll's *Alice's Adventures in Wonderland*, first published in 1865, that someone was Alice. Recently arrived in Wonderland, soaking wet and shrunk to a size little bigger than a mouse, Alice had just enough sweets in her pocket for the host of breathless creatures that pushed around her after winning the Caucus Race - running around on a course of one's own choosing - as the surest way to get dry. The race was presided over by the dodo (*Raphus cucullatus*), a personification of Carroll himself, in reality the Oxford academic Charles Lutwidge Dodgson. The passage alludes to a real summer boating trip when Dodgson first told young Alice Liddell the story that bears her name, in the company of friends and relatives represented by the gathered animals. The dodo, an extinct flightless pigeon endemic to the island of Mauritius, has a special connection with Oxford. A partial head and foot held at the Oxford University Museum of Natural History are all that remain of the only mounted specimen ever known, belonging to the seventeenth-century collector and antiquarian John Tradescant. The museum also houses a painting from the same period of an overly-plump dodo, by the artist Jan Savery (1589-1654), which was probably the model for this rotund and benevolent depiction by John Tenniel (1820-1914), the original illustrator of the *Alice* books.

Polly Morgan

To Every Seed His Own Body, 2006
Taxidermy, chandelier, prayer book, glass, wood, Diam. 20 × 22 cm / 7⅞ × 8⅝ in
Private collection

A blue tit (*Cyanistes caeruleus*) lies peacefully on a small prayer book underneath a miniature chandelier, housed in a glass dome and wooden stand, reminiscent of a religious icon. The colourful blue tit is one of the most recognizable garden visitors, with up to 44 million pairs across Europe and North Africa. In the artist's interpretation, however, the everyday bird becomes a modern *memento mori*, chiming with the work's biblical title, a quote from St Paul's first letter to the Corinthians that likens the death of the body to the seed of

resurrection. The taxidermy, by British artist Polly Morgan (born 1980), was shown in the 2011 exhibition *Dead Time* at Void in Derry, Northern Ireland. Originally an English student, Morgan later trained as a taxidermist, studying with renowned practitioner George Jamieson in Edinburgh before setting up her own studio. She quickly became sought after by collectors including Banksy (see p.66), who snapped up her early pieces and commissioned new ones. Her work has been exhibited at White Cube, the Horniman

Museum and the Saatchi Gallery. Although Morgan is a member of the UK Guild of Taxidermists, her work is much more akin to fine art than to taxidermy, as her animals are placed in staged juxtapositions with props. In 2020 she began to work almost exclusively with snakes, creating a commentary on the superficiality of modern life: 'For years I had been peeling back the skins of animals and taxidermy seemed a good metaphor for artifice vs. truth.'

John Singer Sargent

Studies of a Dead Bird, 1878
Oil on canvas, 50.8 × 38.1 cm / 20 × 15 in
Metropolitan Museum of Art, New York

The same blue tit (*Cyanistes caeruleus*) appears twice in these studies by the American painter John Singer Sargent (1856–1925), depicted at top in flight and below as if it had just crash landed. The bird's oddly crumpled appearance reveals that it is dead, but rather than painting it as deceased – curled up, wings down at its sides – Sargent decided to stage it as if it were alive, propping it up in one view with two sticks and in the other positioning it as if it were getting up after being knocked down. However, rather than trying to cover up this artifice, he embraces it. The 'flying' bird has its wings unnaturally stiffly out to its sides rather than naturally gliding or flapping, and the bird below is even more tragic, slumping to its right, its wings and tail feathers limp and lifeless. Sargent was famed for his high-society portraits of Edwardian grandeur as well as his many paintings of his numerous travels around the world, and these studies are somewhat out of character to his better-known work. Sargent once observed, however, that whenever he painted a portrait he 'looked for the animal in the sitter', so perhaps we should see these birds as character studies. Rather than representing them as realistic birds in their natural habitats, the artist has painted them as sitters posing to have their portrait painted.

Gary Heery

Macaw Wings, 2010
Archival pigment print, 150 × 115 cm / 59 × 45¼ in
Private collection

Capturing the back of the bird rather than the front, this portrait of a red-and-green macaw (*Ara chloropterus*) flies in the face of natural history conventions, and defies the unwritten rules of portraiture by omitting the animal's head altogether. The bold, almost crucifix-like composition, however, preserves a sense of mystery while foregrounding the beauty of the wings and feathers and still conveying something of the bird's personality. For sheer elegance and colour, few birds can compete with macaws, the largest of all parrot species. Originally from South and Central America, macaws were imported to Europe from the early sixteenth century. They are extremely curious birds with strong memories, and were highly prized for their ability to mimic sounds and human words. The birds' rich personalities also made them popular as pets – and today make them challenging subjects to photograph. Before immortalizing birds in creative and original ways, internationally renowned Australian photographer Gary Heery spent years practising his skills on celebrities, including Cate Blanchett, Nicole Kidman and Madonna. After thirty-five years in showbusiness, Heery finally felt ready to tackle birds – some of the most enigmatic sitters in the whole of the animal kingdom. For these restless subjects, whose character is expressed through their entire bodies, he constructed a translucent tent in which they felt secure and could still fly. 'I treated it, not unlike any other portraiture situation, as a kind of controlled spontaneity,' Heery said.

MACROCERCUS ARACANGA.

Red and Yellow Macaw.

Edward Lear

Macrocercus aracanga. Red and Yellow Macaw,
from *Illustrations of the Family Psittacidae or Parrots*, 1832
Hand-coloured lithograph, 54 × 37 cm / 21¼ × 14⅝ in

Edward Lear (1812–88) is perhaps best known today for the marvellous illustrated nonsense poems (including *The Owl and the Pussycat* and *The Jumblies*) created for young children – for whom the painfully shy and delicate Lear felt an affinity – but by profession he was a highly accomplished natural history illustrator. He produced many notable and beautiful works for John Gould's (see p.106) monumental books on ornithology, as well as animal portraits at Lord Stanley's menagerie at Knowsley Hall near Liverpool. However, it was his

own publication, *Illustrations of the Family Psittacidae or Parrots*, for which he deserves greatest credit, particularly in his mastery of the new printing technique of lithography. Lear was only eighteen when he conceived the plan of producing the very first monograph devoted to a single family of birds, and went about the task with remarkable maturity and single-mindedness. He worked directly from the living, screeching specimens at London Zoo's Parrot House, and his birds consequently exude life and character:

this scarlet macaw (*Ara macao*, then known as the red and yellow macaw) is perhaps the most iconic of all parrot images. Keepers would hold the parrots while Lear studied them: an exercise probably resulting in many painful bites. Not surprisingly, Lear's activities often attracted the attention of members of the public in the zoo and, to hide his embarrassment, he would entertain them by drawing lightning-fast caricatures – not always complimentary.

Unknown

Springtime Fresco, c.1650–1550 BC
Fresco, overall: 2.5 × 2.6 m / 8 ft 2½ in × 8 ft 6 in
National Archaeological Museum, Athens

Painted about 3,500 years ago by an unknown artist in a house in Akrotiri, on the Greek island of Santorini, barn swallows (*Hirundo rustica*), heralds of spring in the Aegean, swoop among lilies in a colourful landscape full of light and warmth. But rather than a straightforward seasonal image, this painting is the subject of mystery. Almost every fresco in the Bronze Age town was painted in an upper-floor room, whereas this small chamber is on the ground floor, tucked in among larger spaces, leading scholars to suggest that the room and the fresco had some private cultic purpose. When Akrotiri was destroyed in Santorini's volcanic eruption, however, it was being used as a storeroom, for a bed and domestic utensils. Birds are usually considered religious symbols in Bronze Age Aegean art, sometimes signifying a deity, and this scene has been interpreted as representing a spring festival at which a nature goddess was being worshipped, with the swallows flying in ritualistic courtship patterns. Another theory suggests the birds are engaging in parenting behaviour: in each pair, an adult is feeding a fledgling. A third interpretation is that of a 'feather fight', typical behaviour in spring and early summer, when swallows compete for feathers with which to line their nests. The most recent theory contends that there is no need to choose between these ideas – that the birds, flowers and rocky crags all work together in a depiction of the cycle of life.

Vincent van Gogh

Four Swifts with Landscape Sketches, 1887
Pencil, pen and ink and chalk, 26.9 × 35.2 cm / 10⅝ × 13⅞ in
Van Gogh Museum, Amsterdam

Four swifts (Apodidae) soar effortlessly through the sky, the artist's style endowing them with a sense of urgency and speed. The Dutch artist Vincent van Gogh (1853–90) draws the birds from above, placing the viewer even higher up as we join them in their aerial dance as they wheel and glide next to sketched landscape details of fields and trees. On closer inspection, it is clear that anatomically these birds are rather rudimentary and their wings seem disjointed and not symmetrical, but the drawing comes alive through the marks van Gogh makes to represent the feathers. Using a very loose cross-hatching technique, he efficiently creates a beautiful patina which communicates both dynamic movement and texture. He has repeated the same sketched posture three times, as if practising for the moment when they will be included in a painting – but as far as we know, these swifts did not end up in any of van Gogh's finished works. In fact, he painted very few birds, apart from what was to become one of his most famous paintings and perhaps his last ever: *Wheatfield with Crows* (1890). In this pen and ink drawing made three years before van Gogh shot himself in that same wheatfield, the crow-like deathly black pallor of the swifts – more usually a portent of summer – could be viewed as a symbolic premonition of his impending death.

Andrew Wyeth

Soaring, 1942–50
Tempera on masonite, 121.9 × 221 cm / 48 × 87 in
Shelburne Museum, Shelburne, Vermont

In this remarkable bird's-eye view, the observer feels high in the sky, gazing down with the circling birds to the bare fields and lonely house far below, and out to the rolling hills and distant skyline beyond. The muted colours lend the work a portentous quality. The birds are turkey vultures (*Cathartes aura*), a species common in open country across much of the Americas, from southern Canada to South America. Scavengers, they feed mainly on carrion, using their acute vision and highly developed sense of smell to locate food sources from a great height as they soar on thermal air currents. *Soaring*, begun in 1942, was not completed until 1950, and is the largest painting by the American realist Andrew Wyeth (1917–2009). Born in Chadds Ford, Pennsylvania, Wyeth found his inspiration mainly in the countryside and people in and around his hometown and at his summer home in Cushing, Maine. In his youth he was tutored by his father, Newell Convers Wyeth (N. C. Wyeth), a well-known illustrator. Father and son both felt a great closeness with nature and were much influenced by the writings of Henry David Thoreau and the poetry of Robert Frost. Wyeth's first one-man exhibition, at the Macbeth Gallery in New York City in 1937, was a great success and all the paintings were sold. Wyeth's style, while based firmly in realism, is overlain with abstract qualities that lend it great emotional depth.

Xavi Bou

Ornitography #2
Photograph, dimensions variable

A streak of organic plasticity ripples across the frame. The abstract ribbon of silvers, greys and blues is clearly formed from a dynamic, biological form, but its identity is confused, simultaneously resembling the fronds of an ocean-dwelling invertebrate and the flattened edges of a twirling seed pod. The background, however, makes it clear that this is an aerial display and that we are witnessing the rhythmic pulsations of a bird in flight, elongated into a single, oscillating sheet of feathers. Spanish photographer Xavi Bou (born 1979), began his series of 'Ornitographies' in 2012, joining the long history of photographers using technology to freeze movement. But Bou's work can be seen as subverting the locomotion photography of pioneers such as Étienne Jules Marey (see p.263) and Eadweard Muybridge. Rather than capturing the minute mechanics of locomotion as single atomized moments, Bou records video footage of birds in flight at between 30 and 120 frames per second, splits the video into frames and then stitches the images into a single artwork to present a visualization of flight as a poetic extension of a single form through both space and time. The identity of the bird is not clear, and Bou does not name it. By removing focus from the precise biology of the species, he forces us to consider only the fluidity of the bird's movement, to savour the clarity with which he presents the extraordinary hidden within the ordinary.

Charles Herbert Moore

Peacock Feather, c.1879–82
Watercolour and gouache on off-white wove paper, 30.5 × 24.6 cm / 12 × 9¹¹⁄₁₆ in
Harvard Art Museums, Cambridge, Massachusetts

This extremely delicate watercolour of a peacock's feather is the work of US academic and artist Charles Herbert Moore (1840–1930). Known primarily as a painter of expansive American landscapes, Moore was an ardent follower of the teachings of the British art critic John Ruskin and the style of painting he championed, as practised by the Pre-Raphaelite artists in the nineteenth century. Moore studied for a time with Ruskin in Italy around the time this work was completed. The vastly influential Ruskin nurtured in his followers a deep appreciation for the natural world, exhorting them to 'go to nature in all singleness of heart ... rejecting nothing, selecting nothing and scorning nothing'. Originally from the Indian subcontinent, the Indian peafowl (*Pavo cristatus*) is well known for the spectacular train of the male, which can be dramatically unfurled into a giant fan to impress females. In this drawing, Moore's attention is focused on the tip and 'eye' of one such exquisitely complex feather, and the work is executed in a painstakingly detailed realism outstanding in natural history illustration. Moore's ability to accurately portray the structure of the feather along with its nuanced coloration is a testament to his belief in art and the careful observation of nature as an ennobling activity. That conviction led to his pioneering tenure as the first professor of art at Harvard University, in whose museum collections this work is held today.

Melchior d'Hondecoeter

Peacocks, 1683
Oil on canvas, 190.2 × 134.6 cm / 74⅞ × 53 in
Metropolitan Museum of Art, New York

From the right-hand side of the image, a female Indian peafowl (*Pavo cristatus*) hisses at a monkey, which in turn is distracted by a squirrel from the ripe fruit it was about to eat. At the same time, her annoyed male companion seems to be scolding the passing swallow. The splendour of the male bird is emphasized by some sunflowers. Habitually, they are always turned towards the sun, but here they are reverently turned to the majestic peacock. Peacocks are traditional symbols of pride and vanity, and the real birds are known for their loud, resonant calls, and meat that is not considered tasty by everyone. This is all compensated, however, by the males's colourful feathers and splendid train. In Greek mythology, the peacock was the favourite animal of the goddess Hera. After the hundred-eyed giant, Argus, had been killed by the god Hermes, who was acting on Hera's behalf, she adorned the tail of the bird with the eyes of the watchful giant. Melchior d'Hondecoeter (1636–95) was the most renowned painter of birds in seventeenth-century Holland, serving an international clientele with scenes such as this painting of a palace menagerie, which also includes a sarus crane (*Antigone antigone*), a squirrel, a monkey, a wild turkey (*Meleagris gallopavo*) and a swallow flying past. The crane and the turkey were profoundly exotic subjects, and their presence reflected the cultural status of their owners. D'Hondecoeter was a master in rendering his subjects in fine detail, full of lively action and interaction.

Peter Paul Rubens

The Abduction of Ganymede, 1611–12
Oil on canvas, 204 × 206 cm / 80¼ × 81⅛ in
Musée des Beaux-Arts de Bordeaux

Depicting a myth told in slightly different versions by Homer, Virgil and Ovid this painting by the renowned Flemish artist Peter Paul Rubens (1577–1640) tells the story of Ganymede, son of Tros, the King of Troy. Ganymede was famed for his beauty and worked as a shepherd when he caught the eye of Jupiter – the Roman god of the sky and king of the gods – who fell madly in love with him. Jupiter transformed himself into a great eagle to seize Ganymede. He carried him to Olympus to be his cupbearer, a role that he took over from Hebe, who was daughter of Juno and goddess of youth. There are around sixty species of large birds of prey called eagles belonging to the family Accipitridae, which has its highest species density in Eurasia and Africa. Eagles' eyes have a highly sensitive retina that enables them to spot prey at great distances. They are the apex predators of the avian world, primarily feeding on mammals, though some species will also take fish, birds and reptiles. In this painting, Jupiter takes the form of what seems to be a golden eagle (*Aquila chrysaetos*), a northern hemisphere species with dark brown feathers, with a nape of golden plumage and yellow feet. Rubens often gave animals a central role in his history painting and depicted a diverse array of exotic creatures, including lions, tigers, a crocodile and a hippopotamus.

Attributed to the Pistoxenos Painter

White-ground kylix, *c*.460 BC
Painted ceramic, Diam. 24.1 cm / 9½ in; H. 10.75 cm / 4¼ in
British Museum, London

Unusually, the Greek goddess of beauty, Aphrodite, rides on a goose rather than her normal swan in the bowl of this drinking cup, holding a plant tendril in one hand. White-ground vases, in which the scene is painted in colours on a white background, are thought to reflect the styles of panel paintings once popular in ancient Greece but now lost. Here, details are rendered in a pale brown glaze, with purplish red used for the goddess's cloak and the edges of her tunic. The painter's preliminary sketch is still visible beneath later alterations to the plant and the feathers of the goose's wings. This image may represent the greylag goose (*Anser anser*), ancestor of many varieties of the domestic goose, which was domesticated more than 3,000 years ago; it was known in ancient Greece for its usefulness in guarding premises and for having a low-maintenance diet of grass and other vegetation. The birds were farmed for meat and eggs, occasionally domesticated as pets, bred for specific traits such as calmness or luxurious feathers and associated with a number of deities and heroines. In addition to its links with Aphrodite, the goose was sacred to the Greek goddesses Artemis, Athena, Kore/Persephone, Hecate and Nemesis, and to the Roman gods Juno and Priapus. In Homer's *Odyssey*, the faithful Penelope, wife of Odysseus, had 'twenty geese in the house, that come forth from the water and eat wheat; my heart warms with joy when I see them.'

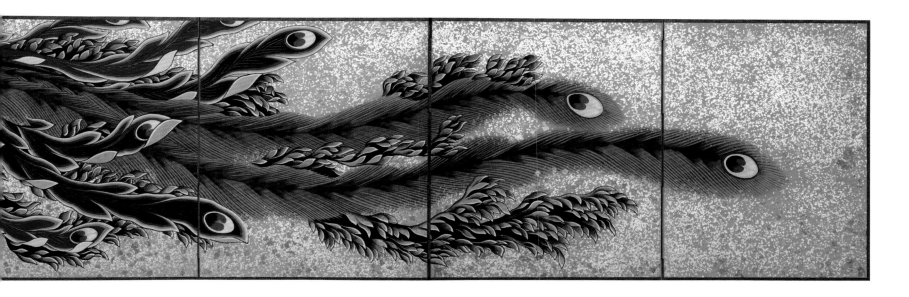

Katsushika Hokusai

Phoenix, 1835
Eight-panel screen, ink, colours, cut-gold leaf and sprinkled gold on paper, 35.8 × 233.2 cm / 14⅛ × 91¾ in
Museum of Fine Arts, Boston, Massachusetts

Although it is compressed into an unusually long and low folding screen format, this large, dramatically rendered phoenix appears about to soar out of its restrictive frame. The myriad patterns that make up this fantastic bird are painted with a wide range of bright colours, which sparkle against the gold background of a screen that would have been used to divide interior space in a Japanese room largely devoid of fixed furniture. When sitting on the floor, the bright colours and immediacy of the phoenix

image would have a startling effect. The renowned Japanese artist Katsushika Hokusai (1760–1849) was a master of many media, including woodblock prints, paintings, illustrated books and board games. He was also technically very skilful, as can be seen with the careful attention paid to the varied feathers that make up this large bird, which is a symbol of the empress and of peace in East Asia. His best works were made during his later years, and this screen was painted when the artist was seventy-five years old.

While Hokusai painted this phoenix without background, close to the foreground and in a relatively flattened and highly graphic manner, as was common in Japanese traditional painting, he employed a subtle degree of modelling to give the bird a sense of three-dimensionality, a technique learned from European prints that had been recently imported to Japan. Conversely, Hokusai's bold woodblock prints exerted a great influence on Impressionist artists in Europe.

PLATE XXIX.

Henry W. Elliott and Robert Ridgway

Plate XXIX, from *A History of North American Birds, Volume II* by Spencer Fullerton Baird, Thomas Mayo Brewer and Robert Ridgway, 1875
Hand-coloured engraving, 28 × 18.2 cm / 11 × 7 in
American Museum of Natural History, New York

This colourful plate of the heads of North American seed-eating birds comes from one of the earliest works to catalogue the avifauna of the region. It shows a selection of New World buntings and relatives, members of the cardinal and grosbeak family (Cardinalidae). Features such as bill size and shape and the pattern and colours of plumage are clearly displayed, with the scientific names listed at the foot of the plate. The names have mostly since been revised, but the distinctive features allow accurate identification. They include male and female examples of lark bunting (*Calamospiza melanocorys*, 2 and 3), blue grosbeak (*Passerina caerulea*, 4 and 5), lazuli bunting (*P. amoena*, 11 and 12) and indigo buntings (*P. cyanea*, 13 and 14). *A History of North American Birds* was first published in three volumes in 1874 and includes 64 plates and 593 woodcuts. Most of the plates of heads were prepared by the artist Henry W. Elliott (1846–1930) and the ornithologist Robert Ridgway (1850–1929). Spencer Fullerton Baird (1823–1887), the first-named author, served as secretary to the Smithsonian Institution in Washington DC, where he helped create the National Museum, of which he became curator in 1850. Baird combined field collection with research and he met and corresponded with many other naturalists, including John James Audubon (see p.177). He established a wide network of collectors and brought together a large body of scientific specimens for display and research in the developing museum.

Duke Riley

The Filmmakers, 2013
Key West reclaimed roof tin, gouache, dimensions variable, each tin approx. 35.5 × 23.5 cm / 14 × 9¼ in
Pizzuti Collection, Columbus, Ohio

Painted onto tin roofing shingles, these twenty-five portraits depict homing pigeons (*Columba livia*) who were involved in a mission to smuggle cigars from Cuba to the United States. Inspired by the long history of smuggling between the two countries, Brooklyn-based artist Duke Riley (born 1972) spent eight months training fifty pigeons to fly between Havana and Key West in Florida as part of his 2013 project *Trading with the Enemy*. Half of the birds were tasked with transporting the contraband, while those shown here documented the dangerous journey with tiny lightweight video cameras strapped to their bodies. The first group were named after notorious smugglers such as Pierre Lafitte and Pablo Escobar, while the camera-carrying birds were given names of filmmakers who have had brushes with the law, including Roman Polanski and Mel Gibson. Not all of the birds participated in the flight across the Florida Straits, and of the fifty trainees only eleven successfully completed the journey. Like a roll of honour, the imagined fate of each bird is described under its portrait. Alongside those who returned safely, we read that Jafar Panahi was lost at sea and Dennis Hopper was killed by a hawk. Riley's relationship with pigeons began in childhood after he rescued and nursed back to health an injured bird. He now owns hundreds of pigeons, which are a constant source of inspiration for his drawings, prints, mosaics, paintings and projects in the public realm.

Jochen Gerner

Beagle Boy Bird, 2020
Vintage notebook paper and coloured felt-tip pens, 16 × 12.5 cm / 6¼ × 4⅞ in
Private collection

This colourful bird stands on a thin blue line of ruled paper. The drawing, made by French artist and illustrator Jochen Gerner (born 1970), is part of his larger series titled *Oiseaux* – an inventory of 200 birds, both real and imagined. Gerner documented his drawings in ten school notebooks, a fitting format for an ornithological study. The small vintage notebooks offer a range of textured papers, and the printed horizontal lines serve as a grounding device while also adding a background layer to the plumage design.

This series is as much about chromatic possibilities as it is about birds: by using felt-tip pens and limiting his palette, Gerner explores the boundaries of pattern, line and colour. For visual references, he turned to François-Nicolas Martinet's plates in Buffon's *Natural History of Birds*, as well as to contemporary photographs and the birds outside his studio window. He also invented new species, creating imaginary shapes, patterns and colour combinations. In this drawing, he references The Beagle Boys, a group of villainous

cartoon characters created by Carl Barks in 1951 for Walt Disney. The bird's shape and colours are based on the faces and clothing of these fictional thieves. Seen in profile – much like an Assyrian relief – alongside small orange abstract circles (perhaps seeds or recently stolen coins), the bird wears boots and looks half human. 'None of them fly,' Gerner points out. 'This is the paradox of this series.'

Unknown

A Common Indian Nightjar (Caprimulgus asiaticus), *c*.1780
Opaque watercolour on paper, 47.3 × 28.3 cm / 18⅝ × 11 in
Metropolitan Museum of Art, New York

This remarkably detailed depiction of an Indian nightjar (*Caprimulgus asiaticus*), with each feather rendered individually against a contrastingly empty landscape and sky, was an early souvenir painted by an unknown local artist for a French soldier living in Lucknow during the early days of European involvement in India. The Indian nightjar is a small, ground-dwelling bird active at dawn and dusk across South and Southeast Asia. Its generic name, *Caprimulgus,* means 'goat sucker', referring to a traditional belief that the birds suckled from goats at night, which probably had its roots in their habit of feeding on insects around domestic goats. The nightjar was sometimes called the 'ice bird' in colonial India for its characteristic clicking call that sounds like a stone skipping on a frozen surface. This work is an example of Company painting, which takes its name from the British East India Company that dominated European trade with India from the late 1600s, and combines elements of traditional Rajput and Mughal painting, such as miniaturization, with Western linear perspective and volumetric shading. Surrounded by interesting monuments and unknown flora and fauna, Europeans sought a visual record of India, and local artists quickly adopted Western techniques to create paintings on paper that could be collected in portfolios or albums – this example is one of 658 paintings of birds commissioned by Major-General Claude Martin. Company painting remained popular until the 1840s, when photography was introduced to India.

Walter Crane

Design for wallpaper, 'Swan, Rush and Iris', 1875
Bodycolour on paper, 53.1 × 53 cm / 20⅞ × 20⅞ in
Victoria & Albert Museum, London

Two swans – stylized, but naturalistic – face each other among bullrushes and iris in a wallpaper design reminiscent of a classical Greek vase by the British artist Walter Crane (1845–1915), a member of the Arts and Crafts movement. The mute swans (*Cygnus olor*) – Crane has painted them with orange bills with characteristic black knobs at the base, so the species is clear – are shown in profile, their exaggerated arched necks and upraised feathers corresponding to the elbow area on a wing giving them the formal symmetry of heraldic emblems. Traditionally, swans are seen as symbols of married love and fidelity, because they mate for life, and Crane's facing pairs of birds may have been intended to refer to this. He was influenced by the work of William Morris and began designing wallpapers in the early 1870s. This design was issued in 1877 by the London wallpaper manufacturer Jeffrey & Co. who also printed for Morris. It is typical of Crane's figurative patterns, which often relate to his illustrated children's books, taking their inspiration from Greek myths, fairy tales and nursery rhymes. Birds of all kinds – from peacocks to parrots – populate Crane's lavishly ornamented wallpapers, and his skilful drawing was much admired by his contemporaries: the authors of the seminal *History of English Wallpaper*, published in 1926, declared that 'Crane's facile handling of gorgeous birds ... has never been excelled.'

58

Unknown

Child's coat with ducks in pearl medallions, 8th century
Silk, 48 × 82.5 cm / 18⅞ × 32½ in
Cleveland Museum of Art, Ohio

In the 700s, this silk coat was the height of luxury, woven for a young prince in either Iran or the neighbouring Central Asian empire of Sogdiana, based in what are now Tajikistan and Uzbekistan. Its alternating panels depict lotus flowers and ducks embroidered in pearl roundels in five bright colours, with pearl collars, flying ribbons and carrying jewelled necklaces – all imperial symbols of the Sassanid dynasty that had ruled Persia, or Iran, until shortly before the coat was created. The duck was an important imperial symbol, and appeared on Persian clothes, pottery and containers for centuries. In a dry region where water was vital, the bird did not just represent nature's plenty – Central Asia's canebrakes were home to millions of wild ducks – but was also a symbol of Anahita, the goddess of fertility and clear waters. A motif that began as a purely naturalistic depiction of an important bird in Central Asian culture became highly symbolic, representing not just the goddess but also imperial rule, before surviving as a purely decorative motif long after its symbolic importance had declined. The coat is lined with silk damask from China, which would have been exported along the fabled Silk Road, the great trans-Asia trade route that linked China with the West, and the silk trousers that accompanied it reflect the influence of contemporary Tang China.

Unknown

Out-of-the-Blue Bird: The Millet-Eating / Panic Bird, c.1866–68
Woodblock print, 35.8 × 52.9 cm / 14 × 20¾ in
Museum of Fine Arts, Boston, Massachusetts

A so-called panic bird attempts to feed on the last remains of wealth and to carry valued possessions to safety in this allegorical print, created at a time of intense civil unrest in Japan. The bird feeds on millet grains made of coins, which also make up the creature's beak. Its wings are made of account books and its tail of a cartwheel and ladders; its body comprises chests and bundles of possessions, and its legs are made of keys. The title is a play on the Japanese word for millet-eating – *awakui* – which sounds like the term for foam-eating

– *awa o taberu* – which refers to panic, frothing at the mouth. The imaginary panic bird resembles a raven from Japanese mythology called *Yatagarasu* (an 'eight-span crow', because of its large size); as the animal that cleans up after battles, it is a symbol of rebirth or rejuvenation. Its appearance is believed to indicate divine intervention in human affairs. The image comes from a deeply unsettled time when all feudal class privileges were abolished during the Meiji Restoration of 1868, which saw the return

of the monarchy to Japan, following more than 250 years of military rule under the Tokugawa shogunate. A *coup d'état*, by young samurai who had chaffed at the feudal rule of the shoguns, was followed by an eighteen-month civil war before the last shogun surrendered and the Emperor Meiji was installed on the throne.

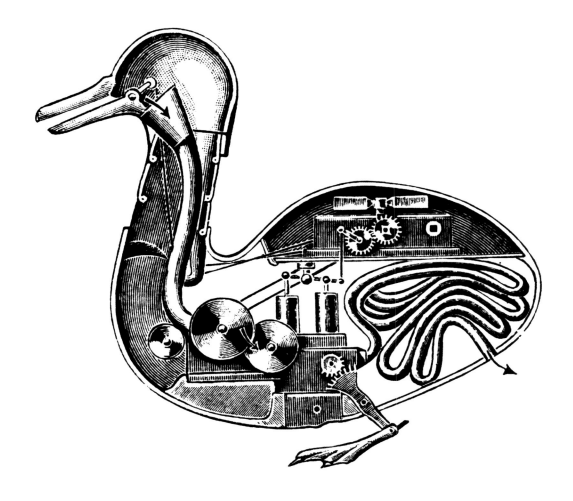

A. Konby

Interior of Vaucanson's Automatic Duck, from *Scientific American*, Vol. 80 No. 03 (January 1899)
Engraving

This diagram from *Scientific American* magazine in 1899 attempts to reconstruct the inner workings of a mechanical duck that the great Enlightenment figure Voltaire once hailed as a reminder of the glory of France for its apparent ability to eat and digest grain, then defecate the waste. When it was created by the Grenoble artist and inventor Jacques de Vaucanson in 1739, the duck was hailed as a triumph, but its novelty soon passed (including for Vaucanson, who sent it on a tour of the country while he designed an automated silk loom, leading enraged silk workers to drive him out of town). The life-sized bird stood on top of a base holding the clockwork needed to make it move its beak, peck at kernels of corn, quack and adjust its position. The bird ended up in the hands of a German collector, where its workings gradually ceased, but it was restored for the Exposition Universelle in Paris in 1844. There, it was examined by an illusionist who revealed that the duck's ability to produce waste was the result, not of mechanical digestion, but of a hidden compartment where the waste was stored, ready to be expelled from the duck's body. The whole thing was an illusion – but the duck itself is said to have been destroyed in a fire in a museum in Poland in 1879, so it is unlikely that its workings will ever be fully understood.

Johann Joachim Kändler

King Vulture, 1734
Hard-paste porcelain, polychrome enamels, 58 × 43 cm / 22.8 × 16.9 in
Art Institute of Chicago, Illinois

Crafted from fine porcelain, this magnificent king vulture (*Sarcoramphus papa*) perches on a tree stump with its head bowed. The large scavenger's distinctive white and black feathers are complemented by its bright, red-tipped beak, purplish blue collar and an orangey yellow caruncle bulging above its nostrils. A native of Central and South America, the vulture feeds on carrion, tearing the meat with its strong beak. This elegant, life-size sculpture was produced by the German artist Johann Joachim Kändler

(1706–75) at the famous Meissen porcelain factory near Dresden, the first European factory to discover how to make luxury hard-paste porcelain, a strong and hard-wearing material previously produced only in China and Japan. It was commissioned by Meissen's principal patron, Augustus II the Strong, Elector of Saxony and King of Poland, who wanted to convey his dominion over the animal kingdom by decorating his Baroque pleasure palace with a fantastic porcelain menagerie. Kändler specialized in lifelike figures of

birds and mammals and at the time of the king's death he had completed more than seventy different models. Among the other birds he crafted are doves, magpies, woodpeckers, wagtails, kingfishers, bitterns, sparrowhawks and jays. Kändler drew this vulture from life at Augustus's aviary in Dresden, enabling him to accurately record its form and re-create its essence in porcelain.

Tim Flach

King Vulture Portrait, 2019
Photograph, dimensions variable

The king vulture (*Sarcoramphus papa*) is an unusual bird. Above its large, sharp bill sits a strange yellow carbuncle, and a bright staring eye set in a red ring that lends the bird a distinctly demonic appearance. In this study, the gaudy yellow, orange, and pink neck emerges beneath a ruff of grey silky plumage, topped by strange growths of coloured skin with a rope-like texture that surround the head. The king vulture is found across much of South America, and north to Mexico. Like other vultures, it soars on thermals – rising currents of warm air – as it searches for carrion, its main food source. Tim Flach (born 1958) is an internationally acclaimed British photographer who specializes in studies of domestic and wild animals. His exhibition *Endangered*, held at the Osborne Samuel Gallery, London, in 2017, is also available as a published volume. This brings together portraits of a wide range of endangered animals and their habitats and contains remarkable portraits for example of primates, big cats, elephants and many species of bird.

Flach studied communication and design at North East London Polytechnic, and photography at Central Saint Martins College of Art and Design. His work has been widely exhibited, notably in Europe and in the USA, China and Japan. Flach has also published several books, including *Equus* (2008) and *Dogs Gods* (2010), both of which illustrate the story of the domestication of two species strongly associated with humans.

Ceal Floyer

Warning Birds, 2002
Self-adhesive 'warning birds' on window
Temporary installation, Kölnischer Kunstverein, Cologne

Dozens of mass-produced adhesive 'warning birds' – stickers traditionally designed to deter actual birds from flying into glass panes they otherwise cannot see – are arranged on a gallery window in such close proximity that they significantly restrict the outside view and block the light entering the room, erasing the basic function of the window and turning the birds from passive actors to protagonists. Identifiable only by their silhouettes, the birds' original purpose as protectors of the transparent glass is replaced by feelings of claustrophobia and danger reminiscent of the disquieting effect of Alfred Hitchcock's 1963 horror movie *The Birds* (see p.35). At the same time, their subversive action may refer to the idea of nature as something that humankind is deluded enough to believe it can control - but that in reality cannot and never will be tamed. British-born, Berlin-based artist Ceal Floyer (born 1968) has a predilection for modifying the public's perception of ordinary objects while respecting their intrinsic characteristics and dimensions. Floyer initially presented *Warning Birds* at Lisson Gallery in London in 2002, with the birds occupying the window on the upper floor. Eventually the piece grew in magnitude and scale, with further representations in 2005 at Fondazione Stelline in Milan, where it took the entire courtyard of a former monastery, and in 2013 at the Kunstverein in Cologne, where it blinded the only source of natural light of the building.

Banksy

Untitled, 2014
Graffiti painting
Clacton-on-Sea, United Kingdom

A group of city pigeons brandish anti-immigration slogans as they confront a lone exotic bird. While its features are more reminiscent of a swallow, the stranger's green colour marks it as a probable reference to the rose-ringed parakeet (*Psittacula krameria*), a species common to Africa and southern Asia that has recently been thriving in Britain and elsewhere in Europe thanks to milder winters. Animals have often been portrayed in satirical ways to comment on social and political affairs. This mural about Britain's reaction to immigrants by the renowned British graffiti artist Banksy (born 1973) ruffled enough feathers to warrant its swift removal. How parakeets first came to the UK is a matter of modern folklore. It has been claimed that a flock was let free in 1951, during the filming of *the African Queen*, starring Humphry Bogart and Katherine Hepburn. Some trace their arrival to Jimi Hendrix, who apparently owned a pair of parakeets while living in London during the 1960s. Others blame the Great Storm of 1987, which destroyed tropical aviaries, setting birds free. Since the start of the twenty-first century, population growth and increased visibility have placed the birds at the centre of a debate about native species and environmental stability. In 2009, the rose-ringed parakeet was added to the list of species that can be lawfully killed in Britain, further polarizing opinion among those who see the birds as a colourful addition to urban wildlife and others who cast them as non-native invaders threatening the survival of British species.

Andrew Garn

Fido the Googly Eyed Pigeon, 2017
Photograph, dimensions variable

Bright orange eyes regard us above iridescent feathers of green and purple in this hyper-real studio portrait of one of New York City's pigeons. The image was taken deliberately to highlight the beauty and individual character of the birds, which are widely considered feral pests in many of the world's great cities. Also known as feral pigeons, *they* are descended from domestic pigeons that have returned to the wild. They perch on the edges of buildings, the urban equivalent of the sea-cliffs and mountains that were home to their ancestor, the wild rock dove (*Columba livia*). As a native New Yorker, photographer Andrew Garn (born 1957) grew up surrounded by pigeons and became fascinated by their reputation as an invasive nuisance, creating a large amount of excrement, carrying disease and destroying crops and property. Garn spent eight years researching a photographic study to depict the bird's appeal and unappreciated expressiveness. He developed a profound respect for their hardiness as well as their apparent paradoxical nature. Why do these birds, able to fly up to 800 km (500 miles) per day and, as demonstrated by Harvard psychologist B. F. Skinner, able to undertake complicated tasks, ranging from tracking missile targets to recognizing individual human faces, appear to thrive foraging for scraps in the often harsh urban environment? Using high-speed strobe photography, Garn also caught pigeons in mid-flight with their wings at full span, underlining their complexity and grace as animals.

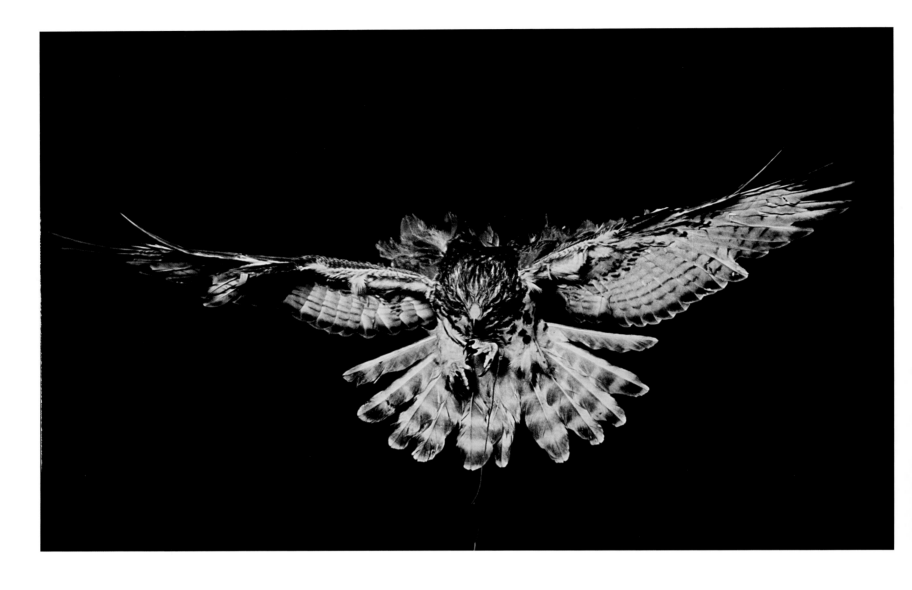

Margaret Bourke-White

Flying Bird, c.1940
Gelatin silver print, 32.4 × 48 cm / 12¾ × 19⅛ in
George Eastman Museum, Rochester, New York

This stunning black and white photograph of a bird of prey – possibly a northern goshawk (*Accipiter gentilis*) – is the work of American photojournalist Margaret Bourke-White (1904–71). Famous for her iconic shots of innovative industrial machinery, Bourke-White also made history as America's first accredited woman photographer during World War II, and as the first authorized to fly on a combat mission. Between 1936 and 1957, she worked as in-house photographer for *Life* magazine, and garnered many awards throughout her career, greatly aided by an eye for unconventional viewpoints that simultaneously ennobled and aggrandized her subjects while casting them in a new light. Animals and flowers often attracted her attention despite their marginality as subjects in photojournalism. A string fastened to the bird's left foot clearly implies it might be captive. Caught in flight, with its wings stretched open, the orientation of the ruffled feathers on its back suggest it might be preparing to land. Widely distributed across the northern hemisphere, goshawks are large raptors, whose long tail and relatively short wings are adapted to the contortions of hunting in forests and thick vegetation. Known as the 'cook's bird' for their prowess at capturing traditional game, including rabbits and pheasants, goshawks are however infamously difficult to train. Their temperamental nature and quixotic deviations from command are well documented, for example in Helen Macdonald's award-winning 2014 memoir *H Is for Hawk*.

Cai Guo-Qiang

Murmuration (Landscape), 2019
Gunpowder on porcelain, 10 × 23 m / 33 ft × 75 ft 6 in
National Gallery of Victoria, Melbourne

This sublime flock of 10,000 starlings filling an exhibition space in the National Gallery of Victoria in Melbourne is the work of contemporary Chinese artist Cai Guo-Qiang (born 1957). Renowned for his interest in the natural world, Cai often creates sculptures of animals from artificial materials rather than taxidermy, in this case working with porcelain – a material invented in China roughly two thousand years ago that embodies quintessential ideas of beauty, grace and fragility. Each of the individual sculpted common starlings (*Sturnus vulgaris*) was cast by the artist and scorched black by explosions of gunpowder – another important Chinese invention. The result is an overwhelming three-dimensional spectacle that captures the phenomenon known as murmuration: a cloud-like, synchronized swooping of birds in flight. Murmuration is a manifestation of birds' ability to manage uncertainty while maintaining consensus among vast colonies. According to scientific research, each starling in the flock syncs with seven nearby birds, forming a small and manageable network among the multitude – but mystery still hovers over the reasons behind this spectacular phenomenon. Some experts believe that synchronized flight-acrobatics help birds to gather in an orderly way in preparation for roosting. Safety is in numbers: starlings spend the night together in large groups, often counting more than 500 individuals per cubic metre. Others believe that murmuration also plays a fundamental role in avian communication.

Henry Stacy Marks

A Select Committee, 1891
Oil on canvas, 111.7 × 86.7 cm / 44 × 34 ⅛ in
Walker Art Gallery, Liverpool

A variety of parrots display distinctly human attitudes as they convene in this whimsical parliamentary meeting. The hyacinth macaw (*Anodorhynchus hyacinthinus*) to the left is apparently delivering a speech. Below, a blue-and-yellow macaw (*Ara ararauna*) turns its head towards the speaker, perched alongside a red-tailed black cockatoo (*Calyptorhynchus banksii*) and a pink Major Mitchell's cockatoo (*Cacatua leadbeateri*), both of which are paying less attention. Opposite sit four cockatoos: the salmon-crested cockatoo (*C. moluccensis*) is animated

and speaking, but the sulphur-crested cockatoo (*C. galerita*) seems bored to the point of slumber. They are flanked by a white cockatoo (*C. alba*) and probably a western corella (*C. pastinator*). In the background two house sparrows (*Passer domesticus*) flutter near the window of what seems to be a grand hall. *A Select Committee* is one of the most famous paintings of Henry Stacy Marks (1829–98), a talented British artist with a particular interest in painting birds. Marks studied at the Royal Academy Schools in London and the

École des Beaux-Arts in Paris and was a founding member of a group of artists known as the St John's Wood Clique, active in the 1870s and 1880s. He observed birds closely, aided by regular visits to the London Zoo and through studying skeletons at the museum of the Royal College of Surgeons. In 1890, he held a private exhibition of his bird portraits, which reflected the great accuracy and attention to detail displayed here.

Elizabeth Butterworth

Lear's Macaw, 2005
Gouache, ink and pencil on paper, 25 × 34 cm / 9¼ × 13⅜ in
Private collection

Lear's macaw (*Anodorhynchus leari*), a large species of parrot found wild only in an extremely limited range in northeast Bahia State in Brazil, is one of only two species of large parrot with entirely blue plumage. Only about 1,250 individuals are thought to survive in just two colonies in a habitat known as *caatinga*, a kind of thorny scrub, where the birds favour stands of licuri palm. The parrots nest in holes in nearby sandstone cliffs, and eat mainly the nuts of the licuri palm. The annotations around this portrait of the head and two feathers of Lear's macaw show the meticulous attention paid to detail by the contemporary British artist Elizabeth Butterworth (born 1949) to achieve the correct colour tone for every feather and patch of skin. A leading bird artist, with a particular interest in painting parrots, Butterworth was born in Rochdale, Lancashire, studying at the local art school and later at the Royal College of Art in London. She now exhibits worldwide. The bird's scientific name honours the famous nineteenth-century nonsense-poet, writer and artist Edward Lear (see p.43) who also painted many species of parrot, including a blue macaw that may well have been this species, at that time undescribed. Butterworth's depictions of parrots are considered among the finest and it is fitting that her work includes this splendid specimen associated with another great artist with a penchant for parrots.

Unknown

Plate III, from *Musurgia universalis sive ars magna consoni et dissoni: in X libros digesta* by Athanasius Kircher, 1650
Engraving, 31.5 × 22 cm / 12½ × 8⅝ in
Private collection

This famous print from 1650 was one of the first attempts to transcribe birdsong into musical notation - but not for its own sake; rather, the illustration comes from a comprehensive two-volume treatise that sets out to show that music reflects the harmony of God's cosmos. At the top of the page is the song of the common nightingale (*Luscinia megarhynchos*), followed by those of the cockerel, a hen calling to her chicks, a cuckoo (Cuculidae), a common quail (*Coturnix coturnix*) and a parrot, saying 'hello' in Greek.

The author, a German Jesuit based in Rome named Athanasius Kircher (1602–80), said of the nightingale that 'its ingenuity mocks the efforts of all musicians'. More than 1,500 copies of Kircher's book were printed in the year of publication, 1650, and widely disseminated by travelling Jesuits. It became a standard work of musicology, influencing composers such as Johann Sebastian Bach and Ludwig van Beethoven, but the correlation between birdsong and music is not as clear as Kircher implies. In the 1770s, when the musicologist Daines Barrington hired a flautist to play the nightingale transcription, he remarked, 'It was impossible to observe almost any traces of the nightingale's song.' Modern researchers suggest any similarity between birdsong and music is purely accidental, with few bird calls matching the regular harmonic intervals of the musical scale. Nevertheless, composers have frequently attempted to replicate birdsong in their works, including most notably the French composer Olivier Messiaen.

Nick Cave

Soundsuit, 2011
Found objects, metal armature, knit head and bodysuit, and mannequin, 307.3 × 106.7 × 83.8 cm / 121 × 42 × 33 in
Museum of Modern Art, New York

There is a suggestion of chaos in the bird figurines of all shapes and sizes caught in the tangle of wires created by the African-American performance artist and dancer Nick Cave (born 1959). This is one of more than 500 Soundsuits he has produced using a range of objects in assemblages that disguise the wearer like a mask - or like armour. Birds, Cave realized as he built the piece, migrate as well as people, and their peaceful cohabitation on top of the Soundsuit, while somewhat mundane, also carries a message about diversity and

how important it is for society to learn from nature if it wants to move forwards. Cave made his first Soundsuit in 1992 in response to the beating of Rodney King by police officers in Los Angeles, assembling it from twigs and other discarded materials he found during a walk in a park in Chicago. The sculpture emitted unpredictable sounds once Cave put it on, which he saw as an opportunity to ensure that his protesting voice could be heard - a motivation echoed here by the inclusion of a gramophone horn. Each of

Cave's Soundsuits has its own peculiarities, thanks to his practice of gathering objects in flea markets and antique malls. Despite their futuristic quality and chromatic intensity, the suits retain a degree of familiarity precisely because of the everyday objects they comprise.

Shaikh Zain al-Din

Indian Roller on Sandalwood Branch, 1779
Opaque colours and ink on paper, 76.2 × 96.5 cm / 30 × 38 in
Minneapolis Institute of Art

This painting of an Indian roller (*Coracias benghalensis*) on the twig of a sandalwood tree was intended as a souvenir of India for Lady Mary Impey, wife of Sir Elijah Impey, who had been made Chief Justice of the Supreme Court at Fort William in Bengal at a time when much of the subcontinent was under the rule of Britain's East India Company. The Impeys loved India, and collected plants and animals, some of which they kept on their substantial estate, where in the late 1770s they commissioned local artist Shaikh Zain al-Din to paint species from their menagerie. Originally from the city of Patna, and trained in the Mughal artistic tradition, Zain al-Din used paper and watercolour paints supplied from England and a style that reflected the influence of British botanical illustration – but combined with the more ornate flourishes of Indian painting. The Indian roller, like its European counterpart (see p.166), takes its name from its twisting and turning display flight; the birds are common throughout India, where they often perch on branches – and today on telephone lines – to study the ground for insects, spiders and other food. Here, the bird is preening tits right wing, which is stretched out to reveal the characteristic shiny blue feathers, contrasting with the sandy pink of its head and back. Indian sandalwood is a tropical aromatic tree famous for its timber, especially the fragrant heartwood, and as a source of essential oil.

Céleste Boursier-Mougenot

From Here to Ear (detail), 2010
Temporary installation
Barbican Centre, London

What at first glance might look like a typical wildlife photograph turns out to be anything but. On closer inspection, these zebra finches (*Taeniopygia guttata*), with their distinctive orange beaks, are seen to be perched on the head and neck of an electric guitar. The situation is a deliberately constructed installation featuring seventy finches and fourteen guitars: face upwards, plugged in and tuned by the French artist Céleste Boursier-Mougenot (born 1961). Each time one of the birds takes off or lands on one of the instruments, its claws pick the strings and produce pre-tuned chords that play out through high-frequency amps placed in the installation. Thus the gallery becomes both a sonic aviary and a concert hall. The 'piece' that the birds are 'playing' has its own particular rhythm and self-generative quality. It is not entirely random, and takes no jazzlike unexpected turns. Rather, it speaks sonically to the organic relationship the finches have to each other. While finches naturally chirp away excessively, we, as spectators, have little understanding of the complex social dance going on in front of our eyes: hierarchies are being tested, warnings of potential predators being sounded and bonds being forged. The sounds that the artist has invited the birds to conjure give audience members a potential artistic (almost painterly) language for understanding what is happening in the space, revealingly weaving together two normally very separate worlds into a fascinating narration of nature's beauty.

Unknown

Meidum Geese, c.2575–2551 BC
Painted plaster on limestone, 27 × 172 cm / 10½ × 67¾ in
Egyptian Museum, Cairo

A row of geese adorn a passage leading to the tomb chapel of Itet, daughter-in-law of the pharaoh Snefru, who founded Egypt's Fourth Dynasty in about 2613 BC. Laid to rest in a mastaba tomb alongside the first true pyramid in Egypt, Itet and her husband Nefermaat were accompanied into eternity by scenes of farming and hunting. Three signifies 'plural' in Egyptian iconography, and these two symmetrical groups of three geese thus symbolize many birds. Shown in accurate detail are two bean geese (*Anser*

fabalis) at either end, two greater white-fronted geese (*A. albifrons*) facing left and two red-breasted geese (*Branta ruficollis*) facing right. The mastaba of Nefermaat was excavated in 1871 by Auguste Mariette and Luigi Vassalli, an artist. In 2015, Francesco Tiradritti, director of the Italian archaeological mission to Egypt, suggested that Vassalli himself may have painted the scene, citing such evidence as paint colours, the equal (unrealistic) sizes of the geese, his belief that the bean goose and the

red-breasted goose were unlikely to have been seen in Egypt and other technical issues. Each of these points was refuted by authorities at the Egyptian Museum, and the painting is usually accepted today as genuine. A full-size facsimile was created of this and other tomb paintings by artists of the Metropolitan Museum of Art's Egyptian Expedition, which excavated in Egypt between 1907 and 1937. These twentieth-century paintings are now invaluable records of works that have deteriorated or been destroyed.

Unknown

Black-figure amphora, *c.*540 BC
Painted ceramic, H. 40.6 cm / 16 in
British Museum, London

Wearing his lionskin and with a quiver slung over his back, the ancient Greek hero Herakles takes aim at a flock of birds in this illustration on an amphora, used to hold water. The scene is depicted in the black-figure vase-painting technique, in which figures are painted in silhouette, with details incised. The sixth of Herakles' twelve labours was to rid the land around the town of Stymphalia, in Arkadia, of a flock of flesh-eating birds, which the second-century-AD traveller Pausanias described as having beaks of bronze, poisonous dung and sharp, metallic feathers that could be launched at their enemies like arrows. The birds were said to resemble ibis (Threskiornithidae) but were the size of cranes (Gruidae), and unlike ibis had powerful, straight beaks. They had established themselves in a marsh and proceeded to destroy crops, orchards and townspeople. Herakles was unable to approach because of the soft ground, so the goddess Athena presented him with a rattle, which he used to frighten the birds into the air, where he shot them with arrows poisoned with the blood of the Hydra, a monster slain in another labour. Those that escaped flew to an island in the Black Sea, where they were later encountered by the Argonauts in another Greek myth. Pausanias describes a sanctuary to Artemis built at Stymphalia, with the birds carved in the frieze below its roof.

Habiballah of Sava

The Concourse of the Birds, from *Mantiq al-tair*, c.1600
Ink, opaque watercolour, gold and silver on paper, 25.4 × 11.4 cm / 10 × 4½ in
Metropolitan Museum, New York

A hunter holding a shotgun so long that it overspills the frame of the image looks on as a common hoopoe (*Upupa epops*), recognizable from its crest as it stands tall on a rock right of centre, addresses a gathering of birds drawn from all over the world, including a magpie, herons, parrots, doves, a white cockerel and many raptors. The illustration by Iranian artist Habiballah of Sava (*fl. c.*1590–1610) accompanied a poem by Farid ud-Din 'Attar, *Mantiq al-tair*, or Language of the Birds, referring to a passage in the Qur'an in which Israeli kings Solomon and David learn the language of birds. Despite the realistic depiction of the birds, they are symbolic: each represents a human shortcoming that stands in the way of attaining spiritual enlightenment. The hoopoe, a symbol of wisdom, exhorts its companions to begin a treacherous journey in search of the simurgh, a mythological bird that symbolized ultimate spiritual unity, but in Din 'Attar's poem the route proposed by the hoopoe was so treacherous that the very thought of it caused some of the birds to die on the spot. Eventually, a smaller flock of thirty birds reached the destination of their quest, only to find out that, in fact, they, together, were the simurgh, which in the Persian language of ancient Iran means 'thirty birds'.

Frans Snijders

Concert of Birds, 1629-30
Oil on canvas, 98 × 137 cm / 38⅝ × 54 in
Museo del Prado, Madrid

A motley group of birds has assembled on the branches of a battered tree, around a wide-eyed little owl (*Athene noctua*) perched on top of a songbook that is tied to a branch with red ribbons. The chances that these birds will sing in unison are next to none, however. The finches, the jays (*Garrulus glandarius*) and the flying Bohemian waxwing (*Bombycilla garrulus*) qualify as songbirds; not so the yellow-crowned Amazon parrot (*Amazona ochrocephala*), common hoopoes (*Upupa epops*), or the owl itself,

which would together produce an inevitable cacophony. Nevertheless, the concert or choir of birds was a popular theme among Dutch and Flemish seventeenth-century painters and their audiences, possibly reflecting a Dutch proverb that translates as 'Every bird sings with the beak it has been given' - in other words, every individual is different. The subject provided an excellent excuse for artists to depict a range of birds in a single painting, and Frans Snijders (1579-1657) showed each one in a natural

pose, although he may have used stuffed birds as models for at least some species. Snijders was the most inventive and influential painter of still lifes and of scenes with live animals of the early seventeenth century. Rubens hired him regularly as a collaborator and he had many followers in Flanders and abroad. This painting must have been sent from Antwerp to Spain shortly after Snijders finished it. It was presented to King Philip IV and first recorded in an inventory of the Alcázar palace in Madrid in 1636.

Hiroshi Sugimoto

Hyena-Jackal-Vulture, 1976
Gelatin silver print, dimensions variable
Private collection

A frenzy of at least four different species of vultures, along with a thick-billed raven and a maribu stork, almost entirely block the view of the carrion upon which they have descended, although the tips of two striped legs identify the victim as a zebra. Other scavengers are waiting their turn, including a hyena and a jackal, while two vultures fight in the foreground: one is tipped on its back, and screeching loudly. This scene from the African savannah is actually a posed diorama of stuffed animals photographed by the

Japanese artist Hiroshi Sugimoto (born 1948) in the American Museum of Natural History in New York. By cropping out the frame and shooting the scene in a unifying black and white, the artist erases the artificiality that would normally be apparent to visitors and reintroduces a dynamic sense of movement. Vultures have commonly conjured up negative cultural associations: apart from being considered 'ugly' birds, with their dull plumage and bald head and neck, they are frequently used as a symbol of death and decay.

Here the birds brawl over scraps of food, emphasizing the combative mood, which Sugimoto suggested was reminiscent of the museum's home city: 'I thought, wow, this is New York.' Despite such a poor reputation and associations, the vulture plays an important role in the ecosystem of their habitats. Images such as this help us to zoom in and perhaps consider for a moment the bird not in isolation but as part of a dynamic system rooted in a balanced natural environment.

William James Webb

The White Owl, 1856
Oil on board, 45 × 26.3 cm / 17¾ × 10⅜ in
Private collection

Statuesque and somnolent, a barn owl (*Tyto alba*) stands upright on a wooden beam next to its rodent prey. The site is probably a ruined building, perhaps a disused chapel or outhouse, its old timbers cracked and overgrown by ivy, a sprig of which clambers upwards. The soft texture of the owl's plumage is captured well, as are the delicate shades of pale orange and grey of the wings and the ghostly white of its underparts. Barn owls hunt on still, dry days, by night and at dawn or dusk, and they sometimes nest in church towers, which explains their prominence in folklore and superstition. The British painter William James Webb (also known as William James Webbe; 1830-c.1912) was inspired by the final two lines of each verse in the 1830 poem *The Owl* by Alfred, Lord Tennyson: 'Alone and warming his five wits, The white owl in the belfry sits.' Born in Cornwall, the son of a Wesleyan minister, Webb had by 1856 moved to the Isle of Wight, where Tennyson was also a regular visitor. Eventually Webb and his wife settled in Ealing, Middlesex, by which time he was well known as an artist who illustrated religious books and stories for children, as well as rustic scenes of country life. Animals feature in many of his paintings, and this detailed study of a barn owl is one of his finest.

Josef Albers

*Owl (II), c.*1917
Ink on paper, 50.2 × 37.5 cm / 19¾ × 14¾ in
Josef and Anni Albers Foundation

Best known for his series of minimalist abstract paintings *Homages to the Square,* and for his seminal work on colour theory, *Interaction of Colour,* the Bauhaus-trained German artist, designer and craftsman Josef Albers (1888–1976) was a leading figure in twentieth-century art on both sides of the Atlantic. His life history reads like a 'Who's Who' of the Modernist movement: Paul Klee and Wassily Kandinsky were his colleagues, and Cy Twombly and Robert Rauschenberg (see p.189) were among his many students. The Bauhaus founder Walter Gropius himself enlisted Albers as a *werklehrer* – handicrafts teacher – on the strength of his practical skills, particularly in stained glass. Despite his rich pedigree as an abstract artist, Albers was a skilled figurative draughtsman, shown by the economical use of loose, expressive marks, perfectly capturing the form and character of this Eurasian eagle owl (*Bubo bubo*). The ability to recognize and explore the artistry in all manner of practical applications, uniting form and function, design and craftsmanship, was one of the tenets central to the Bauhaus movement. For Albers, art itself was the constant, the common denominator that underpinned fields as diverse as album covers and architectural design. Above all, Albers' legacy was as an educator, encouraging an attitude of humility and a desire to learn by direct observation and first-hand experience. 'What counts,' he told his students, 'is not so-called knowledge of so-called facts, but vision – seeing.'

Ken Loach

Kes, 1969
Film, dimensions variable
Woodfall Film Productions, produced by Tony Garnett / United Artists

Falconry may be the sport of kings, but the common kestrel (*Falco tinnunculus*) is a 'bird for the riff-raff of the world', says film director Ken Loach (born 1936), of the bird in his acclaimed 1969 social-realist film, based on the 1968 novel *A Kestrel for a Knave* by Barry Hines. In *Kes*, a misunderstood teen, Billy Casper (played by David Bradley), unfairly written off by his superiors as fit only for work in the local coal mine, captures and trains the titular bird to fly and return, and in doing so finds companionship, joy and a welcome release from frustrations engendered by a lack of freedom or opportunity. This image - widely used on the European posters upon the film's initial release - shows Billy gazing intently at Kes perched on his gloved hand; his tangible concentration offers the bird the focused attention and care that he rarely receives from his own relations. When hunting, kestrels usually hover above the ground looking for prey such as voles, before diving down, which Billy trains his kestrel to do by holding raw meat in his thickly gloved hand. *Kes* displays Loach's enduring themes of social isolation and the disenfranchisement of the most vulnerable, and offers an indictment of social policy in Britain at the time. Despite its sombre themes and at times harrowing narrative, the film was a surprise hit, praised variously for its humanity, authenticity and portrayal of human relations with nature, and it launched Loach's international filmmaking career.

Unknown

Book of the Dead of Hunefer, *c*.1285 BC
Painted and inked papyrus, 46.2 × 57.3 cm / 18 × 22½ in
British Museum, London

In the right-hand panel of this ancient Egyptian papyrus, the god Ra-Horakhty appears in the form of a falcon with a sun-disk on his head, accompanied by seven baboons, with a blue arc possibly representing the sky above; below him stand the goddesses Isis (mother of Horus and restorer of dead souls) and Nephthys (sister of Isis and associated with funerals and embalming), flanking a personified *djed* pillar (a hieroglyph representing stability). This is a section of the Book of the Dead of Hunefer, a royal scribe and steward of the pharaoh Seti I. He appears at left with his wife, Nasha, in poses of adoration. Hunefer might well have inked this hymn to the rising sun himself. Ra was the ancient Egyptian sun god, believed to rule the sky, earth and underworld. He was portrayed as a falcon, and when merged with the falcon-headed sky god, Horus, was known as Ra-Horakhty, 'Ra, who is Horus of the Two Horizons'. The falcon denoted divine kingship, with the pharaoh identified as the human manifestation of Horus. Books of the Dead contained funerary prayers, hymns and magical spells and were interred with the deceased from the early New Kingdom (from *c*.1450 BC) to just before the Roman period in Egypt. The texts were intended to assist the soul through the tests and judgements of the underworld and into a blessed afterlife. The finest examples, like this one, would have been created by master artists and scribes.

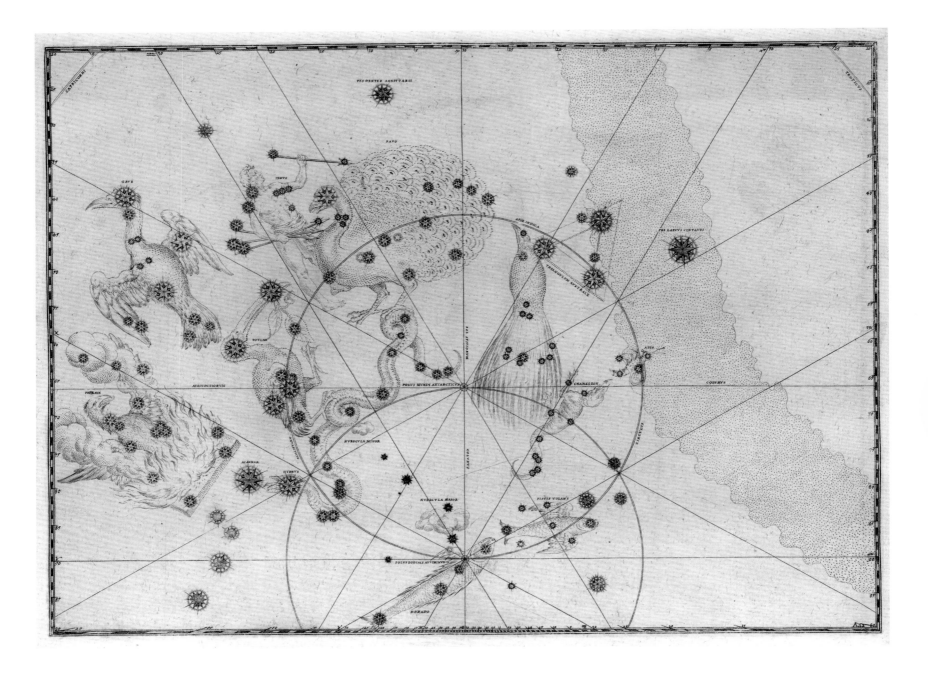

Johann Bayer and Alexander Mair

Constellations: Apis Indica, Hydra, Pavo, Indus, Grus, Phoenix, Toucan, Piscis Volans, Chameleon,
Nubecula Minor and Major, Dorado and Triangulum Australe, from Uranometria *by Johann Bayer, 1603*
Engraving, 29 × 39 cm / 11½ × 15⅜ in
David Rumsey Map Collection, Stanford University, California

This star map from 1603 – the first published of the southern hemisphere – includes five constellations, or star patterns, known collectively as 'the celestial birds'. At left is the mythical phoenix, which lives for 500 years before dying and being reborn in flames; next to it is Grus, the crane, with Tucana, the toucan, beneath. To the right of a figure carrying arrows is Pavo, the peacock whose tail was said to contain one hundred eyes, beside Apus, the bird of paradise, a native of Australia and Papua New Guinea, countries

from which this portion of the sky would be visible. The German lawyer and preacher Johann Bayer (1572–1625) created the first atlas of the whole sky, *Uranometria*, with fifty-one plates embellished with figures illustrated by Alexander Mair (1559–c.1620), based on designs by Albrecht Dürer (see p.166). Forty-eight plates illustrated the individual northern hemisphere constellations listed by the ancient Greek astronomer Ptolemy, but this plate showed all the newstars and constellations mapped by explorers of

the Dutch East India Company on their first voyage to Java and Sumatra in 1594. It is perhaps no surprise that birds should figure so frequently among the constellations, given their traditional symbolism as a link between the earthly world and the heavens. Of the eighty-eight constellations recognized today, nine feature birds: the five mentioned by Bayer plus the older constellations listed by Ptolemy: Corvus, the crow; Aquila, the eagle; Cygnus, the swan; and Columba, the dove.

Unknown

Tile with image of phoenix, late 13th century
Stonepaste with underglaze painted in blue and turquoise and lustre-painted on
opaque white ground, 37.5 × 36.2 cm / 14¾ × 14¼ in
Metropolitan Museum of Art, New York

After the Mongol invasion of Iran in the Ilkhanate period between 1256 and 1335, there was a profusion of links between modern day China and Persia, both of trade and design. Iconography such as lotus flowers proliferated, with some of the best examples in the tiles from Takht-i Sulaymän ('Throne of Solomon') in northwestern Iran. Built as a summer and hunting palace by Mongol ruler Abaqa Khan, it was situated on the site of Adur Gushnasp, one of the three most sacred Zoroastrian fire temples of pre-Islamic Iran, in order to confer legitimacy on the new Mongol rulers. This tile, probably from Takht-i Sulaymän, is a cobalt and lustre-glazed moulded example showing a *fenghuang*, like the phoenix of Greek mythology though from a separate origin. A symbol of virtue and the coming together of yin and yang, it is often paired with a *loong* (Chinese dragon) in weddings and used by royalty to indicate a positive relationship between a man (the dragon) and a woman (the *fenghuang*). The creature is common in many East Asian cultures and found today on the seal of the president of South Korea, in the name of typhoons and in place names throughout China. The bird may also be a reference to a simurgh, another phoenix-like mythological beast from Persian culture dating back thousands of years, which underscores the mix of Mongol, Chinese and Persian influences on Ilkhanate art.

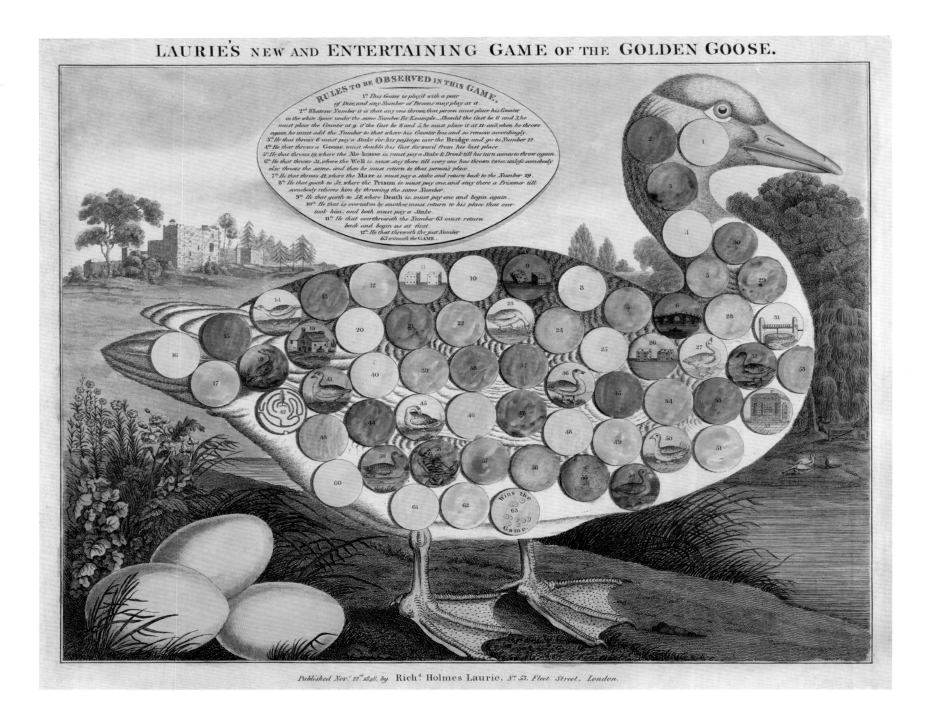

R. H. Laurie

Laurie's New and Entertaining Game of the Golden Goose, 1848
Hand-coloured engraving on paper backed with linen, 35.5 × 46 cm / 14 × 18 in
Wellcome Collection, London

There's a promise of reward to whoever wins the Game of the Goose: three large golden eggs next to the goose on a country riverbank. When it emerged in sixteenth-century Italy, where geese were considered to be lucky – a superstition that perhaps dates back to the Roman belief that geese were a favoured animal of the goddess Juno – the Game of the Goose was the first commercial board game, though its roots can be traced back to an ancient Egyptian forerunner. The Game of the Goose became popular throughout Europe – Francesco de' Medici gave a game to King Phillip II of Spain. This later English design, produced by Richard Holmes Laurie (1777-1858), references Aesop's fable 'The Goose That Laid the Golden Eggs', which famously warns against greed. Yet the game is entirely chance based; as with related games, such as Snakes and Ladders, progress is governed by the roll of the dice. In this version, players start at space 1 by the bird's eye and continue from right to left down its body to space no. 63 above its webbed feet.

While hundreds of variations have been produced over the centuries, the basic gameplay remains the same: scattered across the board are Goose spaces, which contain a small image of the bird; players landing on these lucky spaces earn another roll of the dice. The morally questionable Inn, however, results in losing a turn, while the Death space, denoted by a skeleton, sends players back to the start.

Peter Karl Fabergé

The Hen Egg, 1885
Varicoloured gold, enamel, rubies, H. egg: 6.4 cm / 2½ in, hen: 3.5 cm / 1⅜ in
Fabergé Museum, Saint Petersburg

In 1885 Tsar Alexander III of Russia commissioned the jeweller Peter Karl Fabergé to create an Easter gift for his wife, Tsarina Maria. Inspired by an eighteenth-century ivory egg from the Royal Danish Collection – Maria had Danish heritage – Fabergé created this hen's egg: a white enamel 'shell' that opens to reveal a matt-yellow gold 'yolk' which in turn holds a golden hen containing a replica of the Imperial Crown with a ruby pendant. The opulent gift, crafted in Fabergé's workshops, began an annual tradition in which Alexander, and, from 1894, his son Tsar Nicholas II, commissioned intricate bejewelled eggs containing equally rich 'surprises' as gifts to family members. For Fabergé, who had taken over his family jewellery business in 1882, it was an opportunity to showcase the workmanship and opulence of his *objets d'art*. Alexander III had first seen Fabergé's work at the Pan-Russian Exhibition in Moscow in 1885, and after his first few commissions the jeweller was given increasingly free rein with his creations. He would design more than fifty imperial eggs, but following the Russian Revolution in 1917, Fabergé eggs became symbolic of the extravagance and excess of Russia under the Romanovs. In 1918, the eggs were seized by the communist Bolsheviks before later being sold off and scattered across the globe. In 2004 nine eggs, including *The Hen Egg*, were returned to Russia by businessman Viktor Vekselberg, who spent $100m acquiring them.

TURBITS.
BLACK. RED. YELLOW.

RED PIED POUTER COCK.

FRILL-BACKS.
PLAIN-HEADED AND CRESTED.
SCANDAROONS.
RED AND BLACK PIED.

BRUNETTE.   SATINETTE
BLUETTE.   SILVERETTE.

MAGPIES.

ENGLISH FANTAILS
BLACK. WHITE. BLUE.

ALMOND TUMBLER SUB-VARIETIES.

WHITE CARRIER COCK.

RED & YELLOW BARBS.

JACOBINS.
BLUE   WHITE   BLACK

BLACK CAPUCHINS
AND
DAMASCENES.

RED, WHITE & YELLOW DRAGOONS.
(LONDON FANCY)

J. W. Ludlow

Selection of plates from *The Illustrated Book of Pigeons. With standards for judging* by Robert Fulton, 1876
Chromolithographs, each 28 × 21.5 cm / 11 × 8½ in
Field Museum of Natural History Library, Chicago, Illinois

Although radically different in appearance, all of these remarkable pigeon varieties belong to a single species, the domesticated form of the rock dove (*Columba livia*). The same species is used in pigeon racing, carried messages in wartime and walks the streets of virtually every town and city worldwide – and its variety is remarkable. The British naturalist Charles Darwin, in the opening chapter of *On the Origin of Species* (1859), wrote of these 'fancy' or exhibition pigeon breeds, 'Altogether at least a score of pigeons might be chosen which, if shown to an ornithologist and he were told that they were wild birds, would certainly, I think, be ranked by him as well-defined species.' The sheer diversity of forms that could be created by selective breeding from a single wild ancestor suggested to Darwin a mechanism by which animals might change in nature. A pigeon breeder himself, Darwin's experiments with his own birds and dialogue with other fanciers helped shape his theory of evolution by natural selection. Robert Fulton's *The Illustrated Book of Pigeons* is a classic work and represents all the exhibition varieties popular in England in the late nineteenth century, including Pouters, Fantails, Jacobins, Carriers, Barbs, Scandaroons, Turbits and Tumblers, to name just a few, each in many varieties of colour and pattern. All of these breeds are still kept by fanciers, but none look quite the same as they did in Fulton's time, having evolved by artificial selection in just a few pigeon generations.

Hoang Tien Quyet

Rooster, 2014
Wet-folded from one uncut square of Vietnamese handmade paper, dimensions variable

This remarkable figure of a rooster was folded from a single piece of paper by the Vietnamese origami artist Hoang Tien Quyet (born 1988). Having started folding paper as a young child, Quyet later joined the Vietnam Origami Group, where he learned the technique of wet folding, which allows artists to achieve organic, flowing lines by temporarily dissolving the adhesive that bonds the paper fibres together, enabling the paper to be folded before it sets again. Quyet uses sheets of handmade Vietnamese paper to fashion animals such as pigs, rabbits, lions and foxes. This rooster - one of two he made within a few years of each other - reflects the bird's importance in Vietnamese tradition. Because the rooster crows loudly at sunrise, it is celebrated around the world as a link between humans and the heavens, from which it summons sunlight; in Vietnam it is linked with the supernatural world of genies. The rooster was already an important ritual symbol among the farming peoples of prehistoric Vietnam, when the Dong Son cast images of the bird on their bronze drums and painted it inside temples devoted to the Mother Goddess. Roosters are still sacrificed on New Year's Eve, said to be the darkest night of the year, as a traditional gesture to guarantee the return of the sun the next morning. In rural villages, the family whose rooster crows first on New Year's Day is thought to be blessed with luck.

Unknown

Pendant in the form of a cock, *c.*1600
Enamel, gold, pearl, ruby, 7.5 cm × 4.5 cm / 3 × 1¾ in
Rijksmuseum, Amsterdam

This tiny, delicate cockerel was so valuable that it probably belonged to the Stadtholder, or ruler of the Dutch republic, following its creation by an unknown German jeweller as a housing for a so-called baroque pearl – a pearl that was large enough to be valuable, but not regular enough in shape to be crafted into the sorts of earrings or necklaces that feature so widely in the paintings of Dutch painter Jan Vermeer. The pearl forms the bird's body, while its head, tail and feet are made of gold enamelled in various colours and set with rubies. For the Dutch Protestants, pearls were a symbol of Christianity, and particularly of the purity and chastity associated with Mary and Jesus Christ; they were also often linked to the idea of *vanitas* – the teaching that an attachment to earthly wealth was misguided, as it would surely pass, while spiritual wealth endured. More widely, roosters were symbols of the arrival of good news, thanks to their habit of crowing first thing in the morning, and of both fertility and war, thanks to their propensity for fighting. Merchants imported pearls from the Dutch empire in Asia, particularly from the Gulf of Mannar, between South India and Sri Lanka. Gathered by divers who used heavy stones to pull themselves down to the seabed, perfectly shaped pearls were rare and highly expensive to obtain, so jewellers developed imaginative ways to use irregular stones to their best advantage.

Jim Henson and Kermit Love

Big Bird reads to children during an episode of *Sesame Street*, 2008
Photograph, dimensions variable

This bumbling 2.5 m (8 ft) tall, bright yellow bird has been entertaining and educating pre-school children on the American television show *Sesame Street* since 1969. Some imagine that Big Bird is an oversized canary, others a giant ibis (*Pseudibis gigantea*) or perhaps a unique type of whooping crane (*Grus americana*): the truth is that his species remains a mystery. Big Bird is known for his childlike wonderings and misunderstandings, and for reassuring young viewers not to worry about not knowing everything because he too

has much to learn; 'Asking questions is a good way of finding things out!' he regularly says. The puppet, designed by the puppeteer and creator of the Muppets, Jim Henson (1936–90), is covered with around 4,000 white turkey feathers, dyed yellow. The puppeteer is completely enclosed in the suit and operates the character's head and neck with a raised hand. With no eye holes, the puppet is manoeuvred around the set with the aid of a small television monitor, strapped to the puppeteer's chest. Big Bird was performed by

Caroll Spinney from 1969 until his retirement in 2018, when he was replaced by Matt Vogel. Spinney developed the character, evolving him from a bird-brained hillbilly to a curious six-year-old, to ensure that children could identify more closely with him. The character's cultural and educational impact was recognized by the United States Library of Congress, which honoured him with a Living Legend award.

Florentijn Hofman

Rubber Duck, 2013
PVC, H. 16.5 m / 21 ft
Temporary installation, Hong Kong

An inflatable rubber duck some 20 m (65 ft) high floats in Hong Kong harbour as if it were in some gigantic bath. The bath-time toy's familiar appearance was established in the 1940s – the first rubber ducks, created in the 1880s, were chew toys for infants and did not float – with the design of yellow body and orange bill often credited to the sculptor Peter Ganine, who sold more than 50 million models. Dutch artist Florentijn Hofman (born 1977) first presented his gigantic rubber duck on the Loire River in Saint-Nazaire, France, in 2007, echoing the regular-object-reproduced-oversize concept made popular by Claes Oldenburg in the 1970s. Over the following decade, Hofman made multiple replicas for other locations, and in 2013 *Rubber Duck* was installed in Victoria Harbour in Hong Kong – the city responsible for its creation. According to Hofman, the piece was based on a small duck manufactured by a local company called Tolo Toys. The sculpture also echoes a 1992 incident in which a Hong Kong container ship lost part of its cargo in the Pacific Ocean, including 29,000 rubber ducks. The toys were carried thousands of kilometres, proving of invaluable help to oceanographers mapping marine currents. Since its inception, *Rubber Duck* has raised questions over the merits of public art, its ubiquitous presence challenging the idea that it should be site specific. Hofman's later work – including monumental elephants and rabbits – was never quite able to match the global popularity of the original.

William de Morgan

The Fishing Lesson, c.1890s
Ceramic charger, Diam. 37 cm / 14½ in
Private collection

A protective mother pelican with her wings splayed urges her chick to catch one of the many fish swimming in the river below on this large ceramic plate painted with a dazzling palette of rich blue, green and lustre glazes by the celebrated English potter William de Morgan (1839–1917). Pelicans often fish in groups, often feed in groups where fish are abundant, scooping them up in their capacious throat pouch. Contrary to popular belief, however, pelicans do not store fish in their distinctive throat pouches but swallow them immediately. De Morgan was closely associated with William Morris and the Arts and Crafts movement in the late nineteenth century, and the designs of his Persian-style plates and tiles often incorporated birds and animals, drawing inspiration from Middle Eastern motifs, Italian Renaissance patterns, medieval art and seventeenth-century Dutch engravings. This example typifies his approach, which was inspired by the vibrant ceramics of Iznik in Turkey. Its iridescent finish is known as lustreware, an ancient form of glazing that originated in ninth-century Egypt before spreading through Syria to the Middle East and Europe. De Morgan revived the technique after a period of technical experimentation; he discovered that starving his kiln of oxygen during firing would leave a layer of silver oxide on the plate's surface. The result proved commercially successful and his handmade ceramics were eagerly collected.

Jan Asselijn

The Threatened Swan, c.1650
Oil on canvas, 144 × 171 cm / 56¾ × 67⅜ in
Rijksmuseum, Amsterdam

Bigger than life size, hissing with spread wings, this mute swan (*Cygnus olor*) towers over the viewer as she fends off a scruffy dog (barely visible in the water at lower left) to protect her nest full of eggs. Flying feathers and a contorted shape accentuate the bird's agitated motion, while dramatic lighting and the heavy cloud beyond add to the ominous atmosphere. Perhaps a real-life confrontation with such a swan had made a lasting impression on Jan Asselijn (*c.*1610–52), a painter of the Dutch Golden Age. It is the only

image of this kind among his many Italianate landscape paintings. Several decades after its creation, the painting began to be reinterpreted as an allegory for an event that occurred twenty years after Asselijn's death. Added inscriptions identify one of the swan's eggs as 'Holland' and the dog as 'the enemy of the state'. The swan itself represents Johan de Witt, the republican secretary of state who unsuccessfully opposed the reinstatement of the young William III of Orange as Stadholder. In 1672, de Witt and his brother, Cornelis,

were falsely blamed for an invasion of the Netherlands by a European alliance and lynched by a mob in The Hague. As a political commentary – albeit unintended – the painting came to be considered of great historical importance and was the first work of art to be acquired for the Nationale Kunstgalerij (later the Rijksmuseum), in 1800.

Arthur Rackham

'The Owl and the Birds' from *Aesops Fables*, William Heinemann edition, 1912
Ink and watercolour, 29.5 × 22.9 cm / 11⅝ × 9 in
Private collection

A motley collection of farmyard and wild birds gathers around a barn owl (*Tyto alba*) as it warns them to uproot a tender oak shoot. The owl's audience includes storks, a condor, duck, turkey, cockerel and macaw, as well as a starling and another songbird – possibly a robin – seen only from the back. The illustration by British artist Arthur Rackham (1867–1939) accompanies the story of 'The Owl and the Birds' from *Aesop's Fables*, a collection of tales assembled in Greece over 2,500 years ago.

In the story, the owl – widely known for its wisdom – counsels the other birds not to let the oak grow, because it will produce mistletoe, which can be used to poison birds; it goes on to tell them to eat flax seeds, which will eventually produce fibres for nets to catch birds, and to beware the archer, who will use feathers to make arrows to kill birds. The birds initially ignore the story's message – destroy the seed of evil, before it grows into something that harms you – but come to see the wisdom of the owl's lesson.

Rackham was a talented book illustrator whose haunting, original drawings and paintings adorn many famous publications, especially children's books such as J. M. Barrie's *Peter Pan* (1911) and Kenneth Grahame's *The Wind in the Willows* (1908) and classics such as Shakespeare's *A Midsummer Night's Dream*. This plate is from an English edition of *Aesop's Fables* published by William Heinemann in London in 1912.

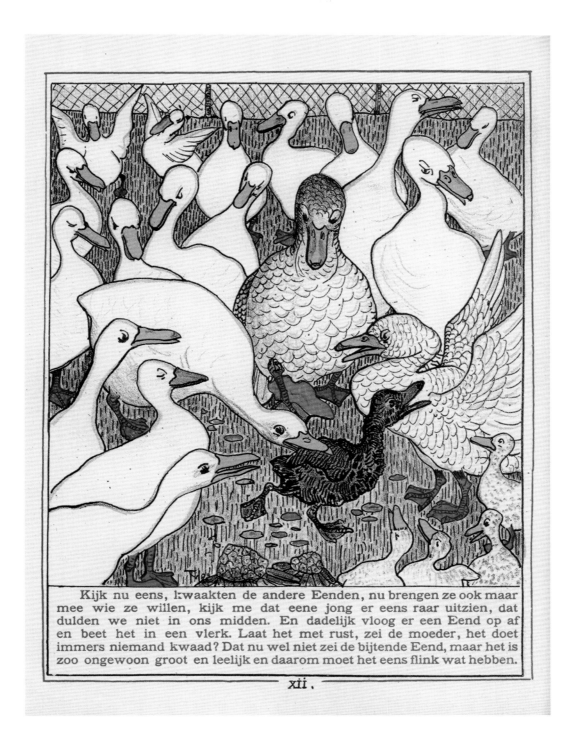

Kijk nu eens, kwaakten de andere Eenden, nu brengen ze ook maar mee wie ze willen, kijk me dat eene jong er eens raar uitzien, dat dulden we niet in ons midden. En dadelijk vloog er een Eend op af en beet het in een vlerk. Laat het met rust, zei de moeder, het doet immers niemand kwaad? Dat nu wel niet zei de bijtende Eend, maar het is zoo ongewoon groot en leelijk en daarom moet het eens flink wat hebben.

xii.

Theo van Hoytema

Page xii, from *Het leelijke jonge eendje* ('The Ugly Duckling'), 1893
Chromolithograph, 29 × 22.5 cm / 11⅜ × 8⅞ in
Koninklijke Bibliotheek, The Hague

An ugly duckling with brown feathers is surrounded by a flock of white ducks that scold him and bite, eventually driving him out of the community, based solely on the fact that he appears different. The bird eventually grows up to be a beautiful swan – a morality lesson for the reader on not judging beauty purely on appearances. This illustration of the celebrated tale 'The Ugly Duckling' by Hans Christian Andersen is by the renowned Dutch artist Theo van Hoytema (1863–1917), as part of the second children's book of his artistic career in 1893. The charm of his illustrations lies in the skilful depiction of the birds in just a few lines. When the third edition was released in 2000, the publisher A. G. Schoonderbeek hailed van Hoytema's work as 'the most beautiful picture book in the Netherlands'. The book was particularly advanced for its time. The thirty-one lithographs are produced in five-colour printing, which meant that a separate stone (lithography means 'stone printing') had to be produced for each individual colour. The artist draws the design directly on the stone slab and so the print bears the direct, graphic character of the artist's handwriting – as is clearly seen in Hoytema's illustrations. In the second half of the nineteenth century in particular, the new printing techniques created a flood of wonderfully illustrated books to delight adults and children alike.

Joel Sartore

Curl-crested aracari (*Pteroglossus beauharnaesii*) at the Dallas World Aquarium, 2013
Photograph, dimensions variable

The arresting, persuasive gaze of the curl-crested aracari (*Pteroglossus beauharnaesii*) strikes the viewer almost as if the bird is beckoning to us. This is the allure of the US photographer Joel Sartore (born 1962), whose work fosters a kinship between humans and his bird and other animal subjects while nurturing a deep reverence for the creatures' physical attributes. The brilliant colours of the bird – a toucan that lives in the humid forests of the Amazon Basin – stand out in stunning detail against a flat black background.

Sartore's ambitious project, *The Photo Ark*, began in 2006 with the aim of creating a broad visual catalogue encompassing the planet's biodiversity. Sartore's intention is to photograph each of the roughly 12,000 species living in zoos and wildlife sanctuaries across the globe. The comprehensive list of species ranges from invertebrates a couple of centimetres long to elephants and giraffes. It is a monumental endeavour that Sartore estimates will take twenty-five years. As a child, Sartore was moved upon learning the story

of Martha, the last known living passenger pigeon (*Ectopistes migratorius*), which died at the Cincinnati Zoo & Botanical Garden, Cincinnati, Ohio in 1914, marking the extinction of her species. Sartore's fervent hope is to inspire protection of the species he features and to prevent further extinction. His work has been widely published, most notably through his partnership with *National Geographic*. Additionally, *The Photo Ark* has been featured globally, including in the documentary series *Rare* on PBS.

John Gilroy

Lovely Day for a Guinness, 1955
Colour lithograph, 60 × 40 cm / 23⅝ × 15¾ in
Guinness Archives, Dublin

Instantly recognizable from its large, brightly coloured bill, a toco toucan (*Ramphastos toco*) perches atop a weather vane, balancing a pint of stout. Despite being native to the rainforests of South America, the largest of the toucans was for more than twenty-five years synonymous in the UK with Guinness, the famous Irish brewery for which this advertising poster was created by the English artist John Gilroy (1898–1985), who worked on Guinness advertisements from 1928 to the 1960s. While working at the advertising agency

S. H. Benson, the former newspaper cartoonist was asked to create a wholesome, family-friendly advertisement for the brand. Inspired by a performing sea lion he saw at the circus, Gilroy swapped the ball it balanced on its nose for a pint of stout, spawning an entire series in which hapless zookeepers had their beer pilfered by an ever-growing menagerie of characters, including a turtle, an ostrich, a crocodile, a kangaroo, a penguin and, of course, the iconic toucan. Gilroy produced around fifty posters for Guinness, creating multiple

designs for each campaign (an earlier version of this poster shows the bird facing in the opposite direction). He also designed a series of posters for the American market with toucans balancing pints on their beaks as they flew over the Statue of Liberty, Mount Rushmore and the Golden Gate Bridge, although these were never used.

Georg Flegel

Still Life of Birds, Insects and a Mouse, 1637
Oil on canvas, 52.5 × 54.5 cm / 20⅝ × 21½ in
Museum der Bildenden Künste, Leipzig

This curious image of a variety of birds, living and dead, is exceptional not only in the oeuvre of Georg Flegel (1566–1638), a still-life painter in Frankfurt am Main, Germany, but in still-life painting in general. Why Flegel painted it – at the age of seventy-one, as inscribed on the painting – is unclear, but it may well have been intended for a cabinet of curiosities. Such encyclopaedic collections of natural specimens and artefacts were assembled by scholars and educated citizens, and could also include stuffed birds. Perhaps

this painting both recorded some of the birds and at the same time became an item in the collection. A Bohemian waxwing (*Bombycilla garrulus*), a common kingfisher (*Alcedo atthis*), a blue tit (*Cyanistes caeruleus*), a northern lapwing (*Vanellus vanellus*), a domesticated pigeon, a common chaffinch (*Fringilla coelebs*) and a hawfinch (*Coccothraustes coccothraustes*) are all shown as if living. The blue tit is eying a caterpillar. The dead woodcock and partridge lying on the table are typical gamebirds that would make a good meal. Only the

turqouise-fronted Amazon parrot (*Amazona aestiva*) at upper right is an exotic curiosity. The exact same bird appears as the only living creature, also near a dish of sweets, in a still life of luxury items that Flegel painted much earlier, in around 1620. Here, the artist has cleverly arranged the birds on a decorative mossy branch, while the hawfinch sits at the front, among some cherries of which it habitually splits the stones for food.

Adriaen Collaert

Columbus plumipes vittatus & Picus cinereus, from *Avium Vivae Icones in aes incisae & edita ab Adriano Collardo*, 1600
Engraving, 22 × 29 cm / 8⅝ × 11⅜ in
Rijksmuseum, Amsterdam

This quarto-sized print depicts *Columbus plumipes vittatus* ('a pigeon with feathered legs') at left and *Picus cinereus*, now the Eurasian nuthatch (*Sitta europaea*), at right, sitting in front of a detailed depiction of a farm and dovecote in the countryside of Flanders. The pigeon is likely influenced by a similar work by the sixteenth-century Italian naturalist Ulisse Aldrovandi (see p.28), *Columba cypria cucullata*, which was widely copied. The breed is probably the ancestor of today's Jacobin fancy pigeons. The plate is one of thirty that illustrated the two volumes of *Avium vivae icones in aes incisae* ('Images of live birds engraved in brass'), probably published around 1600, by Adriaen Collaert (*c*.1560–1618). The son of Antwerp-based engraver and printmaker Jan Collaert I, Adriaen was part of a dynasty of Flemish artists in the sixteenth and seventeenth centuries. Collaert, who worked in Antwerp after spending time in Italy, was not known as a natural history illustrator, and most of his works – which were often based on the illustrations of other artists – were either pastoral or religious, the other exception being his *One hundred and twenty-five plates of fishes*. Though his style was common for the time, the family's legacy as printmakers and publishers enabled it to reach a wide audience. Both his sons, Jan Baptist Collaert and Carel Collaert, continued the family tradition of engraving and printmaking, focusing on devotional and religious subjects.

Unknown

Relief plaque with swallows and quail chicks (front and back), 400–30 BC
Limestone, paint, 15 × 13.8 cm / 5⅞ × 5½ in
Metropolitan Museum of Art, New York

In Old Kingdom Egypt (c.2686–2182 BC), swallows (Hirudinidae) were associated with the souls of the dead. The Fifth Dynasty (2494–2345 BC) Pyramid Texts describe how the pharaoh has 'gone to the great island in the midst of the Field of Offerings, on which the swallow gods alight; the swallows are the imperishable stars', referring to the North Star and the nearby stars that never seem to move. The bird is also depicted on the prow of the solar barque, the boat on which the sun god, Ra, traverses the world. The swallow hieroglyph functions both as an ideogram for the bird and as a phonogram meaning 'great'. Common quails (*Coturnix coturnix*) were popular pets as well as being bred for food; the hieroglyph of a quail chick served to make a word plural. Plaques such as this one, which features two relief carvings of swallows on one side and a pair of quail chicks on the other, along with an ink drawing of a third, date from the Late Period (664–332 BC) and are characterized by their unfinished appearance. Their function remains uncertain. They may have been used as models to train sculptors, or as votives dedicated to the gods and hung in temples – or perhaps both. That this one was indeed used for training purposes might be indicated by the drawing of the quail chick, and the fact that the lower swallow is more complete than the upper one.

Unknown

Inlay depicting Thoth as an ibis with a Ma'at feather, 4th century BC
Faience, 15.5 × 15.6 cm / 6 × 6 in
Metropolitan Museum of Art, New York

Thoth, the ancient Egyptian god of writing, law and justice, philosophy, science and magic, was often shown as a man with the head of an ibis. His Egyptian name ('Thoth' comes from the Greek) means 'he who is like the ibis'. The African sacred ibis (*Threskiornis aethiopicus*) was associated with wisdom, and the Greeks believed Thoth to have originated all knowledge. More than two million mummified ibis have been excavated that were offered as sacrifices at an annual festival in his honour. Texts suggest that ibis may have been raised near the god's temples for the purpose. One priest-scribe records feeding 'clover and bread' to around 60,000 sacred ibis. This piece of inlay appears to have formed part of a royal inscription that included epithets of Thoth and Seshat (goddess of writing and books, and daughter or wife of Thoth). The god appears as an ibis, its beak supported by the ostrich feather of Ma'at, goddess of justice. Ma'at was integral to the Weighing of the Heart ritual that every soul had to undergo after death, when the deceased's heart was weighed in a balance against the feather. If the two sides balanced, Thoth recorded the verdict, and the deceased was presented to Osiris; if the heart was heavier, it was devoured by a demon and the soul destroyed. Kings were often shown with the feather of Ma'at, as a symbol of their role as upholders of law and virtue.

MENURA SUPERBA: Shaw.

John Gould

Menura superba: Lyrebird, from *Birds of Australia*, 1837-48
Hand-coloured lithograph, 52 × 36.8 cm / 20½ × 14½ in
Minneapolis Institute of Art, Minnesota

A flashy male superb lyrebird (*Menura novaehollandiae,* previously *M. superba*) dominates the composition while the more demure female of the mating pair rests upon her perch. The superb lyrebird is a flamboyant bird endemic to Australia, named for the male's striking lyre-shaped tail surrounded by delicate, wispy plumes. The illustration featured in *Birds of Australia,* the culmination of a two-year-long expedition by English ornithologist John Gould (1804-81). Among the 681 plates of this ambitious book, 328 described and named new species. Early exposure to the Royal Gardens of Windsor, where his father was a master gardener, laid the foundation for Gould's fascination with nature. A skilled taxidermist, his work eventually led him to a prestigious position as curator at the Zoological Society of London. As such, he would come to collaborate with the most important naturalists of the era, eventually earning equal esteem among the most significant contributors to modern biology. Gould identified specimens collected from Charles Darwin's voyage to the Galápagos islands aboard HMS *Beagle* (see p.27). His conclusions connecting speciation and location would provide the groundwork for Darwin's theory of evolution by natural selection. Gould's wife Elizabeth (1804-41), who illustrated many of his book plates, was an accomplished scientific artist who contributed some of the most historically significant imagery to the field of ornithology.

Ernst Haeckel

Trochilidae – Kolibris, from *Kunstformen der Natur*, 1904
Chromolithograph, 36 × 26 cm / 14 × 10¼ in

This kaleidoscopic scene of richly coloured humming-birds suggests an imaginary world, but the dozen species depicted here are all very real. They include the horned sungem (*Heliactin bilophus*, top right), the white-vented violetear (*Colibri serrirostris*, left, second from bottom) and the booted racket-tail (*Ocreatus underwoodii*, bottom right), rendered in meticulous detail by the German scientist and artist Ernst Haeckel (1834-1919). Or, more accurately, scientist, artist, zoologist, naturalist, physician,

professor, philosopher and marine biologist... Haeckel made incalculable contributions to each discipline. His concepts formed the foundation of phylogeny, the evolutionary tree, and his desire to describe the rarest forms of plants and animals often led to his discovery of new species. Those species he deemed the most remarkable were named after his late wife, Anna, whose untimely death is said to have led him to eschew orthodox theology. *Trochilidae* was plate 99 (of 100) in Haeckel's most famous work,

Kunstformen der Natur ('Artforms in Nature', 1899-1904), and encapsulates Haeckel's tendency to highlight the parallels between natural form and the human notion of adornment. The dot-eared coquette (*Lophornis gouldii*, left, third from top) mirrors the style of royal portraiture, while the delicate coif of the hooded visorbearer (*Augastes lumachella*, right, second from bottom) competes with the most sophisticated of hairstyles in a way that would probably have made Haeckel's voguish contemporaries envious.

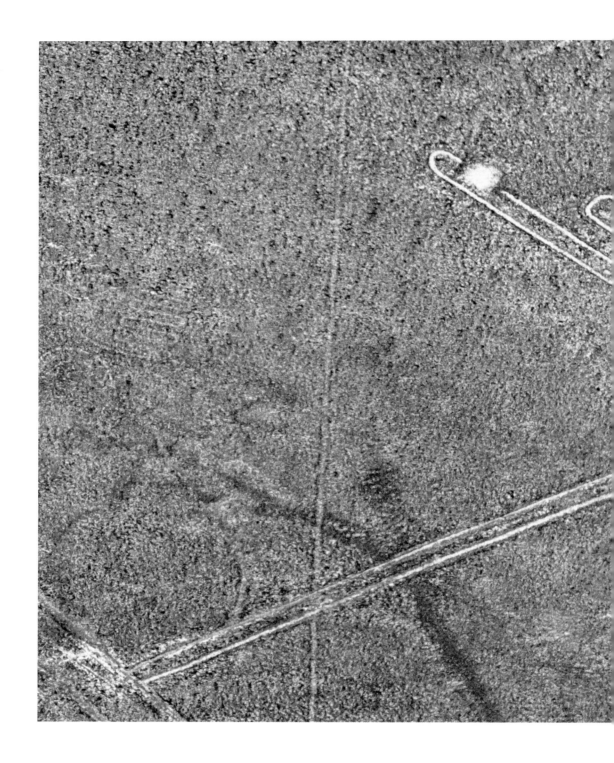

Unknown

Hermit Hummingbird, 500 BC–AD 500
Geoglyph, 97.5 × 65.8 m / 320 × 216 ft
Desert plains of Rio Grande de Nazca, Peru

From eye level, the creators of this outline drawing of what appears to be a hummingbird - one of the features of the renowned Nazca Lines of Peru - would not have been able to see their design as they removed dark, iron-oxide coloured pebbles and gravel from the surface of the desert to a depth of 10–15 cm (4–6 in), to expose the lighter coloured sands and bedrock underneath. Some sixteen birds have been identified among the mysterious designs - many from locations far from the Peruvian desert - but the long beak and other features meant this design was identified as a hummingbird (Trochilidae) from its first discovery in the late 1920s. Detailed ornithological analysis concluded in 2019 that this geoglyph actually represents a species of hermit (*Phaethornis* sp.), a type of hummingbird that exists only in tropical lowland forests far to the north and east. The researchers speculated that the Nazca people encountered the creatures they depicted while gathering food, though its presence in the desert is a mystery. In the 1930s and '40s, it was believed that the geoglyphs had some astronomical and calendrical purpose, possibly representing star groupings or seasonal solstices. Today, however, it is generally assumed that the Nazca Lines were associated with that most precious desert commodity: water. They are believed to have been ritual drawings that established locations for propitiatory events in which the promise of water and fertility of crops would be asked of the gods.

Gary Cook

Female Northern Cardinal Landing, 2018
Photograph, dimensions variable

This remarkable image owes as much to luck as to judgement. American photographer Gary Cook (born 1965) did not expect to capture such a widely lauded image on a November day at his home in Beavercreek, Ohio, where a sudden cold snap brought large numbers of hungry birds to his feeder to take advantage of the freely available food. Cook had already set his camera up next to the feeder to remotely capture what he anticipated would be a frenzy of birds when this female northern cardinal (*Cardinalis cardinalis*) arrived, her crest raised in aggression to ward off the other, smaller diners, as she flew directly at the feeder and the camera, scattering the other birds and creating the remarkable symmetry of Cook's image. Northern cardinals are fairly large finch-like songbirds, with the males being a particularly vivid shade of red while females are never as bright and are usually mostly fawn. The male birds' colours stand out particularly when seen against snow. They are a numerous species across the eastern US and their range also extends into Mexico. They are listed by the International Union for Conservation of Nature as a species of least concern, with a population thought to be around 100 million individuals. Often referred to simply as 'cardinals', they get their common name from the distinctive red hats and robes of the cardinals who are senior officials of the Roman Catholic Church.

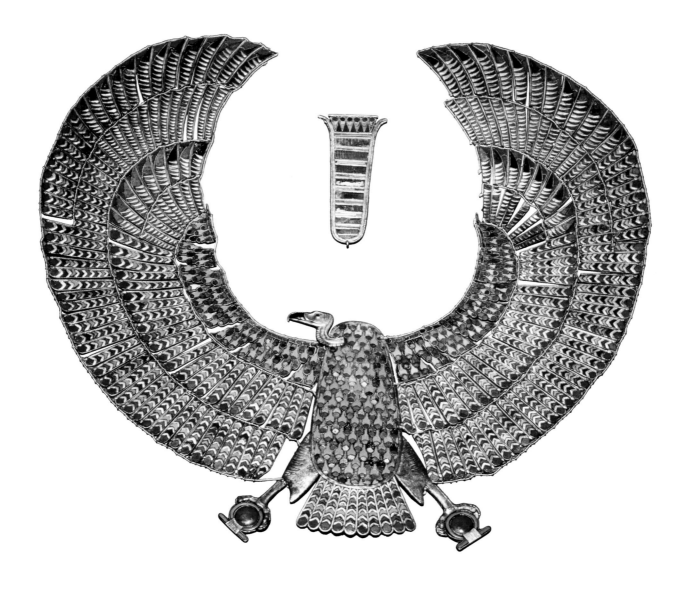

Unknown

Collar from the tomb of Tutankhamun, c.1370–1352 BC
Gold, glass and obsidian, 39.5 × 48 cm / 15½ × 18¾ in
Egyptian Museum, Cairo

Over 3,000 years ago, this flexible gold collar was placed on the chest and shoulders of the most famous of all Egyptian mummies, the young King Tutankhamun. Its elongated wings are composed of gold segments inlaid on the front with 'feathers' of polychrome glass to imitate lapis lazuli, jasper and turquoise, held together with thread and divided by borders of tiny gold beads. The beak and eye are obsidian. A counterpoise in the form of a lotus was attached by gold wires at the back of the mummy. The collar was not merely an object of adornment but a symbol of magical protection that represents the goddess Nekhbet, the guardian deity of Upper Egypt, in the form of a griffon vulture (*Gyps fulvus*) or a lappet-faced, or Nubian, vulture (*Torgos tracheliotos*). Nekhbet is often portrayed with her wings spread protectively over the king, or as a woman with a vulture's head, sometimes suckling the pharaoh. In each talon, she grasps the hieroglyph *shen*, representing infinity. As well as being associated with Upper Egypt, Nekhbet was also linked to the sky god Horus, protector of the pharaoh (see p.85), and she often appears above the king in battle scenes, guarding him and threatening his enemies. Vultures were believed to be entirely female, born without male involvement, making them a symbol of motherhood, and their ability to turn carrion – death – into life symbolized the eternal cycle of transformation, death and rebirth.

Werner Bischof

Penguins from the Zoo taking their Weekly Walk, 1950
Photograph, dimensions variable

What do you do when your penguins accidentally escape? Turn it into a parade, of course! In the 1950s, a keeper at Edinburgh Zoo apparently left a gate open, allowing many of the penguins to wander around. The spectacle proved so popular with visitors that the 'parade' became a unique marketing tool. Edinburgh Zoo was the first in the world to successfully breed king penguins (*Aptenodytes patagonicus*) in captivity, and their daily walkabout was a way to draw in visitors from the streets around Corstorphine Hill.

In this image looking up at the gaggle of king penguins, the Swiss photographer Werner Bischof (1916–54) evokes a sense of exploration as the birds encounter 1950s Edinburgh, much as Antarctic explorers must have felt on the islands and ice sheets of the frozen continent a half-century before. Found on islands throughout the Southern Ocean, king penguins are closely related to their better-known Antarctic counterparts, emperor penguins (*A. forsteri*). They are the most pelagic penguin species, ranging hundreds of kilometres

on a single foraging trip. Bischof was an early member of the photographer cooperative Magnum, joining in 1949, and documented much of post-war Europe before travelling to India, Japan and South America. His photojournalistic style showed both the hardships and the optimism of postwar recovery. The penguins still parade in Edinburgh, inspiring fresh dreams of adventure in new generations of visitors and raising awareness of their conservation.

FOR THE ZOO, BOOK TO REGENT'S PARK OR CAMDEN TOWN

UNDERGROUND

Charles Paine

For the Zoo, Book to Regent's Park or Camden Town, 1921
Chromolithograph, 101.6 × 63.5 cm / 40 × 25 in
London Transport Museum

Like a group of commuters pushed into one another during a particularly crowded train ride, a waddle of penguins stumble into each other in this striking 1921 advertisement for travelling on the London underground. Although the illustration is stylized, the general placement of the orange coloration on the side of the penguins' heads and the patch of colour on the lower jaw suggest these are four king penguins (*Aptenodytes patagonicus*), which were being kept at the zoo by at least 1914 (the first live specimen in the UK

arrived from the Falkland Islands in 1865). The famed Penguin Pool, designed by Berthold Lubetkin, was opened at the zoo in 1934. In reality, king penguins' body plumage is a dusky grey rather than the pale blue chosen by the artist, Charles Paine (1895-1967), and the birds' chests should feature a yellow-orange burst of colour before fading to the familiar white belly – yet there is no question of mistaking these aquatic birds for any other. Trained in stained-glass design and printmaking, Paine worked for clients such as Penguin

Books and the British government, but during the 1920s his work for London Underground could be seen throughout the capital. He produced thirty-one posters for Frank Pick, the visionary CEO who worked with graphic designers and artists to develop a clear, lasting design identity for the underground in the early twentieth century.

Maurizio Cattelan

Untitled, 1997
Male ostrich, 130 × 160 × 70 cm / 51¼ × 63 × 27½ in
Private collection

With its head buried in the floor of an art gallery, this stuffed common ostrich (*Struthio camelus*) represents the familiar idea of burying one's head in the sand, used to convey the foolishness of ignoring problems by pretending they do not exist. For the Italian artist Maurizio Cattelan (born 1960), who produced this sculpture after his work began receiving international attention in the late 1990s, it conveys the feelings of insecurity that accompanied his newfound fame. Ostriches have many curious behaviours. They can't fly, though they can sprint at approximately 70 km/h (45 mph). They fight with their feet and, when it is time to mate, the male's beak, neck and legs turn bright red. However, contrary to popular belief, they do not bury their heads when threatened. This myth probably originated with the first-century Roman naturalist Pliny the Elder, who wrote that these African birds 'imagine, when they have thrust their head and neck into a bush, that the whole of their body is concealed'. Pliny's description was probably based on ostriches' feeding behaviour; they also sometimes swallow grit and small pebbles to help digest fibrous food. Cattelan, who is known for incorporating taxidermied animals in his artworks, often employs humour to address important issues. Here, the ostrich becomes a striking metaphor for the insecurities of both the artist and the viewer, illustrating a tendency with which everyone can identify.

Jean-Lebrecht Reinhold

Têtes de Grandeur Naturelle de L'Engoulevent à Queue Fourchue et son pied,
from *Histoire Naturelle des Oiseaux d'Afrique* by François Levaillant, 1799–1808
Etching and aquatint, 30 × 24 cm / 11¾ × 9½ in
Smithsonian Libraries, Washington, DC

At first glance nothing appears amiss with this striking illustration. It shows the head and foot of a potoo (family Nyctibiidae), a nocturnal relative of the nightjars, with its distinctive anatomical details: the broad gape, unfringed with the nightjars' row of stout bristles; the upturned corner of the closed bill, giving the appearance of a smile; even the structure of the claws. The French naturalist and collector François Levaillant (1753–1824) identifies the species as *L'Engoulevent à Queue Fourchue* – a fork-tailed nightjar

(Levaillant refused to use the more reliable binomial Latin naming system recently introduced by Linnaeus). However, Levaillant included the bird in his monograph on African ornithology, yet potoos are exclusively South American. (He would have been familiar with them from the forests near his childhood home in Suriname.) This plate is preceded by an image of the whole bird sporting a long and deeply forked tail, but potoos have a rounded tail. The list of discrepancies goes on, right the way down to

Levaillant's colourful account of the bird's capture, in a hollow tree in Namaqualand in southern Africa. Did Levaillant plant a false tail on a potoo specimen and try to pass it off as a new species? It is difficult to tell, but the existence of fifty-plus similar discrepancies in Levaillant's work may hint at the answer.

Unknown

Nilotic scene with ducks and frogs, first century BC
Mosaic, 67 × 136 cm / 26⅜ × 53½ in
Museo Archeologico Nazionale, Naples

Ducks and geese were almost as popular in ancient Roman households as dogs, but this scene of water birds swimming among lotuses and waterlilies reveals much more than a preference in pets. It was installed in the House of the Faun in Pompeii, near the famous Alexander Mosaic, and was created in *opus vermiculatum*, a technique using extremely small stone and glass tesserae that enabled the mosaicist to render fine details of colour and light. The presence of seasonally flowering lotuses indicates that this is a depiction of the Nile in flood. The birds are not expertly depicted, but based on their general appearance and on the conspicuous pale forewing, the ducks at front and back left most closely resemble garganey (*Spatula querquedula*), a small migratory species that would have been common in southern Italy, especially on migration; two purple swamphens (*Porphyrio porphyrio*) float at back right. Mosaics in this style are rare in Pompeii, reflecting the taste of the wealthiest citizens. That its sophisticated owner wanted to show off his knowledge of Greek culture is clear from the Alexander Mosaic in the next room; scenes of Egyptian exotica such as this enabled hosts (and guests) to demonstrate their knowledge of natural history and foreign customs. Nilotic imagery evokes luxuriousness, and the lavish lifestyles enjoyed by the elite of the Bay of Naples cities were sometimes compared to the opulence of Egypt.

Steve Torna

Eared Grebes, 2014
Photograph, dimensions variable

Birdwatchers expect to see grebes as singletons, or perhaps pairs tending young. To see a large aggregation is exceptional. This photograph secured the amateur prize for American photographer Steve Torna in the 2016 edition of the Audubon Society's annual photographic competition. In Torna's words: 'In May 2014 I was fortunate to see hundreds, perhaps a thousand, migrating eared grebes floating in a tight flock between the ice and the shore on Yellowstone Lake [Wyoming, USA]. I was drawn to their bright-red eyes, their golden "ears," and the way the flock created a colourful natural pattern. With their heads tucked into their feathers, the birds seemed harmonious and peaceful. They were silent. I never once heard a vocalization.' The eared grebe (*Podiceps nigricollis*) – called the black-necked grebe in the Old World – has a fragmented distribution in western North America, Eurasia and southern Africa. It is possibly the most numerous grebe species in the world; its population in western North America has been estimated at more than four million, and its nesting colonies on marshy lakes may contain hundreds of pairs. Eared grebes catch most of their prey underwater, including insects, molluscs and fish. The striking red eyes are shared with several grebe species and with divers (loons), which also feed underwater. Since modern DNA analysis suggests grebes and divers are not very closely related, it is tempting to wonder whether the red eye somehow facilitates underwater feeding. Quite how remains unclear.

Rosa Bonheur

The Wounded Eagle, c.1870
Oil on canvas, 147.6 × 114.6 cm / 58⅛ × 45⅛ in
Los Angeles County Museum of Art, California

A golden eagle (*Aquila chrysaetos*) struggles to fly with a broken wing in this painting by the French artist Rosa Bonheur (1822–99), unusually depicting the huge and fearsome raptor in a moment of vulnerability and defeat. In Western art, as in classical culture, the eagle is traditionally a symbol of martial triumph and pride, used by armies from the Roman legions to Napoleon's Grande Armée and the forces of the Hapsburg empire. Here, the symbolism of the wounded bird may refer to the defeat and capture of the French ruler, Napoleon III, at the Battle of Sedan during the Franco-Prussian War (1870–1), or possibly to the harm Prussia (again, symbolized by an eagle) had caused itself by beginning the conflict. Bonheur made her name painting highly accurate images of animals at a time when such paintings were considered less important than portraiture or history painting, but her originality was widely recognized. She exhibited many times at the prestigious Paris Salon and was awarded the Légion d'honneur in 1865. With a wingspan measuring up to 2.2 m (7 ft), the golden eagle is one of the largest birds living on the French Alps and one of the most powerful fliers of all raptors as it hunts other birds, reptiles and mammals. Bonheur's representation defies the convention of the triumphantly confident, masculine bird – a symbolic attack on patriarchy by a trailblazing female artist who lived her homosexuality with pride at a time when few dared.

Andy Warhol

Bald Eagle, 1983
Screenprint, 96.5 × 96.5 cm / 38 × 38 in
Private collection

This colourful screenprint portrait of a bald eagle (*Haliaeetus leucocephalus*) by Andy Warhol (1928-87) is confirmation of the bird's iconic status in popular culture. Chosen by the Founding Fathers in 1782 as the Great Seal of the United States, the bird summons ideals of majestic power, confidence and elegance. A bird of prey native to North America, the bald eagle joined the list of endangered species in 1967. Substantial population declines were linked to environmental degradation, and most specifically to the indiscriminate use of DDT for agricultural purposes. While not necessarily deadly to the birds, the insecticide interfered with their metabolization of calcium. This led to them laying brittle eggs that would break under the weight of a brooding adult. In 1983, gallerists and environmental activists Ronald and Frayda Feldman commissioned the renowned Pop artist Warhol to produce a series of screenprints to raise public awareness on the urgency of wildlife conservation. The result, *Endangered Species*, is a set of ten screenprints immortalizing near-extinct animals - including Grevy's zebra, the African elephant, the giant panda - just as Warhol had done for some years with his famed rock stars and actors. Today the bald eagle's numbers have risen to the point that the bird is no longer endangered and it is a widely acknowledged success story for the conservation movement - like another of Warhol's species, the Pine Barrens tree frog. The bald eagle remains protected in the United States under multiple federal laws and regulations.

Melissa Groo

Lilac-breasted Roller, Tanzania, 2020
Photograph, dimensions variable

With its distinctive colouring of lustrous pink, turquoise and blue feathers glinting under a cloak of tawny brown, the lilac-breasted roller (*Coracias caudatus*) can be easy to spot, standing atop shrubs and other vantage points in open woodland and savannah habitats of sub-Saharan Africa. It is from these lofty perches that it swoops to capture its ground-based prey: insects, lizards, scorpions, snails, small birds and rodents. Rollers are a favoured target for visiting photographers, as well as being much loved by local people – the lilac-breasted roller is the official national bird of Kenya. The roller family is related to kingfishers and bee-eaters and found only in the Old World. Rollers are so named because of their aerial territorial and courtship flights that feature dramatic acrobatic twists and turns. The lilac-breasted roller is no different, with the male flying to heights of up to 145 m (475 ft) during his display, then descending in swoops and dives while uttering harsh and discordant cries. In this serene image, the acclaimed writer, conservationist and photographer Melissa Groo (born 1962) has depicted a quieter moment. Groo champions an ethical approach to wildlife photography, rejecting the use of any form of bait to elicit action from animals. She prizes 'the welfare of animals above the desire for great photos', and her results are captivating.

15 MILES WEST
OF
LAKE T'SANA.
APRIL 6, 1927.

Prionops concinnata

NILE HELMET SHRIKE

Louis Agassiz Fuertes

Nile Helmet Shrike: Prionops concinnata, from *Album of Abyssinian Birds and Mammals,* 1927
Watercolour, 32 × 27 cm / 12⅝ × 10⅝ in
Field Museum of Natural History, Chicago, Illinois

One of the best-loved of all American bird artists, Louis Agassiz Fuertes (1874–1927) considered himself first and foremost an ornithologist. Painting birds was a continuation of this passion. An ardent collector, skilled in the preparation of scientific specimens, Fuertes steeped himself in fieldwork and the study of birds, living and dead. In 1926 he was fortunate to be invited to take part in a large-scale collecting expedition to Ethiopia with the Field Museum of Natural History in Chicago. Although well-travelled and a seasoned expedition biologist, his prior experience had been mostly confined to the New World and he greeted the opportunity to study African birds with characteristic enthusiasm. By the time he returned from Ethiopia Fuertes had reached the height of his powers as a draughtsman and watercolourist. Months of continued practice and diligent observation in the field had honed his skills and confidence, enabling him to develop a much freer artistic style. The 108 drawings of birds and mammals he made during the expedition, including this helmetshrike, a songbird that lives in scrub or open woodland, were the finest work of his career. In August 1927, shortly after his return to the United States, Fuertes was driving home after showing his album of Ethiopian drawings to a friend when his car was hit by a train. He was killed instantly. His wife was badly injured, but the collection of watercolour studies from the expedition was thrown to safety.

Utamaro Kitagawa

Sparrows and Pigeons, from *Myriad Birds: A Playful Poetry Contest (Momo chidori kyoka-awase),* 1790
Woodblock, 25.4 × 19.1 cm / 10 × 7½ in
Private collection

In this delightful album by one of the foremost Japanese *ukiyo-e* artists, Utamaro Kitagawa (*c.*1754–1806), bird species are arranged in pairs across facing pages (rather as they are in this book) with a dialogue of light-hearted love poetry purporting to be in the voice of each pair (*kyoka* literally means 'mad verse'.) On these pages, the pigeons symbolize homeliness and fidelity lasting into old age ('Even when we must use canes to walk, like pigeons, our love will never change, and we will eat beans together to celebrate the New Year'), while the sparrows represent restlessness, rumours and illicit romance ('Your fickle notions of love, restless as a flock of sparrows, will lead to secret assignations and gossip'). The popular style of woodblock printing called *ukiyo-e,* developed during Japan's Edo period (1603–1867), involved printing from multiple blocks, sometimes in as many as ten colours, and reached a level of technical mastery never seen in the medium before or since. Despite this, *ukiyo-e* prints – usually depicting actors or courtesans, animals or popular scenes – were derided as mass-produced imagery for the hedonistic tastes of the common towns-people, perhaps the equivalent to comic-book art today; they were never accepted as 'serious' art in Japan. Ironically then, when *ukiyo-e* prints reached a European audience in the second half of the nineteenth century, their artistic influence was profound, helping to shape the very foundations of Modernism.

Matt Stuart

Trafalgar Square, 2004
Photograph, dimensions variable

Although it is out of focus, this feral pigeon (*Columba livia*) is instantly recognizable as it struts in London's Trafalgar Square in front of a chance background of legs within legs, echoing its own movement and shape, as if bird and pedestrians all race towards an unseen finishing line. This image helped make the name of the British street photographer Matt Stuart (born 1974), who had spent half an hour bending almost double on a step, hoping to photograph passers-by against the distant wall, when the pigeon walked into his

viewfinder. There are reckoned to be between about 800,000 and a million pigeons in the British capital, probably descended from birds kept in dovecotes for meat, eggs and fertilizer many centuries ago, or by the resemblance of the tall buildings to the cliffs that were home to their ancestor, the rock dove. The birds congregate in such large numbers that city authorities try various methods of control, including outlawing pigeon feeding and flying Harris's hawks (*Parabuteo unicinctus*) daily in Trafalgar Square to scare them

away. Many people dislike the birds, but in fact their droppings present more danger to stonework, which they corrode, than to human health. For their many supporters, however, London pigeons remain sociable and intelligent icons of the city. Stuart's photograph is part of a body of work – *All that Life Can Afford*, capturing visual oddities of contemporary London – that was first exhibited and published as a book in 2016.

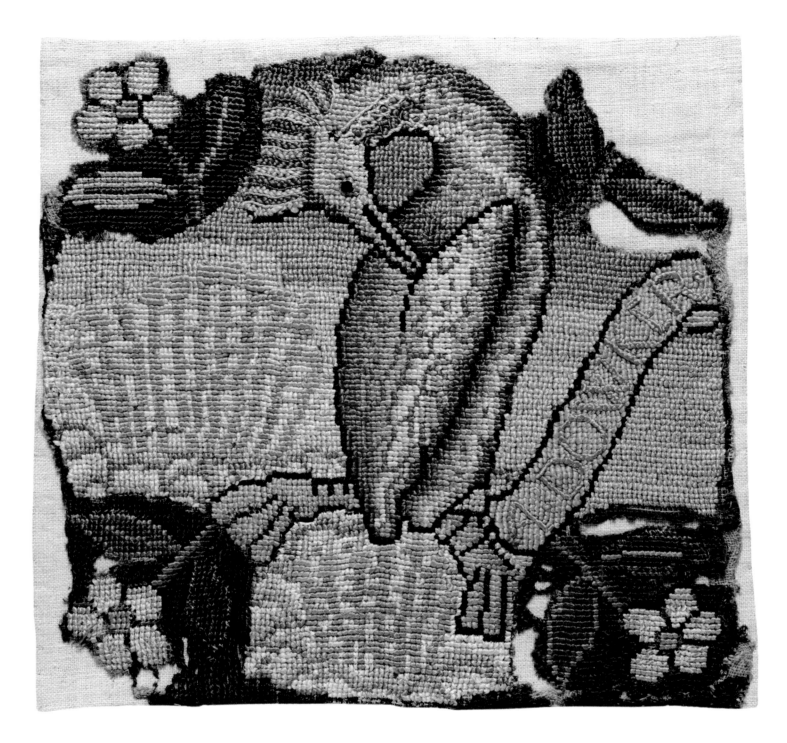

Mary Queen of Scots and Elizabeth Talbot

Fragment of embroidery from the Oxburgh Hangings, 1570-85
Embroidered linen canvas with silks, 26.2 × 26 cm / 10¼ × 10¼ in
Victoria & Albert Museum, London

This fragment of textile showing a great crested grebe (*Podiceps cristatus*) with its ornate head plume, preening its feathers on a lake, plays a part in a national drama. It was embroidered by Mary, Queen of Scots (1542-87), during the eighteen and a half years she spent imprisoned by her cousin, Elizabeth I, before her eventual execution. With a long-held claim to the English throne, the deposed Catholic monarch represented a threat to the Protestant queen. The elegant waterbird - the largest member of the grebe family, noted for its diving skills and mating display - is embroidered in fine blue, green, yellow and brown silks with stitches worked over coarse woven canvas. The panel belongs to a collection known as the Oxburgh Hangings, produced by Mary and Elizabeth Talbot, Countess of Shrewsbury, that includes more than a hundred panels featuring animals, birds and plants, many of which were sewn together to form hangings and bed curtains. Embroidery was a popular pastime for women in England in the sixteenth century, but Mary also used it as a form of communication; her chosen motifs, copied from natural history books, helped to convey her innermost thoughts at a time when her correspondence was closely monitored. This grebe was based on a woodcut in Conrad Gessner's *Icones Avium Omnium* (1560, see p.302), and while its significance is unclear, other emblems in Mary's needlework were cited as evidence that she was involved in plots to unseat Elizabeth.

Rathika Ramasamy

Black-crowned Night Heron – Nycticorax nycticorax, 2013
Photograph, dimensions variable

This fabulous capture by Indian photographer Rathika Ramasamy shows an adult black-crowned night heron (*Nycticorax nycticorax*) alighting on submerged vegetation. This small heron species has a near-global distribution. While the common name suggests they are birds of the night, they are more often crepuscular, flying to and from daytime roosts in the riparian bushes of fresh and salt-water wetlands, where they breed. Night herons habitually stand, stock-still, at the water's edge waiting in ambush for prey, usually small fish,

amphibians, crustaceans and aquatic insects. They have even been known to tackle small mammals and birds that cross their path. In common with several other species of heron, they also demonstrate a rare use of tools, tossing edible or inedible objects into the water within striking distance as bait to attract fish towards them. Black-crowned night herons are attractive birds with red eyes and their eponymous darker feathered cap and back over a body of pale white and grey. Youngsters are less distinctive – mostly a blend of brown with

paler streaks. There are around seven species of night heron, with some superficially similar in appearance. Those found in southern South America and the Falkland Islands, for example, are darker with crown and back feathers of a beautiful sooty blue-grey wash. Ramasamy, a specialist bird photographer, honed her craft in the many birding spots around her New Delhi home, including the Okhla Bird Sanctuary, where this photograph was taken.

Sydney Parkinson

Red-tailed Tropicbird, c.1769
Watercolour, 29 × 31.5 cm / 11½ × 12½ in
Natural History Museum, London

When the Scottish artist Sydney Parkinson (1745–71) painted this image of the red-tailed tropicbird (*Phaethon rubricauda*), it was unknown to science. He created it along with many hundreds more natural history illustrations on HMS *Endeavour* during James Cook's circumnavigation of the globe from 1768 to 1771. Parkinson died from dysentery on the homeward voyage, six months before *Endeavour* returned to England. He had been invited to join the expedition as illustrator by the botanist and patron of natural sciences Joseph Banks, who recorded seeing the bird on 13 March 1769, in the South Pacific: 'I saw a tropick [sic] bird for the first time hovering over the ship but flying very high; if my eyes did not deceive me it differd [sic] from that describd [sic] by Linnaeus, *Phaeton aethereus*, in having the long feathers of his tail red and his crissum black.' Banks named the bird *Phaeton erubescens*. In 2018, Parkinson's depiction of the tropicbird was among images chosen to appear in a set of six Royal Mail stamps commemorating the 250th anniversary of Cook's voyage, which collected thousands of specimens of birds, butterflies, fish, shells and plants. The majority were new to science, greatly enhancing European knowledge of the world's natural history. Parkinson's own name lives on in the Latin moniker of another bird, *Procellaria parkinsoni*, Parkinson's petrel.

Georg Forster

Blue Petrel (Halobaena caerulea), 1777
Watercolour, 53 × 36.5 cm / 20⅞ × 14⅜ in
Natural History Museum, London

This watercolour of a blue petrel (*Halobaena caerulea*) by Georg Forster (1754-94) clearly shows the bird's distinctive plumage, wings extended against a background of sea and sky. Forster was only seventeen when he was commissioned as a draughtsman to accompany his father, ship's naturalist Johann Reinhold Forster, on James Cook's second voyage to the South Pacific, on board the HMS *Resolution*. His role, as the 'camera' of the expedition, was to record the plant and animal specimens collected before their preservation caused them to dry and their colours to fade. In practical terms, this meant a flurry of activity after every shore visit, followed by a window of time while out at sea in which to catch up with journal entries, record data and put the finishing touches to drawings. The *Resolution* penetrated deep into the southern oceans and Antarctic waters where 'tube-nosed' seabirds (Procellariiformes) like this blue petrel would have been plentiful. Petrels travel vast distances at sea, returning to land only to visit their breeding colonies. Despite the difficulties and discomforts, Forster meticulously recorded the necessary scientific details, apparently adding the background setting for purely creative pleasure. Forster justly found fame as a travel writer. He was an attentive observer with a passion for ethnography, and his faithful yet compelling account of the customs and habits of the peoples of the South Pacific, *A Voyage Round the World* (1777), far exceeded the official account in popularity, and influenced generations of explorers to follow.

Unknown

Bird of Paradise Quilt Top, 1858–63
Cotton, wool and silk with ink and silk embroidery, 214 × 176.8 cm / 84½ × 69⅝ in
American Folk Art Museum, New York

We know virtually everything about the creation of this remarkable quilt in New York State around the time of the American Civil War (1861–5), except the name of its creator. Remarkably, the illustrations the quilter cut from newspapers to act as templates for her appliqué have survived with the quilt itself. For all the joyful images of fertility – fruiting trees, a groaning table, pairs of playful animals, butterflies, flowers and birds, either in courting pairs or with nests full of eggs – an artwork that was probably created to celebrate a marriage or betrothal may hide a tragic story. The templates show that the woman harvesting apples and cherries was intended to have a male counterpart in the next panel: instead, it is filled only with scrolls of vegetation. One suggestion is that the woman's intended husband did not survive the war, so he was never included. The birds depicted are heavily stylized but appear to be loosely based on tanagers, robins and red-winged blackbirds (Agelaius), one of the most populous birds in North America, and exotic species including ostriches, peafowl, and, in a central panel, what may have been intended to represent a bird of paradise. Beneath this is a pair of champion racehorses and beneath them the elephant Hannibal, which was a popular attraction with a touring circus in the Hudson Valley region.

128

Christian Lacroix Maison

Birds Sinfonia (colourway: Perce-Neige), from *Histoires Naturelles*, 2018
Digital print on fabric and paper, dimensions variable

Vertical lines fall like dripping paint from the feathers of garden songbirds including robins, exotic parrots and canaries, as well as falcons, hummingbirds, kingfishers and macaws, set against a backdrop of foliage and flowers. The birds are based on the works of key ornithological artists, including John James Audubon (see p.177), Edward Lear (see p.43), John Gould (see p.106) and many others. This rich jumble of colours was created as a wallpaper and homeware design by the renowned French fashion house Christian

Lacroix, under the creative direction of designer Sacha Walckhoff, inspired by the imaginary residence of a botanist for the *Histoires Naturelles* collection of 2018. Lacroix closed his fashion house in 2009, but his homeware continues to tap into similar opulent and whimsical themes as his theatrical *haute couture* and ready-to-wear collections had done for more than two decades, with a rich sense of colour and surface decoration. *Birds Sinfonia* fits into a rich tradition of similar designs from the eighteenth and nineteenth

centuries, when beautiful birds habited chinoiserie papers, firstly in hand-painted paper panels and then later in printed wallpapers. The boom began in the mid-eighteenth century, when woodblock prints were produced in China and exported to the European market, particularly to England, where they survive in historic homes such as Felbrigg Hall and Ightham Mote. A century later, birds became a popular wallpaper motif once more as the Arts and Crafts movement popularized a return to nature.

Richard Barnes

Murmur #25, 2006
Photograph, dimensions variable

What might at first appear to be an abstract black and white image of smudges floating in the atmosphere like smoke is, in fact, a depiction of starling flocks on the southern outskirts of Rome. These gatherings of thousands of birds, known as murmurations, occur at dusk as the birds gather above their communal roosting sites; they are thought to offer safety in numbers from predators such as birds of prey. New York-based photographer Richard Barnes (born 1953) became fascinated by starlings and recorded them in his series *Murmur*, alongside another series *Refuge*, which examined the organic and artificial materials that come together in birds' nests. Native to Europe, Asia and Africa, common starlings (*Sturnus vulgaris*) are small- to medium-size songbirds in the family Sturnidae. Their plumage is dark with a metallic sheen, though they are most awe-inspiring when seen flying as a group than being observed individually. As gregarious birds, they come together in large flight formations within which they wheel and dart, guided by a biological mechanism that is not fully understood. When on the ground, starlings eat insects and fruits, as well as searching for grubs by open-bill probing (exposing prey by forcefully inserting the bill into a crevice). Incorporating noises from their surroundings into their own vocalizations, starlings have been known to mimic the sound of both human speech and car alarms, and it is even possible to recognize individuals by their calls.

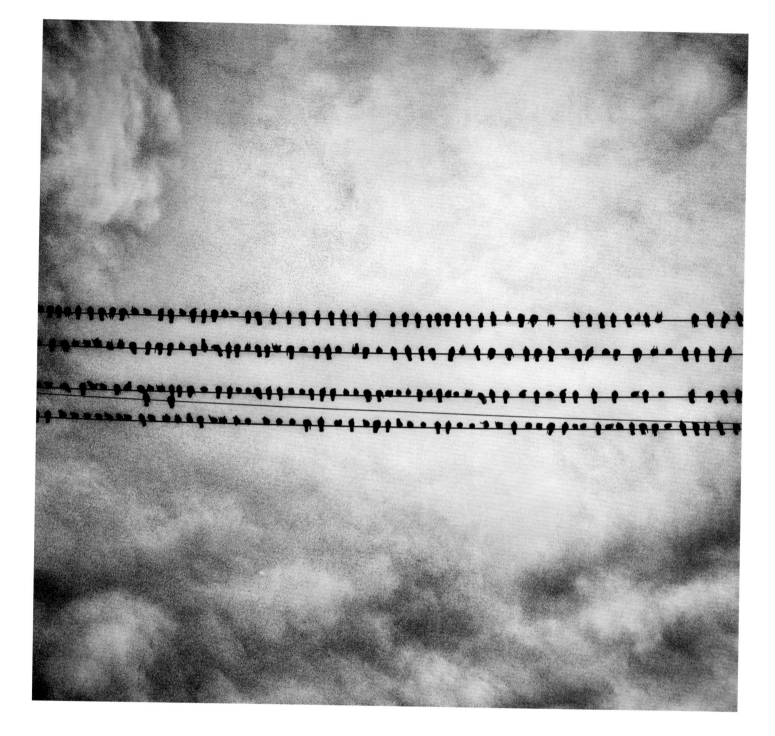

Matt Black

Birds in Tulare, California, 2014
Photograph, dimensions variable

Five electricity cables bisect a troubled sky, most holding dozens of perching birds silhouetted against the clouds, their shapes recognizable as avian, but their species indistinct. Their presence, twinned with the dim exposure and tousled ceiling of clouds, is ominous. They appear waiting, trapped, while the cables act as conduits for high-speed electrons blistering towards their destination, but the cables themselves remain static, gripped between hundreds of toes. The work of the American photographer Matt Black (born 1970) centres on the geography and environment of the Californian Central Valley, as well as the deep inequalities present in his homeland. This image is part of his project *Geography of Poverty*, which, since 2015, has seen him travel 160,000 km (100,000 miles) across 46 states. Many of the images contrast the brutality of the landscape with the plight of those people living within it: travellers leaning exhausted against telegraph poles, workers hiding from the sun under palm-leaf straw hats, mattresses lying in the snow. For all its foreboding atmosphere, *Birds in Tulare* is a respite from the trauma laid bare in Black's other images. For many, birds remain the symbol of peace, serenity and escape and, as we crane our necks backwards, shielding our eyes and contemplating the birds above us, we are given a chance to forget the world we are part of and perch along with these animals, high above the reality we may wish to leave behind.

Willem van Aelst

Still Life with Fowl, 1658
Oil on canvas, 95 × 78.5 cm / 37⅜ × 30⅞ in
Rijksmuseum, Amsterdam

Paintings with dead birds are not best sellers on the art market these days – but they were remarkably popular with artists in the past, partly as a showcase for artistic ability and partly for the more practical reason that dead animals do not run away, so are easier models than live creatures. Today, however, the questionable attraction of dead animals tends to colour the viewer's assessment of the aesthetic value of the work of art itself – especially given that death, including the deaths of animals, is today excluded

from daily life as much as possible. In the work of Willem van Aelst (1627–83), still-life painting with dead birds reached a peak during a period of great popularity in the seventeenth century. Despite its subject, Van Aelst's painting is bursting with liveliness. Even nearly 400 years later, it gives the impression that the two cocks are lying in front of the viewer, who is torn between admiration and revulsion. Small flies testify to the mastery of brushwork, as does the wide variety of feathers:

sometimes shimmering metallic, sometimes fluffy, soft and almost transparent. Van Aelst stages the composition dramatically by directing a spotlight from the front left onto the cocks on the stone plinth, above which a kingfisher and a ruff (*Calidris pugnax*) disappear into the darkness, creating an unexpected alliance of beauty and death.

Irving Penn

Woman in Chicken Hat (Lisa Fonssagrives-Penn), New York, 1949
Gelatin silver print, 38.3 × 36.5 cm / 15 × 14⅜ in
Metropolitan Museum of Art, New York

The Swedish model Lisa Fonssagrives looks out with customary elegance from under an elaborate hat topped with the feathers - and artificial heads - of domesticated poultry, in this 1949 image by the celebrated American fashion photographer Irving Penn (1917-2009). As shortages eased after the end of World War II (1939-45), fashion - guided by Paris - attempted to recapture both the elegance and the excess of the early twentieth century, when the use of feathers in fashion and millinery was commonplace.

The trade in feathers had declined thanks to the efforts of bird conservation movements, particularly Audubon Society members in the United States whose campaigns led to the Migratory Bird Treaty Act in 1918, one of the first federal protections for wildlife. Found in Southeast Asia, the red junglefowl (*Gallus gallus*) was domesticated by humans around 8,000 years ago and is now the most abundant bird on the planet, numbering more than 50 billion individuals. In the wild, the long elaborate tails, dazzling plumage,

red wattle and comb are used as signals of quality and to attract a mate. In a hat, they do much the same, indicating status and money. As the first 'supermodel', Fonssagrives appeared on numerous magazine covers and commanded high fees. She worked regularly with Penn, whom she married in 1950. Penn's sharp contrast and simple backgrounds were a hallmark of his portraiture, and give this image a crisp detail.

Vincent Munier

Dancing cranes, 2017
Photograph, dimensions variable

Two flashes of red – the features that give the red-crowned crane (*Grus japonensis*) its name – provide the only colour in this graceful geometric design of whites and blacks against the grey of heavy snow in Hokkaido, Japan. Cranes dance as part of their courtship display, but also to reinforce their pair bonding; some species dance when they are excited or frustrated, and also to teach young cranes, or colts, to dance. The red-crowned crane is one of the rarest of the fifteen species of crane and is listed as endangered, with a population of only about 2,000 adults; about half of these live on Hokkaido, where a protection programme has resulted in a slow increase in numbers. Elsewhere, the species breeds sporadically in northern China, Mongolia, Korea and Russia, wintering south to Korea and southern China. In Japan, the bird has long been revered as a symbol of immortality and good fortune and features in ancient folk tales and as a recurring motif in Japanese art. French wildlife photographer Vincent Munier (born 1976) honed his skills from an early age photographing the wildlife in the forests close to his home in the Vosges region, and has travelled widely to photograph species and wild habitats for magazines such as *National Geographic*. Munier is the first photographer to have received the Eric Hosking Award (encouraging emerging young talent) three years in succession in the BBC Wildlife Photographer of the Year competition.

Ohara Koson

Egret in the Rain, 1925–36
Colour woodcut, 36.2 × 23.6 cm/ 14¼ × 9¼ in
Rijksmuseum, Amsterdam

An egret's single beady eye, gazing slightly down, regards its current situation. Caught in a torrential rain storm, its back is hunched and its neck drawn in to gather as much of its body up under its wings as possible to keep dry. One of its two spindly legs is also drawn up into its downy feathers as if to keep at least one of its feet off the wet ground. The behaviour is common among wading birds and is thought to be a means of conserving body heat. The oval shape that the egret forms is dramatically set against a solid black background raked with rain. The Japanese woodblock print artist, Ohara Koson (1877–1945), a master of the so-called Bird and Flower school, explores the aesthetic possibilities presented by the shape of the bird as well as by the raindrops that frame it, most of which are stylized as a long single white line, emphasizing both the weight of the drops and the severity of the storm. The artist is also deeply concerned with anatomical accuracy, as can be seen in the details of the skin of the legs, feet and claws, which are faithfully recreated and realistic. The striking power of this image is generated by a dynamic fusion of anatomic and behavioural accuracy with aesthetics that invite us to empathize with the bird while still considering it as a scientific specimen.

Frank Chapman

Florida's Cuthbert Rookery, 1902/1962
Taxidermy and mixed media installation
American Museum of Natural History, New York

This idyllic scene in the Florida Everglades, as the summer sun beats down on herons, ibises and spoonbills, is both a deception and a memorial of a murder. In the early twentieth century, many thousands of the Everglades' herons and egrets were slaughtered for their feathers, destined for the millinery trade in New York, Boston and Chicago, where the plumes would adorn women's hats. In July 1905, at Cuthbert Rookery on Oyster Keys at the southern tip of Florida, Guy Bradley, the first 'bird

warden' employed by the Audubon Society to discourage plume hunters, noticed the schooner of a local feather hunter, Walter Smith. He launched his dinghy from the nearby town of Flamingo to investigate – and never returned. Smith confessed to shooting Bradley, but the trial was far from fair, and he was acquitted. Meanwhile in New York, Frank Chapman (1864–1945), a curator of birds and mammals at the American Museum of Natural History, came up with the idea of displaying taxi-

dermy in expansive dioramas like this to show species and habitats in an era before mass photography and international travel. *Florida's Cuthbert Rookery* is one of twenty such dioramas in the Hall of North American Birds, which Chapman designed as a memorial to Bradley, even using it to persuade President Theodore Roosevelt to enact some of the earliest wildlife protection in the United States. Today, the dioramas remain outstanding examples of early American natural history exhibitions.

Unknown

Cypro-Archaic Jug, 700–600 BC
Painted terracotta, H. 20.2 cm / 8 in
Metropolitan Museum of Art, New York

This stylized rendition of a bird appears on a bichrome jug, a style characterized by decoration in black and red on a white slip. The style was probably introduced from the Levant to Cyprus; the latter was in ancient times a cultural and trading hub of the eastern Mediterranean. Birds on Cypro-Archaic jugs were always shown in profile, with the far wing held above the body. The white eye area and black head may indicate that a specific species was being represented, but the depiction is too stylized for any certain attribution.

In ancient Cyprus, depictions of types of birds are linked with particular locations: vases with painted images of waterfowl tended to be deposited in tombs, while depictions of songbirds are found mostly in sanctuaries, and those of birds of prey in private cultic contexts. In contemporary Greek, Egyptian and Near Eastern art, water birds are often associated with ideas of the afterlife and may be apotropaic, believed to protect the soul after death. Cyprus is an important transit stop for migrating birds, and their presence

in funerary contexts may be a metaphor for the journey of the soul in the afterlife. Migrating birds, which were seen as being able to ascend to heights closer to the gods than humans could achieve, were linked with the cycle of life and death by virtue of their absence and reappearance at various times of the year.

Unknown

Bird (Sejen), 19th–mid-20th century
Wood, iron, twine, 142.9 × 62.2 × 39.4 cm / 56¼ × 24½ × 15½ in
Metropolitan Museum of Art, New York

This heavy wood and iron bird, supporting smaller birds on each outstretched wing, is a mystical symbol of protection and wisdom associated with Poro, a society among the Senufo peoples of West Africa into which men are initiated as they grow older, preparing youngsters to take on responsible roles and overseeing the rituals associated with the worship of the ancestors and the Ancient Mother. The Senufo, who live in Côte d'Ivoire, Burkina Faso and Mali, carry the sculptures in processions during initiation cere-monies and funerals, even using the rounded base to wear them on their heads. When not being used, the birds protect a secret grove considered sacred by the Poro. The long, phallic beak and swollen belly of this bird refer to both male and female forces of procreation and their part in the continuity of the community, while geometric and figural motifs painted on the back of the wings allude to the knowledge and wisdom preserved and passed on by the Poro. Although the sculptures do not necessarily represent any specific bird, the long beak suggests this statue represents the yellow-casqued hornbill (*Ceratogymna elata*), which the Senufo believe was one of the first animals created, arrogant and intelligent, making it a symbol of the knowledge passed on to young initiates by Poro elders. Senufo art influenced twentieth-century European art, significantly the early Cubism of Pablo Picasso and the work of Fernand Léger.

Unknown

Plate LXIII, *Birds of Paradise, Paradisaeidae,* from *Locupletissimi rerum naturalium thesauri accurata descriptio* by Albertus Seba, 1734
Etching, 53.5 × 66 cm / 21 × 26 in

When you own one of the largest cabinets of curiosities of the eighteenth century – the personal collections that were the precursors to today's natural history museums – what better way to show it to the world than by publishing a four-volume description with 449 hand-coloured plates? Dutch pharmacist and collector Albertus Seba (1665-1736) sold his first collection to the Russian emperor Peter the Great on a visit to Moscow, but soon amassed an even larger collection, detailed in his *Thesaurus.* Although Seba produced the text, the plates were created by several artists, and not all plates were signed. Plate LXIII from Volume 1, published in 1734, shows a male greater bird of paradise (*Paradisaea apoda*; Fig. 1), and what is indicated as a female of the same species (Fig. 2), although this is incorrect as females lack the ornate plumes. Fig. 3 is probably a sunbird (Nectariniidae), while Seba's text identifies Fig. 4 as a kingfisher (Alcedinidae). The precise species are difficult to tell owing to the differences in the hand-colouring among copies. Dutch trade and colonization of what are now Indonesia and New Guinea enabled such specimens from far afield to reach the Netherlands, where many were first described to European science. Seba's *Thesaurus* influenced the founder of modern taxonomy and classification, Swedish botanist Carl Linnaeus, and it is best remembered for the high quality of the plates rather than the less remarkable text.

Tim Laman

Male Red Bird of Paradise (Paradisaea rubra) *in Display Pose*, 2013
Photograph, dimensions variable

A male red bird of paradise (*Paradisaea rubra*) displays in a treetop hundreds of feet above the ground. In the words of US wildlife photographer Tim Laman (born 1961), 'When he perches upright, the two flattened, wirelike tail feathers just hang down with a few twists in them. Only when he goes into his inverted position during display do you see how they work, framing and accentuating his body perfectly.' The red bird of paradise is confined to the islands of Waigeo, Batanta, Gemien and Saonek off northwest Papua New Guinea, where it is common in forests and forest edges in the lowlands and lower hills. It was on Waigeo that the pioneering nineteenth-century naturalist, Alfred Russel Wallace, encountered the red bird of paradise and learned the local technique for capturing it. This entailed attaching red arum fruits and a noose to the respective ends of a forked stick, which was then attached to a branch often visited by the birds. The hunter, sitting below, waited until a bird was attracted to the fruit, then pulled the cord to tighten the noose and catch the bird. But patience was needed. If other fruit was available nearby, it might take two days. Birds of paradise, whose distribution is centred on the New Guinea region, commonly display in treetops, so are challenging subjects for photographers. Laman employs rope-work skills he learned while studying strangler figs in Borneo in the early 1990s.

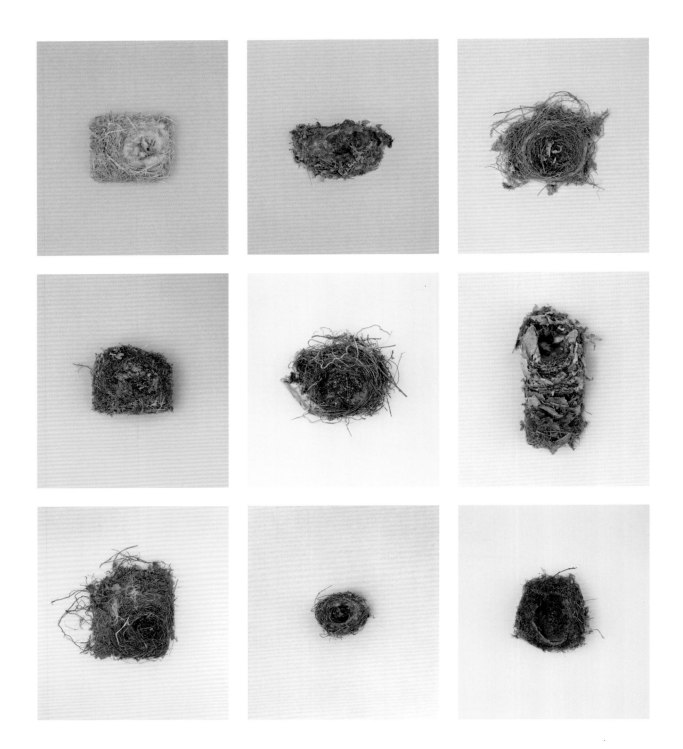

Bianca Tuckwell

The Growth That Is Our Cradle, 2013
Photographs, dimensions variable

Removed from the cloistered confines of the nestbox, or the tangle of thorny undergrowth, these deserted nests shot against coloured paper backgrounds are nine little architectural masterpieces of summers past and objects of immense beauty. Artist Bianca Tuckwell's photography reveals a subject usually almost invisible to us. Birds have honed this knack through millions of years of evolution to hide their vulnerable eggs and young from the prying eyes of would-be predators. Their skulking and secretive behaviour, the often drab colours of incubating birds, camouflaged eggshells and the position and material of nests hidden deep within foliage or safe within a cavity all mean that we seldom see nests even when nesting season is in full swing. Few of us could find them even if we tried. In many countries, bird protection legislation has rightly introduced stiff penalties for disturbing nesting birds – though it seldom prevents the destruction of their habitat – but it has also meant that skills of observation and fieldcraft that were once possessed by every child have been lost. When we do find them, empty and weather-beaten after the young have fledged and the leaves have fallen, we may wonder how we could possibly have missed something so obvious. Even then, however, we seldom stop to admire them. The birds made the nests, but it takes an artist to present them as the poignant works of art they are.

François-Xavier Lalanne

Le Cocodoll, 1964
Brass and canvas on steel frame, 200 × 225 × 100 cm / 78¾ × 88½ × 39⅜ in
Private collection

A whimsical full-size four-poster bed consists of two halves of an egg-shaped white bird. The bottom half contains a mattress in a moulded base sitting on large gilt 'feet', while brass posts support an upper canopy comprising the top half of the bird with a moulded white body and a gilt head with a large beak. Created by the Postmodern French sculptor and artist François-Xavier Lalanne (1927–2008), *Le Cocodoll* nods to Surrealism but also to the artist's belief that art should be functional and an intrinsic part of the home. The association of a bed with a bird suggests a link with nesting, while the toylike appearance of *Le Cocodoll* is also reminiscent of childhood and the nursery. Along with his wife Claude (1925–2019) – the pair worked under the name Les Lalanne, although they were co-creators rather than collaborators – Lalanne would blaze a trail for larger-than-life sculptures that were both playful and provocative. The couple's first exhibition, *Zoophites*, in 1964 displayed their mutual interest in nature, using plants and animals as inspiration for their strange designs, although it was François-Xavier who focused particularly on the large-scale animal pieces. His similarly supersized animal sculptures included a hippopotamus bath tub. Les Lalanne's work became popular with notable collectors, including Yves Saint Laurent and Pierre Bergé as well as interior decorator Jacques Grange, who had a *Le Cocodoll* bed in his Paris apartment.

Christian Heinrich Pander and Eduard d'Alton

Plate IV, *Skeleton of the Secretarybird*, Gypogeranus serpentarius, from *Die Vergleichende Osteologie*, 1828
Engraving and etching, 40 × 55 cm / 15¾ × 21⅝ in

This plate comes from one of the finest but least known works of comparative osteology – the study of skeletons and bones. *Die Vergleichende Osteologie* by Christian Heinrich Pander (1794–1865) and Eduard d'Alton (1772–1840) is a masterpiece of both science and art. Principally devoted to mammals, it contains a short second volume dealing with just two bird groups: the flightless ratites and the birds of prey. The sensitivity of modelling on the bones, achieved with finely engraved hatched lines is outstanding.

Not only is the skeleton itself accurately rendered and observed, but its position, superimposed onto the shallow-etched silhouette of the fully feathered bird, shows a genuine understanding of anatomy. No-one knows for certain how the secretarybird acquired its name, but Buffon's suggestion that its eccentric-looking crest resembles a secretary or scribe with quill pens behind their ear seems plausible. Related to the hawks and eagles, this native of sub-Saharan Africa occupies a family of its own and possesses a number

of anatomical and behavioural idiosyncrasies. As its valid scientific name suggests, *Sagittarius serpentarius* is a snake hunter. Its prodigiously long legs, small toes and claws are perfectly adapted, not just for hunting on foot, but for literally kicking and stamping snakes to death. Unlike almost all other long-legged birds, the secretarybird has a relatively short neck. This keeps the head out of harm's way when tackling snakes – but means the bird has to bend its legs to swallow them.

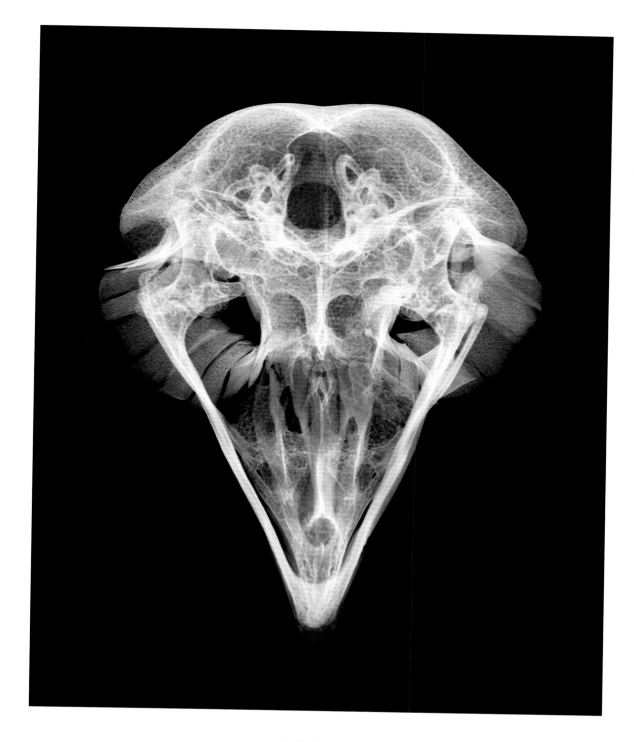

D. Roberts

Eagle Owl Skull, 21st century
Coloured X-ray, dimensions variable

The intricate beauty of anatomical structures revealed by three-dimensional imaging techniques, like this coloured X-ray of a skull of a Eurasian eagle owl (*Bubo bubo*), straddles the boundary between science and art. Owls' distinctive skulls are highly adapted for their nocturnal lives. Their forward-facing eyes are angled slightly apart, giving a wide field of view, and the ring of tiny bones that surrounds the eyes of all birds is, in owls, flattened and enlarged to form a rigid tube, shown here in blue, extending out from the orbits of the skull. In conjunction with the almost spherical lens, this increases the size of the image received on the bird's retina, much like moving a projector away from a screen. Although eyesight is enhanced, the eyes are virtually immovable in their sockets, so owls compensate with a highly flexible neck which allows them to turn their head in almost a full circle. Although owls certainly see well in dark conditions, it is their hearing that truly excels. Most owls have asymmetrically positioned hearing apparatus, which results in a slight time lapse between right and left sides that allows them to pinpoint the precise location of prey, not just in the dark, but completely hidden beneath a layer of snow or leaves. Different owls have evolved different arrangements and in the eagle owl the apparatus lies in the ear openings at the sides of the head.

Erika Giovanna Klien

Diving Bird, 1939
Oil on canvas, 111 × 96 cm / 43¾ × 37¾ in
Belvedere, Vienna

Geometric almost to the point of pure abstraction, this twisting composition of a bird in flight is the work of Italian artist Erika Giovanna Klien (1900–57), who studied and worked in Vienna in the years following World War I (1914–18). The sense of movement the image evokes reflects the aesthetic principles of Viennese Kineticism, influenced by broader European artistic movements – including Cubism, Futurism, Vorticism and Expressionism – that were also exploring ways to depict in art the dynamism, excitement and mechanical quality of the modern world. By the end of the nineteenth century, fascination with movement and bird flight more especially had played a substantial role in the photographic experimentations of Eadweard Muybridge and Étienne Jules Marey (see p.263), who both pioneered the use of new cameras to capture animal movement. A couple of decades later, these technological innovations would prove pivotal to the invention of cinema. Klien's painting shows her ability to incorporate these early experimentations into a thoroughly original, painterly language, translating objective documentation into poetry. In *Diving Bird*, the stark clarity of photographic images is replaced by a subtle layering of monochromatic shades and intersecting lines to convey the elegant complexity of bird flight. In this instance, Klien was not concerned with the realistic portrayal of a specific species but simply with capturing a universal and elusive kind of beauty intrinsic to all birds.

Rebecca Horn

Zen der Eule, 2010
Feathers, brass, motor, electronic device, 70 × 70 × 28 cm / 27½ × 27½ × 11 in
Private collection

A wheel of owl feathers gently unfurls around a deceptively simple mechanical body that repeatedly collapses the feathers to the bottom then raises and spreads them into this perfectly symmetrical crown. The work of contemporary German artist Rebecca Horn (born 1944), *Zen der Eule* ('Zen of the Owl') reflects a longstanding interest in the boundaries of the human body, the animal, and the machine. Horn became interested in creating machines capable of replicating the movement of birds during the early

1980s, while she was filming in Italy. The peacock she had planned to film began to moult a day before shooting was due to begin, prompting her to build a machine that could replicate the unfurling of the bird's spectacular train to realistic effect. To Horn these machines have their own kind of soul - one suspended between naturality and artificiality - and their beauty alludes to humans' fraught relationship with the animal kingdom. On the one hand, *Zen der Eule* can be seen to represent our aspiration to be like

birds and to fly with our own set of wings, a dream that was constantly pursued by the likes of Leonardo da Vinci during the Renaissance. And on the other, it reminds us of our inclination to think about animals in reductive ways, as machines: beautifully complex but ultimately devoid of feelings and lacking in souls, as was infamously claimed by the seventeenth-century French philosopher René Descartes.

Sean Graesser

Tropical Hummingbirds: The Finer Details, 2018
Photograph, dimensions variable

Picked out against a crisp, black background, the opposing tail feathers and upper and lower tail coverts of two neotropical hummingbirds (Trochilidae) dazzle with spectacular colours. This part of the birds' anatomy is rarely focused on, but US photographer and conservation biologist Sean Graesser draws attention to them thanks to his playful arrangement and sophisticated lighting. The deep indigos and purples apparent in gradients across the feathers are visible specifically thanks to this lighting, as they are formed as light refracts and interacts with microscopic ridges and clefts on the feathers, rather than by chemical pigmentation. The peerless hovering ability of hummingbirds is primarily powered by the birds' wings, which move in a figure of eight in order to generate lift, unlike the simpler up-and-down movement of non-hovering birds; this is augmented by the stability afforded by the wide tail feathers, which fan, close and angle forwards or backwards during flight. Rather than singing, hummingbirds rely on their extraordinary coloration and aerial acrobatics to woo potential mates. After initially attracting females with their brightly coloured throat patches, or gorgets, some male hummingbirds then display their flying prowess by performing a hovering dance, using their tails for an unexpected purpose. By diving quickly and fanning the tail feathers outwards as they are pulled through the air, the birds generate a high-pitched whistling trill that scientists have only recently discovered is not made in their vocal cords.

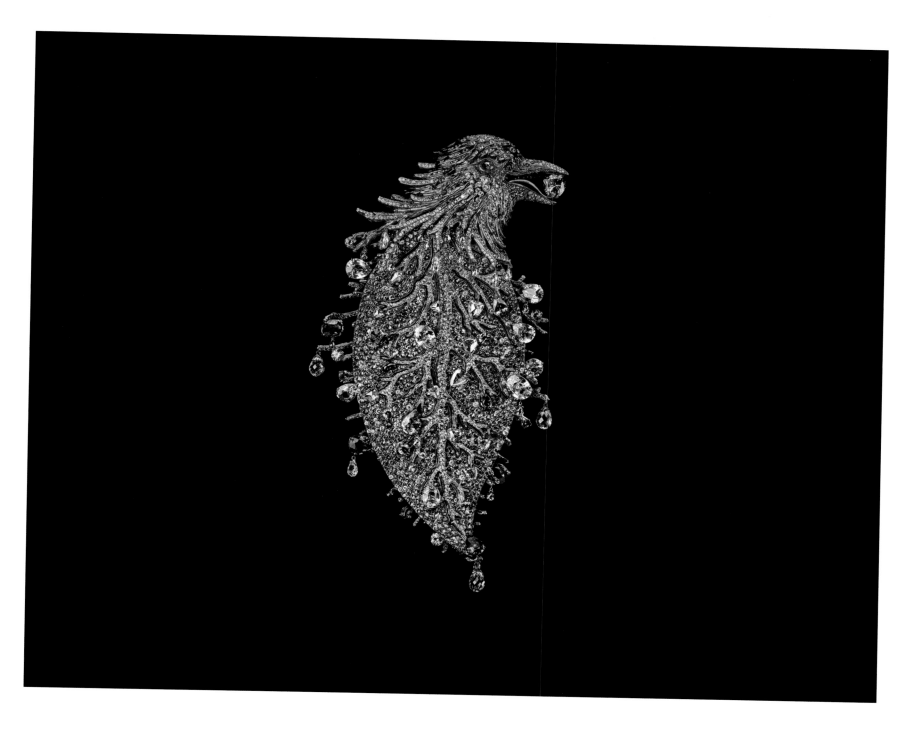

Wallace Chan

The Lark, 2012
Fancy-coloured diamond, fancy-coloured sapphire and tsavorite garnet in titanium setting,
17 × 9 × 4 cm / 6¾ × 3½ × 1⅝ in
Private collection

Perhaps few birds are as deserving of carrying a diamond in their beak as the larks, which have long been celebrated for their melodious song. Male larks sing elaborate calls during so-called song flights, which can serve both to attract a mate and to defend a territory from other males. There are around ninety species in the family Alaudidae, spread across a wide range of habitats around the world, although most live in Africa. In Europe, the birds are celebrated for singing at dawn – hence the phrase 'up with the lark'; in China they are kept as songbirds, and valued for their ability to mimic other birds and for their ability to learn a precise cycle of thirteen songs. The Chinese-born, Hong-Kong-based jeweller Wallace Chan (born 1956), who was brought up in Fuzhou province, was already familiar with caged larks, when he moved to Hong Kong with his family aged eight and began to work with his hands to earn money, first making cheap plastic flowers and then carving religious icons in malachite that he sold door to door. Today one of the world's most exclusive jewellers, in 2015 he produced a diamond necklace named A Heritage in Bloom, which is said to be one of the most expensive in the world, at $200m. This brooch – one of many by him that feature a depiction of an animal – contains diamonds, sapphires and tsavorite garnets set in Chan's signature sculpted titanium.

Portraict de l'amas des os humains , mis en comparaiſon
de l'anatomie de ceux des oyſeaux, faiſant que les
lettres d'icelle ſe raporteront à ceſte cy, pour
faire apparoiſtre combien l'affinité eſt
grande des vns aux autres.

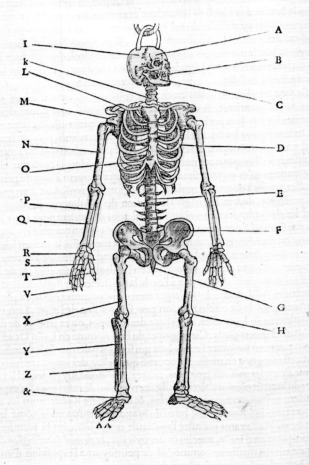

La comparaiſon du ſuſdit portraiẛ des os humains monſtre combien ceſtuy cy qui eſt d'vn oyſeau, en eſt prochain.

Portraict des os de l'oyſeau.

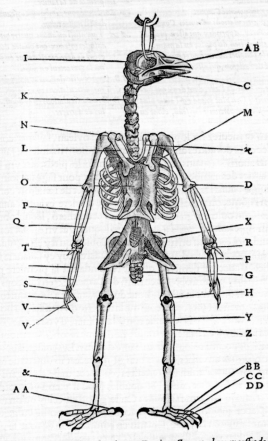

A B Les Oyſeaux n'ont dents ne leures , mais ont
le bec tranchant fort ou foible, plus ou moins ſe-
lon l'affaire qu'ils ont eu à mettre en pieces ce
dont ils viuent.
M Deux pallerons longs & eſtroicts, vn en chaſ-
cun coſté.
ᵶ L'os qu'on nommé la Lunette ou Fourchette
n'eſt trouué en aucun autre animal , hors mis en
l'oyſeau.

D Six coſtes , attachees au coffre de l'eſtomach par
deuãt, & aux ſix vertebres du dos par derriere.
F Les deux os des hanches ſont longs , car il n'y a
aucunes vertebres au deſſoubs des coſtes .
G Six oſſelets au cropion.
H La rouelle du genoil .
I Les ſutures du teſt n'apparoiſſent gueres ſinon
qu'il ſoit boully.
k Douze vertebres au col, & ſix au dos.

d iii

Pierre Belon

The Comparative Anatomy of Avian and Human Skeletons,
from *L'Histoire de la Nature des Oyseaux*, 1555
Woodcut, 21.5 × 32 cm / 8½ × 12⅝ cm

At first glance these two skeletons look remarkably similar. Only the beaked skull and an unusually long neck in the skeleton on the right hints at something birdlike, but closer inspection confirms that this is indeed the skeleton of a bird, suspended to allow it to dangle vertically, with wings and legs drooping to their full extent in an unnatural, hominin-like posture. A casual observer might dismiss this image as a crude attempt at reconstruction, but the French naturalist Pierre Belon (1517-74) deliberately set out to highlight the similarities between the human and avian skeleton, even to the point of identifying shared structures in bird and man. The idea of homology – for example, that a human arm and a bird's wing, were not just similar, but inherited from a common ancestor – would come much later, with the shaping of evolutionary theory in the nineteenth century, but as the first-ever published work of comparative anatomy, this simple illustration was centuries ahead of its time. Belon was a true scientist of the Northern Renaissance. He studied medicine in Paris, botany in Germany and archaeology in the Mediterranean and the Near East. His work on the natural history of fish laid the foundations for the modern study of ichthyology, and his dissections of a dolphin foetus added to his list of distinctions the first published work on embryology. His shining career was ended by his murder in Paris, aged only forty-seven.

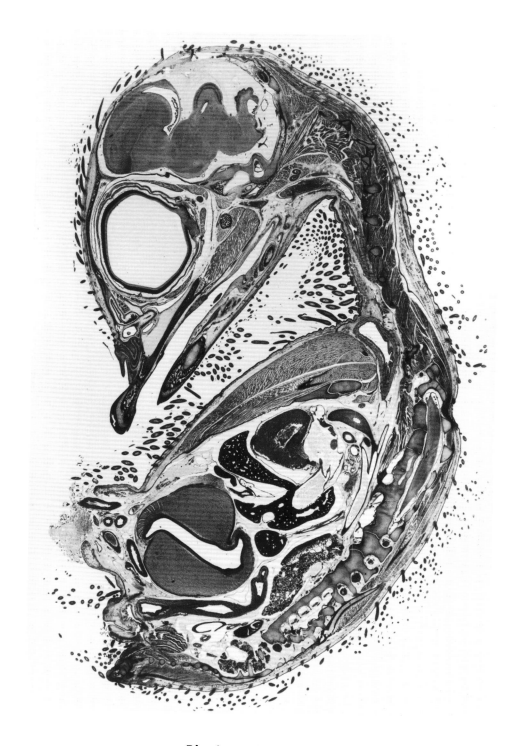

Biophoto Associates

Chicken (Gallus gallus) *embryo in section, c.*2015
Colour-enhanced light micrograph, dimensions variable

Although it's clearly recognizable as a chick, this photo is initially rather confusing, showing just a body and a head, with no legs or wings visible. It is a section sliced through the central axis of a chicken embryo, which is why no limbs are included. The head and beak are clearly defined, as are the brain within the skull cavity, the developing spine, the coiled intestines and the 'keel' of the breastbone. The tiny dots surrounding the embryo are the emerging feathers. This is a 'brightfield' or 'light' micrograph, a microscopy technique in which the slide is illuminated with a beam of light passing through it. It's a cutting-edge technique in more ways than one. For it to work, the object has to be flat and exceedingly thin: just the thickness of a single layer of cells. The whole specimen first needs to be fixed to protect its cellular structure, then sliced into sections using a precision instrument called a microtome. Each section is then stained with dyes so that the structures are clearly visible. Such techniques have revolutionized the study of embryology, enabling scientists to better understand the processes that shape the animal body plan. The study of embryology and the ancient toolkit of genes that control development - evolutionary developmental biology (or evo-devo for short) - has implications not just for a single species, but for understanding the origins of all life on earth.

Unknown

Eagle-headed Genius and Tree, c.883–859 BC
Gypsum alabaster, 2.3 × 1.9 m / 7 ft 6½ × 6 ft 1½ in
Metropolitan Museum of Art, New York

A guardian spirit, or *apkallu*, with an eagle head and human body stands beside a sacred tree in this carved panel from ancient Assyria – now covering parts of Iran, Iraq and Turkey – where *apkallu* were believed to possess exceptional wisdom and to ensure the well-being of the king and his people. The *apkallu* holds a bucket in his left hand and a conifer cone in his right, and makes a gesture that may symbolize either fertilization or protection. The sacred tree to his left (there may have been another to his right) represents the fertility and prosperity of Assyria which, like the king, were under the protection of the *apkallu*. The so-called Standard Inscription lists in cuneiform script the ancestry, titles and accomplishments of King Ashurnasirpal and again probably had a magical, protective function. Throughout the ancient world, the eagle was a symbol of strength, authority and power, its outstretched wings an emblem of protection, especially in regard to rulers. It was believed that *apkallu* helped to build the cities of Mesopotamia, and eagle-headed clay figurines have been found within the walls of Assyrian buildings, probably placed there as protective icons. Eagle-headed deities were often installed at doorways to safeguard those within. This relief is one of many similar carved panels that lined the state apartments of the Palace of Ashurnasirpal II at Nimrud (ancient Kalhu); it would originally have been painted.

Oscar Graubner

Margaret Bourke-White atop the Chrysler Building, c.1932
Gelatin silver print, 34.5 × 26.7 cm / 13½ × 10½ in
Private collection

In this dizzying image, the photographer Margaret Bourke-White (1904–71, see also p.68) perches with her camera on a large eagle's head, high above the streets of Manhattan. The stainless-steel gargoyle is one of four installed on the sixty-first floor of the Chrysler Building – New York City's second most famous skyscraper – where Bourke-White established her studio in 1930. Representing the strength and speed of America's machine age, and symbolic of flight, the bald eagle (*Haliaeetus leucocephalus*) recalls the winged radiator caps that adorned Chrysler's automobiles in the 1920s, as well as referencing the national emblem of the United States and the traditions of Native American art. As President John F. Kennedy remarked in 1962, 'The fierce beauty and proud independence of this great bird aptly symbolizes the strength and freedom of America.' The eagles, together with the building's other imagery, were included by architect William van Alen for his employer, Walter Chrysler, head of the Chrysler corporation. Bourke-White often scaled high scaffolds and endured extreme temperatures to document steel factories and other heavy industry in America and Russia, and this photograph by her assistant Oscar Graubner (1897–1977) was produced as a retort to critics, some of whom alleged that she was really a man. By aligning herself with the jutting eagle, Bourke-White confirmed her reputation as a bold woman unafraid to risk her personal safety for the sake of her craft.

Unknown

Sampler, 1770-99
Embroidered linen with gilt and coloured silks, 30.5 × 38.7 cm / 12 × 15¼ in
Victoria & Albert Museum, London

A combination of inexpert needlework, gilt thread and anatomical inaccuracy makes it difficult to identify the specific birds embroidered in this sampler created by a sewer practising her stitches in Mexico in the late 1700s, together with flowers, a butterfly, a rabbit or hare, a poodle carrying a basket, and various religious symbols. The red bird at top left is a northern cardinal (*Cardinalis cardinalis*), which lives from eastern Canada and the United States as far south as Mexico, Belize and Guatemala. At top right is a chicken, an important food bird in Mexico. To the right of the northern cardinal is what may be a saffron finch (*Sicalis flaveola*), which is common in South America, while the central blue bird resembles the Palawan peacock pheasant (*Polyplectron napoleonis*), which might at first seem unlikely, being native to Palawan Island in the Philippines. However, given that Spain ruled both Mexico and the Philippines in the late 1700s, the inclusion makes more sense, as does the influence on Mexican embroidery of needlework imported from the Philippines. (On the other hand, it may simply be a peacock, a common motif in needlework. Indeed, many of the birds may be imaginary.) The Spanish also introduced their own needlework traditions to Mexico. Samplers gave students a chance to practise as well as being a useful reference of different types of stitches - and a record of their progress.

Huang Quan

Birds, Insects and Turtles, 907–60
Ink and colour on silk, 41.5 × 70.8 cm / 16⅜ × 27⅞ in
Palace Museum, Beijing

These twenty-four animals on a plain background include insects, reptiles and birds common in tenth-century China, represented with such accuracy and naturalism that it is possible to identify each creature with a certain level of confidence. Among others, the artist painted a white wagtail (*Motacilla alba*), a white-cheeked starling (*Spodiopsar cineraceus*), a daurian redstart (*Phoenicurus auroreus*) and, in the middle of the scroll, a scarlet-breasted Mrs Gould's sunbird (*Aethopyga gouldiae*). The attention to detail suggests that the Song dynasty artist Huang Quan (*c.*903–965) observed the birds from nature instead of studying preserved specimens, as was common in the West. The birds are filled with life, as is shown by the accurate portrayal of their behaviour: the white-cheeked starling inquisitively searches the ground for worms and, at right, a baby Eurasian tree sparrow (*Passer montanus*) frantically flaps its wings in anticipation of a meal brought home by its parent. More than just an accurate representation of birdlife, this scene metaphorically anchors the meaning of this hand scroll, which, the inscription details, was created by Huang Quan for his son Jubao to study. The scroll is an outstanding example of the naturalistic *xiesheng* style – literally, 'sketch of life' or 'lifelike painting' – of which Huang Quan was a pioneer. It prioritized realism and accuracy over the philosophical ideas underpinning *xieyi*, the traditional style that expressed concepts through fast and fluid brushwork.

Sam Droege

Collateral Damage, 2012
Photograph, dimensions variable

An intricate pattern of dead birds recalls the form of a stained-glass window in this photograph. From larks and wrens to swallows, crows, yellow cardinals and many more, the shape comprises larger birds placed in the middle of the composition and smaller species at the edge, with colours ranging from green and yellow through brown, red and white. Sam Droege, a biologist who works with the United States Geological Survey, collected birds that had died from colliding into buildings in a small area of Washington, DC.

The photograph's background shade is simply brown craft paper, upon which Droege arranged the birds before capturing them from above, mirroring a bird's aerial view. Combined using computer software, together the images resemble the multi-petal rose windows of Gothic-style churches, perhaps suggesting the godly nature of these creatures, which usually soar above us, seemingly into the heavens. Droege felt the deceased birds were at once 'disturbing and darkly beautiful'. It is estimated that 100 million

neotropical migrants – birds of the western hemisphere that migrate from wintering grounds in the New World tropics to breeding grounds in North America – are killed every year in the United States when flying at night to avoid predators. They crash into buildings, windows or other obstacles when stunned by urban lights. In this sense, Droege's artwork may symbolize just one of the ways these creatures are so unceremoniously killed.

Miranda Brandon

Impact (Tennessee Warbler), 2014
Photograph, dimensions variable

This photograph of a Tennessee warbler (*Leiothlypis peregrina*) colliding with an unforgiving surface immediately brings to mind the hollow thud of a bird hitting a window. It comes from *Impact*, a series of images by Minnesota-based artist Miranda Brandon, created by posing victims of building collisions on sheets of Plexiglass in her studio, photographing them multiple times and then stitching together separate images to form a highly detailed whole up to twelve times larger than the actual bird. Glass on modern buildings, from large mirrored skyscrapers found in large cities to the gable ends of suburban houses, is a double-edged sword: the reflection of sky or habitat attracts birds, but the glass is an invisible, often fatal, barrier. In the United States, as many as one billion birds are killed each year by building collisions, with nearly half of those involving residential houses. *Impact* makes these losses personal and individual. Brandon volunteered for Audubon Minnesota's Project BirdSafe, to record window strikes in Minneapolis; she used the birds she found dead on the pavement – having first gained the necessary permissions from the Bell Museum of Natural History – to explore the broader theme of how the built environment can affect wildlife. Tennessee warblers breed in southern Canada and New England and travel to the Caribbean and Central and South America in the winter. It is during these twice-annual migrations that many birds meet their untimely end, hurtling into their own reflections.

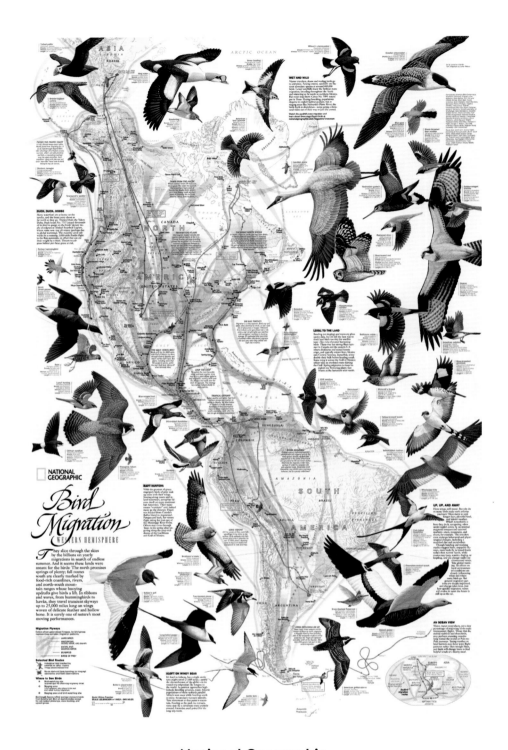

National Geographic

Bird Migration in the Americas, 1979
Printed paper, 91.4 × 58.4 cm / 36 × 23 in
Private collection

This complex thematic map of the paths of bird migration, brimming with bird images and information, at once calls to mind *National Geographic* magazine, which pioneered such richly detailed fold-out supplements. The magazine published *Bird Migration in the Americas* in August 1979 to accompany an article entitled 'Mysteries of Bird Migration'. The map highlights the migratory routes of sixty-seven species, ranging from large raptors to tiny hummingbirds, and includes paintings created by the renowned US wildlife artist Arthur Singer (see pp.236–7). The map uses four colours to represent the migratory routes for four groups of birds: seabirds, gulls and terns (light blue); shore and wading birds (dark green); waterfowl (brown); and land birds and Birds of Prey (light tan). The migration routes connect nesting grounds and wintering areas, and each route is labelled with the name of the bird. One example is the blackpoll warbler (*Setophaga striata*), which flies south over the Atlantic Ocean from eastern Canada to South America – travelling some 4,000 km (2,485 miles) at an altitude of up to 6,400 m (21,000 ft). The map's innovation and popularity launched a whole range of *National Geographic* bird-related products, including migration posters, field guides and picture books.

Jane Kim and Ink Dwell Studio

From So Simple a Beginning: Celebrating the Evolution and Diversity of Birds (detail), 2015
Painted mural, 11 × 24m / 35 × 78 ft
Cornell Lab of Ornithology, Ithaca, New York

This mural, also known as 'The Wall of Birds', provides an impressive and immersive greeting for visitors entering the Cornell Lab of Ornithology. At once artistic and educational, the mural displays avian biodiversity and evolutionary change by featuring bird species from all surviving families as well as selected extinct relatives. Each of the 243 birds shown are painted life-size, in fine detail and full colour and are positioned above their common geographical location. The artist and scientific illustrator Jane Kim (born

1981) and colleagues from Ink Dwell Studio in California created it over four years, starting with sketches from photographs, videos and museum specimens, and taking advice from the Lab's ornithologists. The result combines scientific accuracy with dazzling beauty. Each sketch was transferred to the wall and painted *in situ*, a process taking from a few hours to up to a week for each bird. A photographic record of the wall for an interactive webpage involved combining more than 750 high-definition images into a 2.34 gigapixel whole.

The portion illustrated shows eight Caribbean species, from left to right: Cuba: Oriente warbler (*Oriente teretistris*), Cuban tody (*Todus multicolor*); Haiti and Dominican Republic: palmchat (*Dulus dominicus*), Hispaniolan spindalis (*Spindalis dominicensis*), eastern chat-tanager (*Calyptophilus frugivorus*), black-crowned warbler tanager (*Phaenicophilus palmarum*); Puerto Rico: Puerto Rican tanager (*Nesospingus speculiferus*). Soaring above them floats a red-billed tropicbird (*Phaethon aethereus*).

Eleazar and Elizabeth Albin

The Cock Hoopoe, from *A Natural History of Birds,* 1734
Etching hand-coloured with watercolour, 28.5 × 23 cm / 11¼ × 9 in
Private collection

London may seem an unusual home for a naturalist, but in the early eighteenth century, with ships arriving daily bringing exotic new specimens from around the globe, a well-connected man could find subjects – and patrons – aplenty, without setting foot outside the city. Such a man was Eleazar Albin (*fl.*1690–1742). Primarily an entomologist, he produced several books on insects and spiders as well as two on birds, using the specimens of local collectors. *A Natural History of Birds* was the first bird book to be printed in colour,

and the first to have a woman – Albin's talented daughter, Elizabeth (1708–41) – named as co-author. The pictures were reproduced for publication by etching. It was usual to print the image in black, with additional colours painted onto the finished prints in watercolour by pieceworkers – whose quality of work was a reflection of their abysmal wages. Albin, with characteristic integrity, undertook the colouring of the entire publication himself, assisted only by Elizabeth. He even made his own paints, and experimented with

rather unorthodox ingredients. Although it certainly has an abundance of attitude, this lively-looking common hoopoe (*Upupa epops*), with its crest raised, is just as likely to be a hen as a cock, as both sexes are identical in outward appearance. Hoopoes nest in holes and so do not require camouflage to hide them while incubating their eggs. Instead, they defend their nest hole by secreting a foul-smelling oil which deters predators.

Peeter Boel

*Study of a Crowned Crane, c.*1670
Oil on canvas, 101 × 80 cm / 39¾ × 31½ in
Musée du Louvre, Paris

The nickname of this black crowned crane (*Balearica pavonina*) – the 'royal bird' – reflects its golden coronet but is particularly apt given its link with Louis XIV of France, the 'Sun King'. The bird was kept in the menagerie at Versailles, where the monarch had collected a variety of domestic and exotic creatures in an early zoo in which birds and animals were kept in enclosures surrounding an octagonal pavilion. The Flemish painter of still lifes and animals, Peeter Boel (1622–74), spent much time portraying the inhabitants of the menagerie in life-like studies such as this that were intended to be used as models by the weavers at the royal Gobelin factory, whose tapestries were considered one of the most important artistic expressions of the time. Having moved to Paris in the 1660s, Boel was appointed painter to the king, and from 1669 to 1671 made 400 sketches on paper which resulted in at least eighty-six studies on canvas of a wide variety of birds, a range of mammals – from marmots to tigers – and several reptiles. Some works feature only one animal, while others combine several studies, either of various poses of the same creature or of a combination of species, usually isolated on a plain canvas primed in a reddish tone. Boel devoted several nearly life-size studies to this black crowned crane, with its coronet, bright round eyes and pink facial skin, which had been brought over to Versailles from West Africa, where it originates.

Louis Comfort Tiffany

Hibiscus and Parrots, c.1910-20
Leaded Favrile glass, 66 × 45.1 cm / 26 × 17¾ in
Metropolitan Museum of Art, New York

The translucent glass so typical of the work of American jeweller Tiffany & Co. creates an attractive glow in the creamy-white flowers of the hibiscus, contrasting with the dark blue green of the parrots that perch and bicker on the twigs. Subtle use of shading within the glass lends depth to the petals and the birds, while the mottled background suggests sunlight filtering through the foliage. The shrub is probably a white cultivar of *Hibiscus syriacus*, commonly grown in gardens, and one of several given the common name rose of Sharon.

The identity of the parrots is uncertain; indeed, they are probably fanciful, rather than based on an actual species. Louis Comfort Tiffany (1848-1933) was the son of Charles Lewis Tiffany, who founded the famous company, but originally carved out his own career as a painter, especially of exotic art, partly inspired by his travels in Europe and North Africa, although he was appointed design director to Tiffany & Co. on his father's death in 1902. From the late 1870s he became more concerned with decorative arts and interiors,

especially involving the original use of glass. He developed a method of glass production that involved blending colours in the molten state, thus achieving delicately shaded effects. This process, known as *favrile* (from fabrile, hand-wrought), became a trademark, and features in much of his work.

Ferdinand Bauer

Plate 24, *Trichoglossus haematodus moluccanus,* from *Forty-nine watercolour drawings of animals collected during Captain Matthew Flinders' voyage to Australia,* 1801
Watercolour, 34 × 51 cm / 13⅜ × 20⅛ in
Natural History Museum, London

When the British ship HMS *Investigator* undertook an anticlockwise circumnavigation of Australia between 1801 and 1803 under the captaincy of Lincolnshire-born Matthew Flinders – the first inshore circum-navigation of the island – six scientists were aboard. One was the Austrian illustrator Ferdinand Bauer (1760–1826), who had been selected for the role by the renowned naturalist Sir Joseph Banks, who had himself sailed on James Cook's first voyage and become a grandee of British science. By the time he

embarked, Bauer had been illustrating professionally for some twenty-five years. He adapted his technique to the fact that he could not take on board a full palette of colours, instead capturing animals and plants in preliminary sketches in which the exact colour was indicated by numbers, to be 'coloured in' with watercolours later. This plate showing the rainbow lorikeet (*Trichoglossus haematodus*) illustrates the great success of Bauer's technique. The lorikeet is widespread in many habitats in the eastern part

of Australia, including suburban gardens. Its scientific name, *Trichoglossus,* is derived from Greek words, *tricho-* 'hair', and *glōssa* 'tongue', a reference to the brush-tipped tongue the bird uses for lapping nectar and sucking up soft fruits. Other closely-related *Trichoglossus* species live elsewhere in Australia and New Guinea.

Tom Uttech

Nind Awatchige, 2003
Oil on canvas, 285.7 × 285.7 cm / 112½ × 112½ in
New Orleans Museum of Art, Louisiana

Dusk in a cold, coniferous forest in the Precambrian Shield of North America, the air filled with the rush of beating wings. As the gloaming approaches, a fantastic array of mammals salute the last of the sunlight while a wide assortment of birds including great grey owls, Canada jays, spruce grouse, black-backed woodpeckers and, at the top centre, a northern harrier (*Circus cyaneus*) tear through the forest towards the north. The imagined, but entirely naturalistic, forest scenes of US artist Tom Uttech (born 1942) depict species

that all belong in their environment – but show them in unrealistic numbers. Perhaps the image is like a long exposure, revealing the biodiversity that exists in a single place extended through time. Or perhaps Uttech invites us to contemplate the life that once existed in the ancient forests of the northern United States and southeastern Canada, hinting at the lost biodiversity that flourished before humans made their mark, and echoing the vast flocks of birds, including passenger pigeons (see pp.180-1), that once darkened American

skies. Uttech's decision to name his paintings with words from the indigenous Ojibwe language raises another theme: that of appreciation without understanding. Often chosen merely for their aesthetic or tonal qualities, the Ojibwe words highlight the disconnect between recognizing and knowing a people's culture, mirroring the dissociation between the contemporary inhabitants of North America and the natural world they inhabit.

Mayoreak Ashoona

Tuulirjuaq (Great Big Loon), 2009
Stonecut and stencil, 102.3 × 74 cm / 40¼ × 29 in
Canadian Inuit Art Collection, St Lawrence University, Canton, New York

At 1 m (3¼ ft) across, this highly precise depiction of the great northern diver, or loon (*Gavia immer*), in its breeding plumage is remarkably large for a traditional stonecut print in the Kinnigait or Cape Dorset style of the Inuit of southwestern Baffin Island in Nunavut, Canada. The haunting calls of loons are emblematic of the Canadian wilderness and the lakes of the boreal forests. In the Arctic, loons feed on benthic fish in the ocean and bays. Great northern divers are found throughout Canada, Alaska and Scandinavia, where they breed in wetlands on the tundra and in the northern boreal forests, and they are often hunted by indigenous peoples as a summer food. The Kinnigait artist Mayoreak Ashoona (born 1946) and her husband Qaqaq (1928–96) lived in a remote outpost, finding it brought them closer to their Inuit traditions and their art, where they both drew, made soapstone carvings and produced stonecut prints, teaching themselves new techniques when there was no-one else to learn from. Hailing from a family of celebrated Kinnigait artists, including her husband and her mother-in-law Pitseolak Ashoona, Mayoreak has her works exhibited throughout Canada and internationally. *Tuulirjuaq (Great Big Loon)* was completed in 2009, the fiftieth anniversary of the Kinngait Studio in Kinngait, and is also in the permanent collection of the National Gallery of Canada in Ottawa.

Albrecht Dürer

Wing of a European Roller, 1512
Watercolor and opaque colours, heightened with opaque white, on parchment, 19.6 × 20 cm / 7¾ × 8 in
Albertina Museum, Vienna

From dark blues to bright reds, the remarkable colours of the wing of a dead European roller (*Coracias garrulus*) are displayed in this remarkable study by the renowned German artist Albrecht Dürer (1471-1528), a major figure of the Northern Renaissance who excelled as a landscape painter and printmaker, but who also frequently made detailed studies of wildlife and plants. Here, the structure and texture of each feather are faithfully portrayed, as is the rainbow plumage of the crow-like bird, which was

much more common in the artist's time than it is today. The sole European representative of the roller family - the eleven other species are found in tropical regions - it spends its summers in central and eastern Europe, migrating to sub-Saharan Africa for the winter. Born to a goldsmith in Nuremberg, Dürer was apprenticed to local artist Michael Wolgemut at the age of fifteen, and began to hone his prodigious talent in painting, woodcarving and copper engraving. His reputation brought him to the attention of influential

figures, and he became official court artist to Holy Roman Emperor Maximilian I and to his successor Charles V. As well as producing many religious paintings and woodcuts, Dürer also pioneered the use of watercolour to depict scenes from nature, both as landscapes and in his studies of plants and animals, combining acute observation with the ability to capture accurate likenesses.

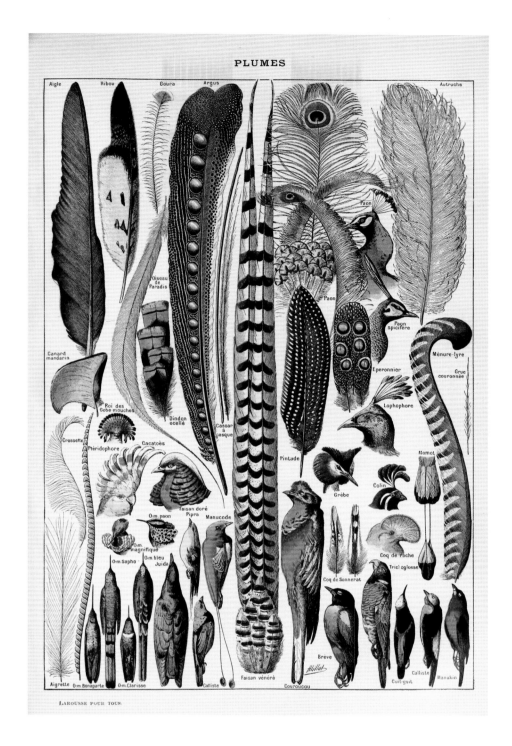

Adolphe Millot

Plumes, from *Le Larousse pour tous: nouveau dictionnaire encyclopédique, vol. II*,
by Pierre Larousse and Claude Augé, 1909
Chromolithograph, 30 × 21 cm / 11¾ × 8¼ in
University of Ottawa, Toronto

Among the finest of the full colour plates in the popular encyclopaedia *Le Larousse pour tous* are the natural history illustrations of Adolphe Millot (1857–1921), naturalist and senior illustrator at the Muséum National d'Histoire Naturelle in Paris. Each plate is composed to illustrate the diversity of nature. This one, *Plumes*, shows both individual feathers and complete specimens (known as museum skins) of an array of bird species: parrots, pittas and birds of paradise; hummingbirds and tanagers; pheasants of all kinds; even the uniquely fan-shaped crest of the royal flycatcher (*Onychorhynchus*). The centrepiece is the complete tail of a Reeve's pheasant (*Syrmaticus reevesii*), which can measure up to 2.4 m (almost 8 ft) – among the longest of any bird. Feathers have evolved a myriad of colours, textures and shapes. Some provide camouflage, while others are elaborately ornamented for courtship displays. Although feathers enable birds to fly, this was only a secondary adaptation. They were present in birds' dinosaur ancestors millions of years before birds evolved (see p.26), and their initial function was probably insulation. *Le Larousse pour tous* represents the very best in early twentieth-century book design, embellished with fine monochrome engravings and full-colour plates. While in these days of internet search engines it is sad to reflect on the redundancy of physical encyclopaedias like this, it is comforting to imagine the countless families for whom these books were once a treasured possession.

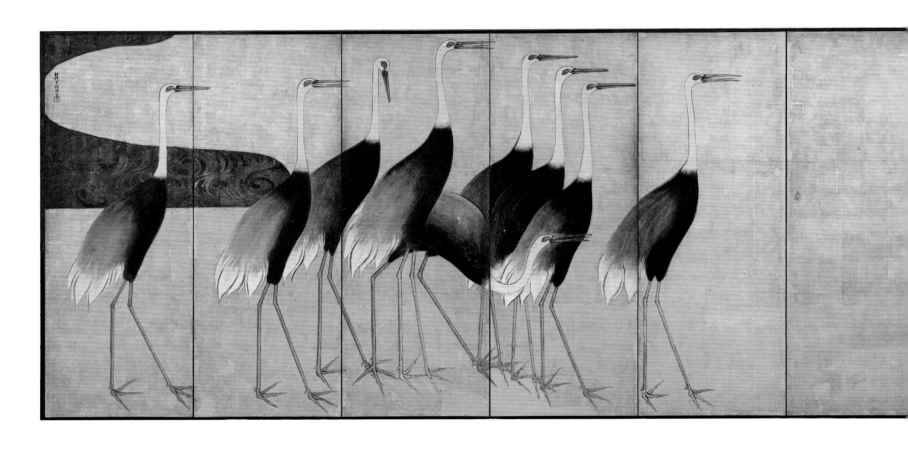

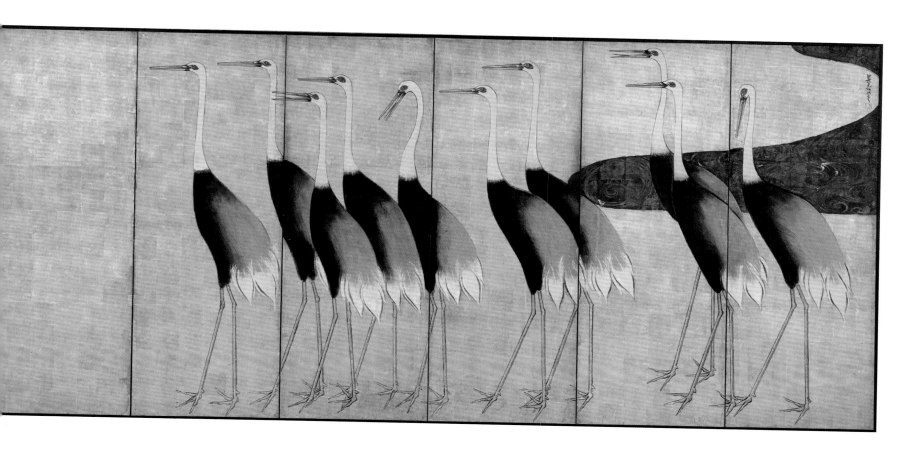

Ogata Korin

Cranes, late 17th–early 18th century
Ink, colour and gold and silver, on paper, each 166 × 371 cm / 65⅜ × 146 in
Freer Gallery of Art, Smithsonian Institution, Washington, DC

This decorative Japanese screen has an apparent symmetry, with two similar groups of cranes facing each other on a mainly gold background: ten cranes on the right-hand screen and nine on the left, the grey, black and white birds forming a striking pattern. On closer inspection, however, the birds are distinct individuals, each behaving differently: most are gazing towards the centre, while others turn their heads downwards and one stoops low. In Japan, cranes are symbols of longevity and fidelity, and

they are popular motifs in art. The species shown here is probably the white-naped crane (*Antigone vipio*) which breeds in north-east China, Mongolia and southeast Russia. A proportion of the population migrates to Kyushu in Japan. It is listed as vulnerable, with a population of around 5,000 individuals worldwide. The artist Ogata Korin (1658–1716) revived a style of art that came to be known as the Rinpa school of painting, prominent in the Edo period (1603–1867), which used vibrant colours in a distinctly

decorative manner, often inspired by the natural world and the changing seasons. Korin was born in Kyoto into a wealthy family of merchants, whose clients included the local nobility to whom they sold high-quality textiles. In 1701 he was awarded the honorific title of *hokkyo*, and by the time of his death he was renowned as an artist of considerable talent. His grave is at the Myoken-ji temple in Kyoto.

169

After Sosus of Pergamon

Doves drinking from a golden basin, first century BC
Mosaic, 113 × 113 cm / 44½ × 44½ in
Museo Archeologico Nazionale, Naples

Despite being familiar and very common, doves nevertheless filled various important roles in Greek and Roman religion and society. They were associated with Aphrodite/Venus, the goddess of love, and with her son, Eros or Cupid, who was often shown with the wings of a dove. The birds also personified the soul or human spirit, and appear as such on tombstones and in allegorical compositions. Aphrodite's temple on the southwest slope of the Athenian acropolis was decorated with relief sculptures of the birds. In his

Natural History, published in the first century AD, the Roman naturalist Pliny the Elder provides the only surviving name of an ancient mosaicist: Sosus of Pergamon, who lived in the second century BC. Pliny describes two of Sosus' most famous works, one of which is 'a dove ... in the act of drinking and casting the shadow of its head on the water; other birds are sunning and preening themselves on the edge of a drinking bowl'. Copies based on this lost original were disseminated widely, with inevitable variations;

the earliest (second or first century BC) comes from the island of Delos and has three birds, and the latest (second century AD) was found at Hadrian's Villa near Rome and shows four; that one is assumed to be closest to the original. This example from Pompeii, with six doves, including two on the table and one in flight, gives its name to the House of the Doves, where it was inserted into the centre of a white mosaic floor in a dining room.

Jacob Epstein

Doves, 1914-15
Greek marble, 64.8 × 78.7 × 34.3 cm / 25½ × 31 × 13½ in
Tate, London

This highly original sculpture by the American-born British artist Jacob Epstein (1880-1959) shows doves mating. The male, on top of the female, pushes his tail toward hers in order to fertilize her eggs. Doves, like most other birds, don't have separate sexual organs. Waste and eggs or sperm pass through one orifice called the cloaca. For this species, sexual encounters are a fleeting matter of superficial contact - here frozen in stone, simplified but instantly recognizable. Epstein was one of the most innovative and contro-versial artists of the last century, whose interest in the linear and bold aesthetics of African and Oceanic sculptures enabled him to prod the boundaries of Western representation. *Doves* poeticized bird-love through a timeless aesthetic linearity, simple volumes and geometrical harmony reminiscent of early Egyptian sculpture. In so doing, Epstein was able to bypass a graphic descriptiveness that would have made the work distasteful or even unacceptable for its time, just after the outbreak of World War I (1914-18). During the Victorian era, romanticized images of animal courtship had become quite common, meta-phorically hinting at the universal naturalness of love across living beings, humans included. However, in Western art, doves are thought of as a symbol of purity and are associated with the Holy Spirit in Christianity. It is likely that Epstein, who thoroughly disrespected the traditionalism of classical art, deliberately wanted to ruffle feathers by tampering with a sacred symbol.

CANARY

ANDES CREEPER

BLUE BACKED MANNIKIN

MADAGASCAN PAROQUET

Sophia May Bowley, for Raphael Tuck & Sons

Canary, Andes Creeper, Blue Backed Mannikin, and Madagascan Paroquet, from Birds on the Wing – Series II, *c.1930*
Chromolithograph on perforated card, 14 × 8.9 cm / 5½ × 3½ in
Museum of Fine Arts, Boston, Massachusetts

This is one of a collection of six delightful postcards in the series *Birds on the Wing* published by Raphael Tuck & Sons featuring the artwork of children's illustrator, Sophia May Bowley (1865–1960). Far more than just two-dimensional images, the cards have the added novelty of pop-out wings, with directions given on the reverse of the card: 'Carefully break through the perforated lines round each bird and bend the wings upwards so as to give the bird a realistic and natural flying appearance.' All the birds in the series are

colourful and, of course, all are depicted in flight. The cards also feature descriptions of each of the birds. In this card, the 'Madagascan paroquet' is actually a rosy-faced lovebird (*Agapornis roseicollis*) from south-western Africa, and not from Madagascar at all. The 'blue-backed mannikin' (*Chiroxiphia pareola*) is correctly identified, though it should be spelled 'manakin', while the 'Andes creeper' is a green honeycreeper (*Chlorophanes spiza*), a lowland species widespread across northern South America … but

entirely absent from the Andes. And the canary is the yellow domesticated variety whose wild ancestor (*Serinus canaria*) from the Canary Islands is green, streaked with black. Founded in 1866, Raphael Tuck & Sons were a prolific London-based printer and publisher, that profited greatly from the 'postcard boom' of the late nineteenth and early twentieth century. The novelty and convenience of sending such colourful notes, without the need for an envelope, were the social media phenomenon of the day.

Shirana Shahbazi

[Vögel-08-2009], 2009
C-print on aluminium, dimensions variable

The photographs of Iranian-born Shirana Shahbazi (born 1974) stand out for their masterly technique which, when coupled with the artist's interest in classical forms of representation, positions them in a close dialogue with the history of art. Most importantly her work offers an update of the grandiose tradition of German photography, filtered through a sensibility inherited from her upbringing in Iranian culture. Her unique style defies codifications and as an artist she strives for powerful visual statements. 'If a mountain is depicted, it has the be the highest, most beautiful mountain,' Shahbazi has said. A vivid example of this practice is *[Vögel-08-2009]*, the result of a period Shahbazi spent venturing into natural history museums around the world to photograph rocks, crystals and animals. The bird in question, an eastern rosella (*Platycercus eximius*), is obviously deceased but it retains traces of its majestic dignity. Placing the brilliant green, blue, white and red feathers of its body against a shocking red background makes the bird look like as if it still sparkles with life, its wings spread in all their glory. The bird becomes an icon with an aura of mystery and royalty – a solitary image removed from everyday uses and functions that reveals itself in all its natural beauty. Rosellas are a genus of six species of Australian parrots, whose name derives from the Rose Hill area of New South Wales, where they were first encountered by European settlers.

Utagawa Hiroshige

Jumantsubo Plain at Fukagawa Susaki, from *One Hundred Famous Views of Edo*, 1856
Woodblock print, 35.7 × 24.1 cm / 14 × 9½ in
Metropolitan Museum of Art, New York

Spilling over the frame of the top half of this woodblock print, a gigantic hawk wheels as it cuts a huge arc through the sky, its body moving to the right as its head turns to the left to spy for its prey on the vast snow-covered marshes of Jumantsubo. The whole scene is set at night in the depths of winter, the cold emphasized by the cloudless sky and twinkling stars. In the distance lie snow-capped mountains and the peak of Mount Tsukuba, with a touch of mist on the highlands; in the foreground trees and marshland, the coastal waters

where an upturned pail bobs and finally the deep sea, indicated by an iridescent dark blue. The precipitous fall as the eye descends through the artist's world from stars to the deep ocean dramatizes the dive that the hawk is about to make as it hurtles through the air. Although the unusual perspective situates the viewer with the bird, the wooden pail links the soaring view to the daily life of Japanese peasants. This is one of more than 8,000 prints produced by the Japanese woodblock master Utagawa Hiroshige (1797–1858),

famed as the last artist in the *ukiyo-e* tradition of the 'floating world'. Hiroshige often produced series of themed prints, and this example comes from *One Hundred Famous Views of Edo*, the former name of Tokyo.

174

Bruno Liljefors

Hawk and Black-Game, 1884
Oil on canvas, 143 × 203 cm / 56¼ × 80 in
Nationalmuseum, Stockholm

Although little known outside his native country, the work of the Swedish painter Bruno Liljefors (1860–1939) has had a profound influence on wildlife artists familiar with it. His understanding of bird behaviour was years ahead of his time and based on many hours' careful observation in the field under conditions that would test the toughest of characters. He worked prolifically, going into the wilderness to paint, often for days at a time, wrapped against the cold in layers of furs and woollen clothes. Liljefors was a hunter

as well as a painter, and embraced nature in all its severity, conveying the stark drama of confrontation between predator and prey with unflinching directness. This painting captures the moment of impact as a northern goshawk (*Accipiter gentilis*), a powerful aerial predator of northern forests, snatches a male Eurasian black grouse (*Lyrurus tetrix*) in mid-air. The presence of so many grouse together suggests that this drama occurred during their communal 'lekking' display, when their attention may have been distracted. Everything

about the artist and his work was uncompromising: the great size of his magnificent oil paintings, his resignation from the Stockholm Academy in protest against lifeless assignments, and his reluctance to undertake commissions of subjects someone else had chosen. Although his subject matter was unpopular in conventional art circles, Liljefors was a fine artist – the equal of any of his peers in the salons of Europe.

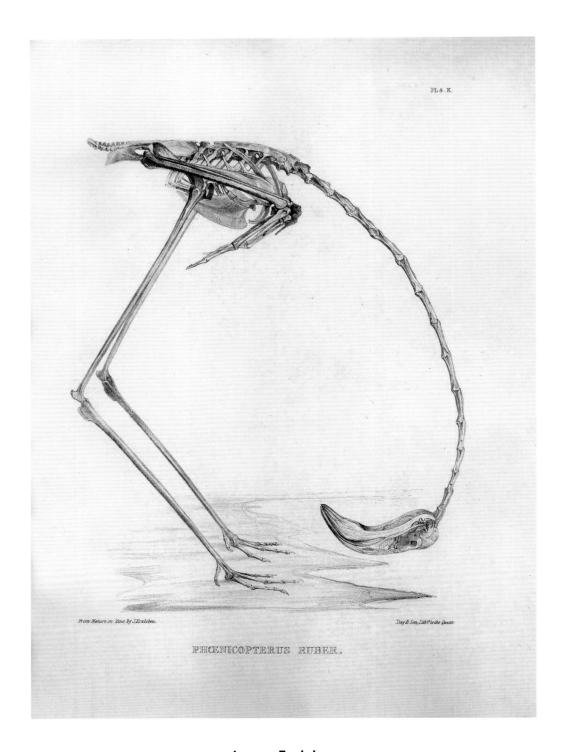

From Nature on Zinc by J.Erxleben.   Day & Son, Lith[rs] to the Queen.

PHŒNICOPTERUS RUBER.

James Erxleben

Phaenicopterus ruber, from *Osteologia Avium or, A Sketch of the Osteology of Birds,*
Vol. 2 by Thomas Campbell Eyton, 1867
Lithograph 29 × 21 cm / 11⅜ × 8¼ in

There is much misunderstanding about the upside-down feeding habits of flamingos. This skeletal reconstruction shows the bird stretching uncomfortably out and down, its legs flexed, to reach the water with head inverted. In fact, flamingos do not feed in this way. Instead, the bird's neck keeps its natural 'S'-shaped curve so the head faces the water with only the bill-tip inverted. This means flamingos can easily reach the mud layer at their feet without needing to bend their legs. Flamingos are filter-feeders, like baleen whales.

Using their large, muscular tongue like a plunger in a syringe, they rapidly suck in and expel water, trapping particles of food in a mesh of comb-like 'lamellae' protruding from the sides of the bill. They have fewer neck vertebrae than many other long-necked birds – seventeen compared with a swan's twenty-four, for example – but the bones themselves are elongated, giving the neck an angular appearance like a dot-to-dot puzzle. Despite the faults of this particular image, the collection from which it comes – *Osteologia Avium or,*

A sketch of the osteology of birds (1867) by the English naturalist Thomas Campbell Eyton – remains a masterpiece of nineteenth-century anatomical illustration. This book retains immense scientific value for its reconstructions of a vast range of skeletons in lifelike, animated postures. The lithographs by James Erxleben (c.1830–90) were made from skeletons mounted in Eyton's own museum, so this odd flamingo can be seen as an accurate drawing of an inaccurate specimen.

John James Audubon (engraved by Robert Havell)

American Flamingo, from *The Birds of America*, double elephant folio edition, 1838
Hand-coloured etching and aquatint, 97 × 65 cm / 38¼ × 25⅝ in

More has been written about John James Audubon (1785-1851) than any other artist in ornithological history. His prodigious talent for drawing birds was matched equally by his natural charisma, his colourful history, a flair for self-promotion and an unwavering determination to bring his 'Great Idea' - a book of all the birds of America printed life-size - to publication. The end result, the 'double elephant folio' edition of *The Birds of America*, is the most magnificent and valuable bird book ever to be produced. This American flamingo (*Phoenicopterus ruber*), perhaps the most iconic of all the plates, nevertheless owes its existence to hair's-breadth timing and good fortune. Audubon saw live flamingos in the Florida Keys in 1832 but failed to obtain the fresh specimen he desired to produce an illustration. Instead he was forced to request that a preserved specimen be sent to him in London, where he was busy overseeing the publication of his work. As the book neared completion, he wrote repeatedly to America, asking, 'When will the flamingos come?' The long-awaited package of dried flamingo skins finally arrived in the summer of 1838. Audubon's hurried watercolour showed the bird alone, animated as best he could to fit the proportions of the 'double elephant'-sized paper, with a note to his engraver, Robert Havell, to add a suitable landscape. Havell completed the engraving just in time for the image to be included in the final five prints of the *magnum opus*.

Alexandre Isidore Leroy de Barde

Still Life with Exotic Birds, c.1810
Watercolour and gouache, 124.5 × 88.5 cm / 49 × 35 in
Musée du Louvre, Paris

The birds in this remarkable *trompe l'oeil* painting are arranged without the modern regard for geographical origin, habitat or taxonomic relationship. There are crakes and cotingas, parakeets and partridges; centre stage, a splendid Eurasian eagle owl (*Bubo bubo*), a bird of cold northern forests, rubs shoulders with a tiny hummingbird from the rainforests of South America. These are unashamedly 'stuffed' birds, with all their imperfections, not an attempt to imitate life. Rather, the paintings are all about the nature of collecting – cabinets of curiosity – rather than about the individual birds, and give the illusion that the viewer is actually looking into a compartmentalized display cabinet, not at a flat canvas. The wood grain and joinery, the interior of each compartment and its shadows have been painstakingly portrayed to create an illusion of reality. Other paintings in this series feature shells, minerals, even Greek vases, rendered exactly as displayed in their museum settings, occupying the same shelves, cases and cabinets where the real artefacts once rested. The painting is one of a series of large compositions made by the French nobleman Vicomte Leroy de Barde (1777–1828) while in exile in England after the French Revolution. The private museums for which these paintings were made no longer exist, and most of the specimens have succumbed to the ravages of time. These images therefore provide an eerily lifelike window on the past, of inestimable cultural and scientific value.

Charley Harper

We Think the World of Birds, 2005
Lithographic print, 58.4 × 13.4 cm / 23 × 34 in

An outsized egg-shaped orb rests upon the Cornell Lab of Ornithology, Ithaca, New York – an institute dedicated to the study and conservation of all things avian – containing a stylized, geometric cacophony of birds, ranging from the miniature ruby-throated hummingbird (*Archilochus colubris*) to the magnificently large whooping crane (*Grus americana*). The birds, boldly rendered with simplified shapes and flat colours, are emblematic of the iconic flat graphic style of the American wildlife artist Charley Harper

(1922–2007). In Harper's chaotic display of diversity of birds from across the globe, the full spectrum of colour adds to a vibrant energy, as if the world can hardly contain the enormous variety of the avian class. The apparently wild amalgamation is misleading: Harper's process was as methodical as it was meticulous, and his aesthetic decisions were as deliberate as the selection of the species to be represented. Each bird represents an individual conservation effort or programme of research carried out by the Lab of Ornithology, representing

Harper's ability to distill a concept to its elemental form while retaining its character and symbolism. Said to be one of his favourite projects, *We Think the World of Birds* was also one of his last. Harper created up until his final days, amassing an enormous catalogue that ranges from *The Giant Golden Book of Biology* (1961) and posters for the National Park Service to mosaic murals. His work remains a source of influence for many contemporary artists.

Falling Bough

Ectopistes migratorius   Passenger Pigeon

Walton Ford

Falling Bough, 2002
Watercolor, gouache, ink and pencil on paper, 154.3 × 303.5 cm / 60¾ × 119½ in
Private collection

The extinct passenger pigeon (*Ectopistes migratorius*) was named for its most memorable behaviour – its migratory habit. It was reported that this North American endemic travelled in massive flocks that blocked the light of the sun and created a deafening cacophony. In *Falling Bough*, American artist Walton Ford (born 1960) illustrates the species *en masse* as they destroy a large branch under the force of their own weight. What first appears to be an innocuous scene of nature's marvel, however, reveals a display of appalling behaviour as the numerous birds victimize one another and wreak havoc on their habitat. Ford sardonically implies that their extinction was a result of their overpopulation and gluttony, suggesting their demise was self-inflicted, whereas in fact the bird is a notable example of a species being decimated as a direct result of human activity. Once one of the most abundant species in North America, its numbers rapidly declined due to aggressive hunting practices and habitat destruction. The species was declared extinct in 1914. Known for subversive commentary on subjects ranging from colonialism to politics to consumerism, Ford masterfully plays with our notions of natural history by employing the techniques of traditional nineteenth-century illustration in allegorical works using flora and fauna to comment on human behaviour. Ford's work has earned him several national honours and is included in esteemed collections such as the Whitney Museum of American Art and the Museum of Modern Art in New York.

Barbara Kruger

Untitled (Let Go), 2003
Chromogenic dye coupler print, 152.4 × 228.6 cm / 60 × 90 in
Private collection

A bird perches in an open hand gazing out at the viewer in this print by the celebrated American artist Barbara Kruger (born 1945). While the contrasting colours of bright red and turquoise comprise the main palette, the bird itself is reproduced in a monochrome green, which makes identification tricky. It appears to be a stuffed example of a variegated canary. The animal is linked to the slogan 'Let Go', an injunction that appeals to the viewer directly; together they encourage the embracing of free will. The hand is open, meaning that a live bird could easily fly away, and yet it stays. In this sense, the work suggests self-oppression and the importance of nurturing the freedom available to us – in the bird's case, to take flight. Kruger is known for her advertising-influenced conceptual art, which challenges the cultural formu-lations underpinning society, from consumerism to identity and sexuality. Often promoting anti-hierarchical ideas, her moralizing words can take the form of criticisms that expose the hypocrisies of our societies. Caught in a freeze-frame, seemingly unable to find liberation, this bird teaches us that freedom is also scary, but we limit our potential if we become comfortable with restriction.

Aaron Wojack

Yellow Tippler Cap. Collection: Pigeon Flying, from *Raising Pigeons*, 2011
Photograph, dimensions variable

In this photograph, taken high above the Brooklyn streets, a tattooed man proudly shows off a domesticated 'tippler' pigeon, bred for its flight performance. The image belongs to the *Raising Pigeons* series by American photographer Aaron Wojack, which documents New York's hidden subculture of 'fliers', who breed and fly their birds from the city's rooftops. Shot amid the weathered coops, Wojack's images show men tending to and releasing their flocks, which are trained to respond to flags and whistles that send them higher or call them back. Wojack considers the series a meditation on masculinity, and many of the photographs reveal the tender relationship between the men and their birds. The tradition of keeping pigeons in New York became popular in the 1950s, introduced by working-class Italian and Irish immigrants and then adopted by African-American and Hispanic communities. It is said that at one time there were fliers on almost every block, with thousands of birds taking to the air each day. Today, this predominantly male community keeps flocks of pigeons by the hundreds. For some fliers from the city's tougher neighbourhoods, the hobby has saved them from a life of crime. Nevertheless, Wojack's photographs document a fading subculture. Gentrification has forced out many coops, with landlords and residents taking a dim view of the birds, which are wrongly perceived as a dirty, disease-carrying nuisance.

Wolfgang Tillmans

Tukan, 2010
Photograph, ink-jet print, 207 × 138 cm / 81½ × 54⅜ in
Private collection

This inquisitive-looking toco toucan (*Ramphastos toco*) was photographed by renowned German photographer Wolfgang Tillmans (born 1968), who for over three decades has documented everyday life through his camera lens. He became the first photographer, and first non-British artist, to win the Turner Prize, one of the most prestigious art awards in Europe. Famous for his distinctive, realist style, Tillmans never tries to romanticize his subjects. His encounters with animals and people are therefore captured with a spontaneity and simplicity that captivate the viewer. In the case of this photograph, Tillmans does not attempt to disguise the tiled floor behind the bird or the feeder on which it perches. This toucan lives in an enclosure, perhaps in a zoo, and it is that context that anthropomorphically charges the expression of the bird with a mixture of mischievousness and sadness. Social and noisy, toucans live in flocks of roughly twenty individuals and tend to lead monogamous lives. Native to the neotropics, from southern Mexico to northern Argentina, in captivity toucans can learn tricks, but they remain wild animals at heart. Their razor-sharp, colourful bill – known for its distinctive shape and size – has baffled evolutionary biologists for over 150 years. While Charles Darwin believed it to be a sexual lure, recent research has revealed the beak might also play an important role in regulating the bird's body temperature.

Central Bank of Suriname

Surinamese gulden banknotes, 2000
Banknotes, each 7 × 14 cm / 2¾ × 5½ in
Private collection

Perhaps it should come as no surprise that birds have long been a popular subject for the design of banknotes from around the world. They are often symbolic of a country, which is one criterion for the choice of subject, but they also have the advantage of being highly attractive, and with enough fine detail in their feathers and features to make the notes hard to reproduce by forgers. In 2000, the former Dutch colony of Suriname issued a set of banknotes featuring endemic birds: the 500-gulden note features a male Guianan cock-of-the-rock (*Rupicola rupicola*), with its bright orange plumage and remarkable half-moon crest. The twenty-five-gulden note depicts a red-billed toucan (*Ramphastos tucanus*), a subspecies of the white-throated toucan. The long-tailed hermit (*Phaethornis superciliosus*) on the hundred-gulden note is a hummingbird from the forest undergrowth in the Guianas, Venezuela and northeastern Brazil, while the five-gulden note shows the red-necked woodpecker (*Campephilus rubricollis*), with its contrasting black and red plumage. The reverse of the notes all show local flowers. Among other notable banknotes to feature birds, many highlight particularly beautiful species – a 2009 two-dollar note from Bermuda featuring the Bermuda type of the eastern bluebird (*Sialia sialis*) was chosen as the International Banknote Society's banknote of the year. Some more unusual birds are also featured in various countries, including the rhinoceros hornbill (*Buceros rhinoceros*) in Malaysia or the African fish eagle (*Haliaeetus vocifer*) in Zambia.

Steve McCurry

A Woman Feeding Doves Near Blue Mosque, 1991
Digital c-print, 68 × 97 cm / 26¾ × 37¾ in

In this image by the celebrated US photographer Steve McCurry (born 1950), a woman crouches down, covered from head to toe in an orange burqa; the only part of her body visible is her hand, which is cupped to allow a dove (*Columba livia*) to feed from it. She is surrounded by hundreds of birds, and the pinkish hue of their beaks chimes with the flowing fabric. One dove stands poised on her head, as if to deliberately display its fine plumage and white tail feathers. These white doves are the same species

as feral street pigeons, and all domesticated pigeons descended from the wild rock dove. The white dove is often used as a sign of love or peace, or as a messenger, and it has an important role in the symbolism of religions including Islam, Judaism and Christianity. The image was taken outside the Ottoman-era seventeenth-century Blue Mosque (or Sultan Ahmed Mosque) in Istanbul, Turkey, the name of which derives from the hand-painted blue tiles that cover the interior. It is a world-famous tourist destination, as well as being

a functioning mosque that holds special Friday noon prayers called *jumu'ah*. Particularly known for his work *Afghan Girl* (1984), a photographic portrait of Sharbat Gula, a young Afghan refugee with remarkable green eyes, McCurry has an approach to representation that aims to capture his subjects in everyday situations that are, nonetheless, wholly unique moments.

Pablo Picasso

The Dove of Peace, c.1950
Pastel on paper, 23 × 31 cm / 9 × 12¼ in
Musée d'Art Moderne de Paris

This deceptively simple drawing of a dove holding a small olive branch in its beak demonstrates the ability of the renowned Spanish artist Pablo Picasso (1881–1973) to convey powerful ideas in a spontaneous way. A confident, bold line defines the shape of one of the most recognizable birds in the world: the dove, universally associated with the idea of purity. A symbol of the divine in Egyptian, Middle Eastern and Greek mythology, the dove became a symbol of peace in the Judeo-Christian tradition. According to the Old Testament story, Noah sent a dove to find land in the aftermath of the flood. The bird returned to the ark carrying a freshly plucked olive leaf – a sign of hope for a prosperous future. In the New Testament gospels, the Holy Spirit manifests in the form of a dove above Jesus's head as he is baptized. Picasso updated the dove to become a symbol of global pacifism. He also made a more realistic version of his dove in 1949 for the The World Congress of Partisans for Peace held in Paris. Soon after, Picasso's more veristic dove appeared on a banner above the stage at the 1952 World Peace Council Congress in Berlin, further consolidating its modern meaning. Picasso was well aware of the dove's positive message. He associated the bird with his childhood and the paintings of pigeon breeds made by his father, José Ruiz Blasco, who taught him to paint.

Lynette Yiadom-Boakye

Strip Lit, 2012
Oil on canvas, 95 × 85 cm / 37⅜ × 33½ in

British artist Lynette Yiadom-Boakye (born 1977) paints realistic works with no tangible reference to reality. Backgrounds are often neutral; the characters she portrays are invented; and their arrangement tends to be ordinary but enigmatic – albeit shaken up by the inclusion of a variant, often in the shape of an animal. These can be cats, owls or birds. In *Strip Lit*, a man who may or may not be looking at the viewer is challenged by the glare of the bald eagle (*Haliaeetus leucocephalus*) that he holds. A master of colouration,

Yiadom-Boakye makes the bird and its holder chromatically complementary. Just as the man is black in a white shirt, the bird's white head towers over brown plumage but the colour the artist chooses for the background does not give prominence to the two figures, instead blurring their defining lines. Inaugurated with her 2009 painting *Bird of Reason*, Yiadom-Boakye's bird paintings have contributed to expand the narrative within her work. Over the years, the types of birds she has depicted have included wrens, skylarks and greenfinches

– but never before a majestic and aggressive bird like an eagle. Given the bald eagle's strong association with the United States (see p.233) and the date of the painting, it is tempting to interpret this composition as a response to the re-election of Barack Obama as US president in 2012. At the same time, with its focus on a bird and feathers, the work may also allude to the tropes of seventeenth-century Dutch paintings, a critical influence that Yiadom-Boakye has often cited.

Robert Rauschenberg

Canyon, 1959
Oil, pencil, paper, metal, photograph, fabric, wood, canvas, buttons, mirror, taxidermied eagle,
cardboard, pillow, paint tube and other materials, 207.6 × 177.8 × 61 cm / 81¾ × 70 × 24 in
Museum of Modern Art, New York

A taxidermied golden eagle (*Aquila chrysaetos*)
– found in a dump by a fellow artist – protrudes
from the base of *Canyon*, one of the most celebrated
examples of the 'combines' that helped make the
name of a founding father of American Pop art,
Robert Rauschenberg (1925–2008) at the end of the
1950s. The works merged painting and collage with
a wide range of discarded objects, here including
fragments of cardboard, a pillow hanging by a string
and a black and white photograph of the artist's then

seven-year-old son Christopher. This latter element
– an unusual personal touch – inspired many observers
to believe that the eagle symbolized the ancient
Greek mythological character of Ganymede (see p.50),
a beautiful young boy from the city of Troy that the
god Zeus had abducted by an eagle in order to have
him serve as a cupbearer in Olympus. The inclusion
of the eagle would prove to be a source of controversy
almost fifty years after the piece's inception, when
the estate of the art dealer Ileana Sonnabend (who

regarded *Canyon* as one of her favourite works by
Rauschenberg) was prevented from selling it due to
the 1918 Bird Migratory Act, which declared the trade
in endangered species such as bald and golden eagles
a crime, even when the birds were no longer alive.
Sonnabend's heirs decided to resolve the dispute
by donating Rauschenberg's iconic combine to the
Museum of Modern Art in New York, effectively
reducing its market value from $65 million to zero.

Lombard Master

Portrait of a Gyrfalcon, Viewed from Three Sides, 1540–60
Oil on canvas, 76 × 100.5 cm / 29¾ × 39½ in
Private collection

'An Eagle for an Emperor / A Gyrfalcon for a King / A Peregrine for a Prince...' The hierarchy in this medieval treatise on hawking - continuing all the way down to 'A Kestrel for a Knave' (see p.84) - leaves no room for misinterpretation: ownership of a gyrfalcon (*Falco rusticolus*), largest of the falcons, a magnificent bird of the high arctic tundra, was the entitlement of only the highest social ranks. Although this bird is shown untethered, without the leather leg straps (jesses) that a falconer's bird would wear for life,

it is certainly a captive, the property of a wealthy man of noble birth. The creature's eyes are full of expression, and the gentle undulations of the wings and mantle, and muted patterns of semi-occluded feathers, reveal an intimacy that can only result from direct observation. Nevertheless, the gyrfalcon has chunky, sausage-like toes altogether uncharacteristic of a falcon, and an oak tree and a poplar - almost certainly symbolic family emblems the meaning of which is now lost - are likewise heavily stylized. Most remarkably,

the artist has shown three views of a single falcon as though it were three birds, perched together in a naturalistic setting. The symmetry of the work leans more towards heraldry than portraiture, although the painting probably functioned as both: a commissioned portrait of a revered and valuable status symbol, a statement of ownership and a declaration of rank.

F. Schumacher & Co.

Bird Zoo, 1940-49
Cotton; hand screen-printed on plain weave, 90.8 × 88.3 cm / 35¾ × 34¾ in
Cooper Hewitt, New York

In this colourful textile design an assortment of birds including a sulphur-crested cockatoo (*Cacatua galerita*), a racket-tailed hummingbird (*Ocreatus*) and a gyrfalcon (*Falco rusticolus*) sit on various perching rods on a tree trunk while a European turtle dove (*Streptopelia turtur*) sits close to her nest containing a couple of unhatched eggs. The pink-bodied bird with the crest is a rosy starling (*Pastor roseus*). The repeat pattern on a lilac-pink ground was created during the 1940s by F. Schumacher & Co., a New York-based textile firm, and is typical of the vibrant designs produced by the company since 1889. Frederic Schumacher had travelled to New York from Paris with the French textile company Passavant & Co. but struck out with his own firm in the same year, importing European textiles and supplying decorative fabrics to a growing market as mansions, apartment blocks and luxury hotels such as the Waldorf Astoria proliferated across the city and America. Tastemakers such as novelist Edith Wharton and heiress Marjorie Merriweather were clients, and after just six years Schumacher bought his own manufacturing facility in New Jersey (moving to twenty-four-hour production of textiles for the war effort). *Bird Zoo* illustrates the popularity of lively, richly coloured textiles for interiors after the World War II (1939-45). The company was also one of the first to ask designers such as the Parisian couturier Paul Poiret to create textile designs; it would later collaborate with Josef Frank, Elsa Schiaparelli and Frank Lloyd Wright.

Francis Barlow

A Decoy, c.1667–c.1679
Oil on canvas, 254 × 346 cm / 100 × 136¼ in
National Trust, Clandon Park, Guildford, UK

Duck decoying is a near-forgotten art. It relies on a tranquil atmosphere and an intimate relationship between hunter, dog and duck. Ducks like to keep ground predators like foxes in sight, so foxlike dogs were trained to gently lure feeding waterfowl deeper and deeper down ever-narrowing waterways ending in a trap. In this scene, behind the back of the decoyman just retreating into his hut, the sudden appearance of a red kite (*Milvus milvus*) has caused havoc among the birds, sending ducks flying in panic

in every direction. Even two Eurasian bitterns (*Botaurus stellaris*), usually shy and secretive, have left the cover of the reeds to keep an eye on the raptor. Far from being fearsome predators, red kites are harmless carrion feeders whose misguided persecution led to their eventual extinction in England in the 1870s. With the exception of a healthy but localized population in central Wales, the kites currently widespread across Britain are descended from birds reintroduced from Spain since 1990.

This intimate portrayal of rural life by the English artist Francis Barlow (1624–1704) offers a rare glimpse into seventeenth-century England but also works at a deeper level. Well known for his political satires and metaphorical undertones, Barlow is believed to have made this painting as an allegory of the perceived threat posed to England by Roman Catholicism after the Civil War. The theme of the painting is hidden versus perceived danger; in fearing the kite, the birds are oblivious to the danger of the decoy.

A. Elmer Crowell

Preening Black Duck, c.1900
Wood, paint and glass, L. 33 cm / 13 in
Private collection

With its raised wing feathers, this preening American black duck (*Anas rubripes*) was painstakingly carved and painted for the purpose of enticing living black ducks to their death. A. Elmer Crowell (1862–1952) lived in East Harwich, Massachusetts, where he started shooting ducks in his early teens in the nearby lakes and coastal bays. After legal restrictions on the use of live decoys to attract ducks were introduced, he began to carve his own from about 1912, gaining a reputation for lifelikeness. The black duck is endemic in eastern North America from Saskatchewan in Canada to Florida, where it lives in tidal marshes, salt marshes and freshwater wetlands, moving between north to south on its annual migration. The 'Crown Prince of the Atlantic Flyway', as it was dubbed by *Sports Illustrated*, appears quietly at dusk and is revered among hunters for being wary and fast-flying – with the result that around a million a year were shot in the 1970s. The numbers of 'blackies' had already fallen, as a result of the drainage of wetlands through urban development as well as the effects of pesticides such as DDT, but also due to hybridization as these ducks mated with incoming mallards. In the 1980s, restrictions limited hunters to one black duck per day; the move stabilized duck numbers, and the limit was raised to two birds in 2017. Black ducks were the decoys most requested from Crowell, whose carvings now change hands for large sums of money. Two of his decoys sold for $1m each in 2007, and this preening duck went for $600,000 in 2018.

WILD TURKEY. *Meleagris gallopavo.* 1.Male. 2.Female. 3.Young.

Alexander Wilson

Wild Turkey Meleagris gallopavo, from *Illustrations of the American Ornithology of Alexander Wilson and Charles Lucian Bonaparte, 1835*
Hand-coloured engraving, 35.2 × 26.5 cm / 13⅞ × 10⅜ in
Smithsonian Libraries, Washington, DC

American Ornithology, a nine-volume work by the artist Alexander Wilson (1766–1813) published between 1808 and 1825, was the first comprehensive work describing and illustrating over 260 native American bird species. Wilson died before its completion, and the final volume, along with later editions, featured the work of other ornithologists. A male and female turkey stand on the trunk of a black locust tree, a species native to the eastern United States and widely introduced further west. Arching above the birds, a twig shows its compound leaves, drooping flower clusters and pea-like seed pod. Below the parent birds are their three chicks, one of which is inspecting a striped beetle. The wild turkey (*Meleagris gallopavo*), the ancestor of the domestic farmed turkey, is found across the United States and Mexico, mainly in open forested habitats. Wilson was born in Paisley, Scotland, into a family of weavers and was a contemporary of the poet Robert Burns. Wilson – a keen poet himself – was an apprentice weaver but used his poems to attack a local mill owner who underpaid his workers, eventually forcing Wilson to emigrate to America to escape charges of sedition. In 1794 he settled near Philadelphia, where he described and illustrated numerous American birds. Several have been named in his honour, including Wilson's phalarope (*Steganopus tricolor*), Wilson's plover (*Charadrius wilsonia*), Wilson's snipe (*Gallinago delicata*), Wilson's storm-petrel (*Oceanites oceanicus*) and Wilson's warbler (*Cardellina pusilla*).

Within the image:

Gentlemen of the Sporting train
Behold brave MADMAN once again.

MADMAN, A Birchen Cock.
Bred in 1830. A Descendent from Mʳ Sewells Stud of Yellow Cocks, whose game & punishing qualities have been so well known for the last 40 Years. — His PERFORMANCES, In 1832 When 2 Years Old he won a match of 2 Sovrˢ. After some disputes respecting his qualities he was matched the same week for 5 Sovrˢ when he defeated his adversary under all these disadvantages in that superior manner which he maintained throughout. In 1833 when 3 Years Old he won an 8 MAIN. In 1834 When 4 Years Old he won another Main under heavy odds, When his present Owner refused 5 Sovrˢ for him, by an admirer of the Sod for a STUD COCK.

Henry Alken

Madman, a Birchen Cock, c.1834
Oil on canvas, 69.2 × 54.7 cm / 27¼ × 21½ in
Private collection

'Gentlemen of the sporting train, behold brave Madman once again': Madman was among the last of the celebrated prize English fighting cocks of the early nineteenth century. Although fighting fowl, known as gamecocks, are the same species as the domesticated chicken (*Gallus gallus*), centuries of selective breeding have produced birds of a very distinctive appearance, with long strong legs, a broad, muscular chest - and a pugnacious character. Cockerels are naturally aggressive to one another and readily fight other males, lashing out with their powerful feet and horny leg spurs. In cockfighting, blades attached to the birds' legs inflict serious injury, with the losing bird dying slowly from blood loss. Although officially illegal almost worldwide, cockfighting is still widely practiced, particularly in Southeast Asia. A year after the British sporting artist Henry Alken (1785-1851) made this portrait, the 'sport' of cockfighting was banned in England under the 1835 Cruelty to Animals Act. Instead of pitting birds against one another in bloody battle, poultry breeders gradually turned their attention instead to competition on the show bench. Two exhibition breeds were created from the traditional fighting strains. One was the 'Old English Game', an attempt by breeders to keep the birds identical to the original cockfighting stock and theoretically fit for its original purpose. The other was the 'Modern English Game', an aesthetic remodelling to enhance the birds' most beautiful features.

Doug Bowman

Twitter Bird, 2012
Logo, dimensions variable

The ubiquitous Twitter Bird is among the world's most iconic logos. Based on the mountain bluebird (*Sialia currucoides*) – a small migratory thrush found in western North America – its design is so recognizable that Twitter has dropped its company name from the logo entirely. As the social networking company's creative director Doug Bowman said at its unveiling in 2012: 'Twitter is the bird, the bird is Twitter.' With nearly 200 million daily active users, including heads of state and high-profile celebrities, Twitter is one of the world's most visited websites. The Twitter Bird symbolizes the short messages known as tweets (named to evoke the chirping sound of a bird), while its open beak and skyward-pointing body reflect the company's values of freedom, hope and limitless possibility. The original Twitter Bird, named Larry after the American basketball player Larry Bird, was designed by British illustrator Simon Oxley and bought for just $15 in 2006. It was replaced in 2009 by a cartoonish design, which was modified and silhouetted the following year. In 2012 the logo was refined further by Bowman, who removed its tufty plumage and streamlined the shape of its wing, which is created from three overlapping circles. Twitter is highly protective of its most recognizable asset, and its brand guidelines stipulate that the logo must never be modified in any way, should always appear with a specified amount of empty space surrounding it and can only be shown in blue or white.

Bob Clampett for Warner Bros.

Tweety, c.1950
Animation, dimensions variable

'I tawt I taw a puddy tat!' Millions of viewers were brought up with the catchphrase of Tweety – a bright yellow canary introduced to audiences in 1942 by American animator Bob Clampett (1913-84) – as he evaded attempts on his life by his hapless adversary, the black and white cat Sylvester. The star of almost fifty Looney Tunes and Merrie Melodies animations, Tweety is one of the most popular characters from the golden age of Warner Brothers cartoons. Originally named Orson and of an unidentified species, he began as a naked pink chick based on a photograph of Clampett as a baby, with a meaner streak than his later congenial incarnation, which was developed by animator Friz Freleng in the mid-1940s and originally voiced by Mel Blanc. Freleng retained Tweety's baby face but made him cuter by adding yellow feathers and large blue eyes. Frelang also paired the bird with Sylvester, whose elaborate schemes are always thwarted, usually by Tweety's owner, Granny, or her bulldog, Hector. The two, who were first pitted together in the 1947 Academy Award-winning cartoon *Tweetie Pie* – Tweety's name was an amalgam of 'sweetie' and 'tweet' – remain one of the most notable pairings in animation history. The Atlantic canary (*Serinus canaria*) was introduced as a cage bird from the Canary Islands to Spain in the seventeeth century, and from there to the rest of Europe. Prized for their bright colour and song, they are still kept in millions of households around the world.

Natalia Goncharova

Peacock in the Bright Sun (Egyptian Style), 1911
Oil on canvas, 129 × 144 cm / 50¾ × 56¾ in
State Tretyakov Gallery, Moscow

A resplendent peacock proudly fans its tail, flooding the canvas with a dazzling patchwork of primary colours. Natalia Goncharova (1881–1962) was a leading figure in the pre-revolutionary Russian avant-garde, working as a painter, illustrator and set designer for the Ballets Russes. Between 1911 and 1912, she produced five paintings of peacocks, each of which uses a different visual style to depict the flamboyant bird, ranging from traditional Russian handicrafts to avant-garde movements such as Cubism. In this composition she combines elements of ancient Egyptian art with Russian folk painting and Rayonism, a type of abstract art she invented with her partner Michel Larionov, in which objects appear fragmented like splintered glass. Employing a stylistic convention common in ancient Near Eastern and Egyptian art, the peacock's head and neck are shown in profile, while its body and legs are depicted frontally. Such composite poses allowed two or more viewpoints to coexist in a single representation. Although the bird is clearly recognizable, the natural colourings of its iridescent blue and green plumage are exchanged for a simple palette of red, yellow, blue, green and brown, which Goncharova has applied as blocks of flat colour. The bird's slender body, painted in purple hues, is enclosed by a green oval, a motif repeated across the fanned tail, replacing the peacock's familiar eyespot markings, while the highly stylized tail suggests the radiant sun, echoing the work's title.

Unknown

Ray crown, 1960-72
Feathers and wicker frame, 40 × 42 cm / 15¾ × 16½ in
Musée du quai Branly, Paris

This crown of feathers - expertly arranged around a wicker frame to achieve a symmetrical design of reds, yellows, greens and greys - was created by one of the world's most remote indigenous peoples: the Rikbaktsa of the Amazon rainforest in the Mato Grosso region of Brazil. The Rikbaktsa had their first contact with outsiders only in the 1940s, when their lands were encroached upon by rubber planting, forestry and mining industries, and the people themselves were subject to attempts by Jesuit missionaries to change their traditional culture. The Rikbaktsa raise birds in their villages to maintain a constant supply of feathers for ornamentation, including parakeets, curassows and guans (Cracidae) - and, above all, parrots and macaws. The people feed the birds brazil nuts and corn, but occasionally pin them in place to pluck out virtually all of their feathers to noisy protests: within a week, the feathers begin to grow again, sometimes appearing even brighter. The drabber brown colours come from birds of prey such as harpy eagles (*Harpia harpyja*), which are kept as mascots in villages, or from chickens. Featherwork is central to Rikbaktsa culture, as it is to other Amazonian peoples, partly because feathers are an important form of ornament in societies that have relatively few clothes. Feathers are also used in rituals, particularly in the form of headdresses, because they are believed to give spiritual strength and protection to the wearer, as well as being beautiful for their own sake.

Brendan McGarry

Buff-breasted Sandpiper Wing, 2015
Photograph, dimensions variable

One of nature's greatest feats of engineering, birds' wings are amazingly complex, diverse, and perfectly suited for their job. They comprise just a few bones, so most of the work is done by the feathers, which are intricately layered and shaped, influencing everything from species' social displays to their hunting techniques. This wing from a buff-breasted sandpiper (*Calidris subruficollis*) is part of a series of images taken in 2015 by freelance photographer Brendan McGarry at the University of Washington Burke Museum in Seattle.

The bottom row of feathers are, at left, the ten primary flight feathers attached to the metacarpal and phalangeal bones and, at right, ten secondary flight feathers, attached to the ulna. These feathers are highly asymmetrical, so that they overlap and interleaf. The four tertial feathers close to the bird's body attach to the humerus. The row above these are the greater coverts, with the lesser coverts and scapular feathers above. The fringed tips of some of the coverts are the result of normal wear and suggest that these feathers

are older than the flight feathers. These so-called moult patterns can be used to determine the age of birds. The overall wing shape also reflects the species' flight patterns. The shape of this sandpiper wing is ideal for rapid take-off to avoid predators, but also well-suited to long-distance migration between breeding grounds in the Arctic and wintering sites in South America.

Unknown

Folio 36v and 37r, from the Aberdeen Bestiary, *c.*1200
Gold, ink and colours on parchment, each page: 30.2 × 21 cm / 11⅞ × 8¼ in
Aberdeen University Library, UK

The Aberdeen Bestiary is a manuscript from around 1200 comprising 103 folios, in Latin, that describe the world from the creation as detailed in the Book of Genesis, through mammals, birds, reptiles, worms, trees, humans and minerals. It is largely based on the style of *Etymologiae* by St Isidore of Seville and the *Physiologus*, a second-century Greek text from Alexandria, functioning as a sort of encyclopaedia. Bestiaries such as this, and the similar Ashmole Bestiary, are analogous to modern-day handbooks in setting out to describe all that is known about species at the time. The volume was likely commissioned by a wealthy English ecclesiastical patron and found its way into the collection of Henry VIII, probably following the dissolution of the monasteries in the 1530s. Since the seventeenth century, it has been in the Aberdeen University library. Embellished with gold leaf and fine paints, the pages shown are among the most richly illustrated of birds. The top of 36v is intended to represent five common hoopoes (*Upupa epops*), whose necks and biting beaks form a complex interlocking design. As migrants that winter in Africa, and now relatively uncommon in England, hoopoes would have been less well-known than the Eurasian magpie (*Pica pica*), being hunted by an archer, and the common raven (*Corvus corax*) on folio 37r. This unfamiliarity may help explain the poorer resemblance as the artist would have relied on descriptions and other illustrations rather than personal experience.

BIRDS

Most birds can fly. Some birds can't fly.
One bird who can't fly lives at the South Pole.
He likes to slide on the ice. Which bird is it?

eagle

hawk

hummingbird

barn swallow

cock

hen

chick

nuthatch

heron

pigeon

woodpeckers

goose

spoonbill

swan

duck

duckling

flamingo

bittern

penguin

pelican

vulture

parrot

crow

owl

toucan

ground dove

puffin

robin

cardinal

jay

sparrow

wren

bluebird

sea gull

tern

sandpiper

bird house

canary

nest

baby birds

bird cage

quail

pheasant

ostrich

woodcock

egret

stork

ostrich egg

74

75

Richard Scarry

Birds, from *Richard Scarry's Best Word Book Ever*, 1964
Printed book, published by Hamlyn Publishing Group by arrangement with Golden Press, 30 × 26 cm / 11¾ × 10¼ in
Private collection

Birds from all over the world fill this colourful spread from best-selling children's book *Richard Scarry's Best Word Book Ever* (first published 1963). Alongside the familiar sparrow, robin and duck are species such as the nuthatch, spoonbill and cardinal. Tropical birds also feature, though no hint of their natural habitat is given. Apart from the woodpeckers clinging to a small tree trunk, nearly every other bird stands on a small patch of nondescript ground. Balanced on a wooden perch, the parrot is evidently a captive bird, as is the canary in its cage. The stylized illustrations, most of which show the birds in profile, display a level of ornithological accuracy unlike the cartoon anthropomorphic animals for which Richard Scarry (1919-94) is best known. The American author and illustrator began illustrating children's books in 1949, and, with *Best Word Book Ever*, writing them, too. The book is divided into different subjects ranging from sports to houses, with each illustrated object or creature labelled to help young readers expand their vocabularies.

A paragraph on each spread challenges readers to find something, such as the bird that 'lives at the South Pole' and 'likes to slide on the ice'. Selling more than 5 million copies worldwide, the book has remained in print for half a century, entertaining and educating generations of young readers.

SEDGE WARBLERS
IMMATURE BIRDS AT PLAY

Henrik Grønvold

Sedge Warblers: Immature Birds at Play,
from *The British Warblers, a History, with Problems of Their Lives* by H. E. Howard, Vol. 2, 1907-14
Chromolithograph, 19 × 28 cm / 7½ × 11 in

Throughout Europe and western Asia, the reedy margins of waterways during the summer months are vibrant with the rasping, chattering calls of small birds. An observer may be lucky enough to catch a glimpse of one as it flits momentarily into view before disappearing almost immediately among the reeds. These are the wetland *Acrocephalus* warblers. Although the majority of these skulking, secretive birds are small, brown and nondescript, they have a subtle beauty all their own. The sedge warbler (*Acrocephalus schoenobaenus*) is one of the more easily recognizable species of the group, with its conspicuous pale eye stripe and streaked upperparts. The juveniles, as seen in this illustration from the early twentieth century, have warm buff underparts and a pretty 'necklace' of spotted feathers on their upper breast. By winter the birds have travelled south to Africa and the reedbeds are silent. Small brown birds have a limited attraction for most artists, but Danish illustrator Henrik Grønvold (1858–1940) had a particular fondness for such understated subjects, as is evident here. An engineering draughtsman with a passion for ornithology, Grønvold interrupted his plans to emigrate to the United States by taking a temporary job at the British Museum of Natural History, and remained there in an unofficial capacity as a natural history illustrator for much of his life. His work was reproduced in a variety of print media, from hand-coloured lithography to photogravure, crossing the boundaries between old and new.

Orsola Maddalena Caccia

Still Life with Birds, c.1596-1676
Oil on canvas, 28 × 40.2 cm / 11 × 15¾ in
Private collection

Despite its rather dull brown background, *Still Life with Birds* harbours some surprises, not least that it was painted by one of the few female artists of the 1600s, the nun Orsola Maddalena (born Theodora Caccia, 1596-1676), or that it sold at Sotheby's in May 2020 for $260,000, fifteen times its estimate. Caccia depicts several common birds, including four members of the tit family: the great tit (*Parus major*); the blue tit (*Cyanistes caeruleus*), one of which lies on its back, apparently dead; the coal tit (*Periparus ater*) standing on a twig of conifer; and the crested tit (*Lophophanes cristatus*). At the centre of the painting is a goldcrest (*Regulus regulus*), one of Europe's smallest birds, with its bright yellow and gold head stripe, while a European goldfinch (*Carduelis carduelis*) is shown in flight. Above the goldcrest is a pale warbler, most probably a common chiffchaff (*Phylloscopus collybita*). The accurate depiction of the characteristic features and plumage of each species allows for easy identification. Theodora Caccia, daughter of the painter Guglielmo Caccia, was born in the Piedmont region of Italy. In 1620 she entered the Ursuline convent of Bianzè before in 1625 returning with her five sisters to another Ursuline convent established by her father in his hometown of Moncalvo, where in due course Orsola became abbess. Her output consisted of altarpieces and other religious paintings, such as *Madonna and Child*, but also included rarer studies of flowers and birds.

Unknown

Great Zimbabwe Bird, 13th–15th century
Steatite, H. *c.*33 cm / 13 in
Groote Schuur Collection, Cape Town

One of eight stone carvings of birds that once stood atop tall pedestals surrounding an altar within the Eastern Enclosure of the ruined city of Great Zimbabwe, this is the only example still in exile from Zimbabwe. It was broken from its 1.5-m (5 ft) plinth by a South African hunter and trader in 1899 and subsequently sold to Cecil Rhodes, founder of Rhodesia (now Zimbabwe and Zambia). It remains in his house, now a museum in Cape Town, despite demands for its return. Great Zimbabwe was built by the ancestors of the modern Shona people, beginning in the eleventh century, and may have been the royal palace. The birds were installed on pillars and walls and are unique to the site. The hybrid sculptures combine human and avian features, with lips instead of beaks and five-toed feet instead of claws. It has been suggested that each bird was carved to mark the reign of a new king, but they seem more likely to represent a totemic animal sacred to the early Shona: the bateleur eagle (*Terathopius* *ecaudatus*). The bateleur, a colourful eagle endemic to sub-Saharan Africa, is a symbol of the Shona protective spirit and a messenger bird between the people, the ancestors and God. The birds are sometimes called Shiri ya Mwari, the Bird of God. The birds of Great Zimbabwe are today the symbol of the modern country, represented on the national flag, stamps, banknotes and coins.

Unknown

Herbalist's staff, mid-20th century
Iron, 67.3 × 16.5 × 16.5 cm / 26½ × 6½ × 6½ in
Smithsonian National Museum of African Art, Washington, DC

This iron staff is topped with a large, stylized bird rising above fourteen smaller birds, each attached by means of a single leg wrapped around a circular iron plate perpendicular to the staff, which was wielded by a powerful local herbalist. In the Yoruba mythology of western Africa, Olodumare, the supreme creator god, instructed Oduduwa, the deity of divine kingship, to create the earth below the sky using a bag of sand and a bird. Oduduwa poured sand onto the primordial sea, and the bird spread it far and wide, producing the land – and confirming the role of the king as intermediary between the gods and his people. Osanyin is the deity associated with the powers of plants, and thus the patron deity of herbalists, who are his priests. The herbalists' staffs are symbols of their power to change into birds in order to commute between heaven and earth. These rods, decorated with a large bird elevated above smaller ones, symbolize the transfer of supernatural powers from the heavenly realms to earth. The number of smaller birds represents the number of basic signs in Yoruba divination, which includes a system of classification for medicinal ingredients. Osanyin and his priests are believed to possess protective powers against illness and disease; the iconography of many smaller birds flocking around a single larger one suggests the role of healers and rulers in assuming control over dangerous forces for the benefit of the community.

Jonas Wood

2 Birds at Night, 2013
Oil and acrylic on linen, 152.4 × 111.8 cm / 60 × 44 in
Private collection

US artist Jonas Wood (born 1977) first became interested in birdcages in 2010, when painting a series of gouaches exploring the subject. He realized that the thin bars that form the structure of the cages could contribute formal density and depth of field simultaneously to a composition – both inviting and resisting the gaze. This visual tension is particularly noticeable in *2 Birds at Night*, where the nocturnal conditions complement Wood's predilection for flat colours, turning the cage into a semi-transparent screen.

The two parrots inside are aligned and viewed from the same angle – an apparently casual position but one that is in fact carefully constructed to showcase both the colours of their plumage in the dark and the way in which two birds within the same order can differ. Adding to the almost cubist confusion of space, these birds establish a spatial dimension that might otherwise be absent, even while the foliage in the background and the coloured squares that may be windows or feeder boxes, challenge basic perspectival rules. Wood's

interest in the more mundane aspects of society and culture – family photographs, sports magazine illustrations, interiors, domestic vegetation and animals – is processed through an urge for typologizing. His works can be seen as attempts to mentally catalogue and capture all the characteristics of a genre or a kind. This is matched with a genuine affection for his 'normal' subjects, which are discretely elevated to a privileged status.

Carel Fabritius

The Goldfinch, 1654
Oil on panel, 33.5 cm × 22.8 cm / 13¼ × 9 in
Mauritshuis, The Hague

The charming simplicity of this painting of a tamed European goldfinch (*Carduelis carduelis*) perched on, and chained to, a feeding box belies the mystery and cultural impact that surround the image. Painted in 1654 during the Dutch Golden Age by Carel Fabritius (1622–54), a student of Rembrandt, it has become, since its rediscovery in 1859, one of the most iconic images of a bird in all of art history. This reputation has only been heightened since its inclusion as a key feature in the eponymous 2013 Pulitzer Prize-winning book by the US novelist Donna Tartt. In the same year this work was painted, Fabritius was killed and most of his work destroyed when the Delft gunpowder magazine exploded. In Tartt's novel, meanwhile, a terrorist bomb kills the central character's mother in the museum where the painting hangs, and the painting becomes a metaphorical link to the deceased. The lack of other paintings and information lends a deep mystery to Fabritius' surviving works. At a time when birds were more often included in paintings as incidental symbols or as dead specimens in still lifes, this work unusually presents the goldfinch as a portrait. It is constructed out of gentle gestural and textured paint strokes that simultaneously make it lifelike yet speak to its materiality. The overall effect is remarkably dramatic for such a small work, leaving viewers to weave their own story as to its meaning and significance.

Charles Frederick Tunnicliffe

Golden Pheasant, 1959
Pencil, ink, watercolour and gouache on paper, 48 × 63.5 cm / 18⅞ × 25 in
Oriel Môn, Rhosmeirch, Llangefni, Isle of Anglesey, UK

Nearly every inch of the paper is covered in this remarkable study of the almost unreal colours and textures of a male golden pheasant (*Chrysolophus pictus*) in full breeding plumage, together with detailed, accurate studies of the different-coloured feathers of the wings, tail and back, with annotations about the dimensions of the bird and the specific details shown. A note at the base records that the study was painted at Euston Hall in Norfolk in January 1959, presumably from a dead bird. This remarkable species, one of the most attractive of all gamebirds, is native to mountain forests in western China, but its beauty has seen it introduced to many other countries, including the Americas and Europe, where it has established populations. In Britain golden pheasants were once frequent in scattered areas of southern and eastern England, notably in Norfolk, but are now rare. Charles Tunnicliffe (1901–79) was one of the most famous artists of British wildlife, best known for his accurate, naturalistic paintings of birds. After studying at the Macclesfield School of Art, he won a scholarship to the Royal College of Art in London. He painted mainly in Anglesey, where he lived from 1947. Among at least 250 books, he illustrated Henry Williamson's famous novel *Tarka the Otter* (1927). This portrait features on the cover of *Tunnicliffe's Birds* (1984), a collection of his measured drawings of dead birds.

Thomas Lohr

Acryllium vulturinum, from *Birds*, 2015
Photograph, dimensions variable

Only a ruffle of feathers alerts us to the fact that this abstract design is actually part of a vulturine guineafowl (*Acryllium vulturinum*), a large bird from northeast Africa related to chickens and turkeys. Specifically, we are looking at an area just in front of the bird's right wrist, the ulna and radius of the guineafowl's forearm, draped in spotted feathers that are overlaid by a sea of soft, electric-blue plumage. The image, taken by the German fashion photographer Thomas Lohr (born 1982) as part of his collection

Birds, presents an abstract landscape of dunes and pools pouring diagonally across the scene, curving in front of the central apex of the wing's base before cascading away. As we look closer, it becomes clear that the smoothness of the surface of the blue and white stripes is scarred by minute ridges, the gaps between the feathers' barbs, the thin elements branching from each feather's shaft and hooking onto its neighbours. On the flat surface of the wing, we begin to see breaks in the spots surrounding the larger

white dots (a marvel of complex, cellular development). The focus on the structure of the feathers is appropriate: the guineafowl's sensational plumage is caused not just by the patterning of pigment but also by the microscopic structure of the feathers, preferentially reflecting and scattering blue light. Lohr's portrait presents us with a novel view of the bird: a motionless study of the intricate architecture of an inherently dynamic creature.

Unknown

Polychrome jar with rainbow, macaw, and floral motifs, 1880–89
Ceramic and pigment, 42.6 × 46.7 cm / 16¾ × 18⅜ in
Art Institute of Chicago, Illinois

A stylized macaw is surrounded by rainbows and plants on this ceramic vessel produced in Acoma Pueblo in New Mexico in the late nineteenth century that encapsulates a centuries-long connection between the peoples of the southwestern United States and macaws. Invading Spanish forces who, in the 1500s, encountered the Pueblo peoples – named for their mud-brick villages, or *pueblos* – noted that they kept scarlet macaws (*Ara macao*) as pets, although the birds' traditional habitat is more than 1,600 km (1,000 miles) to the south. Macaw feathers were traded as part of an extensive barter economy that included goods such as coral, shell and buffalo hides. Many *pueblos* had clans named after birds, including eagles and parrots, and macaws feature in many Pueblo myths. For the Pueblo, red, blue and yellow macaw feathers were so valuable they were tied together to create prayer sticks to be offered to the gods. These feathers also decorated poles and masks for sacred dances and were used to ornament symbolic figures known as *kachinas*. Macaws, which began to appear on Pueblo pottery from around AD 1000, were – and remain – symbols of the sun and of the south, from where rain, important for agriculture and irrigation, often came. They were also associated with the summer and the practice of gathering salt to preserve food. The designs on this pot represent a break from more monochrome earlier Pueblo traditions, perhaps under the influence of embroidered textiles from the east coast.

Diana Beltrán Herrera

Greater Bird of Paradise, 2015
Paper and glue, 25 × 25 cm / 9⅞ × 9⅞ in
Collection of the artist

This striking papercraft model of a male greater bird of paradise (*Paradisaea apoda*) is the work of Colombian designer and maker Diana Beltrán Herrera (born 1987). Her work combines cut, glued and folded paper shapes to create decorative three-dimensional representations of exotic birds and flowers which she then poses and shoots as two-dimensional images against coloured backgrounds. The fabulous plumes of this species actually arise from their flanks, beneath their wings, but are raised up when displaying, giving the appearance of a spectacular fountain of golden feathers over the bird's back. The males display together at dawn in a communal gathering called a lek, while the drab, brown females look on. The energetic dances of the displaying birds are not random, but carefully choreographed to fully exploit the effects of light on their gorgeous plumage. They display from a perch in a favourite tree. Generation after generation of the same species of birds of paradise use the same lekking tree, which is selected to catch the rays of the rising sun. No other tree will do, and if a lekking tree is cut down, the birds move on. It is easy to overlook the females, but despite their drab appearance it is they who run the show. Female choice is the driving force behind the evolution of bird of paradise plumage. In this female-based society, the only use for males is as sexual partners – preferably as eye-catching as possible.

Qi Baishi

*Eagle on a Pine Tree, c.*1940
Hanging scroll, ink on paper, 173 × 54.6 cm / 68⅛ × 21½ in
Metropolitan Museum of Art, New York

This alert and defiant eagle standing at attention on the bough of a pine tree is a powerful piece of patriotic propaganda, produced during a time of war. Rendered only in ink, the large, rapid brushstrokes used for both the bird and the tree create an image of strength and boldness, with a political message conveyed by a poem by the eighth-century Chinese poet Du Fu inscribed at the right: 'Why attack ordinary birds, spraying blood and feathers on the ground?' In Chinese culture, the eagle represents courage and fortitude, and images of

it were given as awards to military officials in the Ming dynasty from 1368 to 1644. The pine on which the eagle stands is an evergreen, symbolizing longevity and perseverance. The Chinese artist Qi Baishi (1864–1957) was inspired to paint this image of defiance and power during the turbulent period of the Second Sino-Japanese War (1937–1945), when China suffered under Japanese military aggression. Qi's eagle guards his home with determination, while the pine suggests that China will endure. This painting also contains

meaningful historical associations apart from its quotation from Du Fu, as it closely resembles ink paintings of eagles made by the renowned artist-monk Bada Shanren in the seventeenth century, not long after the Manchus took control of China and established the Qing dynasty in 1644. In this way, the artist drew on numerous threads of Chinese heritage to express his determination that his country would once again survive.

Eliot Porter

Chipping Sparrow, 1971
Dye imbibition print, 27 × 20.2 cm / 10⅝ × 8 in
Amon Carter Museum of American Art, Fort Worth, Texas

Hungry mouths reach up as a chipping sparrow (*Spizella passerina*) returns to its nest hidden in a conifer tree. This remarkable photograph is the work of American wildlife photography pioneer Eliot Porter (1901–90). While he is well known for his images of landscapes, Porter's 1972 series of bird portraits, published in the book *Birds of North America*, are only more recently gaining the attention they have always deserved. The photographer's ambition set a new artistic model for avian photography. He was strongly influenced by the nineteenth-century natural history illustrations of John James Audubon (see p.177) and thus sought to imbue his images with a painterly quality. Porter's colour palette is bright, the contrast soft and the colour saturation pronounced. To take images of birds frozen in movement, Porter devised a special setup comprising two powerful strobe lamps synchronized to the camera shutter. This enabled him to capture extremely sharp images of small and fast birds in flight. An eager environmentalist and conservationist, Porter used his photographs to make audiences aware of the wonders of the natural world and to promote habitat and species preservation. Chipping sparrows are small birds common in North America. They often lay three or four eggs every spring and nest in pine trees. Their name derives from the sharp 'chip' call they make frequently as they forage and interact with others.

John Leigh-Pemberton

Cover of *Garden Birds*, published by Ladybird Books Ltd, London, 1967
Printed book, 18 × 12 cm / 7⅛ × 4¾ in
Private collection

Two hungry Eurasian bullfinches (*Pyrrhula pyrrhula*) perch in a blossoming apple tree overlooking the bucolic English countryside on a sunny spring day. The male's pink breast draws a striking contrast with the female's duller brown and grey plumage; they both have jet-black crests. Usually found in pairs, the stocky, bull-headed birds are common to woodland but regularly visit gardens and orchards to feed on budding fruit trees and, consequently, can cause a great deal of damage. Based on an original oil painting, this illustration by British artist John Leigh-Pemberton (1911–97) was produced for his Ladybird children's book *Garden Birds*, designed to help children and adults identify visitors to their gardens. The illustrations, which are accompanied by a key and a short description, show more than forty species, from the blackbird to the wren via flycatchers, thrushes and woodpeckers. This small book was the twentieth title in Ladybird's *Nature* series, launched in 1953 to foster a greater appreciation for the natural world in a way that was both entertaining and informative. Leigh-Pemberton's closely observed studies of wildlife – rendered in a naturalistic style – were ideal, and the series also includes his *Sea and Estuary Birds* (1967), *Heath and Woodland Birds* (1968) and *Pond and River Birds* (1969). For many young Britons, Ladybird books were an important introduction to reading, and the titles, both fiction and non-fiction, played a significant role in shaping an understanding of daily life in postwar Britain.

Family *FRINGILLIDAE*.   Finches

CHAFFINCH   Length 6½ in.
Fringilla coelebs gengleri Klein.   Resident

The Chaffinch is one of our most familiar and cheery
birds. The plumage of the male is brown above,
shading to olive on the rump, and there are very conspicuous white bars on the wings. The breast is pink,
and there is slate-blue on the head behind the eye and
on the crown. In winter the plumage is not so bright.
The female appears smaller, and is duller in colour :
olive-brown with white bars on the wings.
HAUNT. Very general, and particularly near
human habitations, though not thriving in the heart
of cities like the Sparrow.
NEST. Very neat and round, of moss, lichens,
wool, feathers and hair, well worked and felted
together ; in a bush or the fork of a tree.
EGGS. 4 to 6, grey, tinged with pink, and with
brown blotches. April, May.
FOOD. Insects, weed-seed and beech-mast.
NOTES. "Pink", and a questioning "weet".
The song is a rollicking cadence, ending up with a
flourish.

34

Family *FRINGILLIDAE*.   Finches

BULLFINCH   Length 6¼ in.
                                               Resident
Pyrrhula pyrrhula nesa Mathews and Iredale

The Bullfinch
is a handsome,
stout Finch with
deep rose - pink
breast, black
head and blue-
grey back. The
female is duller,
lacking the rosy
breast. Both
birds have
noticeable white
rumps.
HAUNT. Rather
general. In
gardens it is
destructive in
pecking off buds
of fruit trees,
but it also does
good by eating injurious insects and the seeds of
harmful weeds.
NEST. Of twigs, roots and hair ; in a tree or
bush.
EGGS. 4 to 6, greenish-blue, spotted with
red-brown, purple and black. April–June.
FOOD. Chiefly weed-seeds and berries ; also
insects in summer.
NOTES. A single, low, plaintive note. There
is also a low but musical song.

35

Archibald Thorburn

Chaffinch and *Bullfinch*, from *The Observer's Book of Birds* by S. Vere Benson, published by Frederick Warne & Co., London, 1937
Printed book, 14.5 × 9.5 cm / 5¾ × 3¾ in
Private collection

The Observer's Book of Birds was the very first of the hugely popular *Observer's* series, originally published by Frederick Warne & Co. and now numbering a hundred titles. Small enough to fit easily into a pocket, accessible, well-illustrated, and affordable, the series inspired and educated in equal measure, and the volume on birds not only founded the series but remained one of its best sellers. The illustrations, however, were vestiges of another era – literally. They were recycled from a much larger seven-volume handbook intended for indoor use: *Coloured Figures of the Birds of the British Islands* by Lord Lilford, published in parts from 1885 to 1897. The principle illustrator was John Gerrard Keulemans (see p.222), who was forced to retire from the project due to ill health and was succeeded by Scotsman Archibald Thorburn (1860–1935), whose work is shown here. Despite its convenient size, the book's uses as an outdoor identification guide were limited. Half of the illustrations were reproduced in monochrome, and the birds were shown in naturalistic habitats with no attempt to guide the viewer to their characteristic field marks. True field guides, specifically designed for identification, would come later, beginning with the ground-breaking publications of Roger Tory Peterson (see p.325). *The Observer's Book of Birds* was nevertheless universally loved. Not only a book for established birdwatchers, it was owned and cherished by countless households with no particular interest in birds, and ignited a passion for the natural world in the postwar generation.

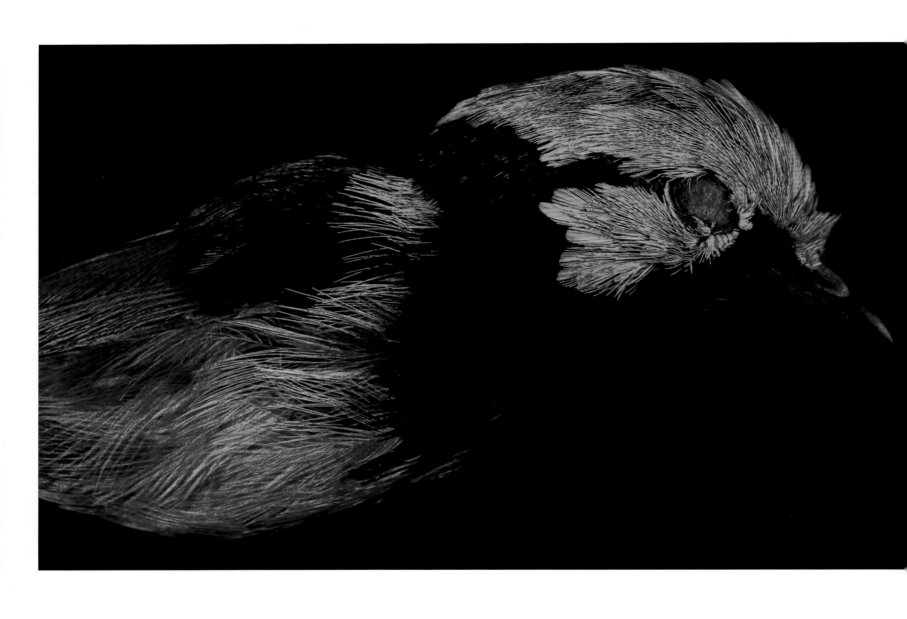

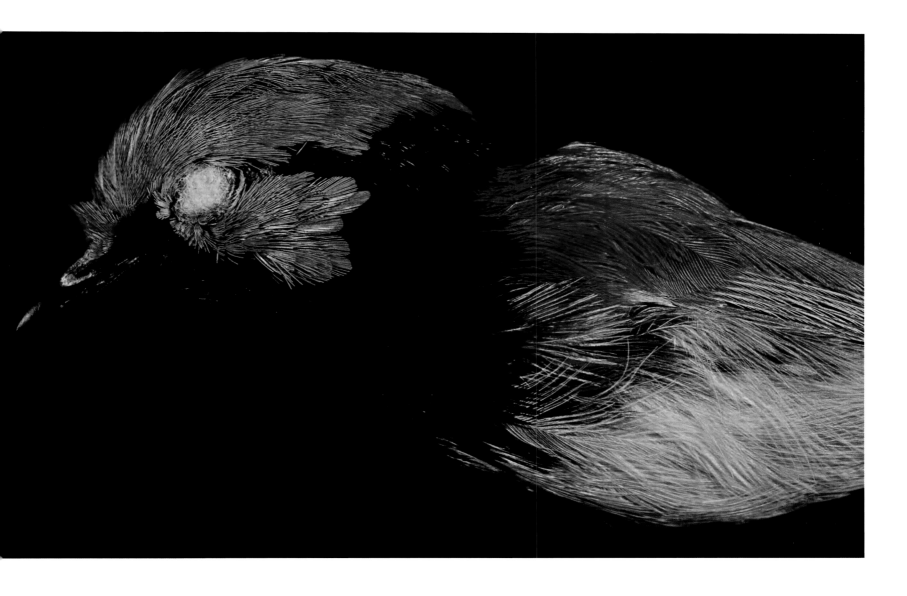

Natural History Museum, London

Project Plumage, 2018
Digital photograph, dimensions variable

A pair of variegated fairywrens (*Malurus lamberti*) face each other, beak to beak, with their feathers – especially those around their empty eye sockets – picked out in strong red and blue light against a black background. While a bird's appearance can be used to determine its species, sex, age and more, what we see differs markedly from what birds actually look like to other birds. Unlike mammals, birds are tetrachromatic. They have four types of cone cells in their eyes, meaning their vision extends into ultraviolet (UV) wavelengths invisible to humans. We have to rely on reflectance under UV light to give us an idea of how birds' plumage might appear in that part of the light spectrum. In these birds from eastern Australia, rather than the vibrant blue head and rufous scapular feathers, the colours appear almost monochrome under UV though still brightly contrasting with the darker feathers of the neck and throat. The birds were photographed by researchers at the University of Sheffield under UV (left) and normal (right) filtered light, at the Natural History Museum's bird collection in Tring, Hertfordshire, as part of 'Project Plumage', a citizen science project that aims to understand the evolution of colours in birds by asking online participants to identify the colours in 50,000 images covering females and males from all bird families. With more than 1 million specimens, the NHM's collection is one of the largest and most diverse in the world, making it ideal for studies spanning the entirety of avian diversity.

Oiva Toikka

Birds by Toikka, 1972–present
Mouth-blown glass, dimensions variable
Iittala collection

Balancing elegant design with expert craftsmanship, these richly coloured glass birds are modern Nordic classics. In the foreground, with dark green stripes hugging its body, resembles an eastern whip-poor-will, which sits next to a transparent glass dove with delicate white markings. Behind these, with its distinctive long beak, stands a green ibis, whose stunning emerald colour is achieved by laying green glass over a milky white base. Among other species, including grouse, terns and ducks, is a graceful white swan and a quirky

brown owl decorated with densely spotted patterning and large orange eyes. The selection represents a tiny fraction of the famous collection created by Oiva Toikka (1931–2019) for the Finnish design brand Iittala. Toikka made his first flycatcher in 1972, adding new birds each year until Iittala established them as a dedicated collection in 1994. Each characterful bird is individually crafted, born from conversations between Toikka and Iittala's master glass-blowers, who respond to the spontaneity of the process rather than to draw-

ings or detailed briefs. While most are inspired by real birds, some are purely imaginative creations, such as the Ruby Bird, seen here with its cranberry colouring and iridescent spots. With several hundred variations, including limited editions like the cobalt glass blue-bird produced between 1991 and 1994, Toikka birds are sought out by collectors worldwide.

J. M. W. Turner

Robin, c.1816
Pencil and watercolour on paper, 14 × 17.7 cm / 5½ × 7 in
Leeds Art Gallery, UK

As a precise depiction of a European robin (*Erithacus rubecula*), this sketch lacks ornithological accuracy, yet it faithfully captures the feisty spirit of the garden bird, which is popular for both its appearance and the fact that it sings nearly all year round. The liveliness of the sketch reflects the genius of its creator: Joseph Mallord William Turner (1775–1851) is one of the most famous English romantic painters, celebrated for his imposing landscapes and seascapes - dramatic representations of such elements as sunshine, storms, high seas and rain - that use a hazy watercolour technique (even though they are oil paintings) to capture effectively the changing moods of the natural world. At the start of his career, Turner made many pencil sketches that were later used as the basis for paintings, often of architectural features such as castles and churches. Aged fourteen he was accepted into the Royal Academy of Art by Sir Joshua Reynolds, and went on to a glittering career, producing famous works such as *The Fighting Temeraire* (1839) and *Rain, Steam and Speed - The Great Western Railway* (1844). Turner's charming study of one of Britain's favourite birds is one of twenty bird portraits prepared for his close friend Walter Fawkes of Farnley Hall near Otley in Yorkshire, which were combined in an album - *The Farnley Hall Bird Book* - in 1850.

John Gerrard Keulemans

Wallace's standardwing, male and female, from *The Malay Archipelago: the land of the orang-utan
and the bird of paradise* by Alfred Russel Wallace, 1869
Engraving, 19 × 23 cm / 7½ × 9 in
Royal Geographical Society, London

The British naturalist Alfred Russel Wallace recorded his delight on first encountering the thrush-sized standard wing in what is now Malaysia: 'I saw a bird with a mass of splendid green feathers on its breast, elongated into two glittering tufts; but, what I could not understand was a pair of long white feathers, which stuck straight out from each shoulder. The four long white plumes ... are narrow, gentle curved ... of a pure creamy white colour. They are about six inches long, equalling the wing, and can be raised at right angles

to it.' Wallace was a commercial collector who shipped specimens to Britain for sale and in 1859, before he returned home, this distinctive bird of paradise of eastern Indonesia had been named in his honour *Semioptera wallacii*, or Wallace's standardwing. While in Malaysia, Wallace also famously sent home a paper outlining the theory of natural selection that was read, alongside that from Charles Darwin, to the Linnean Society in 1858, making him the co-discoverer of the theory of evolution. The female at the top of the

picture is drabber than the male, as is normal for birds of paradise. The availability of food allows females to rear their young independently of males; as a result, female choice over sexual partners pushes the evolution of increasingly elaborate plumage. This print is by John Gerrard Keulemans (1842–1912), one of the six illustrators of Wallace's *The Malay Archipelago* (1869). Dutch by birth, Keulemans lived in England for most of his life.

William T. Cooper

Blue Bird of Paradise, 1991
Acrylic on board, 65 × 50 cm / 25⅝ × 19¾ in
Private collection

'Birds of the gods', as the birds of paradise (Paradis-aeidae) have been called, are some of the most elaborately plumaged, behaviourally remarkable and generally magical birds. Their elaborate mating displays, wild plumage and remoteness – they are found only in the dense forests of New Guinea, eastern Indonesia and northeastern Australia – make them some of the most sought-after species for birdwatchers and naturalists worldwide. This blue bird of paradise (*Paradisaea rudolphi*) is only found in the montane forests of eastern Papua New Guinea. Males have set display locations where they hang upside down, showing two long tail streamers and striking blue tail feathers, bobbing up and down while the female evaluates their performance – and their suitability as a mate. Australian artist William T. (Bill) Cooper (1934–2015) created this image for the 1977 monograph *The Birds of Paradise and Bower Birds* by Joseph Forshaw, showing the distinctive behaviours of each species. Cooper believed that to truly appreciate his subjects, he had to see them for himself. Eschewing painting from photographs, he went on numerous expeditions in Australia, Indonesia and Papua New Guinea to produce detailed illustrations that go so far as to depict the precise species of vegetation and foods linked to each species, aided by his partner the botanist Wendy Price, with whom he often travelled. It is little surprise that Sir David Attenborough called Cooper 'Australia's greatest living scientific painter of birds; he is possibly the best in the world'.

Unknown

Standard ('Alam) in the form of a calligraphic falcon, c.17th century
Perforated gilt copper, 33 × 20.3 cm / 13 × 8 in
Victoria & Albert Museum, London

This 'alam, or standard, would have been mounted on the end of a long staff hung with cloth and carried in religious processions mourning the martyrdom of Imam Husain, grandson of the Prophet Muhammad, at the battle of Karbala in AD 680. Shaped in the form of a falcon, a bird of prey that appears frequently in the literature of Islamic mysticism and was trained to hunt (falconry was practised in Arabia long before the arrival of Islam), they incorporates the tiqe, a sword-like design common to 'alams in the Shia branch of Islam to which Husain belonged. The image of the falcon, made from perforated gilded copper, is created with ornamental calligraphy that praises Ali, son-in-law of the Prophet and father of Husain. The Battle of Karbala, fought against an army loyal to the Umayyad caliph Yazīd, is one of the main historically divisive factors that separate Sunni and Shiite Islam. 'Alams recall the battle standards carried at Karbala by Husain and his followers. This 'alam is believed to have been made in Delhi when India was ruled by the Islamic Mughal empire, between 1526 and 1857. When the dynasty was founded by the Sunni Muslim conqueror Babur, the Deccan - the central part of the subcontinent - had already been ruled for two centuries by Shia sultans. This standard would have been carried by Deccani Shiites in processions during the Muslim month of Muharram, the anniversary of the battle of Karbala.

Unknown

Trophy of an archer's guild, *c.*1500–99
Gold-plated silver, 13.5 × 22 × 3.4 cm / 5¼ × 8⅝ × 1⅜ in
Rijksmuseum, Amsterdam

A silver bird wearing a crown as a choker - a heraldic device signifying a noble rank by marriage rather than birth - raises its wings for take-off. The object originally sat on top of a staff belonging to a civic guard company, likely in the town of Hulst in the Netherlands in the sixteenth century. It was awarded as a prize to the company member who won the annual papegay shooting competition, in which contestants took turns - using a bow and arrow, a crossbow or a gun, depending on the precise nature of the particular 'shooters' guild' - to shoot at a wooden target in the shape of a parrot at the top of a pole. The civic guard were militia, recruited to keep order in towns and to help defend them in times of warfare, so martial skills were highly valued. Here, the silversmith has made the top line of the wings absolutely straight, a nod perhaps towards the accuracy needed to hit the target. The bird is about to take flight as if the archer's arrow itself had been 'nocked', the bowstring taut - just at the moment of the antici-pated release. Finally the tail feathers gently arc, perhaps mimicking the shape of the bow or the flight of the arrow. For these many reasons, and not least because at the time the fletching of the arrow would have been made from goose or turkey feathers, birds and their flight have many metaphorical, and physical, associations with archery.

Maruyama Okyo

Goose and Reeds; Willows in the Moonlight, 1774–1793
Six-panel folding screens, ink, colour and gold on paper, each 153.9 × 354.4 cm / 60⅝ in × 11 ft 7½ in
Metropolitan Museum of Art, New York

Comprising two six-fold screens created twenty years apart, *Goose and Reeds; Willows in the Moonlight* by Maruyama Okyo (1733–95) is an impressive blend of the dominant Kano school of Japanese painting from the mid-fifteenth to mid-nineteenth centuries, with the single-point perspective of European Realism – a style that would be central to the Maruyama and Shijo schools in the late Edo period (1853–67). Okyo was a popular artist during his lifetime, and a well-respected art teacher, founding his own school

in Kyoto in which he trained several well-known Japanese artists. In the right screen, a greater white-fronted goose (*Anser albifrons*) is about to land in a wetland, while in the left screen, willow trees hang over a river whose surface reflects the rippled shape of the moon. Okyo's attention to detail was impressive, and the goose is shown with one brush stroke for each primary flight feather (ten in total). Greater white-fronted geese breed in the Arctic before migrating to temperate areas to winter, relying on bodies of fresh

water, the nearshore and mudflats. As a common winter visitor to most of Japan, numbering in the tens of thousands, the bird would have been a familiar sight in the rivers, ponds and marshes of southern Honshu. The screens capture both the traditional Japanese minimalism and the perspective of the focus, the goose, in true Okyo style.

Raymond Harris Ching

The Kiwi & the Goose, 2010
Oils on composite board, 91.5 × 10.7 cm / 36 × 4¼ in
Private collection

Aesop's Fables have never been illustrated in a more original way than in Raymond Ching's antipodean interpretation, *Aesop's Kiwi Fables*. In this remarkable series, the original animals have been substituted with New Zealand species, all the more bizarre for their vivid hyperrealism. In this tale, the flightless kiwi represents the tortoise who, yearning to fly, asks an eagle – in this case a goose – to carry it aloft. In both cases the burden proves too much, and the luckless passenger spends its final moments regretting its foolish aspirations before falling to its doom. New Zealand artist Ching (born 1939) first sprang to prominence in 1969 as the illustrator of *The Reader's Digest Book of Birds*. Although it was, superficially, just a popular coffee-table book for a general audience, its illustrations were anything but conventional, and they brought to the pages a vibrancy previously unseen in wildlife art. While other artists might have used this initial success as a springboard into regular bird illustration, Ching sprang in the opposite direction. Instead of creating likenesses of birds in their natural environment, he pulls together animals from all corners of the globe in odd compositions, exploring themes of extinction, conservation, folklore and the history of the natural sciences, allowing his imagination and intellect full rein. Never wholly naturalistic but always startlingly real, there is something edgy and rebellious about his work – the artist himself shines through every brushstroke.

227

Charles Francis Annesley Voysey

'Sea Gulls' design for a textile, c.1892
Pencil and watercolour on paper, 5.6 × 5.4 cm / 2¼ × 2⅛ in
Victoria & Albert Museum, London

Although they are reduced to simple shapes and painted as flat silhouettes, these stylized grey gulls (Laridae) with their bright yellow-green bills are instantly identifiable, bobbing along the surface of a blue swirling sea. This textile design is by C. F. A. Voysey (1857–1941), an English architect who was a leading member of the Arts and Crafts movement and a prolific designer of patterns for textiles and wallpapers. Voysey's distinctive designs are characterized by a stylized naturalism, with simple flat shapes in muted colours typical of the movement; natural elements were an important part of interior decoration to counter the industrialized world beyond the home. Birds were among his favourite motifs, and although their forms are simplified for the purposes of his pattern-making they are always identifiable. A review of his work published in 1927 said of his birds, 'We can identify them at once; and the few broad touches and washes by which they are represented usually show us some characteristic of the bird which we had not previously observed. Voysey's version of a particular kind of bird is more like the bird it depicts than the bird itself is.' This design was produced for textile manufacturer A. H. Lee & Sons of Birkenhead, and it was illustrated the following year in the art journal *The Studio*, where Voysey stated his view that birds were acceptable as features of a repeat pattern 'provided they are reduced to mere symbols'.

Martin Parr

GB. England. West Bay: 1996
Photograph, dimensions variable

Two herring gulls (*Larus argentatus*) tuck into a discarded tray of chips as a Union Jack flies in the blue sky beyond in an image that captures an essence of Britishness, rooted in nostalgia for better times. The prolific British photographer Martin Parr (born 1952) has been documenting his homeland for nearly fifty years, visiting seaside resorts, summer fairs and society events, always with a careful eye for images that reveal something about the national identity. It is unsurprising that 2016, the year in which Britain voted to leave the European Union, saw him travelling the country to capture 'Britishness during Brexit'. This older photograph – one of a series from West Bay in Dorset that Parr exhibited in his first commercial gallery show in London – still conveys a sense of rose-tinted sentiment, but it also speaks of the damage humans have caused to the environment and wildlife in recent decades. According to the UK government's Joint Nature Conservation Committee, the number of herring gulls nesting in natural colonies fell by 45 per cent between 1986 and 2018, with changing fishing practices likely to have contributed to this trend. There has been an observed shift inland by these naturally coastal gulls; and their scavenging for food among human detritus is no longer restricted to seaside towns, where they have become bold enough to snatch food from unwary tourists as they eat it outdoors.

Andy Rouse

Kingfisher (Alcedo atthis) *emerging from pool with fish, UK, December, 2015*
Photograph, dimensions variable

Andy Rouse (born 1965) is a British professional photographer specializing in wildlife and aviation. An active champion of conservation, he has been involved in highlighting the plight of endangered species including tigers and mountain gorillas. He is an ambassador for 21st Century Tiger, raising money to fund wild tiger conservation projects, and works with Panthera, an organization devoted to helping protect wild species of cat and their habitats throughout the world. Rouse's dramatic photograph of a common kingfisher (*Alcedo atthis*) makes an immediate impact on the viewer. This species of kingfisher is found through much of Europe and Asia. It is one of some 130 species in this widespread family, only some of which are found in wetland habitats and take a wide variety of vertebrate and invertebrate prey. The bright colours of the common kingfisher seem conspicuous seen close, but provide good camouflage in its reflective watery habitat. The red lower mandible of this stunning bird identifies the individual as a female in full breeding plumage. She has just risen from the water after a successful dive, emerging with a small fish clamped in her bill, probably to take to her brood of hungry young in a nearby nest hole. The shining water droplets gleam like a constellation of stars against the black background, adding an extra cosmic dimension to this instant of wild action.

Arie van 't Riet

Kingfisher Feeding, 2018
X-ray, dimensions variable

With its long, dagger-like bill, disproportionately large head and tiny legs, this bird is instantly recognizable as a common kingfisher (*Alcedo atthis*), even though its dazzling colours have been stripped away in this X-ray image. Once exclusively a tool of the medical and veterinary professions, X-ray photography has an allure that makes it a fine art medium in its own right. Dutch medical physicist-turned artist Arie van 't Riet produces what he calls 'bioramas': X-ray images that re-create the appearance of natural scenes. He

carefully arranges collages of plants and animals that he photographs and colours to create surreal, dreamlike scenarios, reminiscent of shadow puppetry. Although the birds at first glance appear animated, closer inspection shows that these are dead or inanimate specimens positioned to suggest life and movement. Despite their name, the 129 species of kingfisher take a wide variety of prey, including snakes, lizards, invertebrates and even small mammals, and many live nowhere near water. Some inhabit desert

and scrub and a large proportion of the family is found only in tropical forest, far from watercourses. Wherever they live, and whatever they eat, kingfishers predominantly hunt by watching intently from an elevated perch, then dropping down onto their prey. They invariably return with their catch to the same perch and hit it a few times before swallowing. Fish are always turned so that the head end is ingested first, in the direction of the scales.

231

Sarah Stone

*Superb Warbler, c.*1790
Watercolour, 23 × 17.2 cm / 9 × 6¾ in
National Library of Australia, Canberra

It was no mean feat for the British artist Sarah Stone (1760-1844) to capture the characteristic liveliness of Australia's superb fairywren (*Malurus cyaneus*), given that she lived on the other side of the world, in London, had never seen a living specimen and worked only from stuffed examples. During an era of great scientific voyages, when new species were flooding back to England to be classified and catalogued, the talented Stone was one of the very few women to act as a scientific illustrator to depict the new discoveries. She was in her late teens when Sir Ashton Lever engaged her to draw the objects in his renowned natural history and ethnography museum, which became the Leverian Museum. Exceptionally, for a woman, she continued to work as a professional after her marriage in 1789, when she illustrated a collection of birds and other animals shipped from the new colony of New South Wales by surgeon-general John White, for his book *Journal of a Voyage to New South Wales* (1790), hand-colouring the etchings herself. This lively superb fairywren, a male, comes from a different set of paintings, thought to have been made as presentation copies. The bird's vibrant plumage displays Stone's knowledge of pigments – and the bird's suitability as a mate. The fairywren is socially monogamous, but the most promiscuous of birds: males that wear their brilliant blue nuptial plumage longest father the most offspring.

Jeannette Dean Throckmorton

*State Birds and Flowers Quilt, c.*1950
Appliquéd and embroidered quilt, dyed and undyed cotton plain-weave fabrics, cotton embroidery threads,
graphite pencil pattern outlines, 224.6 × 172.7 cm / 88⅜ × 68 in
Art Institute of Chicago, Illinois

Squares of appliqué attached to a large quilt illustrate the forty-eight official birds and flowers of US states existing at the time of its creation. States began selecting official birds in 1927, based on various criteria ranging from birds' ubiquity to their distinctive colour or song. Some choices also had specific historical explanations. Maryland's choice, the Baltimore oriole (*Icterus galbula*), only spends its summers in the state, but its gold and black plumage echoes the colours of the crest of the state's founder, Lord Baltimore. Utah, meanwhile, chose the coastal California gull (*Larus californicus*) because the gulls saved farmers' crops during a cricket infestation in 1848 by arriving in flocks to devour the insects. A few birds represent more than one state: the cardinal (*Cardinalis cardinalis*) has seven, the western meadowlark (*Sturnella neglecta*) six and the northern mockingbird (*Mimus polyglottos*) five, all in the South. A few states also adopted official game-birds, including the wild turkey (*Meleagris gallopavo*, Massachusetts and South Carolina). According to some accounts, the turkey might have been the US national bird, had it been down to Benjamin Franklin, who praised it as 'a respectable bird'. Instead, Congress adopted the bald eagle (*Haliaeetus leucocephalus*), which he condemned as 'a bird of bad moral character'. The quilt's creator, Jeanette Dean Throckmorton (1883–1963), qualified as a doctor in Chicago but had to give up her career at a young age when she lost her hearing.

George Wolfe Plank

Vogue, November 15, 1911
Chromolithograph, 38.7 × 28.5 cm / 15¼ × 11¼ in
Condé Nast, New York

A woman wearing a turban and a long black gown with an ornate bodice and train rides a white peacock whose feathers are styled as a diadem and whose train feathers echo the woman's similarly elaborate garment train in this cover of the fashion magazine *Vogue* from November 1911. This illustration drew on the peacock's long tradition of elegance along with its more contemporary connection with exoticism, which made it a recurrent motif in popular design at the turn of the century and into the 1920s. The woman's clothes reflect the interest in exoticism that swept through the arts and fashion at the time: in 1910 the Ballets Russes had performed *Scheherazade* in Paris and a mania for Orientalism followed. Designers such as Paul Poiret were central to this trend, creating turbans and gowns with a distinctly Ottoman flavour. The Marchesa Casati, an Italian socialite who was legendary for her infamous balls and extravagant and eccentric dress, appeared at one ball as a goddess leading a peacock on a leash. This illustration was created by self-taught American artist George Wolfe Plank (1883-1965), who was a prolific contributor to *Vogue*, working from 1911 until 1936 for both the American and British editions - he moved to England in 1914. The illustration is typical of his fantastical style and of the elongated, sinuous lines of the time, which was influenced by the Aesthetic movement and the ink drawings of Aubrey Beardsley.

Unknown

Uchikake with Phoenix and Birds, c.1868–1912
Silk crepe paste-resist dyed, 174 × 134 cm / 68½ × 52¾ in
Kyoto National Museum

This emerald silk *uchikake*, made in Japan during the Meiji period from 1868 to 1912, features a central phoenix with multi-coloured feathers, surrounded by a flock of other birds including a peacock, dove, hen, herons and other birds. Known as the *hou-ou*, the mythical bird was a popular emblem in Japanese art, having been introduced by the Chinese, most likely during the Asuka period in the mid-sixth to seventh centuries. The phoenix, with its ornate plumage and extravagant tail feathers, was an auspicious symbol of good fortune and longevity and was often associated with the imperial family, particularly the empress. It would remain a popular emblem in the decorative arts, featuring on lacquered boxes and often depicted roosting on paulownia trees or with bamboo. Here it appears on an *uchikake*, a lined robe or outer kimono in silk, often highly decorative and made to be worn by brides or for formal occasions as a loose outer layer. *Uchikakes* were popularized by samurai women in the Kamakura period from 1192 to 1333. Padded or wadded hems would create weight to keep the garment straight and showcase the design to its full potential and the coat was made to trail along on the floor. This flamboyant bird design is created in rice paste-resist applied by hand using what is known as a *tsutsugaki* technique.

Arthur Singer

Hummingbirds, from *Birds of the World* by Oliver L. Austin, 1958–60
Gouache on illustration boards, framed 16.5 × 50.8 cm / 6½ × 20 in
Private collection

Popular books on the 'birds of the world' are rare, and with very good reason: there are around 10,000 species of bird in the world and many of them are small, brown and unremarkable. A book that would satisfy an ornithologist might be too dry and dull for a non-specialist audience, while one that gave over-representation to brightly coloured exotic species would soon be discarded by a serious enthusiast. A classic in its time, *Birds of the World* by Oliver L. Austin was the sort of ambitious book that could be given as a gift to amateur or professional alike and would still be on the recipient's bookcase decades later, well-thumbed and intimately familiar. The idea was so simple it was amazing that no-one had thought of it before: by aiming to include only a minimum number of representative species of most avian families, the book managed to retain its attractiveness and popular appeal while still satisfying the expert. Its principal attraction, however, was the masterly illustrations by the American artist Arthur Singer (1917–90), who grouped species sharing the same habitat, though separated on different continents, into naturalistic tableaux. These hummingbirds, for example, inhabit different geographical areas and altitudes throughout the neo-tropics and would never be encountered together. Because of the book's universal content, it was eminently suitable for a worldwide distribution. *Birds of the World* and all its editions were destined for, and deserving of, their commercial success.

Andy Holden and Peter Holden

Natural Selection, 2018
Mixed media
Temporary installation at Towner Art Gallery, Eastbourne, UK

This monumental arch made of thousands of twigs is an enlarged reconstruction of the bower created by a male bowerbird (Ptilonorhynchidae) transplanted to a gallery and displayed as a work of art. Native to Australia and Papua New Guinea, bowerbirds appear to be creative, and possess a sense of aesthetic beauty. Male birds begin to build a bower early in the mating season, using an elaborate architectural structure and found materials that combine both natural resources and artificial objects discarded by humans. Each male tends to have a favourite colour scheme, which he carefully implements across and around the structure. Not a nest in the traditional sense of the word, the bower is more akin to a stage upon which male birds perform a carefully choreographed dance to attract the females. Through this detailed reconstruction, British artist Andy Holden (born 1982), and his father Peter, an expert ornithologist, emphasize the concept of creativity in animals. Can animals make art? The answer to the question is necessarily inconclusive, but bowerbirds certainly demonstrate that animals can intentionally create objects for aesthetic purposes. In the same way that art objects often display power and status in human society, so the beauty of a well-constructed bower manifests power and status among bowerbirds: females carefully inspect each structure and evaluate their prospective partner's dancing ability before choosing a mate.

Paul Nicklen

Brünnich's guillemots nest in millions along the shores of Cape Fanshawe, Spitsbergen
Photograph, dimensions variable

What could be better than a high-rise with an ocean view? For Brünnich's guillemots (*Uria lomvia*), known as thick-billed murres in North America, it's all part of the routine. Nesting on sheer cliff faces of the circumpolar Arctic in colonies up to 1 million strong, the birds lay a single elongated pyriform egg directly on the rocks, and in colours ranging from white to light blue and turquoise, with spots, streaks or blotches in black, brown or deep violet. With the birds nesting cheek-by-jowl, this variation and diversity in egg colour helps breeding parents know which egg is theirs: females will lay the same colour and pattern through their life. Only fifteen days after hatching, the chicks, then about a quarter of adult size, take their first flight when they leap from the cliffs into the sea below. There, their waiting parents continue to feed them and teach them to dive before migrating to more southerly waters of the northern oceans. This image by Canadian photographer Paul Nicklen (born 1968) shows the huge density of birds on breeding cliffs, and the guano they leave behind. As a Wildlife Photographer of the Year category winner and 2019 inductee to the International Photography Hall of Fame, Nicklen documents the changing Arctic and the conservation of the world's oceans through both his photography and his public speaking and advocacy.

Robert Clark

Flamingo, 2016
Photograph, dimensions variable

American photographer Robert Clark uses his customary sharp focus in his portrait of an American flamingo (*Phoenicopterus ruber*), combined with minute attention to the textures in the bird's brilliant plumage. At rest, the long, flexible neck curves round, allowing the bird to lay its heavy bill amongst the soft feathers of its back. One of six species of flamingo, the American flamingo is found mainly in the islands of the Caribbean, the Yucátan Peninsula of Mexico, along the northern coast of South America and in the Galápagos Islands. Among the largest flamingo species, it grows to a height of 1.5 m (5 ft) and weighs up to 3.6 kg (8 lb). It inhabits shallow salt or brackish water or alkaline lakes, and feeds by filtering algae and aquatic invertebrates, sweeping its large bill from side to side through the water. The bright pink and red colours in its feathers derive from carotenoid pigments found in its food. Clark has established himself as a leading proponent of animal photography. His work can be seen in numerous books, including *Evolution: A Visual Record* (2016) and *Feathers: Displays of Brilliant Plumage* (2016), as well as in leading magazines, including *National Geographic*, for which he has photographed more than forty stories over a period of twenty years, providing several cover images.

Max Ernst

Red Owl, 1952
Oil on canvas, 105.1 × 120.5 cm / 41⅜ × 47½ in
Museum of Contemporary Art, Chicago, Illinois

Two protean forms float amoeba-like in a dense black void. One, as the title indicates, is that of a red owl, although not much of its body is delineated beyond a grey beak and the rough shape of a perched bird. The second form is a shapeless blue blob with two haunted white eyes. This is the creation of the celebrated German surrealist artist Max Ernst (1891-1976), whose work transports his viewers to an otherworldly realm with its own rules. In this alternate reality, Ernst names his owl Loplop

– the name he gives all birds in his paintings, which become something akin to his alter ego or his painted presence in the work. For Ernst, Lolop, and by extension all birds, play a classical role as a transition between his imagination and his fictional world. All owls share large eyes, an adaptation enabling them to see prey, often at night, and adding to their reputation for wisdom. Ernst's red owl has spaces for two large eyes, but the owl's left one is empty and simply reveals the space behind the bird while the

other reflects exactly the colour and texture of the blue form, even echoing one of its 'eyes' with a dash of white. Perhaps this owl, with the bird's traditional associations with knowledge and magic, is bringing a form, an idea or an entity into being, acting as a conduit between its nebulous world and our own.

Konrad von Megenberg

Page 151, from *Das Buch der Natur*, 1481
Woodcut, 31 × 19.3 cm / 12¼ × 7⅝ in
Library of Congress, Washington, DC

The birds in this woodcut from a fifteenth-century compendium are not in every case definitely identified, but they may include (top row, left to right) an eagle, a swan, a European goldfinch (*Carduelis carduelis*) and an Egyptian goose (*Alopochen aegyptiaca*); (second row) a hawk, a stork, a raven and a peacock; (third row) a rose-ringed parakeet (*Psittacula krameri*) and a Eurasian eagle owl (*Bubo bubo*); and (bottom row) a rooster, a common hoopoe (*Upupa epops*) and a Eurasian magpie (*Pica pica*). The plate comes from

Das Buch der Natur ('The Book of Nature'), which was based on a Latin compendium of the same name written by a thirteenth-century Dominican priest, Thomas of Cantimpré. The Bavarian cleric Konrad von Megenberg (1309–74) translated the book into German, making revisions and inserting his own observations, resulting in a comprehensive survey of the natural world as it was known at the time. The eight sections of the book comprise human anatomy and physiology; astronomy and meteorology; zoology; trees; plants;

stones; metals; and bodies of water. These are followed by a section on 'monstrous human races' in the unexplored East. The selection and arrangement of subjects is typical of medieval encyclopaedias. The book was originally a manuscript before being first printed in 1375; these are pages from the second edition. They were printed using a carved block for each page, rather than moveable type. Section Three discusses seventy-two birds, accompanied by this hand-coloured woodcut showing thirteen species.

Maria Sibylla Merian

Heron Encircled by a Snake, with a Worm in his Bill, c.1701–10
Watercolour and white opaque watercolour, with selectively applied gum arabic, on vellum, 37.7 × 30.7 cm / 14⅞ × 12⅛ in
The Morgan Library & Museum, New York

Although its curved bill should be straight, this bird can be identified as a great egret (*Ardea alba*), a species of large heron. It seems remarkably unconcerned by the vivid green snake twining around its neck and body. Certain snakes do adopt this method of defence to the extent of winding themselves tightly around a bird's closed bill, although this egret is more interested in the worm it already holds. There are more than seventy species of heron, including bitterns or egrets, of which about twenty are found in Suriname, on the northeastern coast of South America, where this watercolour was painted by the German-born naturalist and scientific illustrator Maria Sibylla Merian (1647–1717) who noted in the lower right corner that 'This worm-eating bird is named Coximoyanex by the Indians' and that the snake was a 'rat catcher'. In 1699, the fifty-two-year-old Merian moved with her daughter, Dorothea Maria, to the recently established Dutch colony to record its wildlife and plants on behalf of the Burghers of Amsterdam. Merian was already a renowned painter of flowers and insects, having trained under the auspices of her father, the printmaker Matthäus Merian, and stepfather, the painter Jacob Marrel. She published a highly influential treatise on the insects of Suriname in 1705, after an illness forced her return to Europe. Her paintings of the country's other exotic plants and animals, like this example, sold well to Dutch collectors.

Unknown

Cher Ami
Taxidermied carrier pigeon, 24.1 × 27.9 × 14 cm / 9½ × 11 × 5½ in
National Air and Space Museum Archives, Smithsonian Institution, Washington, DC

Celebrated as a war hero, this carrier pigeon (*Columba livia*) was severely wounded during a mission to save a battalion of American soldiers in 1918. Named Cher Ami (French for 'dear friend'), he was one of 600 battlefield messengers employed by the US Army Signal Corps in France during World War I (1914-18). With their speed, agility and remarkable skill for navigating back to their roosts, homing pigeons were valuable military assets. Cher Ami delivered twelve important messages during his service, but it was his last that would make him famous. The 77th Infantry Division had become trapped behind enemy lines in the Argonne Forest without food or ammunition. More than 550 men were surrounded by Germans and being fired on by Allied troops unaware of their predicament. Major Charles W. Whittlesey had already dispatched two messenger pigeons that had been shot down. He released Cher Ami in a last-ditch attempt to call for assistance. An onslaught of enemy bullets left the bird with a pierced breast, a partially severed leg and blind in one eye. But somehow he persevered, arriving at his loft some 40 km (25 miles away) in time to help rescue 194 soldiers. Medics worked furiously to save his life, but were unable to rescue his leg. He died the following year. Cher Ami was awarded the Croix de Guerre medal for his heroism and his body was preserved and mounted; it is now displayed in the Smithsonian Institution.

Neil Armstrong, Edwin 'Buzz' Aldrin and Michael Collins

The Official Emblem of Apollo 11, 1969
Embroidery, Diam. 10.4 cm / 4 in
NASA

In this embroidered patch, a mighty bald eagle (*Haliaeetus leucocephalus*) clutches an olive branch, a traditional symbol of peace, in its talons as it swoops across the moon's surface while, in the background, Earth hangs in space like a small blue marble. This striking image of the national bird of the United States was designed by the crew of Apollo 11 – Neil Armstrong, Edwin 'Buzz' Aldrin and Michael Collins – the first of whom became the first humans to land on the moon on 20 July 1969, while Collins flew the Apollo 11 command module. President John F. Kennedy had announced the historic space mission in 1962, in a bid to demonstrate America's superiority over the Soviet Union in the Space Race during the Cold War. Nevertheless, the patch's design reflects the astronauts' peaceful intentions, and the plaque they left on the moon stressed, 'We came in peace for all mankind.' The eagle image was derived from a *National Geographic* book about birds, which Collins traced using tissue paper, although the initial design, which showed the eagle holding the olive branch in its beak with its talons extended, was considered too aggressive. The final patches were sewn onto flight suits and other pieces of equipment, while the spacesuits carried screen-printed versions of the design. An estimated 650 million television viewers waited as Armstrong guided the lunar module *Eagle* (also named for the national bird) onto the dusty Sea of Tranquillity, announcing its arrival with the words, 'The *Eagle* has landed.'

Attributed to Vincenzo Leonardi

Head of a European Pelican, 1635
Watercolour and body colour over black chalk, 35.5 × 54.4cm / 14 × 21⅜ in
Royal Collection, London

The first of the great seventeenth-century scientific institutions of the European Enlightenment was not the celebrated Royal Society in London, or the Académie des Sciences in Paris. It was the Accademia dei Lincei ('the Academy of the Lynx'), founded in Rome in 1603. Among its associates was Cassiano dal Pozzo, whose high position within the papacy gave him the wealth and connections to pursue his wide-ranging interests – and to achieve a unique ambition. Dal Pozzo had the vision of establishing a collection, not only of rare and curious objects, but also of images of these objects: a picture library as a scholastic resource, containing images of everything from architecture to zoology. He called it his Museo Cartaceo (Paper Museum). Among the thousands of entries were drawings commissioned of living and freshly dead specimens, botanical illustrations, drawings of fossilized wood and some of the first images to be made using a microscope. The emphasis was on the subject matter rather than the artist, and only a single image bears a signature: that of Vincenzo Leonardi (c.1590–c.1646). Nothing is known of the others, though it is probable that Leonardi was responsible for many of the drawings, including this magnificent great white pelican (*Pelecanus onocrotalus*). The pouch of a pelican is the soft, elastic skin called the gular region, between flexible jaws. All birds have a gular pouch, but in pelicans it is much enlarged, and serves as a net for scooping up prey, water and all.

Richard Ross

Booth's Bird Museum Brighton, England, from the series *Museology*, 1986
Photograph, dimensions variable

Most people are familiar with the sublime beauty of taxidermy dioramas that are a highlight of many natural history museums, but far fewer have the opportunity to see behind the scenes. US photographer Richard Ross (born 1947) has travelled around the world to photograph the shelves and drawers that normally only researchers can access. The collection of birds in this image is from the Booth Museum in Brighton. In the mid-nineteenth century Edward Booth, the museum founder, set out to obtain a taxidermy example of every single British bird, resident or migratory. He was about fifty birds short of his target when he died in 1890. Ross's photographs immortalize the contradiction inherent in taxidermy mounts; their 'pretend livingness' and the deadly stillness that characterizes each animal-made object is accentuated by the artificiality of the surroundings. This kind of image asks the viewer to consider the inherent cruelty involved in the study of nature – ultimately, researchers often have to kill the animals they have devoted their lives to studying in order to understand their innermost mysteries. While in the past the study of ornithology required museums to kill large number of birds, many museums today acquire specimens that have died from natural causes. Although the loss of life is lamentable, historic museum collections are of tremendous value to the study of ornithology, and they continue to aid conservation efforts.

Milton Glaser

Birds, 1965
Silkscreen print, 106.7 × 106.7 cm / 42 × 42 in
Private collection

A silhouette of a bird in flight, set against a black background, is filled with smaller bird silhouettes in red, green, blue and white. This silkscreen print was created by legendary US graphic designer and illustrator Milton Glaser (1929–2020) in 1965 and is typical of the graphic Modernism of illustrations and advertising images at the time. Birds are a recurrent motif in Glaser's work – he began working with the Temple University Music Festival in 1968 and would later produce a similar 'peace bird' design as a silhouette filled with exotic flowers. The simple dove silhouette became a popular motif during the middle decades of the twentieth century, reflecting its long history as a symbol of peace in both Christian tradition and ancient Japan. In 1949 a dove designed by Pablo Picasso was chosen as the emblem for the World Peace Congress (see p.187). Glaser co-founded Pushpin Studios in 1954 before setting up in 1974 under his own name, defining the era through work such as a poster of a silhouetted Bob Dylan with a mane of psychedelic hair. His best-known work is probably the 1977 I (heart) NY logo, which was commissioned to help reboot the tarnished image of the city and went on to become an iconic symbol.

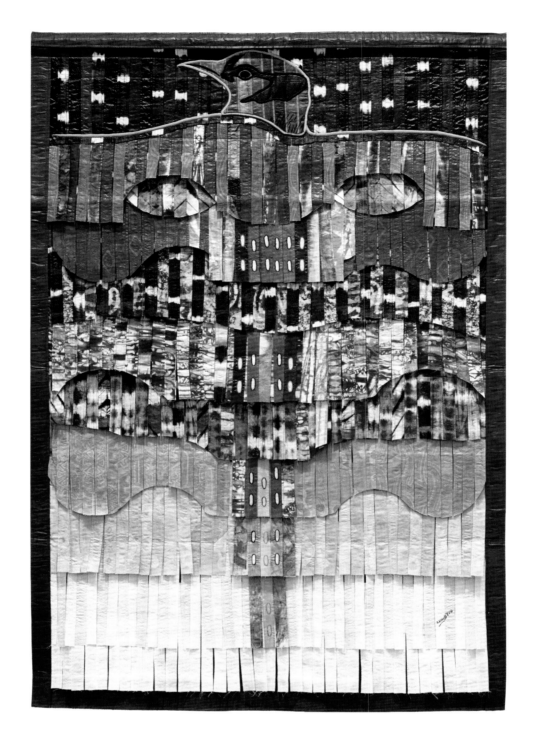

Abdoulaye Konaté

L'Oiseau 2, 2018
Textile, 173.5 × 118 cm / 68¼ × 46½ in
Private collection

A bird ascends into a starry night sky. Its body, defined clearly around its head, beak and shoulders, becomes splintered lower down, as layers of textile tassels hang individually from it. Its wings leave a trail of phantom images behind as it flies upwards, while its body tapers towards its tail, leaving the lighter periwinkle blue below. This colossal abstract work, created in Bamako, the capital of Mali, by the artist Abdoulaye Konaté (born 1953), takes West African textile tradition, deconstructs it and then amplifies it. Each piece is created using formal Malian artisanal techniques and local materials. While the woven cotton and indigo dye speak directly to Mali's cultural heritage, Konaté's works subtly comment on social, religious and political issues in modern-day West Africa, uniting Mali's deep, rich history with contemporary issues such as the AIDS epidemic, globalization and climate change. Konaté's works draw audiences, thanks in part to their vivid colour harmonies: they are beautiful to behold. Yet this beauty acts as a Trojan horse for his critiques of contemporary affairs. Konaté's inspiration from the natural world is clear. The mosaic nature of this piece's fabric mirrors the modular structure of birds' plumage. Just as each feather has its own individual pattern – its own hues, imperfections and errors – so is each piece of fabric, dyed using age-old Malian techniques, unique. Yet, hung together, they act as pieces of a single image, becoming cellular building blocks of a holistic form.

Argnata coccinea Bahamacula. 84

Mark Catesby

The Red Curlew, c.1722-26
Watercolour and body colour over graphite, 37.8 × 27.1 cm / 14¾ × 10½ in
Royal Collection Trust, London

Despite its title – which may reflect the similarity with a curlew's beak – this image actually shows the spectacularly coloured scarlet ibis (*Eudocimus ruber*). The wading bird, which is closely related to the American white ibis (*Eudocimus albus*), lives along the northeastern coasts of South America and nearby islands (it is a national bird of Trinidad and Tobago) and coastal Brazil. The watercolour served as the basis for a plate in the earliest scientific survey of the flora and fauna of the British colonies in the southeast

United States, *The Natural History of Carolina, Florida and the Bahama Islands* (1729-47) by the English-born naturalist Mark Catesby (1682-1749). Catesby travelled widely in Britain's southern colonies, plus Jamaica and the Bahamas, between 1712 and 1726, documenting with great accuracy many plants and animals unknown to Europeans, despite being untrained as an artist. Sometimes known as the 'father of American ornithology', Catesby was one of the first naturalists to suggest that birds migrated; it had been thought

previously that they hibernated. One of the great achievements of eighteenth-century natural science, the *Natural History* was initially acclaimed for introducing Europeans to new species; today, in contrast, it serves as a reminder of how many of those species are now extinct, including the passenger pigeon (*Ectopistes migratorius*, see pp.180-1) and the Carolina parakeet (*Conuropsis carolinensis*).

Unknown

Hand-held clapper with Bird of Prophecy, 16th–19th century
Bronze, 32.5 × 11 × 12 cm / 12¾ × 4⅜ × 4¾ in
British Museum, London

This figure of a bird on a short, cylindrical staff was cast by the Edo people of southern Nigeria, using a wax model to form a clay mould into which the molten bronze was poured, melting and replacing the wax. The object is an ideophone, a musical instrument played by grasping its shaft and striking the beak of the bird with a mallet during the festival of the Bird of Prophecy, held over several weeks before the start of the rainy season. According to the Edo story, in a battle between the kingdoms of Idah and Benin in the early sixteenth century, a bird was heard to utter cries predicting that Benin would be defeated. But the king of Benin refused to accept the prophecy and had the bird killed before going on to win the battle. The Bird of Prophecy, or Bird of Oro, thus testifies to the power of the king to triumph over destiny. It has been variously identified as an African wagtail (*Motacilla aguimp*), a type of kingfisher, an ibis, an African fish eagle (*Haliaeetus vocifer*), a pin-tailed whydah (*Vidua macroura*), a white-tailed ant thrush (*Neocossyphus poensis*), a cattle egret (*Bubulcus ibis*) and, most likely, an African pied hornbill (*Tockus fasciatus*). It has also been assumed to be none of these, but rather a magical construct, combining elements of several different birds.

G. Douanne

I Am a Brave War Hen, 1916
Chromolithograph, 56 × 38 cm / 22 × 15 in
Library of Congress, Washington, DC

A broody black hen sits proudly atop a humorously large pile of fresh eggs beneath an exhortation to 'take care of the farmyard', while the caption below reads 'I am a brave war hen. I eat little and produce a lot.' The poster, issued in the middle of World War I (1914-18) by the French Comité National de Prévoyance et d'Economies, was designed by a sixteen-year-old schoolgirl as part of a competition to use young people's artwork in the propaganda drive to recruit the entire population to contribute toward France's existential struggle against Germany. Signed G. Douanne, nothing else is known about the artist except that she was a pupil of the City of Paris Girls' School. Her simple image is striking in its sophistication, employing bold lines and contrasting colours, with a few blue strokes describing the hen's wings. By 1916, food shortages were widespread in France, with prices skyrocketing in major cities, and conserving valuable resources became increasingly important. Colourful posters by outstanding graphic artists appeared everywhere, encouraging citizens to do their part: whether by depositing their gold, donating to aid organisations or, as here, grasping the importance of agricultural production. Chickens' eggs were a rich source of protein from birds that took up little space, required minimal food and care – and kept laying, unlike animals that had to be killed for meat.

René Magritte

A Variation on Sadness, 1957
Oil on canvas, 50 × 60 cm / 19¾ × 23⅝ in
Private collection

Which came first, the chicken or the egg? Many paintings by the Belgian Surrealist master René Magritte (1898–1967) revel in unanswerable questions: there is a good reason why he is known as the philosopher who swapped the pen for the brush. The likes of Aristotle and Plutarch spent considerable time addressing the 'chicken and egg question' without coming to any sensible conclusion. Is this 'the variation of sadness' to which Magritte refers in his enigmatic title, or is he concerned with altogether weightier questions about

the origin of life itself? Modern evolutionary biology is able to address this conundrum. For millions of years, most terrestrial animals led amphibian lives. While they could temporarily roam dry land to feed, their soft-shelled eggs meant that reproduction could only happen in water. Hard-shelled eggs, lined with amniotic sacs, emerged roughly 312 million years ago. This evolutionary advancement enabled these 'amniotes' to lay eggs on dry land, and thus colonize new territories. From an evolutionary perspective, it is quite clear the

egg came first, and was already present in crocodiles, turtles, snakes, lizards and dinosaurs long before the first birds evolved. The red junglefowl (*Gallus gallus*), native to Southeast Asia, was domesticated roughly 10,000 years ago and was the principal wild ancestor of all domesticated chicken varieties. Unlike other wild birds, hens have been selectively bred over millennia to lay eggs continually, regardless of the time of the year.

Rob Cottle

Jazz Wings – Atlantic Puffin in Flight, 2019
Photograph, dimensions variable

The Atlantic puffin (*Fratercula arctica*) is surely one of the world's most photographed bird species. And the island of Skomer, off the coast of Wales, is one of the most accessible areas for those wanting to photograph puffins, be they non-specialist day visitors or professionals such as the Welsh Rob Cottle, self-avowed lover of tea and hater of rain. Because puffins use their wings for underwater propulsion to depths down to 65 m (210 ft), their wings are smaller than would be ideal for flight, so they need to be flapped fast, around 400 times per minute, to keep the bird aloft. That makes the slower flight speed required for an elegant landing difficult. Even with wings spread and webbed feet thrust forwards to serve as air brakes, this puffin Cottle has captured preparing to land on Skomer will almost certainly topple forward onto its bill when it touches down. An innovative citizen science project coordinated by the UK's Royal Society for the Protection of Birds (RSPB) has capitalized on the puffin's photogenic qualities and its habit of carrying several fish in its bill to the colony. The RSPB invites any photographers to submit images of fish-carrying puffins to its Puffarazzi website. In 2019, 825 people did so, submitting 2,718 photos from 49 colonies. It is hoped that the images will enable researchers to assess how the puffins' diet varies geographically and how it may be changing as seas warm.

Unknown

Hacha, *c.*AD 600–1000
Stone, 25.4 × 53.3 × 6.35 cm / 10 × 21 × 2½ in
Minneapolis Institute of Art, Minnesota

The ring around the eye of this stone bird's head, or *hacha* (from the Spanish word for 'axe') may represent a parrot or macaw, suggesting a link to the mythological Hero Twins Hunahpu and Xbalanque of the Maya creation story. A stone *hacha* represented an ornamental attachment to a U-shaped yoke of leather, cotton or wood, worn around the hips by competitors in Mayan ball games to deflect a hard rubber ball across an I-shaped stone court. Teams of between two and six players used only the right hip, elbow and knee to prevent the ball from touching the ground. The *hacha* originated in Veracruz, though they also occur in Classic Maya art. In the myth, the Hero Twins were asked by the sky god, Huracan, to dispatch a vain, arrogant bird god called Vucub Caquix, or Seven Macaw. Seven Macaw claimed to be the sun or moon, and had amassed a vast following of worshippers. The twins shot him in the jaw with a blowgun while he perched in a tree, but he was only wounded and managed to tear off Hunahpu's arm. The twins then invoked a pair of 'grandparent' gods, who approached Seven Macaw to ask for the return of the arm, saying that they were merely poor peasant dentists. Seven Macaw demanded that his jewelled teeth, which had been loosened by the twins' blowgun, be repaired, but the 'grandparents' replaced his teeth with corn kernels instead, and he died of shame.

Unknown

Bird, c.1950
Earth pigments on two bark panels linked by bamboo rods and cane thongs, 110 × 70 cm / 43¼ × 27½ in
National Gallery of Victoria, Melbourne

The living and the dead are seamlessly linked through the myth and magic of the traditional spiritual beliefs of the people of Papua New Guinea. This painting of a spirit bird, an ancestral or mythological figure, possibly by the artist Wiski Busengin Woknot (c.1920–76), would have been one of many covering the ceiling of a men's ceremonial house in Kambot village; Kambot is home to the Ap Ma people and lies on the banks of the Keram River, a tributary of the Sepik River of Papua New Guinea. The primary figure is in the form of a hornbill, surrounded by sun, waterlily and bird-egg motifs displayed in semi-abstract designs that represent characters and incidents in myths. Kambot village was first visited by Europeans in 1912–13, during the German-led Sepik River Expedition, and since then, Ap Ma tribal art has been collected by museums and galleries around the world; their great ceremonial houses with their significant artwork have all but disappeared. The country's only hornbill is the large, conspicuous Papuan hornbill (*Rhyticeros* *plicatus*). In flight, its wings make a loud rushing noise and its guttural calls carry far though the rainforest. Like all hornbills, it has a unique nesting habit: the female plasters up the entrance to her tree-hole nest, leaving only a narrow opening through which the male feeds her during the incubation and nestling periods. Some tribal groups still hunt the hornbill for food and use its feathers in headdresses and its impressive beak for adornment.

Maude White

The Cormorant, from *Brave Birds: Inspiration on the Wing,* 2018
Cut paper
Private collection

Presented in negative colours, white against a background of black, a cormorant (Phalacrocoracidae) stands erect, with its wings stretched away from its body, its feathers cast downwards, which is a behaviour thought to help the semi-aquatic species to dry its feathers out following a dive to forage eels and other fish. The intricate paper portraits of birds by American paper artist Maude White (born 1986) are all cut by hand, achieving such a remarkable degree of delicacy that some of the birds' wings become translucent.

Her work is inspired by the hidden patterns that abound in nature, but her technique is well suited to birds. The paper interacts with light, in much the same way that birds themselves rely on the diffraction and reflection of light off their feathers to appear as vivid greens and blues. This illustration comes from a book featuring sixty-five cut paper birds, each with an uplifting passage of text to encourage perseverance and hope in the reader. The cormorant, White comments, prompts us to set boundaries, ensuring that we allow

time for enjoyment in our lives; the lyrebird to appreciate different sorts of beauty; the swan to appreciate that we can be many things; the great horned owl (*Bubo virginianus*) to be attentive and flexible. White's use of negative space mirrors the importance of this feature within the skeletal architecture of birds: without the hollow spaces that run through birds' bones, they would be too heavy to fly.

Greg Lecoeur

Cape Gannet Hunting Underwater Sardines Baitball Offshore Port St Johns in South Africa, 2019
Photograph, dimensions variable

Cape gannets (*Morus capensis*) dive in pursuit of sardines that have been herded into a so-called baitball, probably by dolphins, off the coast of South Africa. Baitballs usually only last about ten minutes, but provide most of the fish with safety in numbers in the face of threats. From May to July, sardines – actually Southern African pilchards – move north in the Agulhas Current along the eastern seaboard of South Africa in shoals that may be several kilometres long. The vast numbers attract predators from the deep,

including dolphins, bronze whaler sharks and Bryde's whales, and from the sky, where gannets are prominent. As a breeding species, cape gannets are all but confined to Namibia and South Africa, the largest colony of some 140,000 birds being on Malgas Island, South Africa, the name of which comes from the Afrikaans for the species, which translates into English as 'mad goose'. Comparable derogatory names have been attached to the gannet's tropical relatives, the boobies (see p.279), which were easily hunted at their

colonies by sailors in the past. The cooler-water and similar-looking relatives of the cape gannet are the northern gannet (*M. bassanus*) of the North Atlantic and the Australasian gannet (*M. serrator*) of Australia, New Zealand and some Pacific islands. This image, by acclaimed French underwater photographer Greg Lecoeur (born 1977), won the Silver Award in the Bird Behaviour category of the 2020 Bird Photographer of the Year competition.

Frank Hurley

Victoria Penguin and Nest, c.1913
Photograph, 45.5 × 33.5 cm / 18 × 13¼ in
National Gallery of Australia, Canberra

This seemingly straightforward image of a slightly belligerent southern rockhopper penguin (*Eudyptes chrysocome*) and its nest belies the groundbreaking story behind it. The photograph was taken on the sub-Antarctic Macquarie Island by the Australian photographer James Francis 'Frank' Hurley (1885–1962) during the Antarctic Expedition of 1911–14, led by Douglas Mawson, which tried to reach the Magnetic South Pole. Joining the expedition was a natural step in Hurley's photography career, which began in 1905

in postcards. He developed a reputation for taking risks to secure sensational images, and his appetite for adventure led him to the Antarctic. (Hurley was also the photographer for Ernest Shackleton's ill-fated Trans-Antarctic Expedition, which set sail in 1914 and was marooned until August 1916.) The wind often made conditions for taking images difficult, as Mawson relates in his book *The Home of the Blizzard*: 'To get Hurley and his bulky camera back to the hut, we formed a scrum on the windward side and with

a strong "forward" rush beat our formidable opponent.' Both southern and northern (*E. moseleyi*) rockhopper pengins have red eyes, yellow spiky eyebrows and a bounding gait. Data from historic expeditions such as Hurley's is helping scientists understand how life on earth is changing. The global population of rockhoppers is estimated to have decreased by several million pairs since the early part of the twentieth century, when this image was taken.

Hans Schmoller

Scrapbook pages showing logo designs by Jan Tschichold, 1949–51
Collaged paper with ink annotations
The Penguin Archive, University of Bristol

These characterful penguins are instantly recognizable as the iconic Penguin Books logo. Gathered here on scrapbook pages of production manager and later director of Penguin Hans Schmoller, the stylised black and white birds epitomize the 'dignified flippancy' Allen Lane and his brothers aimed to achieve when they established the British publishing house in 1935. Inspired by the German publisher Albatross Books, Penguin aimed to make book ownership more accessible by introducing inexpensive paperback editions of quality literature. The orange and white colour scheme and original logo were conceived by office junior Edward Young, based on studies made at London Zoo focussing on the birds' black and white 'tuxedo' markings. These are an adaptation, camouflaging them underwater, from predators such as seals and from the fish that they hunt themselves in the wild. Variations of his drawing were used until the late 1940s, when renowned German typographer and graphic designer Jan Tschichold (1902–74) standardized Penguin's visual identity. Tschichold elegantly refined Young's bird, streamlining its pudgy body, raising its head and adding a prominent pupil to its inquisitive eye. Variations, including some with oval frames, adapted the design for spines, covers and title pages. Tschichold also redesigned the logos for Penguin's other bird-inspired imprints: Pelican (non-fiction) and Puffin (children's). Penguin revolutionized publishing and its logo helped it become one of the industry's strongest brands.

Giacomo Balla

Flight of the Swallows, 1913
Gouache on cardboard, 49 × 69.5 cm / 19¼ × 27⅜ in
Kröller-Müller Museum, Otterlo, Netherlands

Painted with a flurry of loose brushstrokes, this dynamic composition captures the darting and diving movements of swallows in flight (though an ornithologist would probably identify them as swifts). Working in an experimental style, the Italian artist Giacomo Balla (1871–1958) painted the birds' trajectory as a sequence of consecutive moments, a technique inspired by the photographs of Étienne-Jules Marey (see opposite), who pioneered a process of making successive exposures on a single photographic plate in order to capture movement. Balla was one of the core exponents of Futurism, an Italian avant-garde movement that sought to celebrate motion and speed through new methods of representation. In seeking to show the birds' rapid movements, he pushed his representation to the edge of abstraction, reflecting the Futurists' desire to establish a new visual language appropriate for the modern age. Balla's addition of undulating white lines adds to the sense of agitated movement, while a limited palette reduces the small birds' blue plumage and red throats into a range of shadowy greys, causing them blend into the building behind. Swallows are agile birds, spending much of their time on the wing, soaring and swooping as they pursue flying insects. Balla has simplified their long, curved wings, forked tails and slender bodies to such an extent that they appear almost like diagrammatic symbols. The image is one of at least sixteen studies of the birds that Balla painted in the years immediately before the outbreak of World War I (1914–18).

Étienne-Jules Marey

Bird Flight, Duck Landing, c.1886
Silver gelatin print, 4.7 × 7.9 cm / 1⅞ × 3⅛ in
Cinémathèque Française, Paris

A fascination with flight, and particularly how bird flight could help human flight, lies behind this remarkable sequence of photographs showing in a single image the rapid contortions of the wings of a duck as it lands. In the 1880s, French physicist Étienne-Jules Marey (1830-1904) pioneered chronophotography, an innovative photographic process that allows multiple exposures to be made on a single photographic plate in rapid succession. The technology, which would become foundational in the development of cinema, helped Marey reveal for the first time details of the locomotion of birds and other animals that had hitherto been invisible to the human eye. Marey originally drew birds in flight using a pantograph, a device that seemed to 'freeze' their movement, but he turned to photography after seeing Eadweard Muybridge's famous sequential photographs of animals in motion. Marey's chronophotographic gun could record twelve consecutive frames per second, and he published his substantial research into wings and flight in 1890 as *Le Vol des Oiseaux* ('The Flight of Birds'). Although not as well known as Muybridge's photographic studies, Marey's images proved inspirational to the Wright Brothers in their pursuit of powered flight, as well as to the work of Thomas Edison, the Lumière brothers, who pioneered the first moving images, Marcel Duchamp and the Futurist painter Giacomo Balla (see opposite).

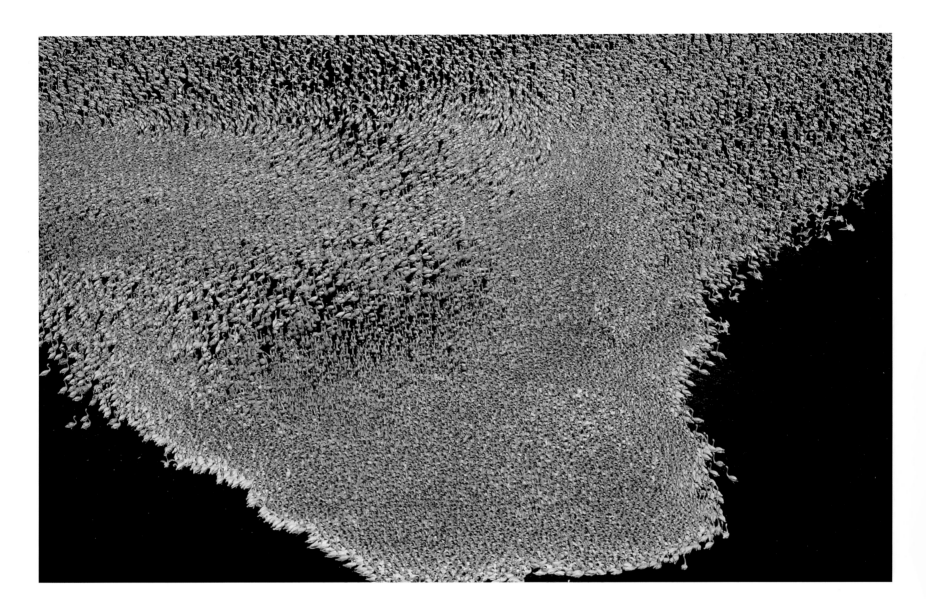

Yann Arthus-Bertrand

Pink Flamingos at Lake Nakuru, Kenya, 2003
Photograph, dimensions variable

A peninsula of pink pours downwards against a colourless background. Patchy in sections, the rosy mass darkens and lightens as the concentration of elements that make up the carpet of colour increases and decreases. At the lighter fringes, unmistakable outlines reveal themselves and slowly it becomes clear that what could easily be a heavily magnified view of microbes or the scaly skin of a reptile actually shows innumerable lesser flamingos (*Phoeniconaias minor*) taken from a great height. The birds are gathered in extraordinary numbers to forage in the shallow waters of Lake Nakuru, part of the Kenyan Lake System, a highly biodiverse area that provides a refuge for thirteen globally threatened species of bird. This image comes from the celebrated *Earth from Above* photographic project by the French photographer and environmentalist Yann Arthus-Bertrand (born 1964). Begun in the 1990s and sponsored by UNESCO, the project uses aerial photographs to highlight the beauty and fragility of the natural world. In a single image, Arthus-Bertrand offers a holistic representation of the whole Lake Nakuru ecosystem. Although the arresting pink of the flamingos draws attention to the huge numbers of birds - at least 2 million gather to feed in Kenya's lakes - this coloration is caused by the beta-carotene pigment deposited in the birds' feathers by the algae they eat. Thus, this mass of colour is directly caused by the smallest members of the ecosystem: the invisible, microscopic animals the flamingos feed on.

Sebastião Salgado

Colony of Chinstrap and Macaroni Penguins with Mount Michael,
an Active Volcano Behind, Saunders Island, South Sandwich Islands, 2009
Silver gelatin print, dimensions variable

Encapsulating life amid bleakness, this image of penguins in the South Sandwich Islands was created as part of the 2004-11 *Genesis* project conceived by Brazilian photographer, Sebastião Salgado (born 1944). The project aimed to offer unblemished images of nature and humanity, and followed Salgado's harrowing 1980s images of workers in Brazil's Serra Pelada gold mine. Penguins are quintessentially birds of the southern hemisphere. Among the eighteen species, only the adélie (*Pygoscelis adeliae*) and emperor (*Aptenodytes forsteri*) nest farther south than the descriptively named chinstrap (*P. antarcticus*). Chinstraps - despite the photograph's title, no macaroni penguins (*Eudyptes chrysolophus*) are visible among the birds in the foreground - largely subsist on a diet of small crustacea and krill, which are also the key food of great whales. Whether commercial harvesting of krill will negatively impact krill - and hence chinstrap - populations remains uncertain. Home to around 1.3 million pairs, the stronghold of the chinstrap penguin is the South Sandwich Islands, in the Southern Atlantic, south of the strong westerly winds known as the Roaring Forties, in the windier-still Furious Fifties. Coupled with South Georgia in a British Overseas Territory, the South Sandwich Islands were first sighted by Captain James Cook in 1775 on his second voyage, and named after the First Lord of the Admiralty of the time, John Montagu, Fourth Earl of Sandwich.

Tracey Emin

Roman Standard, 2005
Bronze, beak to tail: 10.2 × 17.2 cm / 4 × 6¾ in; pole 4 m / 13 ft
Scottish National Gallery of Modern Art, Edinburgh

A nondescript bronze bird – possibly a starling – perches at the top of a pole in this unconventional and yet powerful work. The British artist Tracey Emin (born 1963) subverts the traditional aesthetic of the Roman standard into a monument to feminine vulnerability. Carried into battle by Rome's legions, the standard was an emblem of war. It played an important role as a rallying point on the battlefield, a marker of identity and a symbol of pride. Atop the tall pole often stood a model of a bird, usually an eagle,

a symbol of the power of Rome – and of the masculine. Emin's body of work has usually centred on her own experiences as a woman subjected to violence and abuse. Many of her controversial drawings and quilt works address patriarchal power and invite us to consider the role vulnerability plays in our daily lives. Her *Roman Standard* is a far cry from the imperial pomp of its historic precedent. Substituting the spread-winged eagle of the Roman empire with a very ordinary bird, Emin reinterprets a militaristic

symbol as one of hope, faith and spirituality. The sculpted bird, often at a glance mistaken for a live one, suggests calm, peace and contemplation. Rather than attracting attention to itself, it blends in. As the artist claims, 'I wanted something that had a magic and an alchemy, something which would appear and disappear and not dominate'.

Alec Soth

Cammy's View, Salt Lake City, 2018
Photograph, dimensions variable

In this evocative image by internationally acclaimed US photographer Alec Soth (born 1969), a loose cockatiel (*Nymphicus hollandicus*) looks at the outside world through the windowpane of a conservatory. To the right of the windowsill, a stack of thick religious books counterbalances the lightness implied by the body of the bird. From Christianity to Islam and Buddhism, birds have often symbolized the human soul. Bird wings especially are seen as an incarnation of our desire to free ourselves from material constrictions,

to transcend our earth-bound existence and elevate ourselves closer to God. Soth's image, however, seems to imply a contradiction. In this image the bird is simultaneously kept safe by its captive state – perhaps in an allusion to the rules and limitations religion, as symbolized by the books, might impose upon an individual's life. The cockatiel seems to turn to the viewer in a melancholic way, as if asking for the window to be opened. While parrots have been domesticated for over 5,000 years, cockatiels are a relatively recent

addition to the range of companion birds. Native to Australia, the cockatiel was first classified in 1793 and subsequently imported to Europe as a pet in the early nineteenth century. Like other species of parrots, cockatiels are extremely smart and have sophisticated personalities. They have a good memory, can mimic human language and can problem-solve by using rudimentary tools.

David Doubilet

Chinstrap and Gentoo Penguins, Danco Island, Antarctica, 2011
Photograph, dimensions variable

Among the most aquatic of birds, penguins have long captivated photographers and scientists alike. Although they are not restricted to the cold waters of the Antarctic and Southern Ocean (they live as far north as the Galápagos Islands), they are closely associated with icebergs and the rugged coasts of *Terra Australis*. American underwater photographer David Doubilet (born 1946) has spent fifty years documenting the natural world, above and below water, for *National Geographic*, including a striking series of images from

Danco Island, off the Antarctic Peninsula. Positioning himself at the interface of the sea and sky, Doubilet perfectly captures the environment that is home to these chinstrap (*Pygoscelis antarctica*) and gentoo (*P. papua*) penguins. Danco Island, in the frigid waters of the Gerlache Strait, was named after the Belgian geophysicist Émile Danco, who died during a survey of the region by the Belgian Antarctic Expedition in the late 1890s; it was home to the British Antarctic Survey's Station O from 1956 until 1959. Doubilet's

photograph also captures the harsh Antarctic environment that faced the Belgian and British expeditions, but which for the penguins is their natural element: grey brooding skies and frigid blue waters. The seasonal productivity of these waters, booming in the summer with fish, krill and other marine life, is what draws the penguins to land, as they exploit the natural abundance of prey to feed their chicks.

Carl Cotton

Marsh Birds of the Upper Nile, 1953
Mixed media installation
Field Museum, Chicago, Illinois

For more than seventy years, visitors to Chicago's Field Museum of Natural History have been transported to a clear day on the marshy edge of Lake Kyoga, a shallow lake that forms part of the course of the White Nile in central Uganda, where a collection of thirty-one birds hunt, graze, soar or parent beneath the papyrus and among the floating waterlilies. In this detail from the diorama, a shoebill (*Balaeniceps rex*) peers at visitors, perhaps digesting a recent meal of lungfish and in turn is observed by a group of grey-crowned cranes (*Balearica regulorum*), while a long-toed lapwing (*Vanellus crassirostris*) stands purposefully atop a lily pad, chaperoning her chick. An African openbill (*Anastomus lamelligerus*) searches the shallow water for more snails to prey upon, while an African fish eagle (*Haliaeetus vocifer*) tracks its prey from the sky. The dynamic scene remains as vivid and fresh as when Carl Cotton (1918–71) created it between 1951 and 1953. Cotton was the first African-American to hold a position as a taxidermist at the Field Museum, where he spent twenty-four years crafting detailed work across the breadth of specimens at the museum. He was a talented taxidermist, responsible for outstanding recreations of living creatures both in the Field Museum and elsewhere across North America, where taxidermy and dioramas were popular ways to display natural history specimens. Cotton prepared exhibitions on reptiles, birds and even insects, although this Nile Marsh diorama is considered his masterpiece.

Roelant Savery

Landscape with Birds, 1629
Oil on panel, 42 × 58.5 cm / 16½ × 23 in
Kunsthistorisches Museum, Vienna

Numerous birds from around the globe occupy a pond, its shores and the air above, in a sun-filled, mountainous landscape. The Dutch painter Roelant Savery (1576-1639) was born in Courtrai (now in Belgium) before moving to Haarlem then Amsterdam, finally becoming court painter to Emperor Rudolf II in Prague in 1601. Rudolf's court was a hotbed for arts and sciences and there was an insatiable interest in the natural world. Savery will have seen many of these birds for the first time in the Emperor's

menagerie, and although some of his depictions are a little quirky, most are clearly recognizable. Next to the more common ducks, geese, storks, swans and herons, there are a great bustard (*Otis tarda*), a turkey, a peacock, a cassowary, grey-crowned cranes (*Balearica regulorum*), pelicans, macaws, ostriches and, high in the sky, a pair of birds of paradise. On the shore to the right is a dodo (*Raphus cucullatus*). Reportedly, a live dodo was brought to Amsterdam from Mauritius in 1626, when Savery was living in

Utrecht, and he may have travelled to Amsterdam to see this curiosity. More likely, however, his model was a stuffed bird – perhaps a little too stuffed, as research suggests that dodos were not as plump as Savery would have us believe. While this paradisiacal landscape clearly is the product of Savery's imagination, composed with the aid of numerous studies, he made it look as natural as possible and the result would have filled contemporary viewers with wonder.

Aert Schouman

Head of a Cockatoo, c.1760
Watercolour
Rijksmuseum, Amsterdam

Cockatoos (Cacatuidae) have inspired artists for centuries since their first appearance in Western art in Andrea Mantegna's *Madonna della Vittoria* from 1496, now in the Louvre in Paris. Since then, the white bird with its striking crest has regularly provided an exotic element in history pieces, still lifes, portraits and genre scenes. Cockatoos originate from Australasia and surrounding regions – the earliest mention in Europe dates from the thirteenth century – and the English name derives from the Dutch *kaketoe*, which was adopted in Malaysia by seventeenth-century seafarers as the Dutch built an empire in Asia. The species depicted here is a salmon-crested cockatoo (*Cacatua moluccensis*) from Indonesia, then a Dutch colony. Exotic birds and domestic ones were among the favourite subjects of the prolific painter and draftsman Aert Schouman (1710-92). Schouman often drew from life in various Dutch menageries and aviaries, among them that of the Stadholder, William V, for whom he decorated an entire room with large landscape paintings populated by exotic animals and birds, including a cockatoo. The study illustrated here is part of a series of birds and monkeys that includes similar portraits of various parrots, although Schouman typically drew the entire bird in fine detail, often in a tree or with a landscape background. This study may have been intended as a model for an illustration in a publication on natural history, but eventually does not appear to have been used.

Joseph Cornell

Aviary – Cockatoo and Watches, c.1948
Wood, paint, glass, metal and printed-paper collage, with music box,
41.2 × 43.4 × 11.4 cm / 16¼ × 17⅛ × 4½ in
Private collection

A salmon-crested cockatoo (*Cacatua moluccensis*) perches on a branch surrounded by armless clock faces. This fantastical situation is the work of Joseph Cornell (1903–72), an American artist strongly influenced by Surrealism. Cornell began working with display boxes in the early 1930s, creating a hybrid between natural history dioramas and modern-day cabinets of curiosities, in which disparate found and collected objects are juxtaposed. This box is part of a series called *Aviary*, in which lithographs of parrots cut from books are surrounded by unusual and everyday objects. In place of the romanticized aesthetics that characterized Cornell's earlier boxes, *Aviary* includes more modern and brighter, geometric compositions. This series of boxes, inspired by a visit to a pet shop in Manhattan, is a reflection on rationality, timelessness and the impossibility of knowing what a parrot might be thinking. By juxtaposing a range of everyday objects to images of parrots, Cornell alludes to the mystery of the birds' intellect and the inadequacy of human language to access or represent the complexity of animal minds. Originally from the Australasian region, cockatoos first arrived in Europe as early as the thirteenth century and, because of their bright intelligence and innate curiosity (along with their exclusivity and expense) became popular pets with the aristocracy of the seventeenth and eighteenth centuries. Cockatoos can mimic sounds and human language, something that fascinated Surrealist artists.

Katharina Fritsch

Hahn/Cock, 2013
Fibreglass, 440 × 440 × 150 cm / 173¼ × 173¼ × 59 in
Temporary installation, Trafalgar Square, London

A gigantic, solemn-looking cockerel cast in blue fibreglass gazes out from its plinth over London's Trafalgar Square in a proud stance similar to other statues in the square, including that of Admiral Horatio Nelson on top of the square's famous central column. Created by renowned German artist Katharina Fritsch (born 1956), the sculpture was commissioned as part of a series of public artworks that have occupied the square's empty fourth plinth since 1999. Fritsch's cockerel tells stories of new beginnings and masculine power. The alpha cockerel is the first to sing just before sunrise, with other males following in order, calling from an elevated vantage point to help them spread their message loud and clear. Not only can the cockerel be seen as a celebration of the early risers whose, often unsung, contribution to the life of the city is indispensable, but it can also stand as a commentary on the type of masculinity immortalized by other sculptures in the square. Fritsch said she was inspired by the tailors of nearby Jermyn Street (and their customers), observing that the powerful businessmen in suits she saw in the square were 'posing like cockerels'. In 2013, unveiling the artwork, then Mayor of London Boris Johnson remarked on the irony that a cockerel, the unofficial emblem of France, should watch over a square that commemorates the battle of Trafalgar of 1805, a historic British naval victory over the French.

Jill Greenberg

Purple Chicken Portrait, c.2008
Photograph, dimensions variable

Like a Soviet-era poster celebrating the heroes of Russian industry, a white halo of light lends a statuesque quality to this portrait of the workhorse of the bird world, whose relationship with humans is possibly the closest of any bird: the domestic chicken. The remarkable colours, defiant pose and inquisitive expression of this rooster has been captured by Canadian photographer Jill Greenberg (born 1967), renowned for carefully lit and colourized animal portraits. She highlights the disconnect between the abstract relationship most people have with the bird – as a largely unseen source of eggs and meat – and the chicken's complex character and long history of breeding. First domesticated from the red junglefowl (*Gallus gallus*) between 8,000 and 10,000 years ago in Asia, the chicken has been bred over thousands of generations to improve various qualities: originally, its aggression for cockfighting but later its laying capacity, the amount of meat it yields, its tolerance of harsh conditions – and its pure aesthetic beauty. The result is hundreds of separate chicken breeds from around the world. The enormous Malayan fowl stands over 60 cm (2 ft) in height on powerful long legs, while the dinimutive Japanese bantam or Chabo is a dwarf breed – not just tiny, but with especially short limbs. There are some 25 billion chickens in the world, making it the most numerous bird on the planet.

Unknown

Quail Petroglyph, *c*.12,000–8,000 BC
Pecked petroglyph, L. 40 cm / 15¾ in
Burrup Peninsula, Dampier Archipelago, Western Australia

The stubble quail (*Coturnix pectoralis*), depicted in this millennia-old petroglyph, is Australia's most common species of quail, present across all but the farthest northern reaches of the country. Breeding pairs nest in scrubby undergrowth or, today, among crops, and they are adapted to life in arid regions: they have a high tolerance of saline water, and where green vegetation is available as well as grain, they do not need to drink at all. This image comes from the Burrup Peninsula, an island in the Dampier Archipelago and site of the largest collection of petroglyphs in the world, with up to a million individual drawings; it was made by pecking, the most common technique. When aboriginal people first occupied this part of Australia, some 30,000 years ago, the islands of the archipelago were the tops of a volcanic mountain range on the mainland. The earliest petroglyphs, comprising face motifs, human figures and geometric patterns, may relate to this initial period of occupation, dating to before *c*.18,000 BC. Emus, kangaroos, echidnas and other animals and birds appear after that and until *c*.7,000 BC, by which time the region had become savannah; images of turtles, fish, seabirds and marine mammals testify to rising sea levels after that date, when the islands of the archipelago were created. Indigenous peoples living in the region today regard the images as potent spiritual symbols that represent their laws and customs, embodying beliefs about the ancestor spirits who created the land and sky.

Unknown

Akhenaten sacrificing a duck, *c*.1353–36 BC
Limestone, paint, 24.5 × 54.5 cm / 9½ × 21½ in
Metropolitan Museum of Art, New York

The Egyptian pharaoh Akhenaten wrings a duck's neck in this carved temple relief, realistically wrestling with the struggling creature as he grasps its wings and offers it to the god Aten, the sun disk, whose rays appear at the top of the fragment, each ending in a tiny human hand. One of the hands holds to the king's nose the *ankh* hieroglyph, symbolizing life. The webbed foot of a second duck appears at bottom right, and a related block – now in Copenhagen – shows a female figure offering the duck to the pharaoh; this female was originally Kiya, a minor wife of Akhenaten, but the block was later recarved to show Meritaten, his daughter with his celebrated queen Nefertiti. Birds and other animals were sacrificed in large numbers by the Egyptians as part of religious rituals or celebrations, when their meat would be distributed among participants, and ducks and other waterfowl were both popular as food and symbolic of fertility. Akhenaten replaced Egypt's many gods with a single god, the Aten, creating the world's first monotheistic religion at a newly constructed capital named Akhetaten (modern Amarna); he also abandoned other traditional features of Egyptian life. His portrayal here, for example, with unnaturally elongated features, is a marked departure from Egyptian artistic convention. On his death, his unpopular religious reforms were overturned and his new capital abandoned, many of the building blocks being reused at nearby Hermopolis.

Harland Miller

Bad Weather Painting 4, 2020
Oil on canvas, 236 × 156.5 cm / 93 × 61⅝ in
Private collection

The layering and loose application of paint in this work by British artist Harland Miller (born 1964) suggests a faded, well-thumbed (rather than pristine) paperback novel, and the vertical drips towards the lower section appear as a rainstorm through which a pair of pelicans (*Pelecanus*) are flying. Since the early 1990s, Miller has made paintings based on book-cover designs to which he adds witty and wry invented titles. As well as many based on the iconic Penguin paperback, he has made a series featuring the colour scheme and logo of Pelican Books – the non-fiction imprint of Penguin Books founded in 1937 (see p.261). These books aimed to provide the masses with low-cost access to the latest knowledge across a range of subjects and over 3,000 titles were published in the following five decades. The series is titled *Bad Weather Paintings* – the inclement murkiness at odds with the place names and the slogans' apparent reference to tourism advertisements, which would typically show a perfect cloudless sky. While Scarborough, a fishing village turned Victorian seaside resort in North Yorkshire, is not home to pelicans today, fossils show that Dalmatian pelicans were very common in the area and other parts of the UK around 12,000 years ago. Hunted to extinction during the Roman occupation of Britain, they are now only very rarely sighted further west than their breeding grounds in eastern Europe.

Tui De Roy

Blue-footed booby 'dancing' courtship display, *c.*2015
Photograph, dimensions variable

A striking bird stands balanced on one foot while stretching up its clean, counter-shaded breast against a bokeh, or blurred background, of succulents and outcrops. Towards the peak of its neck, the thick texture of the multi-layered throat feathers becomes clearer, before its head tapers quickly away in the form of a skewering blue beak, flanked by wide-open, forward-facing eyes, as if caught in surprise. The renowned Belgian wildlife photographer Tui de Roy (born 1953) captures the comical appearance of blue-footed boobies (*Sula nebouxii*) on land in the Galápagos islands, but the birds are efficient predators of small fish in the waters of the eastern Pacific Ocean, diving at speed into the sea, aided by their binocular vision, shock-resistant skulls and sealable nostrils. The large, unwieldy feet assist their wings as tools of propulsion under the water and play a key role during courtship while on land. This male is engaged in a courtship 'dance' to advertise the shade of its feet to potential mates. The coloration, derived from carotenoids in their diet, acts as an indicator of an individual's health: the bluer the feet, the better fed and healthier the bird – and the more desirable a mate. The blue-footed booby may not be considered elegant, but its anatomy, perfectly adapted to its lifestyle, and a clarity of sexual advertising is a triumph of evolution.

Beswick

Flying Ducks, 1938–71/73
Hand-painted ceramic, dimensions variable
Private collection

Once mounted on the walls of countless postwar British homes, these flying duck ornaments became the epitome of suburban kitsch. The china mallards (*Anas platyrhynchos*) were first made by the pottery manufacturer Beswick in Stoke-on-Trent, a city famous for its ceramic production. The celebrated design – an open-beaked drake in mid-flight – was created by a freelance artist named Mr Watkin, who modelled a large variety of subjects for Beswick, including flying seagulls, blue tits and pheasants. It was, however, his flying ducks that most resonated with the public. The affordable figurines were produced in five sizes between 1938 and the early 1970s and hand-painted to reproduce the duck's richly coloured plumage, from its iridescent green head and blue 'speculum' wing patch to the warm chestnut of its breast, its white collar and white tail with black curled central tail feathers. In the 1960s and 1970s the flying ducks became a fixture of British popular culture, appearing regularly on the iconic television soap opera *Coronation Street*, where they adorned a tacky mountain vista in the home of the cleaner – and notorious gossip – Hilda Ogden. For viewers who grew up with similar ornaments at home, the association with Ogden's tasteless decor no doubt tarnished the ducks' reputation. Their cult status was confirmed in 2000 when they were given their own Monopoly square in a commemorative *Coronation Street* edition of the boardgame. Original Beswick ducks are now highly collectable, with complete sets commanding high prices.

Lars Jonsson

Eternal Forces, 2012–13
Oil on canvas, 200 × 350 cm / 78¾ × 137¾ in
Private collection

The title of this painting says it all. The eternal forces of wind and water, and the relentless struggle of birds to survive each day in the harshest conditions, are the hallmarks of Lars Jonsson's work. Truly a painter of the outdoors, Jonsson (born 1952) feels most at home drawing directly from nature, filling sketchbooks with artwork of astounding beauty and atmosphere, seemingly oblivious to discomfort. Although they are works of art in their own right, these field sketches often form the basis for large – sometimes very large – studio paintings, like this monumental composition of eider ducks battling the elements on migration. Common eiders (*Somateria mollissima*), the largest of the sea ducks, breed in northern waters, spending the winter farther south. They spend prolonged periods diving for molluscs and crustaceans and are supremely adapted to cold conditions. Their insulating down feathers are famously used to fill eiderdown quilts and duvets. When drawing outdoors, Jonsson uses a telescope with an angled eyepiece, which allows him to observe birds with one eye, while simultaneously drawing what he sees. A highly accomplished birder (a term reserved for the most serious birdwatchers), his intimate familiarity with field marks and those indefinable identification characters that birders call 'jizz' has made Jonsson one of the most respected illustrators of ornithological field guides alive today. It is, nevertheless, his artistic compositions, with their deep personal connection to the elements' eternal forces, that truly set Lars Jonsson apart.

Miles V. Sullivan

Drinking Bird, 1945
Glass, plastic, feathers, metal, felt, H. 19 cm / 7½ in
Private collection

With no obvious power source, this bizarre-looking bird rocks back and forth, dipping its beak into a glass of water as if taking a drink. The classic toy, with its cartoonish eyes, long neck and bulbous bottom, has delighted generations of children and adults alike. Many have tried to uncover its secret and failed, including Albert Einstein, who spent three and a half months studying it to no avail. Patented in 1945 by the American scientist Miles V. Sullivan (1917–2016), the drinking bird is an example of a heat engine, where tiny differences in temperature are harnessed to produce movement. Comprising two glass bulbs joined by a tube, the bird's body is filled with red methylene chloride, a volatile compound that vaporizes at room temperature. The bird's upper bulb, or head, is covered with a fabric that absorbs water from the drinking glass. When the water evaporates, the head cools, causing the vapour inside it to condense. The resulting difference in pressure between the two bulbs forces the red liquid up the tube, filling the head so that the bird tips forwards. When the head drains of liquid, it tips back and the process repeats. A similar toy named the Insatiable Birdie was produced in China from 1910, but it was Sullivan's patented design that captured the world's imagination. Recognized for its educational as well as its entertainment value, it sold in its millions.

Clarice Cliff

Pie funnel in the shape of a blackbird, 1936
Ceramic, H. 11.4 cm / 4½ in
Private collection

With its outstretched neck, this charming ceramic Eurasian blackbird (*Turdus merula*) opens its yellow beak for food, though is itself designed to be baked in pies. The hollow bird funnels steam from a cooking pie, preventing the filling from bubbling over and stopping the crust from sagging. Steam vents for baking were introduced to the Victorian kitchen in the late 1800s, though it was not until the 1930s that they were reimagined in playful ways. The earliest blackbird was produced in Australia by Grace

Seccombe in 1933, though it was British ceramicist Clarice Cliff (1899–1972) who popularized the pie bird in Britain in the mid-1930s. Cliff's whimsical design brought a moment of levity to the family dining table, with the image of a small bird emerging from a pie recalling the nursery rhyme 'Sing a Song of Sixpence', which features the lines: 'Four and twenty blackbirds baked in a pie; When the pie was opened, the birds began to sing.' Responding to the popularity of Cliff's blackbird, competing manufacturers introduced

alternative designs, including owls, quail, ducks, chickens and even elephants. Active from 1922 to 1963 in the Stoke-on-Trent potteries, Cliff was one of the most influential ceramic artists of the twentieth century. The prolific designer sought to provide British homes with bright, colourful and innovative products for daily use. Her famous *Bizarre* wares, to which this pie bird belongs, were launched in 1927 and remain highly collectable.

Ustad Mansur

Great Hornbill, from the *Shah Jahan Album*, c.1540
Ink, opaque watercolour, and gold on paper, 38.7 × 26.7 cm / 15¼ × 10½ in
Metropolitan Museum of Art, New York

This highly realistic painting by Indian artist Ustad Mansur (*fl.*1590-1624) shows a great hornbill (*Buceros bicornis*), a large and colourful bird common in the Indian subcontinent and Southeast Asia. Mansur developed his skills in painting live animals while working as a court painter for the fourth Mughal emperor, Jahangir. Painted on commission for the Emperor to document one of his annual peregrinations, the work accurately portrays the bird's uniquely shaped bill. With a wingspan reaching 1.5 m (5 ft), this species is one of the largest in the hornbill family. Great hornbills tend to be monogamous and are known to build strong bonds with their partners. Their nesting and reproductive cycles are unusual and complex. Hornbills nest in carefully selected tree cavities. When the female becomes pregnant, she begins to seal the entrance with mud, bark, excreta and saliva, finally locking herself in. Connected to the outside world only by a narrow slit through which the male continues to feed her, the female sheds her feathers and becomes entirely dependent on the male's care. The eggs begin to hatch roughly a month later and the female breaks down the seal of the nest a couple of weeks after that, when the chicks are ready to take their first flight. Mansur's works were highly prized for their artistic skill and scientific accuracy, and were copied and even forged by other artists both during his lifetime and after his death.

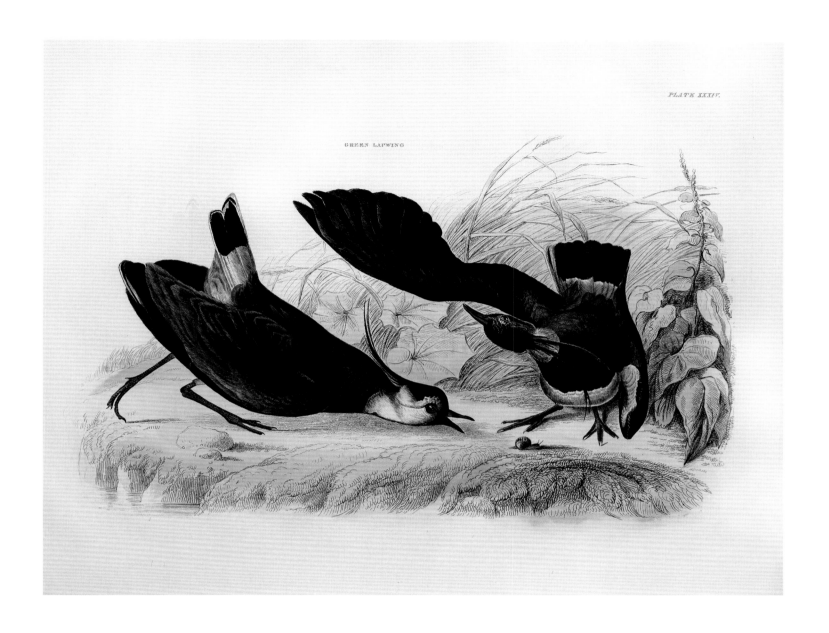

PLATE XXXIV.

GREEN LAPWING

Prideaux John Selby

Green Lapwing, from *Illustrations of British Ornithology*, 1821
Hand-coloured etching, 53 × 63.5 cm / 21 × 25 in
Private collection

For any naturalist making the long journey between scientific meetings in London and Edinburgh, Twizell House must have seemed an oasis. Set in over 200 ha (500 acres) of parkland by the rugged Northumberland coast, it was the home of magistrate Prideaux John Selby (1788-1867) and his wife – warm-hearted hosts, whose drawing room was animated by conversation between the greatest ornithologists, entomologists, geologists, botanists and artists of the day. A respected naturalist, Selby's *magnum opus, Illustrations of British*

Ornithology (1821-34), was one of the first and finest attempts to portray all British bird species life-sized. It was a monumental undertaking, lavishly printed on magnificent elephant folio sheets, and issued to subscribers in nineteen parts over thirteen years. Selby etched most of the large copper printing plates himself, then passed them to the Edinburgh engraver William Home Lizars for adjustments, printing and colouring. Although his work was well received and has retained its value, Selby's name has been somewhat eclipsed by

that of his more colourful contemporary, John James Audubon (see p.177). Nevertheless, the images have tremendous presence and startling beauty. Intensive farming methods have silenced the calls of nesting northern lapwings (*Vanellus vanellus*) through much of the British countryside, but Selby's springtime ramblings over the Northumbrian moors and pastures would have been serenaded by the evocative 'peewit!' calls of these delightful birds as they wheeled and plunged in their aerial courtship displays.

Hector Giacomelli

A Perch of Birds, c.1880
Watercolour over graphite underdrawing heightened with white and gum
on cream, thick, heavily textured wove paper, 17.8 × 48.4 cm / 7 × 19 in
Walters Art Museum, Baltimore, Maryland

This delicate watercolour, which would not look out of place on a chocolate box – albeit a very long and thin one – is an accurate characterization of twenty-four diminutive songbirds of the family Estrildidae, usually known simply as 'estrildid finches'. Despite the name, the birds are more closely related to sparrows than to true finches. Originally birds of open grassland, the 140 or so species are distributed across the Old World from Africa to Australasia. Estrildids are generally sociable, active creatures, accompanied by a pleasant hum of buzzing, chattering calls. Their nests are domes of woven grasses lined with feathers, and the nestlings, raised in the darkness within, have mouths decorated with bright spots that signal 'Feed me!' to their parents. Despite the undisputed attractiveness of these tiny, colourful waxbills, mannikins, cordon bleus and firefinches, this image has a darker side. These would have been captive birds, probably wild-caught and observed by the French artist Hector Giacomelli (1822–1904) in the possession of a bird trader, clustered together out of necessity on a single perch. (A trained eye will notice that the 'fluffiest' individuals in the line-up are actually close to death.) Only a small fraction of wild-caught songbirds would have survived to endure ownership as drawing room pets. For all its apparent sentimentality, Giacomelli's simple but striking *bâton de cage* belies acute observation and a deep affinity for these endearing birds.

Unknown

Falcon box with wrapped feathers, 332–30 BC
Painted and gilded wood, linen, resin and feathers, 58.5 × 24.9 × 33.3 cm / 23 × 9¾ × 13 in
Metropolitan Museum of Art, New York

Carved in ancient Egypt, a falcon guards a painted and gilded box that contains not the mummy of a bird, as might be expected, but a linen-wrapped bundle of what X-rays reveal to be feathers. The falcon was the most common depiction of the Egyptian god Horus, the son of Isis and Osiris who was born after his mother retrieved the dismembered body parts of his murdered father. Using her magic powers, Isis resurrected her husband and was impregnated, giving birth in the marshes of the Nile delta. The living pharaoh had among his titles a royal 'Horus name', and the falcon came to symbolize divine kingship in Egypt. The bird was later associated with the sun god Re and with Montu, god of war, in addition to Horus. Falcon representations are consistent throughout ancient Egyptian history, usually shown in an upright stance with wings folded, but they are ornithologically unrealistic and seem to combine characteristics of several types of birds found in the region. The reddish 'trousers', in combination with the distinctive facial markings and streaked underparts of this depiction indicate that it represents a Eurasian hobby (*Falco subbuteo*), which may have passed through Egypt on its annual migration between Africa and Europe. Like other animals, the falcon was the object of mummification and votive offerings, though sometimes a mummy contained no actual bird, just as the feathers in this elaborate box presumably served as a symbolic substitute for the creature itself.

Unknown

Bird-shaped vessel, 3rd century
Earthenware, 32.7 × 35.2 cm / 12⅞ × 13⅞ in
Metropolitan Museum of Art, New York

Bird-shaped vessels such as this were made in ancient Korea for use as containers for wine or water during rituals. Liquid was poured into the opening in the bird's back and then dispensed through its tail, creating a distinctive spectacle. Although the bird is stylized, the rounded, oblong body, flat and elongated beak, and tall comb on its head resemble those of a duck. Not only are ducks abundant in Korea, but they have long had symbolic meaning. In ancient times, the birds were considered messengers of spirits,

because they can travel on land, water and in the sky. Moreover, because this vessel was made with a finer quality clay than that used for daily ceramics and was fashioned with great skill, it was likely used for rituals, especially funeral ceremonies. While pottery burial containers and figures were crafted to furnish tombs throughout East Asia for centuries, Korean examples are noteworthy for their sculptural quality. Not only is this vessel in the shape of a bird, but the potter has realistically shaped the plump body, exaggerated the

long beak and introduced a dramatic accent with the large comb on top of its head and very un-avian 'ears', creating a container that is as much an expressive statue as it is a practical vessel. Bird-shaped containers such as this one are most often found in pairs in burial sites in southern Korea. During the third century, when this example was made, the region was part of a federation of small semi-independent states known as Gaya.

Carl Brenders

In Mixed Company, 2001
Watercolour and gouache on board, 52 × 67.3 cm / 20½ × 26½ in
Private collection

Exquisitely detailed, and with vivid lighting giving luminosity to the colours, the wildlife paintings of Belgian artist Carl Brenders (born 1937), far from being photorealistic, convey an enhanced vision of nature, reminiscent of the Pre-Raphaelite tradition. The intricate tangle of vegetation, beautifully observed in all its various imperfections, is as much a part of the painting as the animal subjects and shows a deep appreciation of the natural environment. These eight half-grown ducklings, from the same brood, are a

domesticated variety descended from the wild mallard (*Anas platyrhynchos*). Ducks delay incubation until an entire clutch of eggs is laid, so that the ducklings all hatch simultaneously and are able to leave the nest and take to the water together almost immediately afterwards. After several weeks, adult feathers begin to emerge in a distinct pattern called feather tracts, and the birds spend a great deal of time resting and preening. The contrasting textures and subtle colours of the white feathers and yellowish down attracted the

artist to this subject when he spotted this brood during a trip to France. Paintings of domesticated animals, especially young animals with sentimental appeal, are generally frowned on within the specialist wildlife art genre. Conscious of his reputation as a wildlife artist, Brenders therefore added various other animals to the scene, including a dragonfly, a ladybird and a toad, drawing attention to them by entitling the work *In Mixed Company*.

Andrew Parkinson

Mute Swan – Cygnets, c.2017-18
Photograph, dimensions variable

Framed by the cloud-like downy plumage of their own bodies and those of their siblings, three mute swan (*Cygnus olor*) cygnets, still retaining their youthful brownish-grey coloration, lie oblivious to a world that in this moment extends only to their extremities, as mirrored by the composition of the photograph, which has no context or external environment other than comfort and security. This intimate portrait is characteristic of the ability of Welsh photographer Andrew Parkinson to take us into the private worlds of the animals he studies. A contributor to *National Geographic* magazine and a winner of the prestigious Bird Photographer of the Year (for a portfolio including this image), Parkinson's works are never posed or taken with tame animals, which makes his gift for capturing the transient even more impressive. This image was taken while the cygnets rested, utterly exposed, as their parents sat nearby. Parkinson credits his ability to approach so close to the time he spent earning the trust of the parents.

Mute swans have a reputation for being viciously protective of their young, and yet they allowed him to approach their sleeping offspring after they became habituated to his presence and viewed him as being without threat. These cygnets would have remained with their parents for up to five months until their plumage matured to the adult snowy white, eventually breeding after a further two years.

Philip Treacy and Shaun Leane for Alexander McQueen

Bird's Nest Headdress, 2006
Oxidized silver, Swarovski gemstones and mallard's wings
Private collection

This ornate headpiece of wings and gemstone eggs sitting in a silver nest was used by the British fashion designer Alexander McQueen (1969–2010) at the start of his 2006 show, *The Widows of Culloden*. Its reference to the coming of new life was echoed at the end of the show by a similar headdress based on an eagle's skull and black plumes, symbolizing death. This work was created by two of McQueen's long-time collaborators. The jeweller Shaun Leane (born 1969) wove a nest from delicate twigs of oxidized silver and added eggs cast

from silver and studded with Swarovksi crystals. Milliner Philip Treacy (born 1967) mounted the nest on a headband between two wings from a mallard (*Anas platyrhynchos*), displaying the distinctive iridescent blue speculum feathers. Inspired by the Jacobite Risings in Scotland and the subsequent battle of Culloden in 1746, the designer used feathers to refer to Scotland's long association with gamebirds. Birds intrigued McQueen from childhood, when he was a member of the Young Ornithologists' Club of Great Britain and watched birds

swooping above East London. 'Birds in flight fascinate me,' he once said. Birds inspired whole collections; he also used them, sometimes whole, in accessories and clothes, echoing the Victorian obsession with bestiary, when animal parts were incorporated into fashion (see p.300). McQueen's clothes played on the contrast between the romantic and the macabre, the idea of 'savage beauty' that became the title for his posthumous retrospective at the Metropolitan Museum in 2011.

Gregory Crewdson

Untitled, from the *Natural Wonder* series, 1993
Digital c-print, 76.2 × 101.6 cm / 30 × 40 in

The *Natural Wonder* series by the American photographer Gregory Crewdson (born 1962) focuses on animals, but it is the opposite of wildlife photography. The *mise-en-scène* is meticulously planned and photographed in a studio using stuffed animals, not unlike old-fashioned museum dioramas. But rather than being a faithful recreation of authentic animal behaviour and habitat, Crewdson's fidelity is to an idea: his compositions are manufactured, at once mesmerising and disconcerting. Here, one bird stands guard, while four others perch on logs and focus on a perfect circle of eggs standing on ground that has been cleared of grass, reminiscent of humans around a campfire. In the background stands a suburban house with a manicured lawn, a water tower and other human structures, in a palette reminiscent of 1950s films depicting the American Dream in all its technicolour glory. Where in later works Crewdson uses much greater contrast in the lighting of similarly suburban compositions, here both the bird scene in the foreground and the house and garden in the background are well lit and the depth of field is relatively wide, which amplifies the viewer's feeling that these two scenes do not sit comfortably together; that one is impinging on the other; that the threat of human encroachment on the natural world is ever apparent, and the flip side, that this apparent; ritual from the natural world has no place in the suburban garden.

Emperor Huizong, Zhao Ji

Auspicious Cranes, 1112
Silk scroll, 51 x 138.2 cm / 20 × 54⅜ in
Liaoning Provincial Museum, Shenyang

This large Chinese hand scroll is the work not of a professional artist but of a ruler, Emperor Huizong, Zhao Ji (1082–1135) of the Song dynasty. It shows a flock of cranes swirling across a blue sky to commemorate a miraculous event that took place on the sixteenth day of the first month of the lunar calendar in 1112. At right, inscriptions and a poem recount how the emperor saw the flock of cranes gathering above the palace's main gate while auspicious clouds formed around them. It is claimed that thousands of people witnessed the event in awe, thus making it worthy of immortalization on a scroll. The eleventh son of Emperor Shenzong, Zhao Ji was more interested in the arts than in political affairs. He spent most of his youth studying painting and created more than 600 works representing natural themes. He also established an imperial painting academy to promote the realistic style known as *gongbi*, which was particularly suited to painting birds, one of the key themes in Chinese art, where they are used to symbolize specific qualities or as good or bad omens. Red-crowned cranes (*Grus japonensis*) abound in Chinese myths and legends. They are a Taoist symbol of immortality and a commonly acknowledged representation of elegance. With their height and wingspan both approximately 1.5 m (5 ft), red-crowned cranes are among the world's largest cranes.

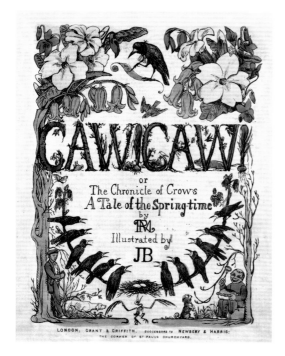

Jemima Blackburn

Caw! Caw!, or The Chronicle of Crows, A Tale of the Spring-time, c.1848
Hand-coloured lithographs, each 24 × 18.9 / 9½ × 7½ in
University of California Libraries, Los Angeles

Caw! Caw! or The Chronicle of Crows, A Tale of the Spring-time tells in verse the story of a colony of rooks (*Corvus frugilegus*) persecuted by a farmer, some even ending up in a pie. Farmers have long battled against rooks and crows, which often feed on sown seeds, traditionally hanging up dead birds to scare off others. At the top of this book's title page, a learned rook writes the story, while beneath the title a dozen birds perch on a curved branch and call towards a nest with eggs. A huntsman and his dog are at lower left,

opposite a figure tucking into bird pie, while the skeleton of a deceased rook performs a macabre dance at the foot of the page. The illustrations set the story on the Scottish borders near North Berwick; the Bass Rock, famous for its enormous gannet colony, is identifiable in the background. The author of the tale, published in London by Grant and Griffith around 1848, is identified only by the initials R. M., and the artist as J. B. The latter almost certainly refers to Edinburgh-born Jemima Blackburn (née Wedderburn,

1823–1909), a talented watercolour painter who became known as one of the foremost illustrators of the Victorian age. Blackburn moved in distinguished artistic and intellectual circles and counted among her friends several eminent artists, including Sir Edwin Landseer, Sir John Everett Millais and John Ruskin. *Caw! Caw!* represents the whimsical side of Blackburn's talent; her more serious illustrations of British birds were published to much acclaim in *Birds Drawn from Nature* in 1862.

Édouard Manet

Design for the poster and cover of *The Raven* by Edgar Allan Poe, 1875
Transfer lithograph on simili-parchment, 32.4 × 28.6 cm / 12¾ × 11¼ in
Metropolitan Museum of Art, New York

This bird's head in profile is a sketched design by the French Impressionist artist Édouard Manet (1832–83) for an 1875 translation by Stéphane Mallarmé of Edgar Allan Poe's *The Raven*, one of most famous poems in the world. Written in 1845, it tells of a lovelorn scholar, visited late at night by a raven, which he questions about his lost love. The raven responds with a repeated refrain, the only word it can speak: 'Quoth the raven, "Nevermore."' Poe's poem hints at the bird's long history as a symbol of death and loss, and as a mediator between life and death, thanks to its black colour and diet of carrion. In Norse tradition, the raven was linked to memory and thought, and a Greek myth told how its feathers were burned black by Apollo after delivering a message that his lover had chosen to marry a mortal. Its ability to 'talk' with a croaking call also linked the bird to prophecy and bad omens; the playwright Christopher Marlowe called it the 'sad presaging raven'. Mallarmé's translation of *The Raven* (*Le Corbeau*) was published in a limited edition of 240 copies and is considered today to be among the finest historic examples of an artist's book. The modernity of Manet's sketchlike transfer lithographs was not appreciated by everyone at the time, however: the Pre-Raphaelite artist Dante Gabriel Rossetti said of the book, 'To view it without a guffaw is impossible.' Sharp-eyed viewers might also take issue with Manet's ornithological veracity – his raven is in fact modelled on the head of a rook (*Corvus frugilegus*).

Myochin Muneharu

Articulated Crow, 19th century
Iron, L. 41 cm / 16⅛ in
Private collection

Although it looks realistic enough to launch from its perch at any moment, this life-sized beady-eyed carrion crow (*Corvus corone*) made in Japan during the late Edo period (1853–67) is actually constructed from numerous overlapping iron plates that have been carefully hammered into shape and joined internally, enabling the bird's body to be moved and arranged in a variety of poses. Each individual feather, from head and wing plumes to those of the tail, has been painstakingly chiselled with detailed markings, while the crow's eyes, beak and claws are crafted with a copper and gold alloy known as *shakudo*, which glints in the light as a counterpoint to the dark body. The sculpture is attributed to a member of the renowned Myochin family, whose reputation as skilled metalworkers dates back to the sixteenth century. Such articulated figures emerged in the eighteenth century during a period of relative peace in Japan, when the demand for samurai armour slowed. The Myochin metalsmiths turned to producing finely crafted decorative and symbolic pieces known as *jizai okimono* (literally 'free display objects') that included reptiles, insects, sea creatures and even mythical beasts, together with many birds, commonly featuring movable wings, heads and claws. After the Meiji restoration in 1868, *jizai* began making its way to Europe and North America; a large eagle exhibited in Chicago at the 1893 World's Columbian Exposition sparked widespread international enthusiasm for the figures, which remain highly prized by collectors.

Christina Malman

*Nothing's Flocking, c.*1939
Graphite, pen and ink, brush and watercolour crayon, 48.8 × 39.3 cm / 19¼ × 15½ in
Cooper Hewitt, New York

If the colourful birds clinging to the leafy twigs of a tree in this cover design for a New York magazine look familiar, it is because the depictions are based on the famous paintings of John James Audubon in his *Birds of America* (see p.177). The bird on the right with blue wings and tail is taken from Audubon's depiction of a female western bluebird (*Sialia mexicana*), below which is a yellow-billed magpie (*Pica nutalli*) in a character-istically twisted posture. The pair to the left imitate Audubon's plate of chestnut-backed chickadees (*Poecile*

rufescens). Ironically these are Western species unlikely to turn up in New York City. The bird at the bottom is probably a house finch (*Carpodacus mexicanus*). Like much of the work of the English-born artist Christina Malman (1912–59), the illustration is a commentary on the social life of New Yorkers, in this case gently mocking an earnest gathering of gentrified ornithol-ogists drawn in cartoon-like silhouettes, who are being scrutinized by the birds above. Malman was born in Southampton, but moved to New York with her family

aged two. After studying fine art, she became a regular exhibitor and contributing artist for *The New Yorker* magazine, for which she provided dozens of covers. *Nothing's Flocking* was designed as a cover for *The New York Magazine* or *Promenade Magazine*, though it was never used.

TAB. XLIIII.

Coccothraustes Indica
cristata.
The Virginian Nightingale.

Coccothraustes.
The Grosbeak or Haw-
finch.

Chloris.
The Greenfinch.

Rubicilla.
The Bullfinch.

Loxia.
The Crosse-bill. after
Edwards 1761

Passer.
A Sparrow.

W. Faithorne sculp.

Francis Willughby and John Ray

Plate XLIII, from *The Ornithology of Francis Willughby*, 1678
Hand-coloured engraving, 36.5 × 24 cm / 14⅜ × 9 in
McGill University Library, Montreal

The species depicted in this coloured plate from an ambitious seventeenth-century attempt to classify the natural world include five more or less familiar European songbirds and, at top right, the Virginian nightingale now known as the northern cardinal (*Cardinalis cardinalis*), a common bird of central and eastern North America. Cardinals were formerly widely kept as cagebirds and today remain the state bird of seven US states. The English parson and naturalist John Ray (1627-1705) and his pupil and friend Francis Willughby (1635-72) toured Europe gathering material for the project, conceived in the 1660s, a complete classification of the vegetable and animal kingdoms. After Willughby's early death Ray took over his notes. Having edited the incomplete manuscript and added his own observations Ray published his friend's work in a Latin version in 1676. A translation by Ray was published two years later with three additional plates, and an expanded text including three further sections, also by Ray, on fowling, falconry and songbirds. This plate comes from a unique, hand-coloured copy of the 1678 book that was apparently presented to Samuel Pepys between 1684 and 1686 during his presidency of the Royal Society. More than 90 per cent of the original engravings of birds are hand-coloured by an unknown painter. The colouring of the 332 bird species on seventy-six hand-coloured plates is mostly accurate – and where it is not, it generally matches the description in Ray's text almost exactly.

Harry Emanuel

Red-legged Honeycreeper Earrings, c.1865
Preserved hummingbird, gold, metal
Metropolitan Museum of Art, New York

We may find it difficult today to comprehend the Victorian taste for jewellery and other adornments made from the preserved body parts of birds, but at the time, brightly coloured tropical birds symbolized the splendours of exotic new worlds. Like jewels, they were rare and beautiful, but they had the additional fascination of having once been alive. The trade in plumes and feathers for women's fashions decimated bird populations worldwide and brought many species to the brink of extinction. By the 1880s,

an estimated 5 million birds a year were being killed for millinery in North American alone. The determination of a handful of inspirational women on both sides of the Atlantic eventually brought this trend to a close and resulted in two of the greatest conservation organizations in the world: the National Audubon Society in the United States and the Royal Society for the Protection of Birds in Britain. Although they superficially resemble hummingbirds, these tiny heads are from two male red-legged

honeycreepers (*Cyanerpes cyaneus*), songbirds of the tanager family. Their purple and turquoise plumage is not due wholly to pigments, but also to microscopic air pockets within the structure of the feather barbs, scattering light to produce an optical effect of gorgeous blues. London jeweller Harry Emanuel (died 1898) was known from the 1850s to the 1870s for using South American birds in necklaces and earrings, and patented a technique for gluing feathers to mounts using shellac.

Martin Johnson Heade

Tropical Landscape with Ten Hummingbirds, 1870
Oil on canvas, 45.7 × 76.2 cm / 18 × 30 in
Private collection

US artist Martin Johnson Heade (1819–1904) described himself as a 'monomaniac' for hummingbirds, and here depicts ten individuals from eight neotropical species, whose iridescent forms lead the eye along vines dotted with crimson passion flowers. Despite the scientific accuracy of the birds, the scene could not exist outside Heade's imagination, as it draws together species such as the red-billed streamertail (*Trochilus polytmus*) and red-tailed comet (*Sappho sparganurus*) that live in different locations from Brazil to Jamaica.

Heade spent much of his career as a landscape painter, specializing in the salt marshes of coastal New England, before travelling in the 1860s and 1870s to Brazil, Central America and the West Indies, where he became interested in tropical flora and fauna. Unusually for a time when artists often favoured minimal backgrounds for their ornithological subjects, Heade painted birds in lush landscapes using advanced lighting techniques to celebrate rainforest biodiversity – albeit an imagined version. Somewhat

of an outlier among his large body of work, this painting comes from a tropical series intended for publication under the title *Gems of Brazil*, but Heade failed to raise funding to complete the project. Unappreciated during his lifetime, Heade benefited from a resurgence of popularity in American art after World War II (1939–45), and today his paintings still turn up as surprise finds at estate sales and thrift stores throughout the United States.

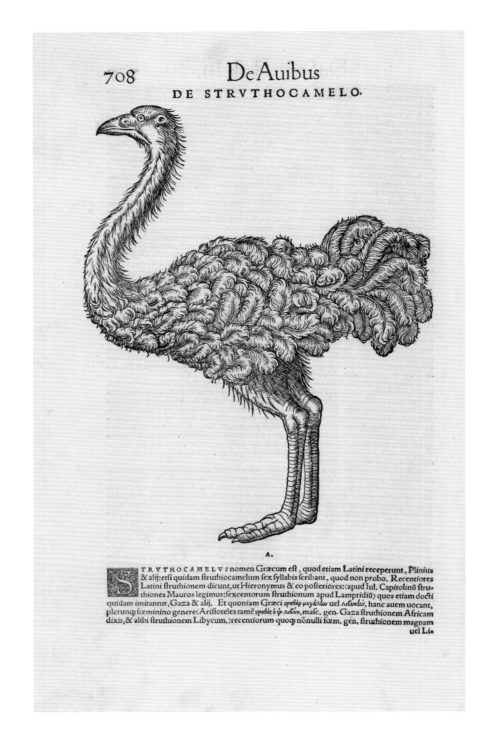

708 DeAuibus

DE STRVTHOCAMELO.

A.

STRVTHOCAMELVS nomen Græcum est, quod etiam Latini receperunt, Plinius
& alij: etsi quidam struthiocamelum sex syllabis scribant, quod non probo. Recentiores
Latini struthionem dicunt, ut Hieronymus & eo posteriores: (apud Iul. Capitolinū stru-
thiones Mauros legimus: sexcentorum struthionum apud Lampridiū) quos etiam docti
quidam imitantur, Gaza & alij. Et quoniam Græci στρουθὸν μεγάλην uel λιβυκὴν, hanc auem uocant,
plerunꝗ fœminino genere (Aristoteles tamē στρουθὸς ὁ ἐν λιβύη, masc. gen. Gaza struthionem Africam
dixit, & alibi struthionem Libycum,) recentiorum quoꝗ nōnulli fœm. gen. struthionem magnam
uel Li-

Conrad Gessner

Ostrich. De Avibus, De Struthocamelo, from *Historia Animalium,* 1551–58
Woodcut, 30.5 × 17.2 cm / 12 × 6¾ in
Minneapolis Institute of Art, Minnesota

Although somewhat crudely drawn, this bird is clearly an ostrich and is labelled as such. The flamboyant tail plumes are characteristic, as are the long, powerful legs with only two toes, though the bill misleadingly looks more like that of an eagle. This somewhat fanciful portrait comes from a sixteenth-century account of the animal world, *Historia Animalium.* The artist of this illustration is unknown, but the book used many sources, including Albrecht Dürer's famous rhinoceros. Under the authorship of Conrad Gessner (1516–65), it was first published in Zürich in five volumes, and is his most famous work. It is the first attempt to describe all the animals known at that time and it became one of the major natural history references of the Renaissance. Based partly on ancient accounts, some of which were mythical, this book is one of the first to apply an objective, scientific rigour to the subject. Gessner was a professor at the Carolinum in Zürich, which later became the University of Zürich. One of the earliest naturalists to describe and document many animals and plants, his name has been honoured in the scientific names of several species, and in the plant family Gesneriaceae. Two species of ostrich are recognized today: the common ostrich (*Struthio camelus*) is still common across the savannahs of central and southern Africa, while the rarer Somali ostrich (*S. molybdophanes*) inhabits parts of Djibouti, Ethiopia, Kenya and Somalia.

Joachim Hiller

Nautilus Cup, c.1600
Silver, nautilus shell, amethyst, 42.4 × 19.7 × 11.5 cm / 16¾ × 7¾ × 4½ in
Rijksmuseum, Amsterdam

As the fastest bird on land – it can run at speeds of up to 70 km/h (43 mph) – the common ostrich (*Struthio camelus*) has long been considered a symbol of virtue, which, like the ostrich in a race, will always triumph. That may explain its choice as the subject of this ceremonial silver cup from seventeenth-century Germany, which is formed by the decorated shell of a nautilus, a mollusc found around the coral reefs of the Indo-Pacific region. Dutch visitors to the East Indies learned the local tradition of stripping the shell to reveal its mother-of-pearl surface. Shipped to Europe, the shells were encased in elaborate mounts of gold and silver to form luxurious drinking cups. Jeweller Joachim Hiller (1573–1613) of Breslau – then in the German empire but now part of Poland – included an amethyst in the head of this example, which was later given to the Tsar of Russia. At the time, ostriches were very rare in Europe, where their eggs were also made into valuable cups. Ostriches are native to Africa, where there are two species: the common ostrich and the Somali ostrich (*Struthio molybdophanes*). As well as its speed, the flightless common ostrich is renowned for being the largest living bird and for laying the largest eggs of any living bird. For centuries, its feathers have been used for decoration and in fashion, while its meat and eggs have been eaten and its skin used to make leather.

Unknown

Thanksgiving Greeting, late 19th–early 20th century
Printed card
Private collection

As every American schoolchild knows, there is no evidence that turkey featured on the menu of the first Thanksgiving in 1621, when the colonists of Plymouth Plantation recorded that they shared a meal with their Native American neighbours. Yet turkey has become the traditional centrepiece of the Thanksgiving meal, as this greeting card suggests. The bronze turkey is shown with other symbols of autumnal harvest - grapes, corn, squash, pumpkins - spilling out of a cornucopia, or horn of plenty. One possible reason why turkey became established as the bird of Thanksgiving is that wild turkeys (*Meleagris gallopavo*) were available in huge numbers to be hunted, while farmed turkeys could be killed without losing out on fresh eggs, which came from hens. Perhaps more straightforwardly, the turkey is one of the larger domestic birds, and it could feed a large family gathering; it was in part for a similar reason that the bird became the accepted Christmas meal in the United Kingdom. The nineteenth-century American writer Sarah Josepha Hale, who campaigned for a Thanksgiving holiday, described a Thanksgiving feast with a turkey in her novel *Northwood* in 1827, but the tradition of sending Thanksgiving cards did not become popular until the 1880s. A typical message was, 'A sincere wish from the sender / That your bird will be plump and tender.' Wild turkeys are native to North America, where they were first domesticated in Mexico around 2,000 years ago. Each Thanksgiving, about 45 million turkeys are killed for the table in the United States.

Kermit Oliver

Faune et Flore du Texas, 2003
Silkscreen print on cashmere shawl, 140 × 140 cm / 55 × 55 in
Private collection

A central illustration of a wild turkey (*Meleagris gallopavo*) with its tail feathers spread is surrounded by a halo of succulent leaves with a barn owl (*Tyto alba*), ring-necked pheasant (*Phasianus colchicus*), birds of prey and smaller songbirds; birds typical of Texas include a greater roadrunner (*Geococcyx californianus*), a greater prairie chicken (*Tympanuchus cupido*) and a plain chachalaca (*Ortalis vetula*). Another square border surrounding this is dotted with with more flora and fauna typical of the region, including various waterfowl, whooping cranes (*Grus americana*) and wild and domesticated mammals, including a puma, a mustang stallion and a Texas longhorn cow. In total, more than fifty native animals and plants are represented in this scarf design created by Texas artist Kermit Oliver (born 1943) for the Parisian luxury firm Hermès, first printed in 1987. The collaboration began in 1980, when Lawrence Marcus of Neiman Marcus introduced Kermit Oliver to Hermès. Over the three decades since his first design, *Pani La Shar Pawnee*, was printed in 1984, Oliver has produced a total of seventeen designs for Hermès scarves. He studied art at Texas Southern University in Houston during the 1960s, and his colourful and intricate work often draws on Texan history, wildlife and mythology in what he describes as symbolic realism. He grew up in the south of the state as the son of a cattle rancher but later moved to Waco, where he combined working as an artist with a job as a mail sorter for the US Postal Service.

Carsten Höller

Four Birds (a set of 9 different images, detail), 2015
Photogravure, each 36.5 × 49.5 cm / 14⅜ × 19½ in
Edition of 18 and 4 artist's proofs
Private collection

German conceptual artist Carsten Höller (born 1961) is best known for his large-scale installations. His work alludes heavily to scientific processes, investigating human emotional responses to stimuli – reminiscent of laboratory experiments in which subjects willingly participate. Lesser known are Höller's photogravure images of caged birds. Superficially monochrome photographs of unremarkable, small, streaked birds, the final artistic work deliberately undermines the identity of the subjects. Although the dark face of a goldfinch (*Carduelis* sp.) is easy to recognize, and a trained eye might pick out characteristics of other small finches and sparrows, these birds cannot be found in any field guide. They are colour variants and hybrids between closely related species, skilfully bred by Höller himself, who is a dedicated aviculturist with a doctorate in agricultural science. Breeders create such hybrids (called mules) specifically for their colour combinations, so reproducing these in monochrome contradicts their purpose and further accentuates their anonymity. More than simply a comment on the human desire to mould new forms from existing species, this work is a thought-provoking reflection on the importance we place on naming and classification, even when no categorization is possible. Evolution in nature recognizes no such categorization; species are not static, and many can even hybridize and produce fertile offspring. Perhaps this work ultimately serves as a comment not just on our attitude to the natural world but also on our understanding of our own species.

Lily Attey Daff

Untitled (Takahe), 1931
Watercolour on paper, 54 × 36.8 cm / 21¼ × 14½ in
Museum of New Zealand, Te Papa Tongarewa, Wellington

This watercolour portrait captures well the upright posture of the majestic takahe of New Zealand, with its powerful deep, red bill and sturdy red feet and legs, as well as the glossy blue and purple of its plumage. The takahe is the largest and strangest of the rails (Rallidae), a family that also contains the familiar coots and moorhens. The South Island takahe (*Porphyrio hochstetteri*) is found mostly in the extreme southwest of New Zealand's South Island, where it inhabits swamps and grassland. A similar species, the North Island takahe (*P. mantelli*), lived in the North Island, but was last seen in 1894 and is considered extinct, now known only from fossils. Takahe are flightless, having evolved in an environment with few natural enemies, and they are thus vulnerable to introduced predators such as stoats. Listed as endangered, their population currently stands at around 450. Although the powerful bill may suggest otherwise, takahe are predominantly vegetarian, feeding mainly on leaves and grasses. This image was painted by the British designer and artist Lily Attey Daff (1885–1945), who moved to New Zealand after studying in London. She was initially in charge of exhibitions in the Otago Museum, for which she painted dioramas. In 1932 she moved to Wellington and was commissioned to paint native birds for the New Zealand Bird Protection Society, many of which have also appeared in book form.

KINGFISHER
TAKAHE
PUKEKO
FANTAIL
YELLOW
HEAD
PIED SHAG
NATIVE
PIGEON
KAKA
TOMTIT
PARADISE DUCK
KIWI
TUI

Penny Griffith

Playing cards featuring New Zealand native birds, 1945–55
Offset print, each 8.6 × 5.7 cm / 3⅜ × 2¼ in
Alexander Turnbull Library, Wellington

The earliest European visitors to New Zealand noted the 'deafening' volume of birdsong, produced often by birds they had never seen before. These twelve playing cards showing distinctive birds of New Zealand come from a pack created in the early 1950s that originally featured four illustrations of each bird (three cards have now been lost). They are copies (perhaps traced) of illustrations in *A History of the Birds of New Zealand* (1873) by Walter Buller, illustrated by John Gerrard Keulemans (see p.222). Penny Griffith (born 1943) combines bold colours with erratic composition, as seen in the depiction of the kiwi that overspills the card. As a remote group of islands, New Zealand is home to dozens of species that are endemic, or found nowhere else. These species include the kakapo (*Strigops habroptila*), a large, flightless nocturnal parrot, along with the New Zealand pigeon (*Hemiphaga novaeseelandiae*), the tui (*Prosthemadera novaesee-landiae*) and the extinct moa (Dinornithidae). The flightless kiwis (Apterygidae) have become an international symbol of New Zealand, and their name a nickname for New Zealanders. There are five species, all of which have hairlike feathers and olfactory apparatus that allow them to hunt by scent. Like other endemic species, kiwis' conservation status is listed as vulnerable, due mainly to habitat loss and predation by introduced mammals such as rats, stoats and dogs. New Zealand is a global leader in developing conservation projects aimed at protecting threatened bird species.

Laurel Roth Hope

Biodiversity Reclamation Suits for Urban Pigeons: Heath Hens, 2014
Crocheted yarn, handmade pigeon mannequin, walnut stand,
35.5 × 50.8 × 30.5 cm / 14 × 20 × 12 in
Private collection

Two carved resin pigeons perch on a walnut stand, wearing playful, hand-crocheted outfits – complete with hoods with eye and beak holes – that disguise them as heath hens, the nominate race of the greater prairie chicken (*Tympanuchus cupido*), a North American grouse. Hunted in large numbers for food from colonial times, the heath hen was the subject of the first formal conservation measures in the United States – a law was passed for its preservation in New York in 1791, but to little ultimate effect. The species became extinct in 1932, due in part to hunting but also to disease and predation. These outfits were designed by US artist and former park ranger Laurel Roth Hope (born 1973), whose work frequently investigates the interaction between humans and the natural world: she describes herself as 'an artist that wishes she was a scientist'. Roth Hope designed her outfits to fit the street pigeon, a bird whose ability to adapt to living alongside people has made it so common in the world's cities that it either goes unnoticed or is classed as a pest. The contrast between the pigeon and the species that had different requirements highlights the vulnerability of the natural world: another design features the passenger pigeon, which once existed in the millions in North America (see p.180-1). Other extinct birds in Roth Hope's series include the Seychelles parakeet (*Psittacula wardi*), Bachman's warbler (*Vermivora bachmanii*), the great auk (*Pinguinus impennis*, see p.318) and the Guadalupe caracara (*Caracara lutosa*).

Elizabeth Boehm

Greater Sage Grouse Fight, 2019
Photograph, dimensions variable

A pair of North American icons come to explosive blows in this image by Illinois-born wildlife photographer Elizabeth Boehm. These adult male greater sage-grouse (*Centrocercus urophasianus*) are competing for mating rights on compacted spring snowpack in Pinedale, Wyoming. Greater sage-grouse, like a handful of other birds, select mates by using a lekking system, whereby a group of males parade, dance and strut around an open amphitheatre, hoping to impress a critical female audience enough to be selected. In these ground-based displays the males attempt to attract the attentions of females not only with their striking back and chest plumage and spectacular, angular tail feathers, but also by inflating huge, yellowish air sacs on their breasts. The remarkable popping sound they make by bouncing and releasing the air in these sacs can carry over 3 km (1.9 miles). Leks demand complex interactions between individuals, and the males fiercely guard their personal position, which is based upon a hierarchy of dominance. Alpha males strut proudly in the centre of the arena and only a small number of dominant males will eventually breed. Greater sage-grouse hens may visit the lek daily for a month before selecting a mate. With stakes this high, contestants jostling side-by-side may fight for dominance between dances, as these two are, throwing powerful blows of their wings against one another.

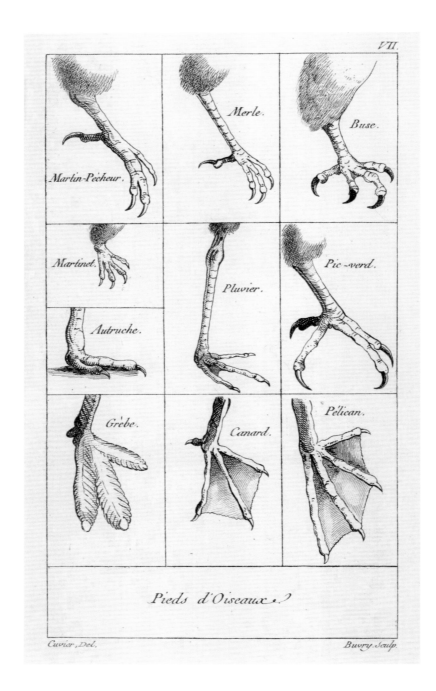

Georges Cuvier

Pieds d'Oiseaux, Plate VII from *Tableau élémentaire de l'histoire naturelle des animaux*, 1797-8
Engraving, 21 × 12.4 cm / 8¼ × 4⅞ in
Smithsonian Libraries, Washington, DC

Perhaps one of the most recognizable ways in which birds have adapted to different environments lies in their feet. Built for perching or for hanging off the side of a tree, webbed for swimming or with deadly talons - the diversity of foot shapes and morphology can reveal much about species' habits and evolution. This illustration of nine different bird feet by the French naturalist Georges Cuvier (1769-1832), from *Tableau élémentaire de l'histoire naturelle des animaux* (1797-8), is an early example of this approach, which is now known as comparative anatomy. From left to right, top to bottom, it shows the feet of a common kingfisher (*Alcedo atthis*), Eurasian blackbird (*Turdus merula*), Eurasian buzzard (*Buteo buteo*), common swift (*Apus apus*), common ostrich (*Struthio camelus*), a plover (*Charadrius* sp.), green woodpecker (*Picus viridis*), grebe (likely *Podiceps* sp.), duck (likely *Anas* sp.) and pelican (*Pelecanus* sp.). The book was a summary of Cuvier's lectures on species classification from the École Centrale du Panthéon (now the Lycée Henri-IV) in Paris, where he taught in the years either side of 1800. Although this is not the earliest depiction of birds' feet, Cuvier was one of the first naturalists to use comparative anatomy to understand the diversity of both living and fossil species. He later extended his methodology of comparative anatomy to humans, leading to a classification of human races and their supposed attributes that would be today condemned as racist.

Audun Rikardsen

Land of the Eagle, 2019
Photograph, dimensions variable

This remarkable image of the moment a golden eagle (*Aquila chrysaetos*) lands on a branch in northern Norway was three years in the making. Audun Rikardsen, a biology professor at the University of Tromsø, deliberately put the tree branch in place to provide what he hoped would be a perfect lookout to attract a golden eagle. Gradually over the next thirty-six months, this eagle did indeed start to use the branch to survey its coastal realm and to enjoy nearby road-kill carrion left by Rikardsen. Finally,

Rikardsen used a motion-sensitive camera trigger to get a photograph of the eagle's arrival, its talons outstretched and its feathers revealed in such fine detail that the bird seems almost superimposed on the background of water and mountains. In Norway, golden eagles live alongside white-tailed sea eagles (*Haliaeetus albicilla*), which are more strictly coastal. Golden eagles often live well inland in their northern hemisphere range, which includes the United States and Canada, and Eurasia from Scotland to far

eastern Russia. The global population is thought to be around 200,000 birds. Since at least the Middle Ages, the power of golden eagles has been harnessed by falconers to bring down prey, varying from hares in the United Kingdom to wolves in Mongolia. This image won the Birds category in the 2019 Wildlife Photographer of the Year competition organized by London's Natural History Museum.

Joseph McGlennon

Florilegium #6, 2016
Giclée digital print on archival Hahnemuhle FineArt Paper, dimensions variable

Hornbills are truly stunning birds, especially the larger species such as these wreathed hornbills (*Rhyticeros undulatus*), which inhabit tropical forests across much of East Asia. Even when the birds are hidden from view by the thick jungle foliage, it's possible to hear the rhythmic, loud thrumming of their wingbeats as they fly above the canopy. The birds' treetop habitat makes it rare to be able to capture such perfectly composed views – but this photograph was not taken of living wild birds, nor

was it intended to appear natural. Australian advertising photographer turned fine artist Joseph McGlennon (born 1957) combines components such as vegetation and bird taxidermy in a studio setting. Hyperreal yet also deliberately unreal, the photographic elements are expertly manipulated to evoke the mystery and romance of the 'perfect' wild landscape, reminiscent of the great historical works of travel and exploration. Hornbills are omnivores, feeding on fruit, insects and a variety of small

animals. Their enormous casqued bill is filled with a spongy honeycomb of bony filaments, making it lightweight and able to be used with surprising delicacy. Food is carefully taken with the pincer-like bill tip, then tossed backwards into the throat with a deft move of the head. These birds, the male with whitish feathering on the face and throat on the right, and the black-feathered female on the left, are carefully picking the eggs from a tiny nest on the branch between them.

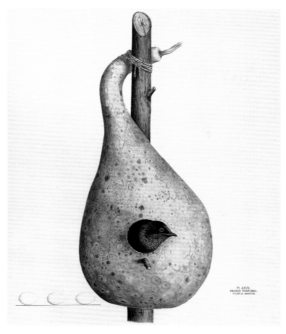

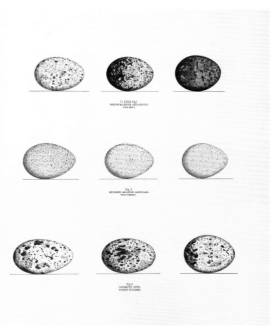

Genevieve Jones and Eliza Jane Shulze

A selection of plates from *Illustrations of the Nests and Eggs of Birds of Ohio: with text,* 1886
Hand-coloured lithographs, 44 × 36 cm / 17⅜ × 14⅛ in
Smithsonian Libraries, Washington, DC

The wistful absence of birds from most of these illustrations of nests and eggs mirrors the poignant life of the US artist Genevieve Jones (1847–79). In 1876 Jones set out to produce a companion to the seminal *Birds of America* by John James Audubon (see p.177), showing the nests and eggs of the species he depicted. She felt it a significant and necessary contribution to the field of ornithology. Originally intending to include all North American species, she eventually limited the project to the nesting birds of her home state of Ohio, filling her family's home with nests and eggs and making fastidious field notes at nesting sites in her determination to achieve scientific accuracy. The ambitious project was to be bound into two volumes, *Illustrations of the Nests and Eggs of Birds of Ohio* (1879–86), but Jones did not live to see the work completed. Typhoid fever caused her untimely death at the age of thirty-two. The project was completed by Genevieve's mother Virginia, her brother Thomas and her friend Eliza Shulze, financed by Genevieve's father, Dr. Nelson Jones, and the work was published in 1886. Although it garnered praise from distinguished ornithologists, it was not widely recognized for its profound contribution to science until some decades later, long after the Jones family had all expired. Few copies remain today.

Peter Scott

Red-breasted Geese Flying over a Ploughed Field, 1974
Oil on canvas, 70.5 × 90.8 cm / 27¾ × 35¾ in
Private collection

A flock of striking red-breasted geese (*Branta ruficollis*) cut through the air, their white, black and ruddy-red tones scattered through the crisp sky, flying alongside greater white-fronted geese (*Anser albifrons*) whose inclusion suggests that this scene comes from a breeding site in Siberia. Individuals within the gliding flock are beginning to extend their feet downwards, slowing their descent as their webbed toes catch the air as they approach the frozen ground. As is usual in the paintings of the British artist Sir Peter Scott (1909–89),

the scene is naturalistically presented from human height, as if we were standing in the field watching the approaching geese. Scott's name is synonymous with bird conservation in the United Kingdom thanks to his founding of the Severn Wildfowl Trust (now the Wildfowl and Wetlands Trust) at Slimbridge – whose captive-breeding programme saved the nene or Hawaiian goose (*Branta sandvicensis*) from extinction in the 1950s – and his presenting of TV nature documentaries through the 1950s to the 1980s. Scott (son

of Antarctic explorer Robert Falcon Scott, see opposite) studied at Cambridge before honing his talent for painting natural history at the Munich State academy and London's Royal Academy, and he would go on to found the Society of Wildlife Artists. By the time Scott painted this image, the threatened red-breasted geese were already facing significant declines due to agricultural change and the extensions of fields such as those on which these geese are landing.

Diomedea melanophrys.

"Discovery". 1901.

Black-browed Albatros.

Southern Ocean.

Edward Wilson

Black-browed Albatross (*Diomedea melanophrys*), 1901
Watercolour, 23 × 29 cm / 9 × 11⅜ in
Scott Polar Research Institute, University of Cambridge

Artist, zoologist, medical doctor and polar explorer, Edward Wilson (1872–1912) was perhaps the closest friend of Captain Robert Falcon Scott, 'Scott of the Antarctic', and accompanied him on two expeditions to attempt to reach the South Pole, in 1901–4 and 1910–1913, an effort that cost both men their lives. These watercolours of black-browed albatross (*Thalassarche melanophris*) were made as their ship the *Discovery* headed southwards towards Antarctica in 1901 across an ocean teeming with bird life. During the later *Terra Nova* expedition, while waiting out the austral winter of 1911, Wilson led a scientific mission from Scott's base camp at Cape Evans to the emperor penguin (*Aptenodytes forsteri*) rookery at Cape Crozier across the Ross Ice Shelf, accompanied by Henry 'Birdie' Bowers and Apsley Cherry-Garrard. The purpose of the journey was to collect the penguins' eggs, based on the mistaken belief that the embryos might shed light on a reptilian origin of birds: a gruelling trek over the Ross Ice Shelf in complete darkness, in temperatures of –40°C, that Cherry-Garrard recounted in his 1922 book *The Worst Journey in the World*. The following spring Wilson was among the five men chosen by Scott to accompany him on the final leg of the journey to the South Pole, which they reached on 18 January 1912, only to find the Norwegian flag of Roald Amundsen's party already flying there. Downcast, exhausted and beset by particularly severe weather, none of the five survived the return journey to base camp.

Harriet Mead

Sole Great Auk, *c*.2013
Scrap metal, H. *c*.75 cm / 29½ in
Private collection

The awkward stance and stubby wings of this sculpture by the British artist Harriet Mead (born 1969) are characteristic of the extinct, flightless great auk (*Pinguinus impennis*). As is true of penguins of the southern hemisphere, the wings were used principally for underwater propulsion, but the great auk was emphatically not a penguin, despite its scientific name. It was a member of the auk family (Alcidae), which also includes such familiar species as the Atlantic puffin (*Fratercula arctica*) and common guillemot (*Uria aalge*). They and the great auk have similar plumage: dark above and white below. Standing around 75 cm (29½ in) tall, the bird once bred across a swathe of the North Atlantic from Newfoundland via Greenland and Iceland to Great Britain – but no more. It was vulnerable to hunting and arguably too trusting for its own good. In the seventeenth century, birds from Funk Island, Newfoundland, were driven up gangplanks onto ships to be killed for their flesh and oil. The last known pair was killed on Eldey, off Iceland, in 1844; a single bird was later seen near Newfoundland in 1852. Harriet Mead specializes in sculpting animals from scrap metal, and her great auk's back is formed by a metal sole or 'tramp' once used to protect a labourer's foot – hence the title *Sole Great Auk*, apt for a species that trod the road towards extinction.

Stefan Christmann

Emperor penguin (Aptenodytes forsteri)*, two males, one with hatching egg, the other with young chick.*
Atka Bay, Antarctica, 2017
Photograph, dimensions variable

In all probability, the first people ever to see emperor penguins (*Aptenodytes forsteri*) were those travelling to Antarctica on James Cook's second voyage from 1772 to 1775, including the German naturalist Johann Reinhold Forster, whose name remains reflected in the species' scientific name. Since that time, the emperors' unique breeding habits and appearance have captivated naturalists and the wider public. This image by photographer Stefan Christmann born 1983), which won the Birds category in the 2019 German Society for Nature Photographers' annual competition, captures the moment when two birds lift their brood pouches to reveal their offspring to each other. In one case, the chick has hatched, in the other it is still cracking its way out of the egg. Christmann writes, 'It was a priceless moment when these two birds met ... and it leaves so much room for coming up with a fictional conversation between the two.' In all likelihood, both adult birds were males, since the nine-to-ten week incubation during the Antarctic winter is undertaken by the male, the female spending this period at sea and only returning to feed the chick around the time of hatching. Both parents then bring food to the growing chick, which sets forth independently to sea when the floating ice fragments in mid-summer. Although recent satellite surveys have added to the number of known colonies, there are concerns that climate change will reduce the extent of floating sea ice so crucial for emperor penguin breeding.

Unknown

Corinthian *aryballos*, *c*.640 BC
Painted ceramic, H. 5 cm / 2 in
Musée du Louvre, Paris

This tiny owl, tilting its head with an expression of curiosity, once held perfume for a wealthy inhabitant of Corinth, in ancient Greece. Owls have a long history in ancient Greek art, dating to the Mycenaean Bronze Age (*c*.1600–1100 BC). They were represented in tombs because their nocturnal habits associated them with death, but owls were also believed to be able to ward off the evil eye – perhaps thanks to their staring eyes. The little owl (*Athene noctua*) was sacred to Athena, appearing on Athens' coinage from the

end of the sixth century BC, and was a symbol of good luck. According to the ancient Greek biographer Plutarch, an owl in flight appeared before the battle of Salamis in 480 BC, raising morale to enable the Greeks to defeat the Persians. The genus *Athene* includes four living species of small owl, as well as several extinct species. This *aryballos* or small flask was created during the Orientalizing period (*c*.725–600 BC), when Corinth was the leading centre for ceramic production, exporting fine wares across the eastern

Mediterranean. The later decades of the period were characterized by the production of miniature vases in the shape of animals, which were moulded with an inner reservoir, a spout in its base and holes for suspension cords. The polychrome technique and the use of incision were both innovative and influential on the black-figure technique of Greek vase painting, which reached its height in the late sixth century BC.

Unknown

Seated albatross netsuke, *c.*1800-50
Ivory and horn, L. 5.1 cm / 2 in
Private collection

This tiny carving of a short-tailed or Steller's albatross (*Phoebastria albatrus*), native to the North Pacific, features the bird's characteristic hooked beak and large eyes inlaid with dark horn. The Japanese word for albatross, *ahodori*, means 'stupid' – perhaps because the creature does not fear humans and is easily caught; it was brought to the brink of extinction in the early twenty-first century and is still critically endangered. This carving is an example of *netsuke*, which became part of Japanese male attire in the

seventeenth century. Men's kimonos had neither pockets nor closed sleeves – as women's did – which could serve as pockets. Instead, men carried personal possessions such as snuff, medicine or other necessities in small containers called *inro*, which were hung from the wide sash (*obi*) that secured the kimono. At the other end of the cord that closed the *inro* was fastened a button-like toggle that acted as a counterweight; over time, this evolved into the tiny sculptures called *netsuke*. All *netsuke*

are small, with holes through which a cord can be passed, and lack any sharp edges or protrusions that might damage a kimono; otherwise, they are as varied as the personalities of the men who wore them and the artists who carved them. Their designs often reflected trends in Japanese art, and those who could afford them amassed large collections, matching them to different kimonos and wearing them to signal mood in the way a woman today might wear a brooch.

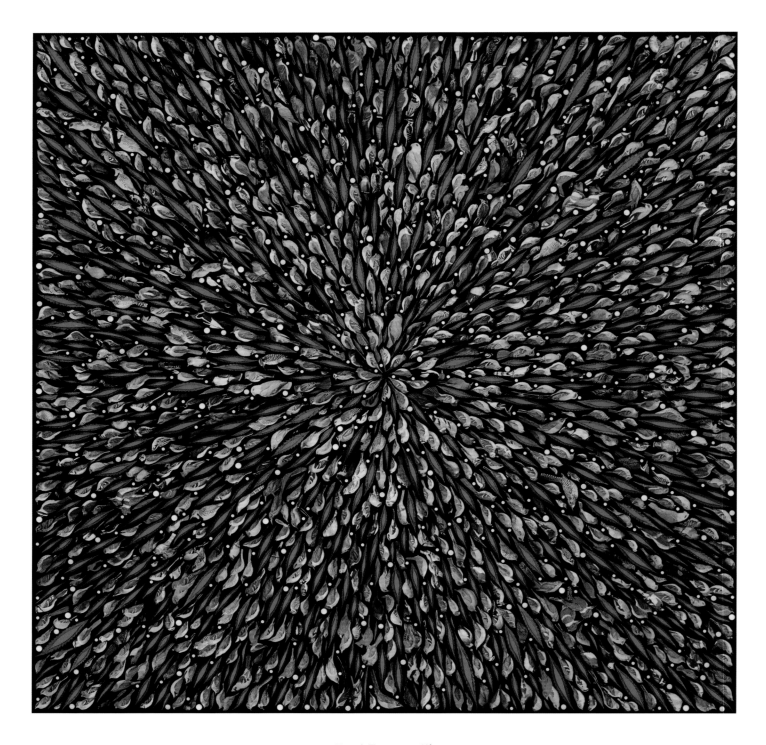

Fred Tomaselli

Bird Blast, 1997
Pills, leaves, collage, synthetic polymer paint and resin on wood panel, 152.4 × 152.4 cm / 60 × 60 in
Museum of Modern Art, New York

A kaleidoscope of colours bursts outwards from a single, central point of origin: a collection of North American birds, dazzling against a black background. Upon closer inspection, the birds are not alone within this intricate radiation of life: hemp leaves, each bearing a single red mark, frame the animals, along with countless white pharmaceutical tablets. The dynamism of the arrangement initially instills in the viewer a sense of vivacity. However, the individual birds are not presented in active, flying form; instead, they are illustrated side-on and motionless. Although the American artist Fred Tomaselli (born 1956) sources these diagrammatic illustrations from field guides intended to be used to identify birds in the wild, the effect is to reflect the type of preserved bird skins maintained in natural history museums across the world. Rather than presenting an explosion of life, Tomaselli offers us an explosion of quiet: a collection from a stilled natural world. His collaged association of the resplendent yet static birds with assorted pharmaceuticals presents an oblique reflection on humanity's impact upon the natural world, particularly by chemical intrusions such as the infamous insecticide DDT, that even after being banned in 1972 in the United States remains a threat to bird populations globally (see p.119). The red marks adorning each leaf may be wounds, while the polished layers of thick epoxy resin coating the work seem to add further distance between birds and viewer.

322

Jean-Baptiste Oudry

The White Duck, 1753
Oil on canvas, 95.3 × 63.5 cm / 37½ × 25 in
Location unknown

The luminous form of a white duck hangs above a table filled with objects selected to highlight the *trompe l'oeil* – or visual illusion – skills of the French painter Jean-Baptiste Oudry (1686–1755), whose name appears on the butcher's label attached to the bird's foot together with the date, 1753. Mostly devoid of colour, *The White Duck's* restricted palette successfully creates an impression of volume and depth in superlative detail, while suggesting a range of textures from feathers and folded linen to the burnished candlestick and white wax. Oudry was often heralded for his ability to animate light, particularly in white forms, and his skill attracted the attention of King Louis XV, of whom he became a favoured court painter. As such, he was often invited to Versailles to paint the royal menagerie and hunting scenes featuring the elite of the Ancien Régime. One of the most revered animal painters of the eighteenth century, Oudry had a strong influence on the visual aesthetics of the French Rococo. Within a year of completing this painting, he suffered a stroke that eventually led to his death in 1755. The allegory of *The White Duck* does not end here. The painting was stolen in 1992 from Houghton Hall in Norfolk, home of the Walpole Collection to which it belonged, by thieves who cut a hole in the roof during a party. It remains missing.

SIBLEY'S BACKYARD BIRDS

EASTERN NORTH AMERICA

ILLUSTRATED BY DAVID ALLEN SIBLEY

David Allen Sibley

Sibley's Backyard Birds: Eastern North America, 2010
Poster, 61 × 91.4 cm / 24 × 36 in

With its minimal design, this wall poster eliminates gratuitous detail, focusing solely on the markings, shape and relative scale observers need to identify the roughly one hundred bird species laid out against a stark white background. The featured species are all frequent backyard birds observed in the United States east of the Rocky Mountains, from perennial favourites such as the northern cardinal (*Cardinalis cardinalis*) to birders' delights such as the painted bunting (*Passerina ciris*) and yellow-throated warbler (*Setophaga dominica*).

The functionality of the work is its genius, as it describes the plumage of both the male *and* the female of the species. This distinction is an important one, as the initial inspiration of US ornithologist David Allen Sibley (born 1961) to create birding guides was born of frustration that females and juveniles were often omitted. Defying convention would prove to be a success. His inaugural volume, *The Sibley Guide to Birds* (2000), quickly became a birding staple. Often referred to as the 'birder's bible', the seminal work made Sibley

one of the leading experts in field identification for North American ornithology. Sibley's admiration for avian species began in early childhood. A self-taught artist, he grew up identifying and drawing birds. His acquired encyclopaedic knowledge has culminated in a prolific ornithological career. In addition to inspiring generations of birders and nature enthusiasts with his guides, his work has appeared in *Science* and *Smithsonian*, and he has been a frequent contributor to *The New York Times*.

Plate 54

KINGFISHER, JAYS, BOBOLINK, ORIOLES AND TANAGERS

BELTED KINGFISHER
Large bill, bushy crest, banded breast.   p. 103

CANADA JAY
Gray; white forehead, black nape.   p. 116

BLUE JAY
Bright blue, with crest.   p. 116

BOBOLINK
Male: Black belly, white patches above.   p. 155
Female: Striped head, buffy breast.

BALTIMORE ORIOLE
Male: Orange; black head.   p. 157
Female: Yellow-orange; wing-bars.

ORCHARD ORIOLE
Adult male: Deep rusty breast and rump.   p. 157
Immature male: Black throat-patch.
Female: Yellow-green; wing-bars.

SCARLET TANAGER
Breeding Male: Scarlet, with black wings.   p. 161
Moulting Male: Red patches.
Female: Yellow green; dusky wings.

SUMMER TANAGER
Breeding Male: Red all over, no crest.   p. 162
Female: Deeper yellow than Scarlet Tanager.

WESTERN TANAGER
Breeding Male: Red face, black back.   p. 161
Female: Wing-bars, Tanager bill.

Roger Tory Peterson

Plate 54, *Kingfisher, Jays, Bobolink, Orioles and Tanagers,* from *A Field Guide to the Birds*
(second revised and enlarged edition), published by Houghton Mifflin Company, Boston, 1947
Printed book, 19 × 12 cm / 7½ × 4¾ in
Private collection

In the nineteenth century, ornithologists – and bird illustrators – often had little choice but to kill birds in order to study them. Today, the modern ornithologist has ready access to a range of tools: binoculars, sound apps and even DNA-based methodologies for distinguishing closely similar species. American naturalist Roger Tory Peterson (1908-96) played a key role in the development of the identification skills of the ornithological community. His first book, *A Field Guide to the Birds* (1934), covering birds of eastern and central United States, went through multiple editions and was followed by companion volumes to western North American birds (1941) and Mexican birds (with Edward Chalif, 1973). In collaboration with Philip Hollom and Guy Mountfort, the Peterson approach was extended to Europe in 1954. Not only was Peterson accomplished enough as an artist to capture the often-distinctive shape and posture of different species; he also realized that quick identification in the field was easier if the observer knew what key features distinguished similar species. Thus he pioneered the use of critical field marks, indicated by the lines shown on this plate. To check whether a female oriole is Baltimore (*Icterus galbula*) or orchard (*I. spurius*), the key need is to check whether the breast is more orange (Baltimore) or plainer yellow-green (orchard). Similarly does a red male tanager have black wings (scarlet tanager *Piranga olivacea*) or red wings (summer *P. rubra*)?

Ostdrossel

Birds of North America, 2018
Photographs, dimensions variable

German bird enthusiast Lisa Cavanary lives in Michigan, USA, and has achieved some celebrity online under her pseudonym 'Ostdrossel', the German name for one of her favourite local species, the eastern bluebird (*Sialia sialis*). She has taken bird photography in an unusual direction by using a static camera to capture the birds that visit the feeding station in her backyard. The result is series of snapshots of the range of local birds that visit for a snack. These images she displays regularly on social media and on her own website, and she has attracted a wide following. The equipment she uses is attached to the bird feeder, which is regularly topped up with a range of food items, and a motion sensor activates the camera, thus securing images without intrusion. A wide variety of birds visit the feeders, and from the thousands of images captured automatically by her camera Ostdrossel selects those with quirky or otherwise appealing portraits. The species displayed here are (clockwise from top left): purple finch, (*Haemorhous purpureus*), male; eastern bluebird, female and male; blue jay (*Cyanocitta cristata*); Baltimore oriole (*Icterus galbula*), male; ruby-throated hummingbird (*Archilochus colubris*), male; common grackle (*Quiscalus quiscula*), male; northern cardinal (*Cardinalis cardinalis*), male; tufted titmouse (*Baeolophus bicolor*); black-capped chickadee (*Poecile atricapillus*); mourning dove (*Zenaida macroura*); red-bellied woodpecker (*Melanerpes carolinus*), male; Baltimore oriole, female.

34,000 BC   Some of the earliest depictions of birds appear on cave walls during the Palaeolithic era. In 2008, an ochre painting of an emu-like bird, thought to depict the *Genyornis newtoni*, a bird that became extinct 40,000 years ago, was discovered in Australia.

15,500 BC   A tiny sculpture thought to represent a passerine bird is carved from a burnt mammal limb bone in Lingjing, China. It is considered to be the oldest East Asian work of art ever found.

15,000 BC   Images of a bird on a stick, a rhino, a bison and a man with a bird's head are painted in Lascaux Cave in southwest France. They may have served as instruction manuals for new hunters, but are more likely to have had symbolic significance, forming part of a prehistoric culture in which birds and other animals had great spiritual value.

c.3800 BC   Early in their history, ancient Egyptians worship Horus, one of many gods associated with the falcon or hawk. The falcon was considered a cosmic deity: its body represented the heavens, and its eyes the Sun and the Moon. Falcons were thought to have special powers of protection.

c.1800 BC   Babylonian artists produce a terracotta relief portraying the goddess known as Queen of the Night, composed of human and bird body parts. Downward-pointing wings and the talons of a bird of prey connect their deity with the underworld.

c.1600 BC   Flying swallows are depicted in Bronze-age frescos at Akrotiri on the Greek island of Santorini (left, p.44).

c.750 BC   Birds are first mentioned in European literature by the Greek Homer in *The Iliad*, in which he describes the Trojan army as being 'like the cranes which flee from the coming winter and sudden rain'.

c.700 BC   The Scythians, nomadic peoples who roam Central Asia, decorate their jewellery and armour with images of birds.

664 BC   In Late-Dynastic Period Egypt, the ibis is worshipped as Thoth, god of writing and knowledge, and is believed to protect the country from serpents and plagues. The birds were often mummified and interred as part of tomb burials (centre, p.105).

c.600 BC   The Celts of central and western Europe possibly believe birds to be reincarnations of highly respected individuals. Birds also symbolize transcendence and freedom because of their ability to take flight towards the heavens. The Celts believed that birds acted as moderators between humans and the gods, with the ability to deliver prophecies and messages of guidance.

c.450 BC   During the Classical period of ancient Greece, the city-state of Athens adopts the owl as a symbol of its patron goddess Athena, representing her wisdom. Images of owls appear on the city's coins.

426 BC   The Greek historian Herodotus compiles his *Histories*, the second volume of which contains lengthy descriptions of Egyptian birds and animals.

414 BC   Ancient Greek playwright Aristophanes writes a comedy titled *The Birds*, which is first performed at the festival of Dionysia in Athens.

c.350 BC   Greek philosopher Aristotle devotes four volumes of his *Historia Animalium* to birds, identifying 170 species. He was the first person to attempt to explain migration. Some of his theories have since been disproven, including the idea that birds hibernate over winter or that some species transmogrify, or change into others.

246 BC   Construction of the mausoleum of Qin Shi Huang, the first Emperor of China, begins near the ancient capital city of Chang'an in Shaanxi Province, China. The 50-square-kilometre (20 sq. mile) compound eventually contained 8,000 life-size terracotta soldiers and thousands of animal artefacts and figurines, including birds.

57 BC   Bird-shaped ceramic vessels are used during funereal and burial rituals on the southern Korean peninsula (right, p.289).

44 BC   Roman senator Marcus Junius Brutus uses carrier pigeons to send messages to his allies during the siege of Modena.

27 BC   Roman legions begin to use the Aquila, or eagle, as an insignia, carried into battle by a standard-bearer known as an Aquilifer. The eagle represented power and courage.

AD 77   Roman statesman and naturalist Pliny the Elder completes his *Naturalis historia*. Book X is devoted to birds and describes – among other things – their harmfulness or usefulness to humans.

79   The eruption of Vesuvius destroys the Roman town of Pompeii in southern Italy. Among the buried buildings is the House of the Faun, which has a wall mosaic depicting a Nilotic scene of ducks and geese swimming among lotuses and waterlilies. Another mosaic of birds in the House of the Doves is based on a lost original by Sosus of Pergamon, described in the writings of Pliny the Elder (overleaf left, p.170).

c.100   The Romans and Greeks produce bird-shaped glass bottles to hold liquids, perfumes and cosmetic powders. The bottles were made with the contents sealed inside, accessed by breaking the bird's tail.

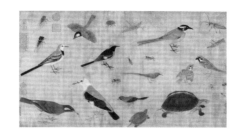

100s   *Physiologus*, is compiled in Alexandria, Egypt, by an unknown author. Covering the characteristics and behaviour of animals, it became a primary source for medieval bestiaries. The text also had a key influence on Christian art. It records well-known stories such as the phoenix rising from ashes and the pelican feeding her young with her blood.

Ancient people in southern Peru begin carving a series of enormous geoglyphs, in the Nazca Desert, including a number of figures of birds. Created over centuries, the Nazca Lines, have been variously interpreted as boundary markers, indicators of spring, and ritual paths for processions.

*c.*200   Roman author Aelian, or Claudius Aelianus, writes *On the Nature of Animals*. The seventeen-volume treatise includes stories of birds and other animals in the form of anecdotes, folklore, or fables with morals.

200s   Nightingales, starlings, ravens, magpies and parrots are popular household pets in the Roman Empire.

355   *Nihon-shoki*, a largely mythical narrative, records the introduction of falconry to Japan from Baekje by the sixteenth emperor, Nintoku. The sport was seen as a status symbol due to the rarity and price of hawks and the time, money and space required to raise and train them.

*c.*400   Falconry is brought to Europe from the Middle East by merchants and travellers. Initially, it is adopted as a way to hunt for food. It was practiced widely throughout Western Europe and Great Britain by the ninth century, and later became a noble pursuit among the privileged classes.

*c.*500   The first quill pens appear in Europe, made using the hollow barrel of a bird's feather to hold ink. They remained the primary writing implement until the mid-1800s. The strongest quills were produced from the moulted feathers of living birds.

*c.*501   A monk named Saint Serf feeds a robin by hand, in Fife, Scotland, marking the beginning of the tradition of feeding garden birds.

*c.*630   Isadore, Archbishop of Seville compiles his *Etymologiae*, a compendium of human knowledge in twenty books. Book XII, 'de animalibus', covers beasts and birds and collates information from sources including Pliny, Servius and Solnius.

842   Benedictine monk Rabanus Maurus begins to compile *De rerum naturis*, a twenty-two book encyclopaedia. The eighth book, on animals, is divided into seven chapters according to animal type: 'beasts', 'small animals', 'serpents', 'worms', 'fish', 'birds' and 'small birds'.

*c.*900   The Pueblo peoples of Chaco Canyon, now in New Mexico, begin importing macaws over long-distance trade routes from their native Mesoamerica.

900s   Chinese Song Dynasty artist Huan Quan accurately depicts a white wagtail, a gull, a white-cheeked starling, a daurian redstart and a scarlet Mrs Gould's Sunbird among twenty-four common Chinese animals on a handscroll for his son to study (centre left, p.155).

*c.*1000   The Islamic polymath Avicenna translates and produces commentary on Aristotle's works of natural history. His arabic versions of the texts are vital sources in the eventual 'recovery of Aristotle' in the West in the middle ages.

*c.*1000   The extinction of the *Aepyornis*, commonly known as the 'elephant bird', is widely believed to have taken place around this time as a consequence of human activity. The large, flightless birds of Madgascar were likely hunted to extinction. Discoveries of shells amongst the remains of human fires suggest their eggs provided meals for entire families.

1112   Chinese Emperor Huizong, Zhao Ji paints a flock of cranes he has seen gathering above his palace gates while auspicious clouds formed around them. It is claimed that thousands of people witnessed the event in awe, making it worthy of commemoration on a scroll.

*c.*1200   A lavishly illuminated manuscript, now known as the Aberdeen Bestiary, is compiled in England. It includes numerous depictions of birds, some more accurate than others (centre right, p.202).

Artisans in the city of Limoges in France begin making eucharistic doves of enamelled metal, which can be hung above altars to symbolize the Holy Ghost.

*c.*1220   Working in the court of King Frederic II of Sicily, the scholar Michael Scot translates Aristotle's *Historia animalium* and various commentaries on it from Arabic to Latin.

*c.*1230   Thomas of Cantimpré begins his twenty-volume encyclopedia *Liber de natura rerum* ('Book on the Nature of Things'). He dedicates Book V to birds.

1240s   Frederick II, Holy Roman Emperor, writes a detailed treatise on falconry, *De Arte Venandi cum Avibus* ('The Art of Hunting with Birds'). It includes a general account of birds based on personal observation, and is considered the first book dedicated solely to ornithology.

*c.*1250   German Catholic Dominican friar Albertus Magnus, also known as Albert the Great, compiles a treatise on birds based on his translations of the writing of Aristotle, including instructions on caring for sick and wounded falcons.

People in Paquimé, Mexico, begin breeding macaws to meet demand for the birds which are culturally important throughout the region.

1478   Canaries are introduced to Europe as pet birds from the Canary Islands by Spanish sailors.

1481   German scholar Konrad von Megenberg publishes *Das Buch der Natur* ('The Book of Nature'), a comprehensive survey of the natural world that includes descriptions of seventy-two different birds.

1492   Italian artist Andrea Mantegna includes a cockatoo in his painting *Madonna della Vittoria*. It is the first time this native of Southeast Asia and Australasia appears in Western art.

1506   Italian Renaissance master Raphael paints *Madonna of the Goldfinch*. It is one of many religious paintings of the period to include the European goldfinch, which variously symbolized the soul, resurrection, sacrifice and death and, following plagues in the fourteenth century, an augur.

*c.*1507   Europeans see the flightless dodo for the first time when Portuguese sailors land on Mauritius in the Indian Ocean.

1512   German artist Albrecht Dürer produces a meticulous study of the wing of a European roller (right, p.166).

1521   Spanish conquistador Hernán Cortés arrives in the Aztec capital of Tenochtitlán and notes that the Aztec keep birds in aviaries.

1544   English priest, physician and naturalist William Turner publishes *The Principal Birds of Aristotle and Pliny*, the first printed bird book. His personal observations on the ancient texts mark the beginning of modern, empirical science. Concurrently, Turner publishes the unfinished *Diologus de Avibus* ('Diologue of Birds') by his friend Gilbert of Longueil.

1555   Swiss naturalist and botanist Conrad Gessner publishes the third volume of his encyclopedia *Historiae Animalium*, which lists more than 182 species of European birds (left, p.302).

French naturalist Pierre Belon publishes *The Comparative Anatomy of Avian and Human Skeletons*, an ornithological encyclopedia and first published work of comparative anatomy.

1570   Imprisoned by her cousin, Queen Elizabeth I, Mary Queen of Scots embroiders the Oxburgh Hangings featuring birds copied from Conrad Gessner's *Icones Avium Omnium*.

1573   Dutch anatomist and physician Volcher Coiter publishes a treatise on bird anatomy.

1599   Italian naturalist Ulisse Aldrovandi publishes his three-volume *Ornithologiae, hoc est, De avibus historiae* ('Ornithology, that is, the history of birds'), which includes detailed descriptions and nearly 700 woodcut illustrations. He claims his images of turkeys and cardinals to be 'among the earliest illustrations of American forms'.

1601   Dutch artist Roelandt Savery becomes court painter to Emperor Rudolf II in Prague, where he is able to paint birds and other animals in the royal menagerie.

1601   Italian scholar Antonio Valli da Todi provides the first written evidence of territoriality in birds, describing the behaviour of nightingales in his book *Il Canto degl'Augelli* ('The song of the birds')

1603   German astronomer Johann Bayer produces a star chart of the 'celestial birds' constellations mapped by explorers of the Dutch East India Company on their 1594 voyage to Java and Sumatra.

German theologian Caspar Schwenckfeld publishes the first list of fauna native to a particular area, including brief descriptions of 150 birds of Silesia.

1605   Dutch botanist Carolus Clusius writes *Exoticorum libri decem* ('Ten books of exotics') the first study published in Europe to focus solely on exotic plants and animals.

1611   Flemish artist Peter Paul Rubens paints *The Abduction of Ganymede*, depicting the Roman god Jupiter in the form of an eagle.

1621   *De formatione ovi et pulli* (On the Formation of the Egg and of the Chick) by Italian embryologist Girolamo Fabrici is published, advancing knowledge of embryo development of birds and their basic reproductive physiology.

1622   The first use of falconry in North America is documented in New England.

1629   Flanders-born artist Frans Snyders paints *Concert of Birds*. Inspired by Aesop's fable 'The Owl and the Birds'. Thanks to Snyders, the motif of the owl as musical conductor was widely disseminated in seventeenth-century Flemish art.

1636   A dead pelican is brought to the antiquarian Cassiano dal Pozzo in Rome, who commissions Vincenzo Leonardi to paint it for his Museo Cartaceo (Paper Museum).

1648   The first scientific study of the flora and fauna of Brasil, the *Historia Naturalis Brasiliae* by Willem Piso and Georg Marcgraf is published.

c.1650   Dutch artist Jan Asselijn paints *The Threatened Swan*. 100 years later, when it is acquired by the Nationale Kunstgalerij, the painting is reinterpreted as a political allegory of the Netherlands defending itself against foreign intervention (centre left, p.97).

Athanasius Kircher publishes *Musurgia universalis sive ars magna consoni et dissoni*, which includes an early attempt to transcribe birdsong into musical notation, aiming to demonstrate that music reflects the harmony of God's cosmos.

1651   English physician William Harvey's study of animal generation is published, correcting certain errors by his teacher Fabrici.

1654   Dutch artist Carel Fabritius paints *The Goldfinch*. Rediscovered in 1859, it becomes one of the most iconic bird images in art history. Almost 360 years later, it was integral to the book of the same name by US writer Donna Tartt.

1658   Willem van Aelst paints *Still Life with Fowl*. The Dutch Golden Age artist was highly influential in developing the bird-still-life genre.

1674   King Louis XIV of France appoints Belgian artist Pieter Boel Peintre Ordinaire. Boel revolutionized animal painting by working directly from live subjects in the King's menagerie at Versailles.

1676   The first truly scientific ornithological text, known as *Ornithologiae libri tres*, is published by English naturalist John Ray four years after the death of his collaborator, the mathematician and natural historian Francis Willughby. An English edition of the book was published in 1678 (centre right, p.299).

1681   The last dodo is killed on the island of Mauritius. The flightless bird later becomes one of the best-known examples of human-induced extinction.

The ambassador of the King of Fez and Morocco presents King Charles II of England with a gift of numerous ostriches, some of which were allowed to roam free in St. James's Park, London.

c.1700   Japanese artist Ogata Korin paints a pair of folding screens featuring nineteen cranes, which symbolize longevity in East Asia, on a golden background.

1721   An encyclopaedia known as *The Compendium of Birds* is produced for the Kangxi court by painter Jiang Tingxi. The album features 360 carefully observed drawings of birds. The systematic approach employed to classify and describe each species makes the work highly unusual for the time.

1729   English naturalist Mark Catesby, later known as the father of American ornithology, publishes the first part of *The Natural History of Carolina, Florida and the Bahama Islands*, which documents the flora and fauna of the southeastern United States and the Caribbean.

1731   English naturalist and illustrator Eleazar Albin and his daughter Elizabeth complete 306 illustrations for *A Natural History of Birds*, one of the first lavishly illustrated ornithological books.

1731-33   Chinese bird-and-flower painter Shen Quan visits Japan, where he teaches traditional Chinese realist painting, leading to the formation of the Nagasaki School.

1734   German sculptor Johann Joachim Kändler produces a ceramic king vulture as part of a porcelain zoo commissioned by Augustus II, Elector of Saxony and King of Poland (right, p.62).

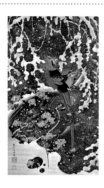   

1735 Swedish naturalist and explorer Carl Linnaeus publishes his *Systema Naturae* ('The System of Nature'), developing a new system of classification for natural species. The classification of birds follows the system devised by John Ray.

1737 Italian naturalist Giuseppe Zinanni publishes the first book devoted to the subject of birds' eggs and nests *Delle uova e dei nidi degli uccelli* ('Some eggs and some birds' nests').

1739 French inventor and artist Jacques de Vaucanson designs a mechanical duck he claims eats and digests grain before defecating.

c.1740 German pastor and ornithologist Johann Heinrich Zorn authors a landmark two-volume study on ornithology and theology.

1743 George Edwards publishes the first section of *A Natural History of Uncommon Birds*. His detailed descriptions are celebrated for their accuracy.

1747 Mark Catesby presents a paper titled 'Of Birds of Passage' to the Royal Society in London, one of the first scientific studies into the migration of birds. Before the seventeenth century, it was generally thought that they hibernated.

1761 Japanese artist Ito Jakuchu begins his masterpiece, *Colourful Realm of Living Beings*, a series of thirty hanging scrolls featuring birds, such as mandarin ducks, sparrows, roosters and chickens, alongside other animals and flowers (left, p.25).

1768 British naval captain James Cook leads an expedition to the South Pacific Ocean on the HMS *Endeavour*. The naturalists accompanying Cook, Joseph Banks and Daniel Solander, collect many bird specimens new to science.

1769 Sailing with Cook on HMS *Endeavour*, Scottish artist Sydney Parkinson documents the red-tailed tropicbird for the first time, among hundreds of other natural history illustrations he makes on the voyage.

1770 Preeminent French naturalist, mathematician Georges-Louis Leclerc, Comte de Buffon publishes the first instalment of his landmark *Histoire Naturelle des Oiseaux* ('Natural History of Birds'). It includes 1,008 hand-coloured plates across thirty six volumes and is translated into many different languages.

The Falconers' Society of England is founded.

1773 James Cook introduces chickens to New Zealand on his second voyage to the country.

1774 Influential bird-and-flower painter Maruyama Okyo completes the first of a pair of folding screens featuring a greater white-fronted goose about to land in a wetland, blending the dominant Kano school of Japanese painting with single-point perspective common to European painting.

1777 German scientist Johann Reinhold Forster names the broad-billed prion *Procellaria vittata* during James Cook's second voyage around the world. It is the first published scientific name given to a New Zealand bird.

1778 Jesuit priest and naturalist Juan Ignacio Molina publishes *Saggio sulla storia naturale del Chile*, which includes the first descriptions of many South American birds.

1780s Lady Mary Impey, wife of the British colonial official Sir Elijah Impey, commissions the Indian artist Shaikh Zain ud-Din to paint birds and other animals of the Subcontinent in their private menagerie (centre left, p.74).

1782 Following a lengthy dispute between members of Congress, the bald eagle is chosen as the national bird of the United States. It still appears on the Great Seal and on official documents, flags, military insignia, and one-dollar bills today.

1791 Japanese artist Kitagawa Utamaro produces the two-volume woodblock printed book *Momo chidori kyōka-awase* ('Myriad Birds: Picture Book of Playful Verse'). Each double-page spread features two species of bird and a poem written in the voice of one of the birds illustrated.

1797 British artist Thomas Bewick publishes the first volume of *A History of British Birds*, which includes detailed descriptions and meticulous wood engravings of each of the major British bird species. A second volume was published in 1804 (centre right, p.16).

1801 British navigator Matthew Flinders sets off on an expedition to map the coast of Australia. Among those on board is Austrian illustrator Ferdinand Bauer, who documents the local flora and fauna, bringing back more than 2,000 drawings.

1802 English naturalist George Montagu publishes *Ornithological Dictionary, or Alphabetical Synopsis of British Birds*, which helps to popularize ornithology in Britain.

1806 French explorer, ornithologist and author François Levaillant publishes *Histoire Naturelle des Oiseaux de Paradis et des Rolliers* featuring 114 illustrations of exotic birds by renowned bird artist Jacques Barraband.

1808-14 Pioneering Scottish ornithologist Alexander Wilson publishes *American Ornithology*, which establishes him as a founder of American ornithology.

1820 English ornithologist William Swainson uses the new printing process of lithography ("drawing on stone"), developed for transcribing musical notation, in his work 'Zoological Illustrations'.

1827 American writer Sarah Josepha Hale campaigns to have Thanksgiving established as a national holiday in the United States and describes a Thanksgiving feast with a turkey in her novel *Northwood*.

1829 The octagonal Raven's Cage is erected at London Zoo to house macaws and later vultures and ravens. Designed by architect Decimus Burton, it remains an iconic part of the zoo, but is no longer used because it is considered too small.

1830 British artist and verse writer Edward Lear publishes the first part of his *Illustrations of the Family Psittacidae or Parrots*. It is thought to be the first monograph on a single family of birds (right, p.43).

1831 British naturalist Charles Darwin embarks on a voyage to South America on the HMS *Beagle*. The finches he discovered during an expedition to the remote Galápagos Islands – now known as Darwin's finches – were connected to his groundbreaking insight that natural selection is the mechanism behind evolution.

1834 Prideaux John Selby publishes the final section of *Illustrations of British Ornithology*, which includes the first set of life-sized illustrations of British birds.

1835 Japanese artist, ukiyo-e painter and printmaker Katsushika Hokusai paints an eight-panel folding screen featuring a phoenix.

The 'sport' of cockfighting is banned in England under the Cruelty to Animals Act.

1838 — American artist and naturalist John James Audubon publishes the fourth and final volume of *Birds of America*. The double elephant folio edition, featuring 435 life-size watercolours of North American Birds, is considered the largest and most beautiful bird book ever made.

1840 — English ornithologist and bird artist John Gould publishes the first part of his seven volume landmark book *The Birds of Australia*. It includes depictions of all 681 Australian bird species known at the time, many illustrated by Gould's wife, Elizabeth.

1844 — The last pair of great auks is killed on Eldey Island, off the coast of Iceland. The species had been hunted initially for meat and feathers and from the 1830s onwards, for scientific study and for museum display.

1845 — American writer Edgar Allen Poe publishes his narrative poem 'The Raven' to wide acclaim, bringing him international fame.

1848 — Scottish artist Jemima Blackburn illustrates *Caw! Caw!, or The Chronicle of Crows, A Tale of Spring Time*, which tells the story of a colony of rooks and their persecution by a farmer.

1849 — Blaise Bontems, opens his own workshop in Paris after successfully repairing a snuffbox with a mechanical bird. He becomes a specialist in the manufacture of automata, renowned for the realism of the bird song they produce (left, p.31).

1850 — English Romantic painter J. M. W Turner produces numerous illustrations for an ornithological study by Walter Fawkes known as *The Farnley Hall Bird Book*. It depicts some of Britain's best-loved birds, including a robin, a kingfisher and a white barn owl.

1856 — British painter William James Webbe exhibits his painting *The White Owl* at the Royal Academy in London.

1858 — English explorer and naturalist Alfred Russel Wallace collects an unknown bird of paradise on the island of Bacan in Indonesia. The following year, it is named *Semioptera wallacei*, or Wallace's standardwing, in his honour. Eleven years later, an illustration by John Gerrard Keulemans appears in Wallace's *The Malay Archipelago: the land of the orang-utan and the bird of paradise*.

English naturalist Thomas Campbell Eyton publishes the first part of *Osteologia avium, or, A sketch of the osteology of birds*, featuring meticulous anatomical illustrations of bird's skeletons arranged in lifelike, animated postures.

1859 — The first issue of *The Ibis*, the scientific journal of the British Ornithological Union, is published.

1860s — The mounting of small birds, such as hummingbirds, in necklaces, earrings and other jewellery is highly fashionable.

1861 — The first fossilized specimen – a single feather – of *Archaeopteryx*, a genus of feathered dinosaur, is discovered in Bavaria, Germany.

1865 — A new edition of Lewis Carroll's *Alice's Adventures in Wonderland* is published in which English illustrator and cartoonist John Tenniel immortalizes the dodo (centre left, p.39).

The first living penguin specimen arrives at London Zoo from the Falkland Islands.

1866 — English Pre-Raphaelite artist William Holman Hunt completes *The Festival of St Swithin (The Dovecote)*, which he paints from life after buying some pigeons and a dovecot.

1867 — With twelve favourite specimens laid out in his bedroom, future US president Theodore Roosevelt establishes the Roosevelt Museum of Natural History aged eight, beginning his lifelong interest in conservation and nature.

1869 — The Seabirds Protection Act in the United Kingdom, one of the first pieces of legislation in the world designed to protect wildlife, is passed following a campaign by Alfred Newton and local clergy and naturalists to save the birds of Flamborough Head in Yorkshire, England.

1870 — The North American Labrador duck becomes extinct, possibly as a result of human competition for the mussels and other shellfish on which it feeds.

French artist Rosa Bonheur, acclaimed for her depictions of animals, paints *The Wounded Eagle*. It is her only known painting of a bird (centre right, p.118).

Robert Fulton publishes *The Illustrated Book of Pigeons with Standards for Judging* following the success of his *Illustrated Book of Poultry* with the aim of producing a 'full and trustworthy treatise for the Pigeon Fancier'.

Homing pigeons are used to carry messages during the Siege of Paris

1874 — *History of North American Birds* by Spencer Fullerton Baird, Thomas Mayo Brewer and Robert Ridgway is published. It features 64 plates and 593 woodcuts by the artist Henry W. Elliott.

1875 — British artist and book illustrator Walter Crane paints one of his first wallpaper designs, which features two swans. Two years later, a wallpaper featuring the design is issued by Jeffrey & Co.

1876 — American artist Genevieve Jones begins work on *Illustrations of the Nests and Eggs of Birds of Ohio*, with the intention of producing a companion volume to John James Audubon's *Birds of America*.

1878 — London-based publisher Cassell, Petter, Galpin & Co., issues *The illustrated book of canaries and cage-birds, British and foreign*, reflecting the popularity of keeping and breeding birds at the time.

American artist John Singer Sargent produces a study featuring two views of a dead blue tit posed to look as though it is still alive.

1880 — The first large-scale aviary in a zoological garden is built at Rotterdam Zoo in the Netherlands.

c.1880 — French artist Hector Giacomelli depicts twenty-four finches in his painting *A Perch of Birds*, which exemplifies his most popular subject, the 'bâtons de cage', showing birds for sale as cagebirds by birdsellers.

1880 — Luxury Parisian jeweller Joseph Chaumet introduces a series of inventive silver, diamond, ruby and feather hummingbird aigrettes, or hair ornaments (right, p.18).

1883 — The American Ornithologists' Union is founded by William Brewster, Elliott Coues and Joel Allen to promote bird conservation and interest in developing ornithology in North America. The Society's official publication, *The Auk: Ornithological Advances*, is established the following year.

1884 — Swedish artist Bruno Liljefors paints a hawk and a grouse he has shot and mounted in the forest of Ärentuna, north of Uppsala. He sought to depict birds and other animals in their habitats as accurately as possible.

1885 — Tsar Alexander III of Russia commissions jeweller Peter Carl Fabergé to create an Easter gift for his wife, Tsarina Maria. Inspired by an eighteenth-century ivory egg in the Royal Danish Collection, Fabergé creates an egg with a white 'shell' that opens to reveal a golden 'yolk' containing a golden hen.

1886 — King Leopold II of Belgium gives the British Royal Family a number of racing pigeons. They are used to establish a pigeon racing loft on the royal estate at Sandringham that is still in existence today.

1889 — English artist Henry Stacy Marks exhibits a collection of his bird paintings, many of them developed from observational drawings he made at London Zoo, at the Fine Art Society in London (left, p.70).

American cigarette company Allen & Ginter issue their Birds of the Tropics cigarette trade cards to promote the brand.

1890s — The first rubber ducks appear on the market after Charles Goodyear develops a process for making rubber easy to use. The modern iconic 'rubber' duck, which is actually made of vinyl, was patented by Russian-American sculptor Peter Ganine in the 1940s.

1890 — French scientist and chronophotographer Étienne-Jules Marey publishes *Le Vol des Oiseaux* ('The Flight of Birds'), featuring pioneering photographs that capture the different phases of flight in a single image.

Danish teacher and ornithologist Hans Christian Cornelius Mortensen has the idea of fastening a ring with a number and address to a bird's leg. In 1899, he began a more systematic approach to ringing birds to gather more information about their behaviour.

1891 — The Society for the Protection of Birds is founded in Britain after the merger of two organizations established to protest the feather trade for women's hats. The organization was granted a Royal Charter fifteen years later, becoming the Royal Society for the Protection of Birds, or RSPB.

1893 — Dutch illustrator and graphic designer Theo van Hoytema publishes *The Ugly Duckling*, an illustrated version of the Hans Christian Anderson fairy tale.

1899 — American bird artist Louis Agassiz Fuertes joins the Harriman Alaska Expedition, during which he documents numerous birds and animals. The illustrations he makes during the expedition propel him to the forefront of wildlife illustration.

1901 — The Australasian Ornithologist's Union is established to promote the study and conservation of native birds in Australia.

1903 — American President Theodore Roosevelt establishes the first Federal Bird Reserve on Florida's Pelican Island.

1904 — German scientist and artist Ernst Haeckel publishes the final instalment of his most famous work *Kunstformen der Natur* ('Artforms in Nature'), which features more than a hundred detailed illustrations of birds, other animals and sea creatures (centre left, p.107).

The Smithsonian Institution commissions the largest ever flight cage for the World's Fair in St. Louis, Missouri. Inside were some 1,000 domestic and exotic birds, ranging from partridges, doves and canaries to gulls, geese and swans. It was intended to be moved to the National Zoo in Washington after the fair, but the residents of St. Louis liked it so much they rallied to keep it, and it remains an iconic part of Saint Louis Zoo today.

1904 — German ornithologist Magdalena Heinroth begins rearing birds in the Berlin apartment she shares with her husband Oskar, assistant diretor at the Zoologischer Garten Berlin. Over the next twenty-eight years, she raises 1,000 birds of 286 species. The couple studied the birds' behaviour and development, publishing their findings between 1924 and 1933.

1905 — Florida game warden Guy Bradley is killed by commercial plume hunters while protecting a bird rookery in Florida Bay.

The National Audubon Society is established in the United States to protect waterbirds from the millenery trade.

1908 — Inspired by one of the ducks on her farm and by the illustrations of Jemima Blackburn, English writer, illustrator and natural scientist Beatrix Potter writes and illustrates *The Tale of Jemima Puddle-Duck*.

1911 — Photographer Frank Hurley joins the Australasian Antarctic Expedition on which he photographs penguins on the sub-Antarctic Macquarie Island (centre right, p.260).

1914 — Martha, the last passenger pigeon, dies in the Cincinnati Zoological Garden.

1914-5 — American-British sculptor Jacob Epstein produces a series of three sculptures of mating doves.

1915 — The Cornell Lab of Ornithology is established by Arthur A. Allen when he joins Cornell University in Ithaca, New York, as one of the first professors of Ornithology in the US.

1918 — In France during World War I, despite its grave injuries carrier pigeon Cher Ami delivers a rescue message from a battalion that has become isolated from other American forces, saving the lives of 194 soldiers.

1918 — In the United States, the Migratory Bird Treaty Act is passed to protect wild birds from illegal trade and hunting. It is one of the first federal protections for wildlife and remains America's most important bird-protection law, credited with saving many species from extinction.

1919 — Edinburgh Zoo in Scotland becomes the first zoo in the world to breed king penguins in captivity.

1920 — The Whitney South Sea Expedition explores the islands of the South Pacific to collect bird specimens. Celebrated as the longest ornithological voyage in history, it enabled naturalists to collect around 40,000 birds, plants and other specimens.

1922 — The International Council for Bird Preservation, the world's first international conservation organization, is formed. It became BirdLife International in 1993.

Ornithologist and photographer Ernest G Holt leads the first-ever bird photography expedition to Venezuela in search of the wintering populations of birds migrating to North America in the summer. He returns with images of more than 3,000 birds, including 486 species.

1929 — The American state of Kentucky selects the northern cardinal to be its official state bird. It is the first state to designate a state bird and the first of seven states to choose the cardinal as its emblem.

1932 — The British Trust for Ornithology is established for the study of birds in the British Isles.

1934 — American ornithologist and wildlife artist Roger Tory Peterson publishes *A Field Guide to the Birds*. The first of many books he wrote and illustrated, it revolutionized field identification and stimulated popular interest in birds (right, p.325).

1935 — British publisher Allen Lane releases the first books of the Penguin imprint, intending to make quality literature accessible to all. A visit to London Zoo inspired the iconic Penguin logo created by graphic designer Edward Young.

Artist John Gilroy designs the first Guinness advertisement to feature a toco toucan, launching one of the most memorable beer advertising campaigns in history.

1937 — British publisher Frederick Warne & Co. issues *The Observer's Book of British Birds*, which describes 243 species and features more than 200 illustrations – popularizing bird watching as a hobby for the postwar generation.

1938 — British pottery manufacturer Beswick issues its first flying duck wall plaques. They were produced in sets of three in five different sizes until 1973, and they remain popular as collector's items (left, p.280).

c.1940 — Chinese artist Qi Baishi paints *Eagle on a Pine Tree* during the turbulent period of the Second Sino-Japanese War.

1941 — The iconic cartoon canary Tweety Bird makes his first appearance in animator Bob Clampett's *Caged Canary*. The character went on to star in forty-seven cartoon shorts, and the short 'Tweety Pie' won the first Warner Brothers Academy Award for animation in 1947.

In the United States, a count finds only twenty-one whooping cranes living in the wild. Through captive breeding, wetland management, and a program that involves teaching young cranes how to migrate, numbers have risen to around 600 today.

Mexican artist Frida Kahlo paints a self-portrait featuring four parrots just after she remarries Mexican muralist Diego Rivera.

1943 — The Museum of Modern Art, New York, hosts an exhibition of pioneering colour photographs of birds by Eliot Porter.

1948 — Artist and ornithologist Peter Scott founds the Severn Wildfowl Trust, which will become the international conservation charity the Wildfowl & Wetlands Trust.

1947 — African-American taxidermist and artist Carl Cotton joins the Field Museum in Chicago, where he spends almost 25 years preparing exhibitions of the museum's collections.

1948 — The flightless South Island takahe, which was previously thought to be extinct, is rediscovered in the Murchison Mountains in New Zealand.

1949 — A dove designed by Spanish artist Pablo Picasso is chosen as the World Peace Congress emblem and becomes a popular symbol of peace.

American artist Joseph Cornell exhibits his most celebrated series, *Aviary*, for the first time in New York. The show features twenty-six bird-themed 'shadow boxes' hanging on ledges of various heights to create the impression of birds in trees.

1951 — A keeper at Edinburgh Zoo in Scotland accidentally leaves the gate to the penguin enclosure open, and the collection of gentoo penguins follow him around the zoo in single-file. The parade is so popular with visitors that it becomes a daily tradition (centre left, p.112).

Thought to be extinct for three hundred years, around eighteen pairs of Bermuda Petrels, or Cahow, are discovered on rocky islets in Castle Harbour, Bermuda. By 2005, following intensive management, the total number of birds was estimated to be 250.

1957 — Belgian surrealist artist René Magritte paints *A Variation on Sadness*, which refers to the age-old question of which came first, the chicken or the egg?

1961 — American bird painter Arthur Singer publishes *Birds of the World*, a survey of 27 orders and 155 bird families. It sells hundreds of thousands of copies, and it is later translated into eight languages.

1962 — Nature writer and former marine biologist Rachel Carson publishes *Silent Spring*, which documents the catastrophic effects of pesticides on the environment in general and on birds in particular.

1963 — American artist Martin Johnson Heade travels to Brazil on the first of three expeditions he will make to Central and South America. During the trip, he makes forty paintings of different species of hummingbirds in their natural habitat.

The Birds, a film by British film director Alfred Hitchcock, is released. Loosely based on a book of the same title by Daphne du Maurier, it tells the story of a series of violent bird attacks on the people of Bodega Bay, California.

1964 — Indian ornithologist Salim Ali, also known as the 'Birdman of India', publishes the first of ten volumes of the *Handbook of the Birds of India and Pakistan* with American ornithologist and conservationist Sidney Dillon Ripley II. The landmark series, featuring 1,200 different species, remains one of the most important reference works on the region's birds.

1966 — The French artist François-Xavier Lalanne designs an idiosyncratic four-poster bed in the form of an egg-shaped white bird.

1968 — Australian artist William T. Cooper publishes *A Portfolio of Australian Birds*; it is the first of many books featuring native Australian birds and their habitats.

1969 — The British film director Ken Loach releases *Kes*, the touching story of a boy's relationship with a hawk based on the 1968 novel *A Kestrel for a Knave* by Barry Hines.

New Zealand artist Raymond Harris-Ching creates 250 painted illustrations for the *Readers Digest* and Automobile Association's *Book of British Birds*, a revolutionary large-format coffee-table ornithological study (centre right, p.227).

Big Bird, a larger-than-human puppet created by American puppeteer and filmmaker Jim Henson, makes its debut on children's television program *Sesame Street*.

Neil Armstrong, Edwin 'Buzz' Aldrin and Michael Collins – design the official emblem for their Apollo 11 mission to the moon, which features a bald eagle carrying an olive branch (right, p.245).

1970 — American painter and graphic artist Robert Rauschenberg designs the first Earth Day poster for the American Environment Foundation featuring the American national bird, the bald eagle.

1972 — Finnish glass designer Oiva Toikka designs his first hand-blown bird named *Sieppo (Flycatcher)*. He goes on to create more than 300 glass birds of different species.

1980 — A fostering programme is developed to rescue the New Zealand black robin from extinction (only five birds were left on Little Mangere Island, which is part of the Chatham Islands archipelago). The scheme was a success, and by 2013 the population had increased to 250.

1982	2001	2011	2016

1982 A series of postage stamps featuring paintings of state birds and flowers by Arthur Singer becomes the most popular special issue in US postal history, selling more than 500 million sets of fifty stamps.

1983 American pop artist Andy Warhol creates a portfolio of prints featuring ten endangered animals, including a bald eagle.

1986 French luxury goods manufacturer Hèrmes produces a silk scarf designed by Texas painter Kermit Oliver featuring a wild turkey surrounded by more than fifty native Texan animals and plants.

1988 The first Californian condor chick is hatched in captivity at the San Diego breeding centre. By 1991, the project had raised a population of more than fifty birds. The following year, two captive-born juveniles are released at the Sespe Condor Sanctuary.

1992 *The White Duck*, a 1753 painting by French painter Jean-Baptiste Oudry is stolen from Houghton Hall, Norfolk, UK.

1999 French contemporary artist Céleste Boursier-Mougenot installs the first iteration of his long-running series *From Ear to Here* at MoMA PS1, New York. His installations featuring live finches allow visitors to get close to the birds, whose activity creates a live piece of music.

2000 Ornithologist and self-taught artist David Allen Sibley releases *The Sibley Field Guide to Birds*, which is celebrated as one of the most comprehensive guides to North American ornithological field identification ever published.

Suriname issues a set of banknotes featuring endemic birds, including the Guianan cock-of-the-rock and the red-billed toucan (left, p.185).

2001 British artist Elizabeth Butterworth exhibits her paintings of macaws and cockatoos at the Natural History Museum, London.

Belgian artist Francis Alÿs sends a peacock to represent him at the Venice Biennale. Accompanied by a guard, the bird wanders around the Giardini and stands in for Alÿs during events.

2005 British artist Tracey Emin creates her sculpture *Roman Standard*, which features a single bronze bird perched atop a 4-meter (13 ft) pole.

2006 German Artist and keen ornithologist Casten Höller produces a series of photographs that document a project in which he selectively breeds birds to create new 'customized' varieties.

US photographer Joel Sartore begins The Photo Ark, an ongoing project intending to photograph each of the roughly 12,000 species of animals and birds living in zoos and wildlife sanctuaries worldwide.

2007 Dutch artist Florentijn Hofman presents the first of a series of giant inflatable sculptures in the form of rubber ducks in Saint-Nazaire, France. Later versions appear in Sydney, Hong Kong, Seoul and Toronto.

American artist Laurel Roth Hope designs the first in a series of her Biodiversity Reclamation Suits for Urban Pigeons.

2009 Social networking platform Twitter introduces 'Larry the Bird' as its logo. A revised version of the logo based on a mountain bluebird is released two years later, and it is still in use today (centre left, p.196).

The mobile game *Angry Birds*, in which players launch birds as projectiles is released for iOS devices, eventually selling more than 12 million copies worldwide.

2011 US-based photographer and biologist Tim Laman and ornithologist Edwin Scholes complete their eight-year quest to photograph all thirty-nine species of bird of paradise.

2013 German artist Katharina Fritsch unveils her monumental rooster sculpture, *Hahn/Cock*, in Trafalgar Square, London, as part of the Fourth Plinth Program.

Publication of *The Unfeathered Bird* by Katrina van Grouw, featuring hundreds of anatomical drawings of birds including reconstructed skeletons in lifelike, active postures.

Ten songbirds new to science are discovered off the coast of Sulawesi, an Indonesian island east of Borneo, the most new bird species identified in a specific area in more than a century.

2014 A mural by British street artist Banksy, depicting a group of city pigeons holding anti-immigration placards, is removed following a complaint that the work is 'racist'.

2015 German fashion, portrait and still-life photographer Thomas Lohr releases the book *Birds*, featuring close-up images of birds' feathers.

Renowned Australian photographer Gary Heery, best-known for his celebrity portraits, publishes his first book of bird photographs (centre right, p.42).

Contemporary artist Joseph McGlennon wins the annual William and Winifred Bowness Photography Prize for *Florilegium #1*, an image of two parrots perched on tropical foliage inspired by Joseph Banks' botanical drawings.

2016 National Geographic photographer Robert Clark publishes *Feathers: Displays of Brilliant Plumage*, which captures the diversity and beauty of feathers.

2016 The Cornell Lab of Ornithology launches 'Wall of Birds', an interactive web project featuring species from each bird family alongside a select group of extinct ancestors (right, p.159).

2017 The Royal Academy of Art in London hosts 'Second Nature: The Art of Charles Tunnicliffe', which features a number of the twentieth-century British artist's bird etchings, wood engravings and woodcuts.

2018 French fashion house Christian Lacroix produces Birds Sinfonia, a wallpaper and fabric design featuring a range of garden and exotic birds designed by creative director Sacha Walckhoff.

Paper artist Maud White publishes her book *Brave Birds: Inspiration on the Wing*, featuring 65 intricate paper-cut birds.

2019 Chinese Artist Cai Guo-Qiang exhibits a flock of 10,000 porcelain birds titled *Murmuration (Landscape)* at the National Gallery of Victoria in Australia.

The Cornell Lab of Ornithology publishes a study 'Decline of the North American Avifauna' that details a staggering decline in population of nearly 3 billion breeding adult birds in the US and Canada since 1970.

2020 Inspired by John James Audubon's *The Birds of America* and American racial politics, contemporary artist Kerry James Marshall begins a new series of paintings titled *Black and part Black Birds in America*.

A painting by nun and Renaissance artist Orsola Maddalena Caccia featuring a marsh tit, chiffchaff, chaffinch, blue tits, goldcrest, crested tit and a great tit is sold at auction for the record sum of £212,500 ($260,000), around five times above the estimated price.

Bird Classification and Orders

Jen Lobo
Artist and Educator
2020 Bartels Science Illustrator, Cornell University
—

One of the most appealing aspects of the class Aves, or birds, is its sheer diversity. Birds inhabit almost every environment on earth and have developed unique physical and behavioural adaptations enabling them to not only survive but to *thrive*. These adaptations provide a unique glimpse into evolutionary history.

The Linnaean system of classification assigns organisms to a grouping based on their relatedness. This places them within a hierarchical taxonomy. Individual species that are most similar belong to a genus. Related genera form a family. Families are collected in orders, which make up classes, until the highest rank, comprising the entire animal kingdom.

Aves includes roughly 10,000 species of modern birds. Bird orders are generally divided into between twenty-nine and forty-one taxonomic groups, based on shared traits. However, the avian phylogenetic tree, which depicts evolutionary connectivity, is in constant flux, particularly now that advancements in genetic technologies allow modern avian systematists to pinpoint differences and similarities in birds' DNA sequence. Through the betterment of technology, along with fossil discoveries, we can expect further changes as we better understand birds' relationships to one other as well as their relationship to ancient birds, giving a clearer reconstruction of their lineage and evolutionary history.

The class Aves is divided into two clades, Palaeognathae and Neognathae. Palaeognathae includes all the ratites, which are flightless. Neognathae includes all other living birds, including the largest order, Passeriformes, which is comprised of more species than all other orders combined.

In evolutionary biology, a divergence occurs when the population of an interbreeding species branches into two or more descendant species. As taxa diverge, species become more disparate as they adapt to their environment. The following lists the orders of the class Aves in order of the earliest to diverge, starting with the Palaeognathae.

STRUTHIONIFORMES (Ostriches)
This order contains a single family, Struthionidae, including two species: the ostriches. The largest living birds, strictly terrestrial and flightless, ostriches are found in open, semi-arid plains, desert, and open woodlands in Africa. They are mainly herbivorous.

RHEIFORMES (Rheas)
The lesser and greater rhea are South America's largest bird species. Although they lack the capability of flight, rheas are very fast runners. Omnivorous, they graze in groups and nest in scrapes on the ground.

TINAMIFORMES (Tinamous)
A diverse order of one family and some forty-six species. The South American birds are elusive. They can fly, but spend most of their lives on the ground.

CASUARIIFORMES (Cassowaries and Emu)
Cassowaries and emus are found in Australia and New Guinea. Cassowaries inhabit rainforests and have a distinctive bare blue head and casque. The emu is found in a variety of habitats in Australia, ranging from woodland to open country.

APTERYGIFORMES (Kiwis)
Petite and charismatic, the kiwis are a small group of flightless, nocturnal birds endemic to New Zealand.

ANSERIFORMES (Ducks, Geese, Magpie Goose, Screamers and Waterfowl)
The Anseriformes are a large and diverse order found worldwide, inhabiting wetlands from the Amazon to Arctic tundra. Possessing multiple adaptations for life on water, members of this order are generally good flyers and adept swimmers.

GALLIFORMES (Chachalacas, Curassows, Grouse and Allies, Guans, Guineafowl, Megapodes, New World Quail, Pheasants)
A large order including five families and roughly 295 species. Several members of this group, such as the greater sage-grouse (*Centrocercus urophasianus*), practice a courtship ritual known as lekking.

PHOENICOPTERIFORMES (Flamingos)
Six species of flamingo make up the sole family of this order, Phoenicopteridae. They feed on plankton, tiny fish, and crustaceans by filtering water and sediment through their bills.

PODICIPEDIFORMES (Grebes)
Podicipediformes contains one family, the grebes, waterbirds whose bodies have adapted, for example with legs set further towards their backside, to make them far more agile on water than on land.

GRUIFORMES (Coots, Cranes, Finfoots, Flufftails, Gallinules, Limpkins, Rails and Trumpeters)
Species in this order can be found worldwide. Many have widely recognizable vocal displays and members of Gruidae, the cranes, are known for their elaborate courtship displays. Rallidae including flightless rails was once thought to be the most diverse family.

CHARADRIIFORMES (Auks, Gulls, Jacanas, Oystercatchers, Plovers, Sandpipers, Sheathbills, Skuas and Jaegers, Stilts and Avocets, Terns and Skimmers, Thick-knees)
Members of this large and diverse order have one prevailing commonality: life near or on the ocean. Often referred to as 'shorebirds', these species can be found worldwide. The order includes many long-distance migrants and pelagic species.

OPISTHOCOMIFORMES (Hoatzin)
Comprised of a single family and sole species, Opisthocomiformes are found in South America, where the hoatzin (*Opisthocomus hoazin*) nests in shrubbery above still waters.

CAPRIMULGIFORMES (Frogmouths, Hummingbirds, Nightjars and Allies, Oilbird, Owlet-nightjars, Potoos, Swifts, Treeswifts)
Both nocturnal and diurnal birds, make up this diverse order of eight families and roughly 597 species, including the Trochilidae, the hummingbirds, with roughly 349 species in a single family.

OTIDIFORMES (Bustards)
A single family within this order contains the twenty-six species of bustards. Long-legged and sleek-necked, these terrestrial birds are found throughout Eurasia and Africa in open areas ranging from grasslands and plains to savannah and semi-arid desert.

MUSOPHAGIFORMES (Turacos)
Inhabiting forests, woodlands, and savannahs of sub-Saharan Africa, the turacos are some of the most brilliantly coloured species, with feather pigments exclusive to the order.

CUCULIFORMES (Cuckoos)
Cuckoos have a wide global distribution, mostly preferring forested and woodland habitats. The order contains one very diverse family with roughly 147 species. Some cuckoo species are known particularly for their brood parasitism: the habit of depositing their eggs in the nest of other birds.

COLUMBIFORMES (Doves and Pigeons)
With some 348 species, this order is represented globally in a variety of habitats, from the feral rock pigeons (*Columba livia*) of the world's great cities to the Victoria crowned-pigeon (*Goura victoria*).

MESITORNITHIFORMES (Mesites)
This small order contains a single family, the mesites. These small, secretive birds have a very limited range in declining rainforests of Madagascar.

PTEROCLIFORMES (Sandgrouse)
The roughly sixteen species of sandgrouse are dove-like birds that inhabit arid environments of the Old World and travel up to 70 km (45 miles) to find water, which they can hold in their belly feathers.

PHAETHONTIFORMES (Tropicbirds)
A sole pelagic family of three species of tropicbirds makes up this order. They feed on fish and aquatic invertebrates and breed on isolated islands.

EURYPYGIFORMES (Kagu and Sunbittern)
An order of two families, each with a single species. Sunbittern have ornately patterned chestnut, black, and gold wings that they spread when threatened.

GAVIIFORMES (Loons)
Five species of loons within a single family form Gaviiformes. Spending their lives in cold waters, loons have adapted for efficient foot-propelled diving. They feed primarily on fish.

SPHENISCIFORMES (Penguins)
The Spheniscidae family with eighteen species of penguins makes up this order. Marine-dwelling and flightless, penguins have made unique adaptions for their specialized lives. Their denser bones make it easier for them to dive in water than to fly.

PROCELLARIIFORMES (Albatrosses, Petrels and Storm Petrels, Shearwaters)
Highly proficient at soaring, these oceanic species have the narrowest and longest wings of all birds.

CICONIIFORMES (Storks)
This order contains a single family with nineteen species. Storks are large wading birds that can soar great distances, with long legs and elongated bills.

SULIFORMES (Anhingas, Boobies, Cormorants and Shags, Frigatebirds, Gannets)
Found across all the world's oceans, four families with roughly fifty-nine species form this order. Several species lack external nostrils, an adaptation for plunging into water to catch schooling fish.

PELECANIFORMES (Hammerkop, Herons, Ibises, Pelicans, Shoebills and Spoonbills)

There are five families and more than 100 species with a worldwide distribution in this diverse order that prefers wetland habitats and marine environments where their appetite for aquatic vertebrates can be met.

CATHARTIFORMES (New World Vultures)

With one family and seven species, this order includes the North and South American vultures and the largest soaring birds, the condors. Relying on rising thermals of warm air, these birds can soar for up to 160 km (100 miles) without flapping their wings.

ACCIPITRIFORMES (Hawks, Eagles, Kites, Osprey and Secretarybird)

This order, which contains the diurnal raptors, has a global distribution and a variety of habitats, from the Amazon rainforest to sub-Saharan Africa. It includes the varied Accipitridae family, containing roughly 250 species of hawks, eagles and kites.

STRIGIFORMES (Owls)

Owls are divided into two families: Tytonidae and Strigidae. Tytonidae contains the species with one of the largest distributions of all living birds, the barn owl (*Tyto alba*). Nocturnal hunting has evolved many unique adaptations in owls.

COLIIFORMES (Mousebirds)

One family with six species, the mousebirds of African woodlands and savannahs, makes up this order. They are highly social, gregarious birds, which huddle together in extended family groups.

LEPTOSOMIFORMES (Cuckoo-roller)

A solitary species makes up this entire order. Neither a cuckoo nor a roller, the cuckoo-roller (*Leptosomus discolor*) is endemic to Madagascar.

TROGONIFORMES (Quetzals and Trogons)

This order contains one family with around forty-three species. Trogons and quetzals are tropical-dwelling species with diverse markings and vivid colours.

BUCEROTIFORMES (Ground Hornbills, Hoopoes, Hornbills and Woodhoopoes)

Four families with some seventy-two species comprise this order. Hoopoes sport a fan-like crest atop their crown while hornbills have large bills which in some species extends into a casque formation.

CORACIIFORMES (Bee-eaters, Kingfishers, Motmots, Rollers and Todies)

This is a varied order with six families and 183 species. They have a worldwide range and are found in a variety of habitats from rainforests to savannah. Most species are brilliantly coloured.

GALBULIFORMES (Jacamars and Puffbirds)

Two neotropical species, each belonging to their own family. Puffbirds are sedentary hunters, striking at prey, while jacamars prefer chasing flying insects.

PICIFORMES (Barbets, Honeyguides, Toucans and Woodpeckers)

With seven families and 378 species, this order has a near worldwide distribution. Bill diversity is a key component in this order, as each family has evolved for diverse foraging and predation methods.

CARIAMIFORMES (Seriemas)

There are two species within a single family in this order. Seriemas are long-legged birds with short toes that inhabit South American grasslands where they feed on everything from insects to snakes.

FALCONIFORMES (Caracaras and Falcons)

This order includes sixty-six species of falcons and caracaras within one family: Falconidae. With nearly a global range, these birds inhabit a multitude of environments with most preferring open habitats.

PSITTACIFORMES (Cockatoos, Parrots and New Zealand parrots)

This large and diverse order with three families and over 350 species includes many unique birds, notably the critically endangered kakapo (*Strigops habroptila*), a flightless and nocturnal endemic of New Zealand.

PASSERIFORMES (Perching Birds)

With a whopping 141 families and well over 6,000 species, Passeriformes include more species than all other orders combined. Members of this order are commonly known as perching birds or passerines. More specifically, they share a foot adaptation that allows for grasping and perching on tree branches.

Taxonomists divide Passeriformes into two suborders, Tyranni (suboscines) and Passeri (oscines). The key disparity between the two groups is that members of Passeri possess a complex set of throat muscles allowing them the capability for more intricate vocalizations. Their songs are learned from listening to birds within their species, in much the same way that humans develop speech.

Avian Phylogenetic Tree

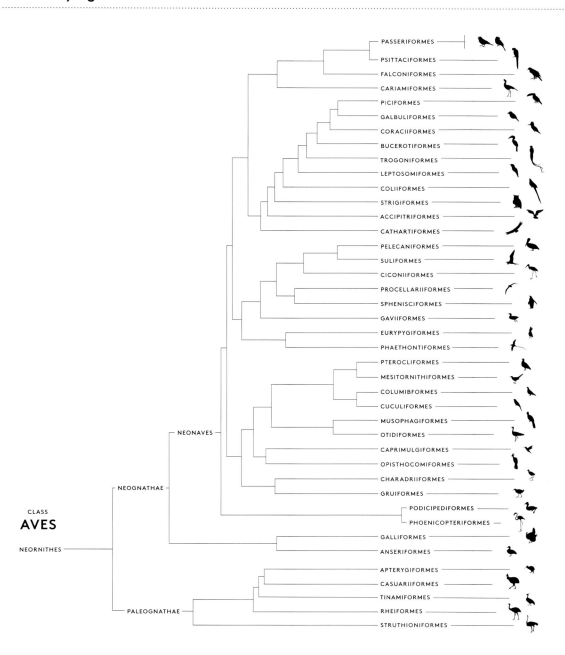

Bird Topography

Jen Lobo
Artist and Educator
2020 Bartels Science Illustrator, Cornell University
—

For the birder, researcher or artist, an understanding of the elements that comprise the avian form is key to identifying and describing species. While colour, shape and size vary, all bird species share remarkably similar structural anatomy from one taxonomic group to another. All extant birds evolved from a flying ancestor, even species that now lack the ability to fly. This shared ancestry leads to mutual traits that support the demands of aerodynamics. Lightweight anatomy, solid bills, strong hindlimbs and two wings are ubiquitous among the class Aves. Similarly, most birds share a common arrangement of feathers. This external anatomy is known as topography. Feathers grow in distinct groups following patterns that support a streamlined shape. Facial feather groups radiate away from the base of the beak. There is some variation across orders.

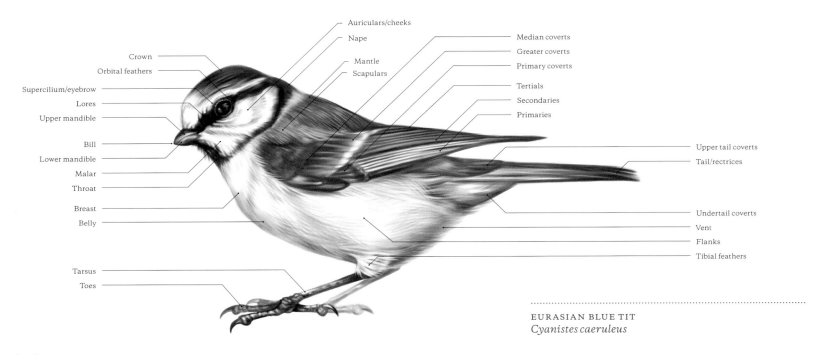

EURASIAN BLUE TIT
Cyanistes caeruleus

Bill Morphology

Although there is much consistency across all bird species, evolution has moulded unique physical adaptations and specialized features to accommodate a bird's particular habitat and ecological niche. The most notable example of this is the avian bill. The bill or beak – in ornithology the terms are synonymous – is a multi-faceted tool of form and function. Along with its obvious use for obtaining food, a bill is used for nearly every aspect of a bird's life from preening to courtship display, from building nests to defence. The study of bill morphology – its shape, structure, size and overall form – is perhaps the clearest means for understanding a bird's ecology. It is little wonder that the bill morphology of the Galapágos finches played such a critical role in the inception of Charles Darwin's theory of evolution by natural selection (see p.27).

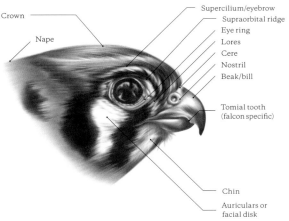

AMERICAN KESTREL
Falco sparverius

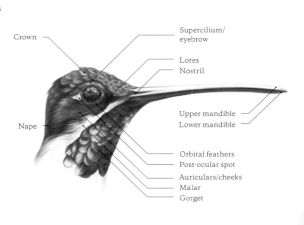

LONG-BILLED STARTHROAT
Heliomaster longirostris

NORTHERN WHITE-FACED OWL
Ptilopsis leucotis

Urban Bird Watching

David Lindo aka The Urban Birder
Broadcaster, speaker and writer
Ambassador – Leica Birding and London Wildlife Trust
Founder – Britain's Vote National Bird Campaign 2015
—

Bird watching as a pastime was born out of dubious beginnings. In the days of Thomas Bewick (see p.16), the keenest observers of birds were upper-class gentlemen who strolled the countryside with guns and birch walking sticks. They were not birding, but bird collecting, shooting birds to be mounted and displayed in the drawing rooms of country mansions. Lower on the social scale, people collected finches for the pet trade. Egg collecting from nests in the wild was also rife. It remained an accepted pastime until the 1970s, even after the creation of the Royal Society for the Protection of Birds in the late 1800s paved the way for the effective conservation of birds in Britain and throughout the world. In the United States, conservation movements took off in the early 1900s after public outcries over the extinction of the passenger pigeon (see pp.180-1) and campaigns against the trade in feathers (see p.300).

It wasn't until the twentieth century that bird watching as a pastime really flourished and the close study and appreciation of birds as some of the planet's most remarkable creatures could be enjoyed by a mass audience. And it's not hard to see why. Think of a colour and there will be a bird out there sporting it. The variety of shapes, sizes and behaviours makes birds endlessly fascinating. From the early classics that catered for and helped to develop the popular interest in birding, such as Roger Tory Peterson's *A Field Guide to the Birds* (1934, see p.325), to the modern popularity of David Allen Sibley's guides (see p.324), birding field guides are delightful objects to leaf through in their own right.

The enjoyment of birds has come a long way since our prehistoric ancestors gazed up to witness groups flying overhead, but for many, birds remain potent symbols of the wild, and life that is untamed beyond our cities and civilization. The truth is that birds are everywhere: from the impenetrable centres of tropical forests to the middle of our own concrete jungles.

Urban environments might seem a challenge for new birders, but they simply need to open their mind to possibility. In reality, there aren't that many differences between an urban environment and the countryside. Of around 620 species on the British list of birds since the early 1900s, around 95 per cent have been seen in an urban environment. Similar levels are true across the world, with bird watchers in a city such as Nairobi in Kenya recording more than 600 species.

If you know what to look for, you will find fascinating birds right on your doorstep, and birding in the city actually has some advantages. Birders can get a lot closer to species that are used to being surrounded by people. Urban habitats also tend to be smaller and more fragmented, which means that wildlife is often more concentrated in one area. It allows the curious to get first-hand experience of otherwise difficult-to-see species.

Today, urban birding has become a fashionable pastime enjoyed by people from all walks of life (its popularity rose during the coronavirus pandemic of 2020 and 2021, as it became clear that watching birds has positive benefits for mental health). All you need to get started are a pair of binoculars and a bird book. You don't have to go far: watching your garden or sitting in a park could easily result in seeing up to twenty different species. If you visit the same place regularly, you will begin to see how population dynamics change with the seasons, especially when you receive visits from migrants in transit.

The motto of the urban birder is that anything can turn up anywhere, at any time. Look at every bird, even if you think that you recognize it. It may well be doing something unexpected – or it may be a species you were not expecting at all. So, get outside and enjoy the birds around you – and don't forget to look up!

The urban birder can expect to encounter birds that are familiar in urban environments – but also much rarer city inhabitants. These are some favourites.

Barn swallow (*Hirundo rustica*, p.44)
This species is the archetypal global representation of a swallow. This is understandable, as it is the most widespread swallow species in the world: it is found in Europe, Asia, Africa and the Americas, and has even been recorded as a vagrant on the coasts of Antarctica. The swallow is very distinctive, with a mostly blue body, deeply forked tail and sweeping flight. It is a migrating bird lauded in many societies as the harbinger of spring. Frequenting open country, swallows often use artificial structures to nest in and commonly live within close proximity of humans.

Blue jay (*Cyanocitta cristata*, pp.326–7)
While the blue jay prefers mixed woodland for a habitat, these little birds can thrive wherever their confident, almost bullish nature takes them and are commonly found in wooded parks and gardens throughout eastern and central North America. Their blue, lilac, black and white colouring is stunning and certainly helps pick them out of a crowd. They may also do the job for you, having been known to bellow out a tactical alarm call, scattering other birds so they can move in to an area to feed.

Common grackle (*Quiscalus quiscalus*, p.36)
This dark, long-tailed bird is common in urban environments in eastern North America. Commonly referred to as a blackbird, it is not a thrush but an Icterid, from a family of songbirds found exclusively in the Americas. This species is recognizable by the male's iridescent black plumage, with the female being browner. They are often to be found on streets and in parks looking for food. Common grackles are gregarious birds instantly recognized by loud calls that sound both mechanical and squeaky.

Common kingfisher (*Alcedo atthis*, p.230)
Encountering a kingfisher on an urban waterway, as the blue, green and rich rusty orange of its body zips from bank to bank, can be a truly magical experience. The iridescence of the kingfisher's feathers, and its long, dagger-like beak protruding from an oversize head, give it the air of a visitor from another world. They favour slow-moving water for hunting small fish and invertebrates and hence can be found around rivers, canals and even ponds throughout Asia, Europe and North Africa. The best time to spot them is early in the morning during the summer months.

European robin (*Erithacus rubecula*, p.221)
This familiar bird needs little introduction. The red-breasted robin was made the United Kingdom's national bird in 2015. Related to Old World flycatchers, it has an extensive distribution from Eurasia to western Siberia and south to Algeria, but it nowhere better known than in Britain, where it is a common garden bird that boldly approaches humans.

Northern Goshawk (*Accipiter gentilis*, p.175)
This large alpha predator will take down any prey, including other predators such as buzzards. Surprisingly, the best place on the planet to see goshawks is the German capital Berlin which hosts more than a hundred pairs. At the height of summer, the piercing, begging calls of the juveniles cut through the noise of human activity in the Tiergarten. Resembling buzzard-sized sparrowhawks, they can be seen dashing through the trees or sitting quietly within the foliage. Despite their apparent confidence, they are inherently wary, melting away once they realize that they are being watched.

Long-eared owl (*Asio otus*)
This medium-sized owl has a near global distribution and is thought to be the most numerous of its family in the world. That said, being a woodland denizen, it can be highly secretive. It has an appealing appearance that at times can look very cat-like. The ear-tufts can be raised or flattened depending on the bird's mood. Northern Serbia – particularly the town of Kikinda – is the best place in the world to see this owl. During winter months, hundreds assemble in daytime roosts, sometimes in the middle of the towns, before drifting off to hunt rodents after dark.

Peregrine falcon (*Falco peregrinus*)
This impressive predator is king of the urban jungle. Peregrines live on every continent, excluding Antarctica, and are the fastest animals on the planet, being able to attain speeds of over 300 kph (200mph) during its hunting stoop. Recently, they have taken to residing in some of the world's cities, nesting on tall buildings and feeding mainly on the abundant pigeons. New York has at least twenty pairs, while peregrines also nest on the ledges of Málaga Cathedral above the busy tourist streets below. These birds belong to the Mediterranean subspecies, which is smaller, with a bluer back and peachy breast.

Sedge warbler (*Acrocephalus schoenobaenus*, p.204)
This innocuous little brown warbler is a summer migrant from Africa to Europe, western and central Asia. It has streaky brown upperparts, whiter underparts and a creamy white eyestripe. It frequents waterside vegetation but is found away from water while migrating. Its scratchy, jittering song is similar to the quite different looking brown Eurasian reed warbler. However, they are discernible by their use of a song flight in which they launch themselves aloft from within a riverine shrub.

Terns (Sternidae, p.158)
Terns are seabirds found throughout much of Asia, Europe and North America. They are the harrier jump jets of the coastal birds: agile, streamlined animals who perform everything from rapid darting manoeuvres to hovering over water as they hunt for fish. No wonder they are nicknamed the 'sea swallow'. Their bodies are mostly white or light grey and they sport a distinctive black cap and orange-red legs and thin beak. They nest on relatively flat surfaces near to coastal waters, so common, Arctic and little terns can be spotted in towns and cities by the ocean or even further inland when migrating.

Select Biographies

Eleazar and Elizabeth Albin
(Germany, c.1690-1741/2 and 1708-41)
Little is known of Eleazar Albin's early life, but he was probably born in Germany. By 1708 he was living in London, where he worked mainly as an art teacher. His *Natural History of Birds* (1731-8) appeared as three volumes with 306 etched plates, which were the work not just of Albin himself but also of his daughter Elizabeth. Albin prided himself on drawing from life, and his connections meant he had access to exotic birds owned by the Duke of Chandos, among other English nobles.

John James Audubon (United States, 1785-1851)
Born in Haiti and brought up in France, Audubon moved to the United States in 1803. He tried various business ventures before combining his skill as an artist with his lifelong interest in ornithology in a fourteen-year project to find, identify and draw the birds of North America. Each bird was placed against a background of plants, depicted either by Audubon or by his assistant, Joseph Mason. The resulting book, *The Birds of America* (1827-38), with its huge etchings of nearly 500 bird species, is a landmark of natural history illustration.

Jacques Barraband (France, c.1767-1809)
Jacques Barraband followed in his father's footsteps by working in the local tapestry factory, before moving to Paris to study art at the l'Académie Royale de Peinture. Highly regarded for his natural history paintings, Barraband was commissioned by Napoleon Bonaparte to produce a series of watercolours of birds and flowers between 1801 and 1804. Collaborating with the naturalist François Levaillant, Barraband produced *Histoire naturelle des perroquets* ('Natural History of Parrots', 1801-5). Working from mounted specimens, Barraband's remarkably skilful renderings were reproduced widely in later books about birds of paradise and toucans, also produced in collaboration with Levaillant.

Ferdinand Bauer (Austria, 1760-1826)
Orphaned as an infant, Ferdinand Bauer was brought up with his brother Franz by the monk, anatomist and botanist Dr Norbert Boccius, who taught them natural history and illustration. The brothers worked at the Royal Botanical Garden at Schloss Schönbrunn in Vienna before Ferdinand accompanied Professor John Sibthorp of Oxford University to Greece and Turkey. Bauer later became the natural history artist on Matthew Flinders' expedition on HMS *Investigator* to circumnavigate Australia (1801-5). He brought back hundreds of pencil drawings of the native flora and fauna, including images of many bird species that were previously undescribed.

Pierre Belon (France, 1517-64)
The French naturalist, writer and explorer Pierre Belon studied botany before travelling through the eastern Mediterranean, observing and recording the local flora and fauna. He wrote several notable books, including works on zoology such as *La nature et diversité des poissons* ('The Nature and Diversity of Fishes', 1551), in which he discussed the dolphin in great detail, and *L'histoire de la nature des oiseaux* ('Natural History of Birds', 1555). These in-depth studies and comparisons between the skeletons of birds and humans were the earliest examples in the field of comparative anatomy.

Pieter Boel (Belgium, 1622-74)
The Flemish still-life and animal painter Pieter Boel introduced a revolutionary approach to animal representation by drawing and painting his subjects from life at the menagerie at Versailles, at a time when most artists worked from taxidermy models. This innovation allowed him to capture the characteristic movements and poses of animals and birds. Boel was also a member of Charles Le Brun's team of painters for the French royal tapestry-maker, the Manufacture des Gobelins, for which he provided the animal and bird motifs.

Jakob Bogdány (Hungary, 1658-1724)
Born in the Kingdom of Hungary, Jakob Bogdány moved to Amsterdam before settling in London in 1688. He worked for the court of Queen Anne as an artist specializing in still lifes and depictions of birds. His patron, Admiral George Churchill, was the brother of the Duke of Marlborough, and the duke's aviary at Windsor Park may have been a major source for the exotic birds Bogdány painted, which included cockatoos, macaws and mynas. Bogdány did not limit himself to exotic birds: he also painted more familiar domestic species, such as blue tits. His landscape paintings were often crammed with birds.

Mark Catesby (Britain, 1682/3-1749)
Born into a wealthy family in Essex, Mark Catesby studied natural history in London before moving to the colony of Virginia. He supplied seeds to London nurseries, and in 1722 the Royal Society sponsored his collecting of plant and animal specimens in Carolina and the West Indies. Back in London, Catesby spent more than twenty years preparing his *Natural History of Carolina, Florida and the Bahama Islands* (1731), including learning how to etch. The early plates showed only animals and birds, but Catesby later included plants, both as backgrounds and as subjects in themselves.

Raymond Harris Ching (New Zealand, 1939-)
Seeing a collection of stuffed hummingbirds on a childhood visit to a museum began Ray Ching's lifelong love affair with birds. After dropping out of school aged just twelve, Ching tried several careers before turning to painting birds. His 1966 exhibition, *Thirty Birds*, sold out instantly. The keen ornithologist Sir William Collins, of Collins publishers, persuaded Ching to move to London, but before the two men could discuss collaborating, Reader's Digest had hired Ching. In under a year, he produced 230 full-colour portraits of birds for *The Reader's Digest Book of British Birds*. Published in 1969, the book remains the world's best-selling bird guide.

William T. Cooper (Australia, 1934-2015)
Working first as a painter of landscapes and seascapes, William Cooper found fame with his precise scientific illustrations, particularly those of birds. A qualified taxidermist, he drew from life rather than photographs, and his subject matter often took him into the wild, where he drew birds in their natural environment. A prolific illustrator, his first book, *Portfolio of Australian Birds*, appeared in 1967. The only Australian to win the gold medal of the American Academy of Natural Sciences, in 1992, Cooper was also awarded the Order of Australia in 1994. His birds appeared on postage stamps for Papua New Guinea.

Carl Cotton (United States, 1918-71)
Carl Cotton's childhood passion for preserving animals turned into a ground-breaking career as the first African-American taxidermist at Chicago's Field Museum. As a child growing up on the South Side of Chicago, Cotton practised his taxidermy on squirrels, birds and deceased pets. He petitioned the Field Museum to take him on and persisted until he was hired as a volunteer in 1947. Quickly promoted to full-time paid taxidermist a month later, Cotton remained at the museum until his death. His mission to make taxidermy an art form is clear in the bird hall where he mainly worked. His most famous work, *Marsh Birds of the Upper Nile*, is on permanent display.

Mark Dion (United States, 1961-)
The work of artist Mark Dion looks at the role of institutions and thought systems in the way we approach the fields of science, natural history, ornithology and knowledge. He uses scientific methodology in collecting and displaying specimens in order to explore the idea of public knowledge. Dion often collaborates with natural history museums, aquariums, zoos and other public institutions to develop his critical approach. He was born in Massachusetts and studied fine art at the Hartford Art School and the School of Visual Arts in New York, before taking part in the Whitney Museum's Independent Study Program. He lives and works in New York.

Max Ernst (Germany, 1891-1976)
One of the foremost avant-garde artists of the early twentieth century, Max Ernst was involved in the Dada art movement in Cologne before moving to Paris and becoming a founding member of the Surrealists in the early 1920s with Paul Éluard and André Breton. He pioneered forms of art originating from the unconscious, called Automatism. In order to stimulate imagery from the unconscious mind, Ernst used techniques such as frottage (pencil rubbings over different materials) and decalcomania (pressing together and pulling apart two canvases with liquid paint between them) in order to create chance images, which would then induce an instinctive response. Ernst fled to the United States in 1941 and married Peggy Guggenheim a year later. After they divorced, he married Dorothea Tanning and relocated to France in 1954.

Walton Ford (United States, 1960-)
Trips to the wild Canadian forests with his father as a child, combined with a love of underground cartoons, inspired Walton Ford's large-scale outsized watercolours, which owe a debt to the Naturalist Illustration movement. Originally influenced by Robert Crumb's satirical cartoons, Ford attended the Rhode Island School of Design, graduating in 1982 with a filmmaking degree. Despite having drawn since a child, his move into art happened later, and his first major show was not until in 2006. He pioneered large-scale multi-

layered etchings that are so detailed they are often mistaken for paintings; the details frequently contain hidden jokes and social critiques.

Georg Forster (Germany, 1754-94)
Explorer and traveller Georg Forster was one of the pioneers of modern scientific travel literature. He moved with his father to England in 1766, and they both accompanied the explorer James Cook on his second voyage to the Pacific between 1772 and 1775. Forster's account, *A Voyage Round the World*, appeared in 1777. Based on his father's journals and his own botanical and scientific observations, the book inspired, among others, the German naturalist Alexander von Humboldt. The work furthered knowledge of the flora and fauna of the South Seas and led to Forster being admitted to the Royal Society at the age of just twenty-two.

Louis Agassiz Fuertes (United States, 1874-1927)
Inspired by Audubon's *Birds of America* as a boy, Louis Agassiz Fuertes was one of the most acclaimed of all American ornithologists. By the age of seventeen, his drawings made him the youngest ever member of the fifty-member American Ornithologist Union. Fuertes drew birds in their natural habitat, traveling widely to broaden his knowledge of birds and their environments. A prolific illustrator, his work appeared in many publications, including the seminal *Handbook of Birds of the Western United States* (1902). He was killed in a car accident at the age of fifty-three.

Conrad Gessner (Switzerland, 1516-65)
A naturalist and physician, Conrad Gessner was a prolific writer best known for his compilations of information on animals and plants. He was born in Zurich to a poor family, his schooling funded by a great-uncle. He showed such promise that after the death of his father, some of his teachers sponsored his further study. He found a teaching position in Zurich, then left to study medicine in Basel. He spent the majority of his career practising medicine in Zurich but also wrote notable works, including the monumental, five-volume *Historiae animalium* ('Histories of the Animals', 1551-87).

John and Elizabeth Gould
(Britain, 1804-81 and 1804-41)
The husband-and-wife team worked as ornithologist and illustrator to produce some of the most influential books of the nineteenth century. John Gould is the father of bird study in Australia, writing the seminal *Birds of Australia* (1840-8), for which Elizabeth illustrated eighty-four plates before her premature death after the birth of her eighth child. She also worked on the plates for Charles Darwin's *The Zoology of the Voyage of HMS Beagle* (1838-43), while her husband, the first curator of the Zoological Society of London, identified the birds now commonly known as Darwin's finches.

Melissa Groo (United States, 1962-)
Melissa Groo's route to becoming a wildlife photographer stretched from working in school reform in Ohio to studying bioacoustics. She spent six years as a research assistant to Katy Payne at Cornell's Center for Conservation Bioacoustics, where she learned to wait, watch and listen. A digital photography class at a community college provided the catalyst for her subsequent career, in which she emphasizes the animals' and birds' welfare. Having learned from its song that a particular bird is in an area, she will spend as long as it takes to capture the image she wants without recourse to using bait.

Ernst Haeckel (Germany, 1834-1919)
The biologist Ernst Haeckel was an enthusiastic supporter of Charles Darwin's theory of evolution, and his research led him to coin many important biological terms, including 'ecology' - the study of the way that organisms relate to their environment. Several of his evolutionary claims turned out to be wrong, however, and he was accused of faking his research into embryology. He nevertheless remained a major scientific figure of his day. A talented artist, Haeckel made hundreds of sketches and watercolours of plants, birds and animals.

Oskar and Magdalena Heinroth
(Germany, 1871-1945 and 1883-1932)
Born in Berlin, Magdalena Heinroth volunteered at the city's Zoologisches Museum at the age of sixteen. There she met her future husband, Oskar, who became the zoo's assistant director in 1904, the year they married. Interested in anatomy from an early age, Magdalena became a skilled taxidermist and passed her passion for studying birds in captivity to her husband, who studied geese and ducks. Over twenty-eight years, the couple made observations on more than 1,000 birds, which they raised from chicks to adults in their Berlin apartment. Their findings appeared alongside Magdalena's taxidermy in their four-volume *Die Vögel Mitteleuropas* ('The Birds of Central Europe', 1928-33).

Melchior d'Hondecoeter (Holland, 1636-95)
Born in Utrecht into a family of painters of animals and still lifes, Melchior d'Hondecoeter's obsession with religion as a young boy led his mother to doubt he would follow the family's profession. However, he began a career painting seascapes before acquiring celebrity status as a painter of exotic and game birds. Breaking with tradition, d'Hondecoeter depicted living rather than stuffed birds, capturing them in motion or fighting. A pupil and later assistant of the painter Jan Weenix, he was greatly in demand for murals and large-scale park scenes, but his real talent lay in his bird paintings.

Huang Quan (China, 903-65)
As the Tang dynasty collapsed, Huang Quan's birthplace, Chengdu, became a centre for painters fleeing the capital at Chang'an. Aged twelve, Huang began studying with the bird-and-flower painter Diao Guangyin, who arrived in the city in 903. Huang developed his own style by combining the strengths of his different teachers. He was a pioneer of the *mogu hua* or 'boneless' style of painting - applying light colours with a delicate skill that did away with the brush outline - that was followed for centuries.

Carsten Höller (Belgium, 1961-)
Better known for playful installations such as the slide at London's Tate Modern, artist Carsten Höller worked as an agricultural entomologist until 1994. The son of German parents who worked for the European Economic Community, he was born and grew up in Brussels and studied for his doctorate at the University of Kiel, only turning to art in the late 1980s. In 2011, he incorporated his passion for birds into an exhibition at New York's New Museum. He had spent several years collecting birds from across Europe for his personal aviaries, meticulously photographing them from egg to old age.

Frank Hurley (Australia, 1885-1962)
The self-taught photographer Frank Hurley bought his first camera at the age of seventeen, by which time he had already run away from his suburban Sydney home to work in a steel mill. He soon gained a reputation for striking images, many of which involved him placing himself in extreme danger. He took several trips to Antarctica, where he served as the official photographer for Sir Ernest Shackleton's ill-fated 1914 expedition, which was marooned until 1916. Hurley joined the Australian Imperial Force in 1917, photographing the Battle of Passchendaele. A pioneer, he was an early adopter of colour photography and made many documentaries later in life.

Ito Jakuchu (Japan, 1716-1800)
Also known as Jokin, Ito Jakuchu was active from the middle of the Tokugawa (Edo) period, and one of the foremost animal painters in Japan. He is known particularly for his bird-and-flower paintings, which combined natural history with Buddhist scenes. He kept fowl at home so that he could observe them from life and better depict them in his realistic style. In later life he became a recluse and was known as Tobeian (Bushel Monk), because it was said that he traded paintings for two bushels of rice.

Martin Johnson Heade (United States, 1819-1904)
The son of a shopkeeper, Martin Johnson Heade was born and raised in Lumberville, Pennsylvania. Trained by a local folk artist, Edward Hicks, Heade created his first known painting in 1839. His move from portraiture to landscape painting was fuelled by trips to Europe and his friendship with artists who belonged to the Hudson River School. By 1863, his interest had switched to the tropics and the birds and flora there. A move to St Augustine, Florida, in 1883 after he married, saw his subject matter change to tropical flowers, particularly magnolias, and the Floridian landscape.

Genevieve Jones (United States, 1847-79)
The 'other Audubon', Genevieve Jones was brought up in Circleville, Ohio. An outstanding student, she graduated from high school in 1865, but anxiety brought on by the Civil War led to a period of ill-health that did not improve during Reconstruction. An ill-fated love affair, ended by her parents and brother, led to her becoming silent and withdrawn. In 1879, she started to illustrate the 130 nesting birds of Ohio, but completed only five illustrations before contracting typhoid fever. Three weeks later she was dead at the age of thirty-two; her work was continued by her family and a friend.

John Gerrard Keulemans (Holland, 1842-1912)
From an early age, John Gerrard Keulemans was an eager collector of animal specimens for museums in Holland. In 1864, he travelled to West Africa at

the behest of the director of the Natural History Museum of Leiden. Five years later, he moved permanently to England, where he stayed for the rest of his life. There he illustrated Richard Bowdler Sharpe's *Family of Kingfishers* (1868-71), and embarked on a prolific career as a painter of birds – estimates suggest he created as many as 5,000 illustrations - working for multiple publications, including *The Ibis: The International Journal of Avian Science*.

Frans Lanting (Netherlands, 1951-)
The recipient of the London Natural History Museum's inaugural Lifetime Achievement Award in 2018, Frans Lanting has spent over fifty years photographing wildlife. His photography began as a hobby when he was an economics student at the Erasmus University in Rotterdam, his birthplace. Moving to study environmental planning in Santa Cruz, California, where he still lives, Lanting realized his hobby could become his job. He has spent three decades documenting wildlife across the planet. Working with his wife, Chris Eckstrom, often for *National Geographic*, his images have set the standard for other wildlife photographers to follow.

François Levaillant (Suriname, 1753-1824)
During the first ten years of his life, in Suriname, François Levaillant was a keen collector of birds and insects. Back in France, where he was rejected by the army, he moved to Paris in 1777 and traded natural history specimens. His reputation was established following a trip to the Cape of Good Hope in 1780, when South Africa was relatively unknown, to study birds and animals in their natural habitat. Levaillant returned to Paris with more than 2,000 specimens of bird, animal, insect and plant life. In the 1790s, he published a number of best-selling books about his travels and the bird life he encountered.

Edward Lear (Britain, 1812-88)
As a teenager the English artist, illustrator and author Edward Lear made a living from drawing, working for the Zoological Society of London and for the ornithologist John Gould, and making illustrations of the Earl of Derby's menagerie. In 1832 he published *Illustrations of the Family Psittacidae or Parrots* with 42 hand-coloured plates demonstrating his pioneering use of lithography. Lear subsequently became better known for his nonsense poems, such as 'The Owl and the Pussy-Cat' and his limericks. After 1837, he travelled extensively and lived abroad, including Greece, Egypt, Syria and India and finally settling in Italy.

Bruno Liljefors (Sweden, 1860-1939)
Born into a poor family in Uppsala, Liljefors' talent for drawing was spotted early, and local shopkeepers kept him supplied with art materials. He studied at the Royal Swedish Academy of Arts in Stockholm before leaving for a tour of Europe from 1882 to 1883. He taught briefly at the Valand Academy in Gothenburg. Between 1917 and 1932, he worked out of his studio in Österbybruk, where he kept hares, foxes and eagles in an enclosure, so he could paint them from life. A lifelong hunter, he would go to extremes for his art, trekking into the wilderness to paint.

Ustad Mansur (India, *fl.*1590-1624)
Also known simply as Mansur (Ustad means 'master'), Ustad Mansur was a leading painter in the court of the Mughal emperor Jahangir. He was known for his paintings of birds and animals and earned the title Nadir al-Asr ('Wonder of the Age') from the Emperor. Mansur, who painted from life, frequently depicted the animals that arrived at court, including gifts of birds. With other court artists, he often accompanied his patron on trips, and was charged with painting specimens of plants and animals for posterity.

Étienne-Jules Marey (France, 1830-1904)
The physiologist Étienne-Jules Marey's scientific interests were broad. In his early career he studied the circulation of the blood, before branching out into cardiology and respiration. He was also practical, and helped to invent an early sphygmograph to take blood pressure and record the pulse. He is best known today for his contributions to early cinematography, in which he captured images of birds and other animals in motion. He would later pair these images with drawings of the muscular and skeletal systems of animals to show how they moved.

Maria Sibylla Merian (Germany, 1647-1717)
Maria Sibylla Merian learned to paint when her stepfather introduced her to miniature flower painting. In Nuremberg in 1680 she published *The New Book of Flowers*, intended as a model book for artists and embroiderers; it was followed by *The Caterpillar Book*, illustrating butterflies and moths. Merian later moved to Amsterdam, where her daughters Johanna Helena and Dorothea Maria also became noted natural history artists; in 1699 Dorothea accompanied her mother to Suriname, where they collected specimens for *Metamorphosis Insectorum Surinamensium* ('The Metamorphosis of the Insects of Suriname', 1705), a work that ensured Merian's reputation as a pioneering entomologist.

Adolphe Millot (France, 1857-1921)
Born in Paris, Adolphe Millot was a member of the prestigious Salon des Artists Français. His precisely detailed drawings of vegetables, insects, birds' eggs and flowers featured in the illustrated encyclopaedia *Le Petit Larousse*, which first appeared in 1905. Millot was responsible for illustrating its natural history section. A well-known and highly regarded lithographer and entomologist, Millot worked as a senior illustrator the Musée Nationale d'Histoire Naturelle in Paris. The museum was established by King Louis XIII in 1635 as the royal garden for medicinal plants.

Jean-Baptiste Oudry (France, 1686-1755)
A painter and tapestry designer in the Rococo style, Jean-Baptiste Oudry is widely considered to be one of the foremost animal painters of the eighteenth century. He trained in portrait painting with Nicolas de Largillière and became a member of the Académie de Peinture et de Sculpture in 1719. By 1720 he was mostly painting animals, hunts and landscapes. Oudry was a favourite of King Louis XV, who often called on him to paint the royal hounds at court. In 1734 he was appointed director of the Beauvais tapestry manufacture, to the north of Paris.

Sydney Parkinson (Britain, 1745-71)
The Scottish artist Sydney Parkinson was the first British artist in Australia, where he drew native plants, birds and animals and Aboriginal peoples. An apprentice draper, his skill at botanical illustration earned him a position with Sir Joseph Banks, one of the leading naturalists of the day. Parkinson accompanied Banks as botanical artist on the first expedition to the Pacific aboard HMS *Endeavour* led by James Cook in 1768, reaching Tahiti and New Zealand as well as Australia. He made hundreds of drawings of collected specimens in difficult conditions on board ship, but died of dysentery on the voyage home, and his work was prepared for publication by others.

Roger Tory Peterson (United States, 1908-96)
The field guides of Roger Tory Peterson inspired a popular fascination with nature that helped to kick start the environmental movement in the United States. Raised in Jamestown, New York, in an immigrant family, Peterson was just ten when he went to work in a mill following his father's premature death. He then worked as a travelling salesman. An interest in birds led to his first published article in 1925. In 1934, he published *A Field Guide to the Birds*, the first modern field guide, which quickly sold out its initial 2,000-copy print run. It included his innovative Peterson Identification System to more easily identify birds. Peterson would go on to create a renowned series of more than fifty Peterson Field Guides, covering other aspects of the natural world, including birds, plants, insects and geographical features.

Rathika Ramasamy (India, *c.*1975-)
With a degree in computer engineering and an MBA, Rathika Ramasamy seemed destined to follow a traditional educational path, which culminated in working as a software engineer for five years. However, after photographing birds at the Bharatpur Bird Sanctuary during a family picnic in January 2004, she switched professions. Self-taught, she has since produced dynamic images of birds in India's national parks and further afield in Africa. One of the best-known female wildlife photographers, not just in India (where she is based in Chennai) but worldwide, Ramasamy uses her photographs to convey her conservation message.

Roelandt Savery (Belgium, 1576-1639)
The Flemish painter and printmaker Roelandt Savery often painted rocky landscapes with animals and figures drawn from life - including allegedly a living dodo - and still lifes of flowers influenced by the work of Jan Brueghel the Elder. His family moved to Haarlem in the Netherlands in 1585 to escape the religious upheaval of the time. Savery joined the painters' guild there in 1587 and moved to Amsterdam with his brother Jacob in 1591. He travelled to Prague under the patronage of Emperor Rudolf II, but ultimately returned to the Netherlands.

Sir Peter Scott (Britain, 1909-89)
The only child of Robert Falcon Scott, the explorer of Antarctica, Peter Scott's career was in many ways as illustrious as his father's. A skilled painter, particularly of birds, Scott was an Olympic

medal winner, broadcaster, conservationist and ornithologist. A life-long passion for birds led him to establish the Severn Wildfowl Trust in 1946. Between 1955 and 1969, his natural history series for the BBC, *Look*, made him a household name in Great Britain. In 1961, he was one of the founding members of the World Wildlife Fund (now the Worldwide Fund for Nature), the world's largest conservation organization, for which he designed its panda logo.

Albertus Seba (Netherlands, 1665–1736)
The Dutch pharmacist Albertus Seba, who was born in Germany but spent his life in Amsterdam, created a renowned collection of curiosities. After amassing a huge number of specimens, he commissioned illustrations that he incorporated into a four-volume catalogue, *Locupletissimi rerum naturalium thesauri* ('Thesaurus of Natural Things', 1734–65). The catalogue recorded everything from birds and butterflies to snakes and crocodiles, and even fantastical creatures such as dragons and a hydra. Seba's early research on natural history and taxonomy influenced Carl Linnaeus. His collection was sold at auction in 1752, and much of it was later confiscated by Napoleon and taken to the Museum of Natural History in Paris.

Prideaux John Selby (Britain, 1788–1867)
By the age of thirteen, Prideaux John Selby had written and illustrated notes about the most common birds found in his home county of Northumberland. His drawings were notable for their accuracy and life-like representation. Returning to Northumberland after Oxford University, he entered local politics and served as high sheriff of Northumberland in 1823. However, his main interest remained natural history, particularly ornithology. Starting in 1821, he produced the *Illustrations of British Ornithology*, finishing in 1834. He illustrated more than two hundred plates, sourcing the birds from his private collection and engraving the copper plates himself.

Shen Quan (China, 1682–1760)
Instrumental in the establishment of the Nagasaki school of painting in Japan, Shen Quan was actually Chinese. Born in Deqing, Zhejiang province, under the Qing dynasty, he specialized in bird-and-flower painting. In 1731, a Japanese official invited him to Nagasaki, where he taught his Japanese students the traditional Chinese style of realist painting. He remained in Japan for two years and became a popular and influential teacher. Back in China, paintings in his style continued to be imported in Japan. Shen's influence on Japanese painting continued into the late nineteenth century.

David Allen Sibley (United States, 1961–)
After dropping out of college in 1980, David Allen Sibley started to watch birds in Cape May Point, New Jersey, having begun birding as a child with his father, the Yale University ornithologist Fred Sibley. A largely self-taught artist, Sibley decided to write and illustrate his own bird guides after leading tours in the 1980s and '90s and finding the existing guides inadequate. His Sibley guides soon became indispensable for any birdwatcher. In 2002, he received the Roger Tory Peterson Award for his contribution to the promotion of

birding. In 2006, he was awarded the Linnaean Society of New York's Eisenmann Medal.

Frans Snyders (Spanish Netherlands, 1579–1657)
The Flemish Baroque painter Frans Snyders was the foremost painter of animals in the seventeenth century, pioneering the animal still life, featuring market and pantry arrangements. He also painted sporting scenes such as hunts, and animals in combat. He studied under Pieter Brueghel the Younger and travelled to Italy in 1608 to view works of art. After returning to Antwerp, he became immersed in the local art world, joining a circle that included Peter Paul Rubens and Jan Brueghel the Elder.

Sarah Stone (Britain, 1760–1844)
At the age of twenty-one, London-born Sarah Stone was invited to show four of her paintings – including one of a peacock – at the Royal Academy of Arts, at a time when women were prohibited from exhibiting. A professional painter from the age of seventeen, she learned her colouring skills from her father, a fan-maker, and taught herself draughtsmanship. Sir Ashton Lever, who wanted her to illustrate objects for his natural history museum, including specimens brought to England by Captain James Cook, was one of many to commission her. She drew more than a thousand illustrations, including for John White's *A Journal of a Voyage to New South Wales* (1790).

Hiroshi Sugimoto (Japan, 1948–)
Tokyo-born and raised but resident in New York since 1974, Hiroshi Sugimoto has created work that extends from photography to art installations and architecture. He studied politics and sociology in Tokyo in 1970, then retrained as an artist. In his first work, *Dioramas* (1976), he photographed displays at the American Museum of Natural History, returning for further shoots in 1982, 1994 and 2012. His photography has been widely exhibited, as has his architecture – his 2014 glass tea-house was initially exhibited at the Venice Biennale. In 2018, his architectural firm completed the redesign of the lobby of the Hirschhorn Museum and Sculpture Garden in Washington, DC.

Charles Frederick Tunnicliffe (Britain, 1901–79)
Raised on a farm in Cheshire, Charles Tunnicliffe drew farm animals on the walls of black creosoted farm buildings with white chalk before winning a scholarship to the nearby Macclesfied School of Art and Design in 1916. Another scholarship took him to London's Royal College of Art. In 1923, he trained as an engraver. Returning north in 1928, he initially worked as an engraver and illustrator before concentrating on painting birds from the 1930s. As well as illustrating books for the Royal Society for the Protection of Birds (RSPB) and the children's Ladybird series, he also wrote and illustrated his own books from his Anglesey home in North Wales, where he lived from 1947 until his death.

Alexander Wilson (Britain, 1766–1813)
Called the founder of American ornithology, Alexander Wilson spent the first part of his life in his native Scotland, where he worked as a peddler and weaver while trying to become a poet. In 1794,

impoverished, he emigrated to the United States and settled in Pennsylvania. Unable to get work as a weaver in Philadelphia, he became a teacher. In 1804, influenced by the naturalist William Bartram, who encouraged his interest in ornithology, Wilson decided to publish a collection of illustrations of every bird in North America.
The result was the pioneering *American Ornithology*. Published in nine volumes between 1808 and 1814, it contained twenty-six species never recorded before.

Edward Wilson (Britain, 1872–1912)
A scientist and medical doctor, Edward Wilson was also a talented artist, and he joined Robert Falcon Scott's expeditions to Antarctica in 1911 and 1912 as the scientist and expedition artist. Wilson was only twenty-nine when he first set sail for the South Pole on HMS *Discovery*. He had overcome tuberculosis in 1901 and was recruited to the expedition only three weeks before it sailed. As the expedition ornithologist, he would paint animal specimens before they were preserved for collection, recording details such as colour that would otherwise be lost. On their second expedition, on HMS *Terra Nova* in 1912, Wilson died with Scott as they battled through bad weather to return to the ship.

Francis Willughby and John Ray
(Britain, 1635–72 and 1627–1705)
First meeting at Trinity College, Cambridge, in 1653, Francis Willughby and his tutor John Ray – known today as 'the father of natural history' – became collaborators, lifelong friends and travelling companions. In the 1660s, the two men travelled around Great Britain and Europe, collecting specimens as part of a project to produce a complete record of the continent's flora and fauna. After Willughby's untimely death in 1672, Ray undertook to publish his friend's findings. *The Ornithology of Francis Willughby* (1676) was a pioneering three-volume scientific study on the birds of Great Britain. Dividing birds into land or water birds was part of the taxonomic system the men developed, helping to lay the groundwork for today's classification of plants and animals.

Shaik Zain al-Din (India, *fl.*1777–83)
Patna-born Muslim artist Shaik Zain al-Din worked for the British expatriate elite at a time when the East India Company's control of India was growing. Trained in the Mughal style but influenced also by Western painting, Zain al-Din combined his illustrations of birds with typically English botanical backgrounds. The Chief Justice of Bengal, Sir Elijah Impey, and his wife, Mary, commissioned the artist to catalogue their private menagerie at their Calcutta home, which included several bird species. Working in watercolours and on paper brought from England, between 1777 and 1783 Zain al-Din meticulously drew and illustrated most of a total of 326 paintings, helped by two other artists.

Glossary

Anatomy The physical structure of an organism and its constituent parts. The branch of biology concerned with studying the structure of an organism.

Apotropaic Believed to have the power to guard against harm from evil.

Aviary A confined space used to house captive birds for display. Usually quite large, so as to allow the birds space to fly.

Avifauna The bird species present in a particular location or region, or within a geological time period.

Beak A pair of light, bony structures covered in keratin sheaths found in a range of animals, including birds. The upper and lower parts (mandibles) may have evolved for eating particular kinds of food, such as fruit, carrion or nuts, and may include teeth-like lamellae along the edge of the mandibles.

Behaviour Responses to stimuli exhibited by an individual. Behaviours may be shared by members of a species, and may be voluntary or involuntary.

Biodiversity Biological diversity, or the variety of life on Earth, considered at all levels. This includes genetic variety within species, the variety of species themselves and habitat variety within an ecosystem.

Breed A population of animals within a species that has been selectively bred to emphasize certain physical or behavioural attributes.

Call A vocalization made by an animal (in birds, via the syrinx) to advertise its presence. This may be to attract mates, to warn off rivals or to declare territory. Bird calls may incorporate repeated patterns of pitches to generate 'songs'.

Carotenoid An orange-red pigment found in many plants that, when ingested in high quantity, may be expressed in, for instance, feathers or skin colour.

Carrion The decaying body of a deceased animal. Usually used to refer specifically to flesh as a food source.

Chick A young bird, usually requiring substantial care from its parents. In early stages of growth, some chicks that are relatively well-developed are covered in down feathers that assist in retaining heat.

Chromolithograph A colour lithograph.

Clade A group of organisms that comprise all the evolutionary descendents of a common ancestor.

Claw A curved, tapering keratin structure found on the end of birds' toes and, in some species, on fingers within their wings. Referred to as talons in raptors.

Cloaca Literally a 'drain' (Latin): the single opening at the posterior of birds used to discharge fecal and urinary matter as well as to transfer sperm. The latter process is colloquially called a 'cloacal kiss'; it does not occur with birds that have evolved phalluses, such as ducks and swans.

Colony A population of individuals of the same species living in close proximity. In birds, colonies are often formed seasonally and assist in mate choice.

Covert (tectrix) A feather that covers other feathers. Coverts assist in the smooth flow of air over the wings and tail.

Dance A ritualistic behaviour exhibited by some species of birds such as cranes and birds of paradise, wherein either one or both sexes perform elaborate sequences of movements to encourage pairing or to reinforce mate bonding.

Decoy A replica of an animal used by hunters to lure other animals.

Diorama A three-dimensional replica of an environment populated by taxidermy models of animals found within it, usually for museum display.

Ecosystem The system or web of movement of energy and nutrients between living (biotic) organisms and the (abiotic) environment.

Endangered A classification bestowed by the International Union for Conservation of Nature, indicating that a species is in danger of extinction.

Endemic An indigenous species that is found only in a specific region, owing to factors that limit its distribution and migration.

Engraving A technique by which a design is scored into a surface such as stone, leather or wood by the use of a sharp tool, called a burin. Also the name for a print produced by transferring ink from this incised surface onto paper.

Extinction The termination of a species. Extinction may occur for many reasons, such as competition by an invasive species, or over-hunting by humans.

Falconry An ancient form of hunting by proxy, whereby humans shelter and train birds of prey that are used to hunt wild prey.

Family The level of taxonomic classification below order and above genus. The family Strigidae, for example, includes all twenty-two genera of true owls.

Fauna The animal life contained within an environment, as opposed to flora.

Feather A complex set of structures consisting of a central shaft (rachis), and paired barbs forming a flat surface (vanes). Feathers assist in maintaining thermoregulation, in non-verbal communication (via coloration) and in generating lift for flight. They may be asymmetric and used for flight (e.g. primary and secondary feathers), symmetrical (e.g. central tail feathers), or very soft to capture heat (e.g. filoplumes and down feathers).

Field Guide A book designed to assist in the identification of plants, animals or minerals when in the 'field' where wildlife is found. Detailed descriptions are usually accompanied by diagrammatic images of the organisms or rocks described.

Flora The plant life (sometimes including fungi and other non-animal life) contained within an environment, as opposed to fauna.

Fossil The remains of deceased organisms within rock, usually slowly altered through geochemical processes. Fossils are generally formed from hard organic tissue such as bone, but soft tissues such as collagen and feathers may be fossilized under excellent conditions. Footprints and burrows are also classed as types of fossil.

Habitat A type of area defined by its particular environment, incorporating both living and non-living factors within which organisms live. A freshwater pool is an example of a habitat.

Hide A built structure from which viewers can observe wildlife without being visible to the animals they are studying.

Insectivorous A carnivorous dietary preference consisting mainly of insects.

Iridescence The appearance of a surface which appears to change colour as the viewer's angle alters. Iridescence is caused by the phase shift and refraction of light (among other phenomena) as it interacts with the surface's microstructure.

Keratin A protein found in vertebrates, the key structural element in the feathers, beak and claws of birds.

Lekking A behaviour exhibited by some bird (and other) species whereby a cohort of males engages in similar repetitive behaviours within a contained area in order to attract a mate, usually via non-aggressive competition.

Lithograph A printing technique developed at the turn of the nineteenth century, in which an image drawn onto a flat surface (initially a stone tablet, hence lithograph, 'drawing on stone') is transferred to a paper sheet.

Markings Pigmentation or structural coloration found on the feathers and skin of birds. Hues and saturation of markings may indicate health (truthfully or otherwise) of an individual, and assist in the identification of other members of a species.

Migration The large-scale movement of animals from one area to another, often seasonal. Migration can result when individuals pursue food sources, more suitable temperatures or mating opportunities.

Monogamy The continued association of a pair of birds following mating, usually combined with joint caring of offspring, for a significant period of time. This may be seasonal or last for several years.

Non-native Not historically found in an area, having been introduced recently into an ecosystem.

Order A level of taxonomic classification hierarchically below class and above family. For example, the order Strigiformes contains barn owls in addition to all true owls.

Passerine Any bird of the order Passeriform (from the Latin: 'sparrow-shaped'), which includes over half of all bird species.

Perch A structure used by birds as a substrate on which to stand. Due to the backward-facing first (and, in some species fourth or second) digit, even thin structures such as tree branches may be grasped and balanced upon.

Phylogeny A diagram illustrating a hypothesis of how species are related to each other, usually resembling a 'family tree', in which the tips of the branches represent individual species. Phylogenetic techniques use data such as genetic or morphological characteristics to compare multiple species against each other through highly complex computation.

Plumage The feathers that collectively cover a bird. Plumage may be duller in one sex and may alter in tone through the seasons.

Pouch (gular) A flap of elastic skin between the two sides of the beak's lower mandible that connects it with the throat and may be used in certain species to hold food, or be expanded as a signal.

Preening The action by which birds use their beaks to rid their feathers of parasites and other detritus, as well as to align the barbules of their feathers to maintain a smooth aerofoil for flight.

Psittacofulvins A set of pigments found only in parrots, responsible for their bright orange and red coloration. They are derived from the carotenoid pigments found in plants.

Raptor A group of hypercarnivorous birds that have evolved anatomical traits such as tearing beaks and sharp eyesight, allowing them to hunt vertebrate prey. Phylogenetically raptors are not a natural clade though the term is usually used to collectively to refer to the unrelated groups the Falconiformes and Accipitriformes.

Ring A small, lightweight plastic or medal band with numbers or lettering, placed around the leg of wild birds in order to help identify and track the movements of individuals.

Social As opposed to solitary birds, social birds spend time in large groups in order to defend themselves against predators or to feed. Some species, such as emperor penguins, rely on social gatherings to protect them from harsh conditions.

Songbird A group of small, globally diverse birds within the Passeriformes (perching birds) that are able to form repertoires of highly complex, repeatable song sequences to advertise their presence.

Species A population of organisms more genetically similar to each other than to organisms outside the group. Variations within this population may be classed as subspecies. In many vertebrates, 'species' is classically defined as the largest population of a group of animals that is able to produce fertile offspring by breeding (the 'biological species model'), but this is complicated in birds, which are able to hybridize between 'species' very easily.

Specimen An example of a species, or any material related to it (e.g. faeces, tracks, fur, DNA etc.), usually acquisitioned into a museum or private collection for reference. 'Type' specimens (or holotypes) are the specimens after which species are described and named.

Syrinx The vocal organ of birds. Sound is created by air flowing through the syrinx, producing vibrations of the syrinx walls and of a cartilagenous bar, the pessulus, within the organ.

Taxidermy The preservation of the external surface of an animal's body, often for museum displays. Preserved bodies or skins may be mounted around an artificial body, historically in order to illustrate natural behaviour, and occasionally to model them in anthropomorphic poses.

Taxonomy The branch of biology concerned with the classification, naming and identification of organisms.

Wader A bird in the order Charadriiformes found near or on shorelines, which uses its long beak to probe damp sand and mudbanks for invertebrate prey. Waders often have long, gracile legs and well-spread toes to assist locomotion in these environments.

Wingspan The overall measurement between the tips of both wings when held outstretched.

Attenborough, David and Fuller, Errol. *Drawn from Paradise: The Natural History, Art and Discovery of the Birds of Paradise*. London: HarperCollins, 2012.

Balmer, Dawn E., et al. *Bird Atlas 2007-11: The Breeding and Wintering Birds of Britain and Ireland*. Thetford: British Trust for Ornithology, 2013.

Birkhead, Tim. *Bird Sense*. London: Bloomsbury, 2014.

Birkhead, Tim. *Ten Thousand Birds*. Princeton: Princeton University Press, 2014.

Brewer, David. *Birds New to Science: Fifty Years of Avian Discoveries*. London: Bloomsbury, 2018.

Bugler, Caroline. *The Bird in Art*. London: Merrell Publishers, 2021.

Cocker, Mark and Tipling, David. *Birds and People*. London: Jonathan Cape, 2008.

Elphick, Jonathan. *Birds: The Art of Ornithology*. London: The Natural History Museum, 2017.

Garcia, Joëlle. *Birds in Paradise*. Paris: L'Ecole School of Jewellery Arts, 2019.

Hyland, Angus and Wilson, Kendra. *The Book of the Bird: Birds in Art*. London: Lawrence King, 2016.

Jackson, Christine E. *Dictionary of Bird Artists of the World*. Woodbridge: Antique Collectors Club, 1999

Lederer, Roger J. *The Art of the Bird: The History of Ornithological Art Through Forty Artists*. Chicago: The University of Chicago Press, 2019.

Lindo, David. *Tales from Concrete Jungles: Urban Birding Around the World*. London: Bloomsbury, 2015.

Lindo, David. *The Urban Birder*. London: Bloomsbury, 2018.

Mynott, Jeremy. *Birds in the Ancient World*. Oxford: Oxford University Press, 2018.

Singer, Robert T. and Kawai, Masatomo. *The Life of Animals in Japanese Art*. Princeton: Princeton University Press, 2019.

Sung, Hou-Mei. *Decoded Messages: The Symbolic Language of Chinese Animal Painting*. New Haven: Yale University Press, 2009.

van Grouw, Katrina. *Unnatural Selection*. Princeton: Princeton University Press, 2018.

van Grouw, Katrina. *The Unfeathered Bird*. Princeton: Princeton University Press, 2012.

Walters, Michael. *A Concise History of Ornithology*. London: Bloomsbury, 2003.

Wepler, Lisanne. *Animal Fables*. Petersberg: Michael Imhof Verlag, 2021.

Index

Page numbers in *italics* refer to illustrations

Publisher's Acknowledgements

A project of this size requires the commitment, advice and expertise of many people. We are particularly indebted to our consultant editor Katrina van Grouw for her vital contribution to the shaping of this book and her exhaustive knowledge, and to Tim Birkhead, Jen Lobo and David Lindo for their editorial input and guidance during the development of the project.

Special thanks are due to our international advisory panel for their knowledge, passion and advice in the selection of the works for inclusion:

Dawn Balmer
Head of Surveys
British Trust for Ornithology (BTO)

Tim Birkhead FRS
Professor of Zoology in the Department of Animal and Plant Sciences, The University of Sheffield
Author of *The Wisdom of Birds: An Illustrated History of Ornithology*

Dr Alexander Bond
Senior Curator in Charge of Birds
Natural History Museum at Tring

Gordon Campbell
Lecturer and Assistant Professor of Ancient Classics, Maynooth University

Dr Sylke Frahnert
Curator of Birds
Museum für Naturkunde
Leibniz Institute for Evolution and Biodiversity Science, Berlin

Joëlle Garcia
Conservatrice en chef des bibliothèques
Bibliothèque Forney

Elizabeth Hammer
Asian art historian and educator
Executive Director – Hammond Museum and Japanese Stroll Garden and Founder – Hammer Fine Art Services LLC

David Lindo aka The Urban Birder
Broadcaster, speaker and writer
Ambassador – Leica Birding and London Wildlife Trust
Founder of Britain's Vote National Bird Campaign 2015

Jen Lobo
Artist and educator
2020 Bartels Science Illustrator, Cornell University

Fred G. Meijer
Independent art historian and expert of Dutch and Flemish seventeenth-century painting

Sabine Meyer
Photography Director
National Audubon Society

Penny Olsen
Honorary Professor, The Australian National University
Author of *Feather and Brush: Three Centuries of Australian Bird Art*

Oliver Rampley
Wildlife guide and consultant specializing in European birds, roe deer and wild boar
Founder of Altana Europe

Katrina van Grouw
Ornithologist, author, illustrator, and artist
Author of *The Unfeathered Bird* and *Unnatural Selection*

Dr Lisanne Wepler
Researcher in the Visual Arts, Rijksmuseum Amsterdam

We are particularly grateful to Rosie Pickles for researching and compiling the longlist of entries for inclusion. Additional thanks are due to Jen Veall and Jenny Faithfull for their picture research, and to Caitlin Arnell Argles, Vanessa Bird, Lynne Ciccaglione, Tim Cooke, Diane Fortenberry, Rebecca Morrill, João Mota, Michele Robecchi and Caroline Taggart for their invaluable assistance.

Finally, we would like to thank all the artists, illustrators, photographers, collectors, libraries, institutions and museums who have given us permission to include their images.

Text Credits

The publisher is grateful to the following writers for their texts:

Giovanni Aloi: 35, 37, 42, 48, 66, 68, 69, 79, 118, 119, 146, 147, 155, 171, 184, 187, 215, 238, 247, 253, 266, 267, 273, 274, 284, 294; **Sara Bader:** 56; **Dr Alex Bond:** 28, 32, 87, 103, 112, 133, 137, 140, 157, 165, 201, 202, 219, 223, 226, 239, 269, 312; **Dr Michael Brooke:** 11, 27, 30, 117, 141, 163, 222, 255, 259, 265, 299, 313, 318, 319, 325; **Tim Cooke:** 21, 31, 59, 61, 72, 86, 92, 93, 123, 128, 149, 154, 185, 193, 199, 212, 233, 243, 275, 296, 303, 304, 309, 310; **Clare Coulson:** 40, 89, 129, 143, 191, 234, 235, 248, 292, 305; **Nick Crumpton:** 18, 22, 23, 47, 113, 131, 148, 164, 211, 249, 258, 264, 270, 279, 291, 311, 316, 322; **Louisa Elderton:** 12, 50, 67, 130, 156, 182, 186; **Diane Fortenberry:** 24, 26, 44, 51, 57, 60, 77, 78, 85, 104, 105, 109, 111, 116, 138, 139, 152, 170, 206, 207, 224, 242, 250, 251, 256, 276, 277, 288, 320, 321; **Carolyn Fry:** 126, 229, 260; **Elizabeth Hammer:** 25, 53, 214, 289; **David Lindo:** 110, 120, 125; **Jen Lobo:** 15, 100, 106, 107, 179, 181, 301, 315, 323, 324; **Fred G. Meijer:** 10, 49, 80, 97, 102, 161, 271, 272; **David B Miller:** 158; **Rebecca Morrill:** 278; **Penny Olsen:** 232, 257; **Michele Robecchi:** 34, 36, 65, 73, 95, 173, 188, 189, 208; **Gill Saunders:** 58, 228; **James Smith:** 41, 45, 75, 81, 135, 174, 209, 225, 241; **David Trigg:** 14, 55, 62, 88, 94, 96, 101, 114, 124, 153, 183, 196, 197, 198, 203, 216, 220, 244, 245, 252, 261, 262, 263, 280, 282, 283, 297; **Katrina van Grouw:** 16, 17, 19, 29, 33, 39, 43, 83, 91, 115, 121, 122, 127, 142, 144, 145, 150, 151, 160, 167, 172, 175, 176, 177, 178, 190, 192, 195, 204, 213, 217, 227, 231, 237, 246, 281, 285, 287, 290, 300, 307, 314, 317; **Martin Walters:** 46, 54, 63, 70, 71, 74, 82, 98, 134, 159, 162, 166, 169, 194, 205, 210, 221, 230, 240, 295, 298, 302, 308, 327; **Isabella Wing-Davey:** 84, 293; **Dr Lisanne Wepler:** 13, 38, 99, 132.

Additional thanks go to Katrina van Grouw for writing the introduction, Jen Lobo for the texts on bird orders and bird topography and their illustrations, David Lindo for the essay on urban bird watching, Rosie Pickles for compiling and writing the timeline, Tim Cooke for writing the biographies and Nick Crumpton for compiling and writing the glossary.

Picture Credits

Every reasonable effort has been made to identify owners of copyright. Errors and omissions will be corrected in subsequent editions.

Abrams/From BRAVE BIRDS by Maude White. Text and artwork copyright © 2018 Maude White. Photographs copyright © 2018 Laura Glazer. Used by permission of Abrams, an imprint of ABRAMS, New York. All rights reserved: 258; ADAGP Images, Paris, 2021: © Photothèque R. Magritte/© ADAGP, Paris and DACS, London 2021 253; akg-images: Erich Lessing 271, Liszt Collection 122; Alamy Stock Photo: Album 140, Authentic-Original 16, 331rc, Artiz 70, 301, 333l, Artokoloro 72, Chronicle of World History 294, Adam Eastland 170, 329l, Everett Collection Inc. Licensed By: Warner Bros. Entertainment Inc. All Rights Reserved 197, funkyfood London - Paul Williams 116, Heritage Image Partnership Ltd 43, 331r, incameraphoto 166, 329r, INTERFOTO 61, The Natural History Museum 126, Nature Collection 156, The Picture Art Collection 25, 331l, Pictures Now 160, Alberto Rigamonti 185tl, 185bl, 185br, 335l, Philip Scalia 108–109, Ivan Vdovin 185tr, Woodfall Films/Entertainment Pictures 84, Zoonar/Ingo Schulz 26; © 2021 The Josef and Anni Albers Foundation/Artists Rights Society (ARS), New York/DACS, London. Photo Tim Nighswander/Imaging4Art: 83; © American Museum of Natural History/Denis Finnin: 136–137; Amon Carter Museum of American Art, Fort Worth, Texas: 215; Arader Galleries, Philadelphia, PA: 285; Artimage: © Tracey Emin. All rights reserved, DACS 2021. Image: © National Galleries of Scotland 266, © Polly Morgan. All Rights Reserved, DACS 2021 40; Art Institute of Chicago: Harry and Maribel G. Blum Endowment Fund, Restricted gift of the Antiquarian Society, Kate S. Buckingham Fund, Charles H. and Mary F. Worcester Collection Fund, Auction Sales Proceeds Fund, Centennial Major Acquisitions Income Fund, Robert Allerton Trust, The Mary and Leigh Block Endowment Fund, Ada Turnbull Hertl Fund, Restricted gift of Harry A. Root, Wirt D. Walker Trust, Gladys N. Anderson Fund, Pauline Seipp Armstrong Fund, Edward E. Ayer Fund in Memory of Charles L. Hutchinson, European Decorative Arts Krehbiel Fund, Restricted gift of Mr. and Mrs. Stanford Marks, Helen A. Regenstein Endowment, Samuel A. Marx Purchase Fund for Major Acquisitions, Laura T. Magnuson Acquisition Fund, The Marian and Samuel Glasstorner Fund, Maurice D. Galleher Endowment, Robert Allerton Purchase Fund, Bessie Bennett Fund, European Decorative Arts General Fund, Edward Johnson Fund, Elizabeth R. Vaughn Fund, Annette Mathby Chapin Fund, Wentworth Greene Field Memorial Fund, Director's Fund, Restricted gift of the Edward Byron Smith, Jr. Family Foundation, Samuel P. Avery Fund, Hugh Leander and Mary Trumbull Adams Memorial Endowment, Restricted gift of the G-Bar Charitable Foundation, Betty Bell Spooner Fund, Restricted gift of Elizabeth Souder Louis, Irving and June Seaman Endowment Fund, Charles U. Harris Endowed Acquisition Fund, S. DeWitt Clough Fund, Restricted gift of the Woman's Board of the Alliance Française of Chicago, Grant J. Pick Purchase Fund, Restricted gift of Ghenete Zelleke 62, 330r, Ethel T. Scarborough and Major Acquisitions funds; Gladys N. Anderson Endowment 212; Photograph © Yann Arthus-Bertrand: 264; Artis Gallery, 280 Parnell Rd, Auckland, New Zealand: 227, 334rc; Photo © Alexandre Bailhache/© ADAGP, Paris and DACS, London 2021: 143; © Richard Barnes: 130; Diana Beltrán Herrera: 213; © Belvedere, Vienna: 146; Biodiversity Heritage Library: 30, 54, 115, 121, 144, 176, 194, 312, 315; Courtesy the artist and Niels Borch Jensen Gallery, Copenhagen/© DACS 2021: 306–307; Elizabeth Boehm: 311; Courtesy of the artist and Tanya Bonakdar Gallery, New York/Los Angeles: 32; © Xavi Bou: 47; © Miranda Brandon: 157; © Carl Brenders, by arrangement with Ansada Licensing Group, LLC: 290; Bridgeman Images: 27, 37, 102, 221, 323, Photo © Christie's Images 82, 195, 297, Photo © Christie's Images © The Joseph and Robert Cornell Memorial Foundation/VAGA at ARS, NY and DACS, London 2021: 273, Photo © Christie's Images/© Dafila Scott 316, Photo © Christie's Images/© 2021 The Andy Warhol Foundation for the Visual Arts, Inc./Licensed by DACS, London and Ronald Feldman Fine Art 119, / © DACS 2021: 262; © Fry Art Gallery Society/© The Estate of Edward Bawden 17, Oscar Graubner/Prismatic Pictures 153, Look & Learn 39, 332cl, © Museum of Fine Arts, Boston/Leonard A. Lauder Postcard Archive—Gift of Leonard A. Lauder 172, Museum of Fine Arts, Boston/William Sturgis Bigelow Collection 60, Photo © National Gallery of Australia, Canberra 260, 333cr, National Gallery of Victoria, Melbourne 257, National Gallery of Victoria, Melbourne, Australia/Courtesy Cai Studio 69, National Trust Photographic Library 192, William Sturgis Bigelow Collection 52–53, © Succession Picasso/DACS, London 2021 187, © UPRAVIS/DACS 2021 198, © Sandro Vannini 76–77; © The Trustees of the British Museum: 51, 78, 85, 251; © Elizabeth Butterworth: 71; Cabinet des Estampes et des Dessins de Strasbourg. Photo Musées de Strasbourg, M.Bertola: 29; Courtesy, Maurizio Cattelan's Archive: 114; Photo courtesy of Caviar20 / © Milton Glaser - Permission Estate of Milton Glaser: 248; Courtesy Wallace Chan: 149; Collection Cinémathèque Française/Copyright Étienne-Jules Marey: 263; © Robert Clark: 240; The Cleveland Museum of Art/Purchase from the J. H. Wade Fund: 59; © Gary Cook, www.garycookphoto.com: 110; © William T. Cooper: 223; Photograph courtesy of Copley Fine Art Auctions: 193; Courtesy the Artist, Corvi-Mora, London, and Jack Shainman Gallery, New York/Photo Marcus Leith: 188; Rob Cottle (social media @robcottle images): 254–255; © Mike Donaldson, Wildrocks Publications, 2020: 276; David Doubilet: 268–269; © the artist. Reproduced with the permission of Dorset Fine Arts: 165; Dreamstime.com: Ac Manley/© DACS 2021 274, Geoffrey Welsh/Courtesy of Pest Control Office, Banksy, Clacton-on-Sea, 2014 66, Zzvet 44, 328l; © Eames Office, LLC/Photograph by Charles Eames: 14; Courtesy, Field Museum/(Z94461_05d): 270; The Fine Art Society/Image courtesy of Michael Whiteway: 96; All rights reserved by Fiskars Finland Oy Ab/Photographer Timo Junttila, Designer Oiva Toikka: 220; Tim Flach: 63; Photo courtesy of The Forbes Collection: 89; © Frederick Warne & Co., 1937: 217; Freer Gallery of Art/Purchase - Charles Lang Freer Endowment. F1965.20-21: 168–169; Courtesy Gagosian: Image courtesy the artist 180–181, © Gregory Crewdson 293; © Andrew Garn: 67; Courtesy of the George Eastman Museum/© 2021 Estate of Margaret Bourke-White/Licensed by VAGA at Artists Rights Society (ARS), NY: 68; © Jochen Gerner - Éditions B42: 56; Getty Images: Carl De Souza/AFP via Getty Images/© ADAGP, Paris and DACS, London 2021 75, Bettmann 111, Royal Geographical Society 222; Courtesy of the artist and Marian Goodman Gallery/Copyright Hiroshi Sugimoto: 81; © Sean Graesser: 148; Jill Greenberg courtesy ClampArt Gallery, New York: 275; © Melissa Groo: 120; Reproduced with permission from Guinness Archive, Diageo: 101; © Charley Harper Art Studio. www.charleyharper.com: 179; HarperCollins UK/Illustrations from Richard Scarry's Best Word Book Ever by Richard Scarry, copyright © 1963 and renewed 1991 by Penguin Random House, LLC. Used by permission of Golden Books, an imprint of Random House Children's Books, a division of Penguin Random House LLC. All rights reserved: 203; Harvard Art Museums/Fogg Museum, Gift of Dr. Denman W. Ross, accession no. 1917.6. © President and Fellows of Harvard College: 48; gary@garyheery.com: 42, 335cr; Heritage Auctions, HA.com/© Hermès Paris, 2021: 305; © Nils Herrmann - Chaumet: 18, 332r; All Rights Reserved, courtesy Studio Florentijn Hofman: 95; Andy Holden/Photograph by Alison Bettles: 238; © 2021 Rebecca Horn/VG Bild Kunst/DACS 2021/Photographer Heinz Hefele, Darmstadt: 147; The Illustrated Book of Pigeons, Publisher London,Cassell, Petter & Galpin: 90–91; Photo courtesy Ink Dwell Studio: 159, 335r; © Lars Jonsson/The Eternal Forces, Northern Eiders, Oilpainting by Lars Jonsson: 281; Kyoto National Museum: 235; Christian Lacroix Maison: 129; © Ladybird Books Ltd 1967: 216; © Frans Lanting/lanting.com: 11; Courtesy Shaun Leane for Alexander McQueen *The Widows of Culloden* AW06, in collaboration with Philip Treacy & Swarovski Gemstones. Photo Simon B. Armitt: 292; Greg Lecoeur/www.greglecoeur.com: 259; Library of Congress: 28, 242; Thomas Lohr: 211; Los Angeles County Museum of Art www.lacma.org/Gift of Jane and Justin Dart (M. 78.37): 118, 332cr; Magnum Photos: © Werner Bischof 112, 334lc, © Matt Black 131, © Steve McCurry 186, © Martin Parr 229, © Alec Soth 267; Mauritshuis, The Hague: 209; © Brendan McGarry: 200–201; Courtesy of the artist and Kate MacGarry, London. Copyright the artist: 23; McGill University Library, Montreal, Blacker Wood Natural History Collection, Rare Books and Special Collections: 299, 330cr; Courtesy Harriet Mead/Photograph by Jody Lawrence: 318; The Metropolitan Museum of Art: Purchase, Lila Acheson Wallace Gift, 1997 289, 328tr, The Jefferson R. Burdick Collection, Gift of Jefferson R. Burdick: 20-21, The Cesnola Collection, Purchased by subscription, 1874–76 138, Fletcher Fund, 1963 79, Mary Griggs Burke Collection, Gift of the Mary and Jackson Burke Foundation, 2015 226t, 226b, Harris Brisbane Dick Fund, 1924 296, Purchase, Edward S. Harkness Gift, 1926 105, 328c, Gift of Samuel H. Kress, 1927 49, The Howard Mansfield Collection, Purchase, Rogers Fund, 1936 174, The Harry G. C. Packard Collection of Asian Art, Gift of Harry G. C. Packard, and Purchase, Fletcher, Rogers, Harris Brisbane Dick, and Louis V. Bell Funds, Joseph Pulitzer Bequest, and The Annenberg Fund Inc. Gift, 1975 24, Gift of J. Pierpont Morgan, 1911 104, Gift of John D. Rockefeller Jr., 1931 152, Rogers Fund, 1912 87, 288, Purchase, Rogers Fund and The Kevorkian Foundation Gift, 1955 284, Gift of Norbert Schimmel, 1985 277, Louis E. and Theresa S. Seley Purchase Fund for Islamic Art, 2004 57, Alfred Z. Solomon-Janet A. Sloane Endowment Fund, 2013 300; Minneapolis Institute of Art: Gift of Elizabeth and Willard Clark 74, 331lc, The William Hood Dunwoody Fund 256, The Minnich Collection The Ethel Morrison Van Derlip Fund, 1966 106, 302, 330l; The Morgan Library & Museum: 243; Collection Museum of Contemporary Art Chicago/gift of Joseph and Jory Shapiro (1998.38)/Photo Nathan Keay/© MCA Chicago: 241; © Vincent Munier: 134; Museum of New Zealand Te Papa Tongarewa (1992-0035-2361): 308; NASA: 245, 334r; National Air and Space Museum, Smithsonian Institution: 244; National Gallery of Art, Washington DC: Gift of Mrs. Walter B. James 177; National Geographic Creative: Arthur Singer 158; The National Library of New Zealand/Griffith, Penny, 1943-. Ref: Eph-F-GAMES-1950s-02. Alexander Turnbull Library, Wellington, New Zealand: 309; National Museum of African Art. Smithsonian Institution/Photograph by Franko Khoury, Gift of Herbert Baker: 207; ©The Trustees of the Natural History Museum, London: 218–219; Nature Picture Library: Stefan Christmann 319, Tui De Roy 279, ©Tim Laman 141, Andy Rouse 230; The New York Public Library/Rare Book Division: 19;© Paul Nicklen/paulnicklen.com: 239; Image courtesy of Oriel Môn, © The Estate of Charles F. Tunnicliffe: 210; Ostdrossel (www.ostdrossel.com): 326–327; Courtesy Maureen Paley, London: © Wolfgang Tillmans 184; Andy Parkinson: 291; From the Penguin Book Archive at the University of Bristol Library Special Collections, DM1294/13/19/1: 261; R. T. Peterson/Published by Houghton Mifflin Harcourt: 325, 333r; Tom Poulsom, (lego.cuusoo.com/ideas/view/16897): 22; Courtesy of the artist and Primo Marella Gallery: 249; © Rathika Ramasamy: 125; Image courtesy of Joseph McGlennon and Michael Reid Sydney + Berlin: 314; Rijksmuseum, Amsterdam: 38, 93, 97, 103, 132, 135, 225, 303, 330cl, / Gift of Mrs Brandt, Amsterdam and Mrs Brandt, Amsterdam 272; © Duke Riley: 55; © Audun Rikardsen: 313; © Richard Ross: 247; © Laurel Roth Hope/Photo by Andy Diaz Hope: 310; The Royal Collection Trust: 246, 250; David Rumsey Map Collection/David Rumsey Map Center, Stanford Libraries: 86; ©Sebastião Salgado/nbpictures: 265; © Joel Sartore/National Geographic Photo Ark: 100; Scala, Florence: Album/© Banco de México Diego Rivera Frida Kahlo Museums Trust, Mexico, D.F./DACS 2021 12, American Folk Art Museum/Art Resource, NY. Photo: Gavin Ashworth 128, The Art Institute of Chicago/Art Resource, NY/© The Saul Steinberg Foundation/Artists Rights Society (ARS), NY/DACS, London 2021 15, The Art Institute of Chicago/Art Resource, NY 233, Cooper-Hewitt, Smithsonian Design Museum/Art Resource, NY 298, Photo Josse 50, Image © The Metropolitan Museum of Art/Art Resource 41, 139, 162, 214, Photo: © 2021. The Metropolitan Museum of Art/Art Resource/© The Irving Penn Foundation. *Woman in Chicken Hat (Lisa Fonssagrives-Penn)*, New York, 1949. 133, Digital Image, The Museum of Modern Art, New York/© Robert Rauschenberg Foundation/VAGA at ARS, NY and DACS, London 2021 189, © 2021. Digital image, The Museum of Modern Art, New York/© Fred Tomaselli 2021. Image courtesy of the artist and James Cohan, New York 322, RMN-Grand Palais: Photographer Gérard Blot 178, Photographer Claude Germain 199, Photographer Hervé Lewandowski 320, Photographer René-Gabriel Ojeda 161, Photo © Smithsonian Institution. New York, Cooper-Hewitt - Smithsonian Institution Design Museum. © 2021. Cooper-Hewitt, Smithsonian Design Museum/Art Resource, NY/Gift of John D. Nicholson (2000-10-3): 191;Courtesy the artist and Esther Schipper, Berlin. Photo © Amélie Proché/© DACS 2021: 64–65; Science Photo Library: Biophoto Associates 151; Natural History Museum, London 33, 127, 163, Arie van 't Riet 231, D. Roberts 145; Scott Polar Research Institute, University of Cambridge, with permission: 317; © Nick Cave. Courtesy of the artist and Jack Shainman Gallery, New York/Photo by James Prinz Photography: 73, © Kerry James Marshall. Courtesy of the artist and Jack Shainman Gallery, New York 36; Courtesy the artist and Sprüth Magers. Permission obtained from Barbara Kruger via Sprüth Magers, Los Angeles: 182; © Shirana Shahbazi: 173; Shutterstock: ANL 282, Associated Press/Mark Lennihan 94, George Wolfe Plank/Condé Nast 234, Universal Pictures/Kobal 35; Sibley's Backyard Birds of North America wall poster copyright © David Allen Sibley and Scott & Nix, In. Used with permission: 324; © Lorna Simpson. Courtesy the artist and Hauser & Wirth. Photo James Wang: 34; The Estate of Arthur Singer: 236–237; Photo © Sotheby's: (detail) 205; Photograph Courtesy of Sotheby's, Inc. © 2014: 31, 332l; Courtesy of Sotheby's Auction House, New York: 190; © Matt Stuart: 123; Photo © Tate / © The estate of Sir Jacob Epstein: 171; © TfL, from the London Transport Museum collection: 113; Photo courtesy of The Old Design Shop: 304; © Hoang Tien Quyet: 92; © Steve Torna: 117; Bianca Tuckwell: 142; Twitter, Inc.: 196, 335lc; UCLA Library Special Collections/Charles E. Young Research Library, UCLA. [Caw caw; or, the chronicle of crows]. Children's Book Collection: 295; © University of Aberdeen: 202, 329rc; Van Gogh Museum, Amsterdam (Vincent van Gogh Foundation): 45; © Victoria and Albert Museum: London 58, 124, 154, 224, 228; The Walters Art Museum, Baltimore: 286–287; Wellcome Collection: (Attribution 4.0 International CC BY 4.0) 88; White Cube/© Harland Miller/Photo © White Cube (Ollie Hammick): 278; Wikimedia Commons: (CC0) 155, 329lc,, 167, 204, Illustration by G. Douanne/Lithograph by Comité national de prévoyance et d'économies, Paris (CC0) 252, Oskar Heinroth/Staatsbibliothek zu Berlin (CC by SA 4.0) 13, Koninklijke Bibliotheek (CC0) 99, Kunstformen der Natur (CC0) 107, 333lc, Museo Nacional del Prado, Madrid (CC0) 80; Nationalmuseum Sweden (CC0) 175; © Aaron Wojack: 183; Artwork copyright © Jonas Wood/Photographer Brian Forrest; Courtesy the artist and Shane Campbell Gallery: 208; © Andrew Wyeth/ARS, NY and DACS, London 2021: 46; Sold at Gallery Zacke since 1968 © November 2018: 321.